Spirited Things

The Work of "Possession" in Afro-Atlantic Religions

Edited by

PAUL CHRISTOPHER JOHNSON

The University of Chicago Press
Chicago and London

Paul Christopher Johnson is professor of history, Afroamerican and African studies, and director of the Doctoral Program in Anthropology and History at the University of Michigan, Ann Arbor. He is the author of *Secrets, Gossip, and Gods: The Transformation of Brazilian Candomblé* and *Diaspora Conversions: Black Carib Religion and the Recovery of Africa*.

The University of Chicago Press, Chicago 60637
The University of Chicago Press, Ltd., London

Printed in the United States of America

23 22 21 20 19 18 17 16 15 14   1 2 3 4 5

ISBN-13: 978-0-226-12262-5 (cloth)
ISBN-13: 978-0-226-12276-2 (paper)
ISBN-13: 978-0-226-12293-9 (e-book)
DOI: 10.7208/chicago/ 9780226122939.001.0001

Library of Congress Cataloging-in-Publication Data

Spirited things : the work of "possession" in Afro-Atlantic religions / edited by Paul Christopher Johnson.
pages cm
Includes bibliographical references and index.
ISBN 978-0-226-12262-5 (cloth : alk. paper) — ISBN 978-0-226-12276-2 (pbk. alk. paper) — ISBN 978-0-226-12293-9 (e-book) 1. Afro-Caribbean cults. 2. Spirit possession—Latin America. 3. Blacks—Latin America—Religion. I. Johnson, Paul C. (Paul Christopher), 1964–
BL2565.S757 2014
299.6'898—dc23

2013031084

♾ This paper meets the requirements of ANSI/NISO Z39.48-1992 (Permanence of Paper).

CONTENTS

PAUL CHRISTOPHER JOHNSON
INTRODUCTION / Spirits and Things in the Making of the Afro-Atlantic World / 1

PAUL CHRISTOPHER JOHNSON
ONE / Toward an Atlantic Genealogy of "Spirit Possession" / 23

STEPHAN PALMIÉ
TWO / The Ejamba of North Fairmount Avenue, the Wizard of Menlo Park, and the Dialectics of Ensoniment: An Episode in the History of an Acoustic Mask / 47

PATRICK A. POLK
THREE / "Who's Dat Knocking at the Door?" A Tragicomic Ethiopian Spirit Delineation in Three Parts / 79

KRISTINA WIRTZ
FOUR / Spiritual Agency, Materiality, and Knowledge in Cuba / 99

BRIAN BRAZEAL
FIVE / The Fetish and the Stone: A Moral Economy of Charlatans and Thieves / 131

STEPHEN SELKA
SIX / Demons and Money: Possessions in Brazilian Pentecostalism / 155

ELIZABETH McALISTER
SEVEN / Possessing the Land for Jesus / 177

KAREN RICHMAN
EIGHT / Possession and Attachment: Notes on Moral Ritual Communication among Haitian Descent Groups / 207

RAQUEL ROMBERG
NINE / Mimetic Corporeality, Discourse, and Indeterminacy in Spirit Possession / 225

MICHAEL LAMBEK
TEN / Afterword: Recognizing and Misrecognizing Spirit Possession / 257

Notes / 277
Bibliography / 303
Contributors / 331
Index / 333

Introduction: Spirits and Things in the Making of the Afro-Atlantic World

PAUL CHRISTOPHER JOHNSON

A spirit . . . may return again, incarnate in an electric streetcar.

—Machado de Assis

Parameters of Possession

Few problems are more central to the history of anthropology, or to the study of religion more broadly, than the ungainly catchall "spirit possession." Though the phrase seems cozily familiar, it gestures toward the unsettling and uncanny. "Possessed" action connotes unfree, nonautonomous, irrational, even possibly dangerous sorts of comportment—actions performed by bodies carrying multiple interior guides whose identities may or may not be transparent or discernable through everyday sensory cues. In the history of European encounters with peoples of Africa and the Americas, possessed action came to be viewed as the opposite of *individual* action—accountable, contract-worthy, transparent, and properly civil—in early modern social theories that became the template for almost all political states.[1] In fact, one might say, the figure of "the possessed" helped define the proper sort of individual in relation to which the state was imagined at all, beginning with the writings of Hobbes and Locke in the mid-seventeenth century.

The time is ripe for spirit possession to be realienated from its liminal status of being at once overly familiar as a category and overly strange as a phenomenon. In this volume, we invert these values: we examine the strange work of the category "spirit possession" (hereafter in quotes only when referring to the name of a generic comparative category), and the everyday nearness of spirit possession practices in Afro-Atlantic religious worlds. To achieve this, we revisit "spirit possession" to explore the ways in which the second part of the phrase, *possession*, weighs down and concretizes the ephemeral first term, *spirit*. "Possession" points relentlessly toward the material, the world of things, bodies and earth, its terrestrial dominion indexing original demonic connotations, especially though not only in the Christian West. When invoked as a noun, it never quite stands free of an implied preposition: possession connotes ownership *by*, control *over*, or physical occupation *of*. In this sense, possession directs, grounds, and localizes the sensations, experiences, and interpretations named as "spirits." The awkward conjunction "spirit possession," cues us right from the start that the historical and ethnographic study of spirits must begin with the materials to which those prepositions emphatically point—the land, flesh, words, and things through which spirits become recognizable, perceptible, and plausibly efficacious in the worlds of those who serve them.

If "spirit possession" is a founding anthropological category, for reasons elaborated in chapter 1, perhaps the most prominent category guiding the anthropology of religion today is "materiality," the crescendo of a generation's attention to the body, the senses, place and space, the visual, and the global circulation of commodities. This volume takes as its point of departure the premise that the old anthropological problem of spirits and the new one of materiality are only artificially, and mistakenly, held apart. We propose the examination of, on the one hand, the material dimensions and mediations of spirit possessions and, on the other hand, the diverse animations of materials, as intertwined and properly inseparable projects (Miller 2001; Modern 2011; Promey 2014; Stolow 2013).[2]

This makes intuitive sense. For example: I walk out the front door of an apartment in Paris. Around the corner is Henry Miller's former abode, where he composed his anything-but-triste *Tropiques* in the early 1930s, and there is the studio where the reclusive Chaim Soutine painted his unforgettable portraits and still-life carcasses. Across the street is the apartment Lenin occupied from 1909 to 1912. The intersection gives me pause. I am not quite transformed to the degree that my body feels owned or occupied, at least not to the point of forfeiting everyday, self-possessed consciousness, but I am surely transported as I pass this crossroads. I am "back there and here at the same time" (LaCapra 2001: 90) and in that sense possessed by early twentieth-century personages.[3] My reliance on multiple *trans-* verbs (*transform, transport*), with their shared root of "crossing over," serves to give spatial form to the otherwise inchoate shift of sensation. Presences pour into things, the street, bricks, and doors that mediate Soutine and Miller and Lenin and make them available to awareness. Their pasts infiltrate and tilt the here and now. They saturate my walk, slowing it down and coloring it with a patina of a specific time-place, a time-place, however, that I know only through the things they lived with and left behind. Books, paintings, and dwellings extend their former owners to my awareness, even from the grave (see, e.g., Gell 1998; Promey 2014).

Even as these walls and doors and pavement stones are permeated *by* the spirits of history, they also work *on* spirits and take part in producing, presenting, and shaping them, and this is the less intuitive perspective presented in the chapters of this volume. Notice the metaphors to which I am forced to resort in the previous paragraph: presences "pour" into things, and "saturate" my walk. Such formulations grant spirits a liquid form that is moving and fluid but at least provisionally able to be contained or blended. The aqueous fusibility endows the spirits of the dead with different characteristics than were they fitted with cosmic, electrical, or telluric terms, to name a few of the obvious alternatives. But the very materials and technologies that signaled and then channeled their metonymic influx also impinge on spirits and the particular ways they can appear: for example, house number 18 on Rue Villa Seurat, where Henry Miller penned his descriptions of precarious bohemian rambles, looks downright comfortable. The house mediates the spirit of Miller in a way that conflicts with his authorial voice, toning down its persona of hungry authenticity.

Why "Spirit Possession"?

The reader may rightly object that this affective registering of historical presences is not quite like spirit possession, which often implies the dramatic displacement of everyday consciousness. She may point to the several analogous words that make their appearance in this introduction, like "mediation" and "incarnation" and wonder why, given these rival candidates and many others, "spirit possession" deserves this much attention. After all, religious practitioners' descriptors for the arrivals of gods or ancestors may include "possession" but are as likely to include words like "manifest" or "descend" or phrases like "being turned," "rolled," "mounted," or "leaned on." There is just as little consensus on proper terminology among anthropologists and historians of religions. I. M. Lewis (1971) and then Erika Bourguignon (1976), most notoriously, preferred the terms "trance" or "dissociation" as neutral phenomenological descriptors, with spirit possession or shamanism standing as second-order interpretations of more primary psychic events. Gilbert Rouget refined the nomenclature even further, parsing "crisis," "trance," and "possession," with the latter two each presented as a subset of the former (1985: 3–62). In this volume, Karen

Richman's chapter points to the harmful misrecognitions "spirit possession" has generated when too easily applied to Haitian Vodou.

For these reasons and others, sophisticated recent critiques of the phrase "spirit possession" have called for its permanent demotion from scholarly use (e.g., McNeal 2011). Yet despite its wounds, "spirit possession" is still in active service, for better or worse. It remains the standard anthropological classification for ritual events in which a nonhuman entity is understood to displace the human person in a given body, with every invocation renewing, at least implicitly, the perennial problems of how to define the "person" in relation to the "body." Poignant for our concerns is the fact that the issues raised by "spirit possession" are especially sedimented in the literature on African and Afro-Atlantic religions.[4] In this volume, we take the geographic patterns of theoretical categories—the ways certain parts of the world are yoked to certain analytical frames—as an invitation rather than a foreclosure. Rather than lament the use of "spirit possession," we take it as an opportunity to interrogate theoretical genealogies as they are deployed in descriptions and interpretations of Afro-Atlantic religions. We are interested, furthermore, in the infiltrations of the phrase into religious practice itself, the ways in which the perceived presence of a deity or ancestor is transformed when understood, and performed, as "possession" instead of as something else (P. Johnson 2011).

Spirit possession warrants its starring role in this volume for at least three intersecting reasons. First, it has been long applied as the defining and even constitutive feature of Afro-Atlantic religions. Raymundo Nina Rodrigues, the first ethnographer of Afro-Brazilian religions, for example, asserted that in possession resides "the essence of all the religious practices of negros" ([1932] 2008: 215). Melville Herskovits (1941: 125, 221, 246) and Roger Bastide (1953: 30) likewise characterized spirit possession as the key feature and fundamental link between the religions.[5] A term like "shamanism," by contrast, has rarely been applied to African or Afro-Atlantic religions. Rather, shamanism has often played the foil for spirit possession and vice versa, with the two types juxtaposed in terms of ecstasy/enstasy (e.g., in Eliade 1964)—sending one's own spirit "out" versus receiving other spirits "within" (De Heusch 2006), with this varying physiology of spirits sometimes understood as an expression of differing ecologies of nomadic versus sedentary agricultural societies (e.g., Berti and Tarabout 2010)—or, alternatively, in terms of the relative subjective control over spirits versus being overwhelmed by spirits (e.g., Lewis1971). Spirit possession indexed the absence of control, the body without will, and, by extension, the figure of the slave. Shamanism connoted at least the partial control of spirits and mastery over space. Its mythohistorical figure was the Native American, who roams as freely as the horsemen of the Siberian steppes (whence *saman*, from Tungus), whereas the African slave was possessed, in multiple senses, and bound in place.

Second, spirit possession contains within it layered significations related to gods, things, bodies, ownership, and property, making it a crowded entrepôt for the exploration of religions formed and re-formed in the context of chattel slavery. In plantation societies, human bodies *were* very often things and property, or possessions, about which I say more in the next section. Third, possession or possession-like events conveying these intersecting religious and material significations are in fact valued in many Afro-Atlantic ritual practices and were both before and after Emancipation.

Persons, Things, and Person-Things

Modernity, it has been argued, was the name for the attempt to strictly separate agents from nonagents and persons from things (Latour 1993; Chakrabarty 2000; Keane 2007; Taylor 2007). The uniqueness of the Afro-Atlantic network that linked Europe and the Americas lay in the application of this dualism to human beings. Slaves were mostly regarded as things, though they were also on occasion, and in certain respects, considered persons (for example, as juridically responsible for their acts, and thus punishable by law). This contradiction produced legal oxymorons of thing-human hybrids, manifested in the United States in 1787 as the three-fifths calculus of personhood (Ghachem 2003). Such anthropological dualism was a basic foundation of the modern and endured for roughly four hundred years, from the end of the fifteenth century until 1888 and abolition in Brazil, the last slaving society in the Americas.

If slavery was its foundational institution and system of exchange, spirit possession provided a key category that helped affix the great ontological and social divide, parting those capable of ownership from those who could by right be owned, as bodies without will, or automatons. For example, the law governing France's slave trade, the Code Noir of 1685, stated, "We declare slaves to be incapable of possessing any thing except to the use of their master; and whatever they may acquire, either by their own industry, or the liberality of others, or by any other means, or under whatsoever title, shall be and accrue to their respective master in full property" (article XXVIII).[6] Slaves could not possess things or engage in contract making. In part, this was because they were possessed by spirits, proof positive of deficient personhood or capacity to act as agents or to act as rational authors of present and future contracts.

To be sure, many Africans and, once the slave trade was under way, Afro-Americans *were* possessed by spirits, though not usually with that precise nomenclature. Sometimes the spirits were even the possessors of what to Europeans were inanimate things or vacant lands. "The land is owned by a vast family of whom many are dead, a few are living, and countless hosts are still unborn" one seventeenth-century Gold Coast chief is reputed to have replied to European claims to land ownership (in Daaku 1970: 50). The question of colonial occupation of territory was therefore a question not only of the economic value of land but also of spirits and their ongoing presence, the "problematic presence of the properly absent" (Ivy 1995: 169). Metaphysics as well as physics were involved, and this was as true for Europeans as for Africans.[7] Africans and Afro-Americans had their own notions of agency and the parts spirits could play in extending or restricting personhood or packing land with ancestors' force, though they were little understood by Europeans and most often severely misrepresented. The chapters of this book interrogate the frictional encounters between European and Euro-American notions of spirit possession on one hand and Afro-Atlantic engagements with spirits on the other, and the effects of early modern and then anthropological classifications on the practice of those religions even today.[8]

The history of slavery hovers over and chains together the tropes of spirit possession, material possessions, and possessable persons. That legacy may not determine contemporary ritual performance, but at least in the context of the religions of African Americans it is often present, sometimes overtly and consciously, sometimes as a barely audible drone or a scar only just visible. We might go so far as to discern in this linkage a uniquely Afro-Atlantic religious ontology, though that must remain an empirical question to be decided inductively rather than simply asserted.[9] Toward the objective of discerning overlapping possession paradigms in the Americas, as well as salient differences, the chapters in this volume present comparable phenomena across a range of religions in Cuba, Haiti, Brazil, Puerto Rico, and the United States.[10] Taken together, they suggest an Afro-Atlantic ontology of personhood that relativizes and provincializes the premise of the autonomous modern individual and the strict distinction between persons and things. They announce that the autonomous individual was and is a fiction, a mis-en-scène whose successful staging hinged on the work of slaves and women and enslaved women (Lukes 1985: 299). As a bodily technology of history making, spirit possession events aid their practitioners in building a notion of personhood from out of the wreckage and body count of Atlantic slave history rather than by its effacement or elision. Attending to the materiality of spirit possession, these essays propose, provides a point of entry into the distinction between agents and things as that distinction played out against the backdrop of slavery in the New World, a backdrop that supplied the material conditions for and conceptually cast into relief the appearance of the rational, autonomous individual in Europe. In the history of the Afro-Atlantic, material possessions and spirit possessions *must* be related theoretically, then, not least because they were imbricated in the historical record—even in an occidental historical record that by definition excludes spirits as historical actors (De Certeau 1975: 3–4; Chakrabarty 2000; Palmié, forthcoming).[11]

The ways in which material and political contexts exert force on spirits' presence are this book's main concern, not the phenomenology of possession experiences. The latter have been long oversold as fascinating exotica. The essays of this volume pay attention to the politics, the economies, and the governance of spirits in order to understand the *means* of, *conditions* of, and *mediations* of spirits' presence. Spirits are never perennial or omnipresent, notwithstanding frequent claims to the contrary. There are always limits to their extension in space and to their duration in time, even in religious practice itself. The rituals that broker spirit appearances do not endure forever, after all; spirits arrive and leave, are present and then gone (Lambek 2009), and both their arrival and their departure depend on specific technologies of emergence and retreat, as well as legal and institutional affordances and restraints.

With this in mind, let's briefly return again to the spirits of a neighborhood in Paris: In 2003 the plaque that once marked and mediated Lenin's occupation of his apartment was removed by new owners unwilling to have his memory attached to their building, leaving only a square stain on the facade. Official memory ceased with the removal of the material thing through which Lenin remained. Though the trace left behind still announces that he is missing, in another decade even the stones will have forgotten. Spirits, even spirits of history[12] like Lenin, Soutine, and Miller, are known and perceived through things that extend their presence but also limit it in time and space. Conscious registering is always also an emplotment, in which spirits are made ever anew, and limited anew, by the material resources at hand.

Scrambling for purchase on this dialectical exchange between spirits and things, a dialectic that renders "history" present in the form of various "possessions," we might call another member of the "trans-" repertory into service, *transduction* (Keane 2012). Transduction describes how spirits are rendered sensible through processes of materialization and dematerialization and the power derived from shifts in semiotic modality (Keane 2012: 2). In this volume, we attend to transductions of a particular kind. Perhaps they can be captured in an even more awkward term, *explectation*, an Old French word recuperated by Raymond Williams that signified both explication—to spread out and arrange—and exploitation, the prospect of the seizure of lands, persons, and goods (Williams (1976) 1985: 130). Explectation gestures toward the politics of purification and to the ways Afro-Atlantic religions were interpolated through a massive asymmetry in power. When spirits and spirit possessions are purged, rationalized, or academically seized for comparative and theoretical purposes, the authors of this volume ask, what are the consequences of such translations, or transductions—the movement of words beyond the circuits that formed them into new sites and situations of use? Chapters by Elizabeth McAlister, Karen Richman, Patrick Polk, and Raquel Romberg raise the question of how "spirit possession" has been constituted by groups in power in order to stereotype, regulate, and exploit but also to mimic and appropriate subaltern groups' religious capacities.

The question of regulating the conditions of spirits' appearance means that spirit possession is entwined with issues of governance. Consider, for example, the early twentieth-century report filed by the German ethnographer of West Africa Leo Frobenius: "Thus, a few years ago such a possessed person, as he was called, burnt a whole village in the Gaboon district without anyone preventing him. . . . When the Government forces arrived there was a great row, and the arrest of the poor idiot almost led to a war. A similar incident would have caused still greater mischief, if the French officer on the spot had not shot down the maniac just in time" (1909: 156). We see in this brief passage how spirits present an indelibly *historical* challenge. Frobenius gropes for words to translate spirit actions into a more recognizable and familiar European frame, with the insertion of "as he was called" after the word possessed, not to mention the less effortful translations of the possessed as "poor idiot" and "maniac." The villagers in Gabon, meanwhile, strive to keep their spirits *in* history, thus the near war against government forces arriving on the scene to remove the possessed or shoot him down. In reading reports like that submitted by Frobenius, we realize that a shortsighted focus on the experience of spirit possessions, much attended to by anthropologists, travel writers, and filmmakers for over a century, does not tell us much without further material and political contextualizations. The more important story issuing from Frobenius's anecdote, and from the essays in this volume as well, is of how mutually constituting categories of accountable man[13] and possessed woman (and man) were played out through ideas of the civil risk. Afro-Atlantic possession religions were potentially dangerous, as the revolution in Haiti (1791–1804) made clear, because of the histories they "worked" and the potential inversions they promised. For that reason they were restricted in the Americas, everywhere from Surinam in the 1770s to Brazil and Cuba in the 1890s and to Trinidad with its prohibition against Shouters in 1916.

The policing of Afro-Atlantic religions required systematic misrecognitions to justify and ideologically undergird it, at least after the emancipation of slavery in a given state. Karen Richman's chapter takes stock of some of these misrecognitions, albeit ones that served a different kind of master than the colony. She explores how local possession experiences in Haitian villages were transduced into writing destined for an international readership by the author and filmmaker Maya Deren. Vodou experiences recounted in Deren's book and movie *Divine Horsemen*, among the most infamous published and filmed accounts of spirit possession, produced a comfortably appealing idea of the deities (*lwa*) as "nature spirits." This allowed Deren the conceit of constituting, through Vodou, a universal spiritual unity with nature and establishing rapport with European and North American readers on the basis of that appeal. But this was achieved on the backs of rural Haitians, whose notions of spirits' "speaking (or dancing) in the head" are anything but universal. To the contrary, serving the lwa is densely interwoven with specific relations to family and to land, a precious union of blood and soil called "heritage" (*eritaj*).

To counter such exoticizing depictions of the experiences of possession, in this volume we afford universalist rhapsodies like Maya Deren's little truck in their own right. Rather, the essays attend to possession experiences as specific, local forms of rhetorical and bodily encoding and as perceptual cultures able to discern spirits in things—in Kristina Wirtz's chapter, especially—or as the bundling in ritual practice of an interwoven sensory load that is named, at least when done according to code, "a spirit." So Raquel Romberg's essay brings into play the sensorial excesses of possession ritual dramas that transform corporeal manifestations into spiritual realities. Taken as a group, the chapters investigate spirit possession experiences as themselves a question of materials and materiality and of the body's remarkable capacities to "body forth" spirits (Jackson 2012: 71).

Fakery and Mimesis

The opposition between those who possess property and those who could be possessed *as* property was a crucial fulcrum of the Afro-Atlantic modern. Contemporary ritual events represent and intervene in that history, sometimes through the deliberate mimesis of colonial rule and enslavement, as Raquel Romberg's essay here suggests. She calls attention to the fact that exoticism is a form of misrecognition but also a medium of knowledge, and one not solely exercised by the dominant. There exists, rather, a "reciprocal shock" entailed by the encounter between different religions, even encounters wildly imbalanced by coercive force. Romberg's chapter is attentive to the productive uses of mimesis in possession performances and to the fractal potentialities of appropriations of the Other's representations of "us," especially as these have played out in the history of Puerto Rico.

Gods and ancestors may be caused to appear in various performative modes, of which spirit possession is only one. Another, for example, could be called the mode of the tableau vivant, in which various traditional activities—music, dress, food, locomotion, and so forth—are layered densely enough to generate an aesthetic of ancestral recollection or even presence (P. Johnson, forthcoming). These modalities can each be approached as mimesis. In the *Poetics*, Aristotle described art, like ritual, as mimesis, the craft of imitation or representation. Its mode can be direct, as in the imitation of a character with one's own voice, or even becoming another personality (section I, part 3), as occurs in spirit possession. Mimesis can also occur through a gradual rounding into form. In place of a direct representation, the object of mediation can be created through a harmony of parts, or even a synesthetic conversion, as when rhythmic dance with the feet is felt as an emotion of longing for return (section I, part 1) or when foods are coded to represent different places and times such that one eats, as well as dances, a history. We might think of two distinct mimetic modes applied in Afro-Atlantic religions: In one, the spirits are presented by *becoming* them through their incarnations in persons, as in possession. In the other, a sensibility of presence emerges gradually but progressively from a harmony of diverse actions executed well—performed, that is, "traditionally," or "properly." This latter persuades through display rather than through argument or direct evidence (*Rhetoric* I: 9). It is, that is to say, epideictic. Its goal is not to prove or persuade anyone of anything so much as it is to amplify something, a vague but valued sensibility. Yet Aristotle also invokes more directly technological methods of spiriting things, or thinging spirits, as when he recalls Daedalus's use of quicksilver to animate a figure of Aphrodite and cause her to move in *De Anima*.

What is distinctive about the mimetic mode of rendering a being present through spirit possession, the form given close attention in this volume, is that it entails a forensic claim: here in *this* woman's body *now* incarnate is Martino Amaya (or Ogun or Ezulie or Maria Padilha or the Holy Spirit). The forensic claim of incarnation that spirit possession often proffers may be disputed or even rejected outright as chicanery or other false representation ("She just wants attention" or "She's had too much to drink, as usual"). The mimetic mode of spirit possession may also allow for the surprising appearance of new, heretofore unknown ancestors or deities that abruptly shift the idea of family or the people or history.[14] An open comparative question is whether these different modes of ritual mimesis—the mode of possession, the mode of tableau vivant, or others—produce different ideas of the relevant dead, even *different gods, spirits, and ancestors*. Several chapters in this volume (including McAlister's and Selka's) consider spirit possession in its role as such a shifter that mediates and redirects between spirits and the Holy Spirit, between Afro-Atlantic religions and Pentecostalism, and between "black" and "white" genres of theatrical performance (Polk's chapter).

Other chapters (those of Brazeal, Romberg, and Palmié) give special attention to the topics of fakery and authenticity, an opposition that has inhabited the convention called spirit possession from its first appearance. In spirit possession events, the gap between the forensic claim of a god's true presence and the inchoate means and measures of determining such is consequential. While the accusation of fakery may be intended to demystify spirit possession, it also helps to constitute real possession through the "interpretive ferment" (Wirtz 2007) its opacity marshals. Authentic possession, after all, can only be determined by reading the *surfaces* of bodies as ciphers of what dwells within. Alongside spirit possession, fakery registered and helped to inaugurate a concern with transparency, the continuous, knowable identity of the person—the problem of "identity" in the most literal sense, as continuity across time and space. The problem of the fake and the challenge of distinguishing true versus counterfeit enactments helped conjure a purified class of religion and the role of the professional specialist able to decipher it.

In the early modern moment of the early encounters of Europeans with African religions, the specialists able to discern authentic from fraudulent possession were Christian priests and pastors. In consequence, the immediate source of the generic anthropological category of "spirit possession" as it was applied in Africa and the Caribbean was the Christian demonic script. The demonic script was established and standardized through a series of very public and widely circulated cases in Europe around the turn of the seventeenth century. Being *legitimately* possessed was not merely a subjective experience. It had to properly persuade, by sufficiently matching the convention of "being possessed." A persuasive case always included a familiar repertoire of symptoms legible on the body's exterior, on the skin, eyes and mouth. These served as narrative cues for otherwise "inner" events.

Besides a script and an established anatomical map, the effort to specify the invisible, internal workings required the refining of classificatory terms. Cotton Mather, for example, wrote that in one case "enchantment" by evil spirits seemed to be growing very far toward an actual "possession" (1697: 9). "Possession" and "obsession" were distinguished during the same period. During the seventeenth century, argued Ernst Benz (1972), the beatific and demonic notions of possession were firmly divided, Ergriffenheit/Bessenheit (pneuma/daimon). Through the refinement of terms interpreting and evaluating the body's surface, possession was generated from the beginning through the prospect of counterfeit, and a class of specialists able to expose it. Fakery *had* to be part of possession's discourse, not least because possession required matching thoroughly underdetermined symptoms whose source was finally unverifiable. For Ignatius Loyola, to take an even earlier example, only by the closest observation within oneself of the *after*effects of spirits' comings and goings could it be determined whether the visitation had been good or evil, God or a dissimulating demon.[15]

In light of this insurmountable indeterminacy, Foucault suggested, the progressing medicalization of demonology engendered a novel hermeneutics of the self. Determining who, and what, possesses you required and hailed a sophisticated reckoning of interior life (Foucault [1962] 1999: 76). Here we near the inaugural moment of the "modern" making of the individual, where Descartes begins the *Meditations* with the question of his own possession: "There is some unidentified deceiver . . . who is dedicated to deceiving me constantly. Therefore, it is indubitable that I also exist, if he deceives me" (24). Alongside the standard Cartesian quip, "I think therefore I am," we must take account of this other Cartesian line of thought, namely: "I may be *deceived*, therefore I am."

The essays in this volume explore the issues of fakery and authenticity in various cases, presenting valuable resources for comparison. Romberg's chapter gives close attention to present-day theories and practices of mimesis and fakery as well as the mirroring between marginalized and master classes enacted in possession events. Brian Brazeal's chapter describes the cross-referencing between claims of authentic and fake gemstones and claims of authentic and fake possession by *orixás*, the gods of Afro-Brazilian Candomblé in Brazil's northeastern interior. Patrick Polk shows how whites would portray blacks on stage in US minstrel theater, but spirits in Spiritualist séances would sometimes portray whites portraying blacks. These chapters remind us that if "spirit possession" was born from questions of authenticity, transparency, and legitimacy, which defined the new European figure of the autonomous, rational individual vis à vis the opaque, irrational Other (as I describe in chapter 1), its contemporary practices remain thoroughly enmeshed with, and even dependent upon, the prospect of the fake.

Spirited Things

Kristina Wirtz's essay in this volume directly addresses the set of exchanges by which certain things come to stand for otherwise intangible spirits' presence, since spirit actions must by necessity be registered in the form of sensible experiences. In what representational economy do spirit materializations in bodies come to make objective sense? The answer to that question, she finds, has important consequences for religious practice. Working in the Cuban city of Santiago, Wirtz explores what she calls the "aesthetics of sensibility," the ways practitioners of Afro-Cuban religions develop particular techniques of discernment and skills of perception—*perspicience*, in Wirtz's nomenclature—beginning with bodily sensations like shivers or prickling on the skin and ascending to full-blown sensations of possession. "To discern spirits," Wirtz shows, "requires being inculcated into a culturally specific phenomenology in which the material effects of immaterial agencies become sensible experiences." The ways esoteric registers are shifted to material registers and back again is key to the question of thinking about spirits' relation to things. Anthropologists and others must try to "travel back up this chain" if we hope to understand what spirit possession entails for a given group.

Patrick Polk's moving chapter in this volume describes the close relations between theater and spirit possession or, to be more specific, between minstrelsy and Spiritualism, in the United States of the nineteenth century. The theater of blackface racial representation used spirit possession for the stereotypical evocation of African American characters. Even more surprisingly, Polk shows that the black spirits conjured during Spiritualist séances were often directly drawn from the repertory of minstrel theater—spirits who sang and danced, played the banjo, told jokes, and generally entertained the audience with highly conventional pejorative scripts of blackness. Based on the evidence presented by Polk's chapter, we might even say that spirit possession in Spiritualist practice was mediated by minstrel theater. Spiritualism relied for its technê bringing forth not only on devices like the alternation of light and darkness or a narrative beginning and end but even on minstrel theater's cast of African American characters. It relied on theater, but it was also a form of theater, a racialist, and usually racist, show staged in darkened salons for elite groups of whites.

A somewhat different "theatrical" approach to spirit possession can be seen in the notion of "possession-performances," to take Karen Brown's (1991) phrase, where spirit possession itself is used as a dynamic subaltern historical theater (Leiris 1958; Métraux 1958; Drewal 1992; Stoller 1997; Lambek 2002). From this perspective, spirits gather and re-present critical historical episodes, rendering them present to experience, conscious scrutiny, critical commentary, and revision. European colonial officers are common spirit figures, as Jean Rouch's film *Les maîtres fous* famously depicted in a Hauka possession ritual in Niger (Romberg's chapter in this volume recalls that Rouch himself was entranced while filming, according to his own report), but spirits traverse more recent history too. In Brazilian Candomblé, African kings jostle with spirits of twentieth-century figures like prostitutes, Asian immigrants, cowboys, and even anthropologists—after all, the French photographer Pierre Verger has become an *egungun*, a living ancestor in one house of Brazilian Candomblé.[16] The revolutionary general Dessalines, who declared Haitian independence in 1804, appears in Haitian Vodou spirit possession ceremonies, but so does the notorious "president for life" François Duvalier (dictator from 1957 to 1971; P. Johnson 2006). Among the Garifuna of Honduras, Belize, and Guatemala, spirits are usually memorable deceased grandparents or great-grandparents who left multiple progeny.

The process of becoming an ancestral spirit is at least in principle democratic. "Spirits are for all, and everyone becomes a spirit," wrote Malinowski (1948: 69). All ancestors are potential spirits and potential representations of history that are available for activation by the living, with this florid multiplicity itself suggesting a kind of irony to possession performance not wholly unlike that of modern theater proper (Lambek 2002: 266–71).[17] Yet in practice becoming a spirit is rare, the provenance of a restricted elite. Activating a spirit, making a piece of history move, dance, and speak, takes enormous work. It requires memory work but also aesthetic, material, and even mechanical work. Even if everyone *may* become a spirit, as Malinowski claimed, few actually do, at least ones that are remembered beyond a generation. Given the high degree of selectivity applied in possession performances, the essays here are attuned to the question of possession as embodied history making and how history making is contingent on material questions of spirit possession's selective staging.

Stephan Palmié's astonishing chapter unfolds the uses of fin-de-siècle sound technologies in mediating, announcing, and quite literally amplifying the power of spirits to impinge on human sensory perception. Spirits possess, but they are themselves bound into human regimens of apperception, language, and technology. The need to materialize spirits through bricolage in relation to the materials at hand, including things, bodies, and places, means that spirit possession performances function not only as a theater of history but as a place for working out the relation *to* historical conditions. Spirits appear in relation to stones in Brazeal's chapter, in relation to sound technologies in Palmié's essay, in relation to bodies for Romberg, in relation to certain kinds of perception of and speech about the saturation of things for Wirtz, in relation to Haitian land for Richman and McAlister, in relation to minstrel theater for Polk, and in relation to Pentecostal church networks for Selka. Possession performances are ritual events in which ancestral personages are brought face to face with contemporary constraints and opportunities, even as they are conjured as practical tools or go-betweens for negotiating material crises. This close attention to the material economy of spirit possession may appear obvious, yet it has not been the usual course for interpreting spirit possession. All rhetoric to the contrary, the usual course has been to apply a superstructural notion of religion—possession performances as coded sites of "expressive culture" rather than as a bodily technology applied to the transforming the very conditions of life. Working with spirits, the authors of this volume show, is itself a form of material practice, an expenditure or wager of resources toward aspired-to benefits of health, wealth, love, and other signs of flourishing, and a technology for making and adjusting the boundaries of "selves" and communities.

Spirit possession is a theater of potential pasts, selectively activated by ritual performers for purposes in the present. Because it is tuned to address current needs, it is as hypermodern as the use of virtual-body avatars used by computer whiz kids to live in and through multiple characters, such that the question of who, and where, the "author" of action is, is unclear. An author may fuse with his avatar, an idea the blockbuster movie *Avatar* profitably explored, or may not. In short, the fulsome post- or late-modern attention to spirits and possession by scholars writing today is in part driven by "possession's" intersections with ideas and technologies of mediumship and by the fascinating mélange of ciphers of the ancient and contemporary media. Michael Lambek names this the "mediated belonging characteristic of the ancestral chronotope" (2002: 237). What is important to note for our purposes is that the bringing forth of the sense of ancestrality may be carried out by engaging the most avant-garde materials and technologies.[18]

Palmié's chapter, to wit, recounts an instance when the presence of Écue, the origin spirit of Afro-Cuban Abakuá, was produced through "sonic enchantment." Closely examining the documentation of Abakuá ritual performances by Cuban émigrés the Leal brothers in Philadelphia shortly after the turn of the twentieth century, Palmié examines the sound amplification technologies through which the voice of Abakuá origins, Écue, was enabled to speak to the streets of Philadelphia. The voice of Écue was manifested through its "sonic mask." Most remarkable in this case, however, is not just the uses of sound engineering to enchant by sonically projecting and amplifying Écue into the streets of Philadelphia but the fact that the very enchantments that produced Écue were built into the period's revolutions in sound recording. Telegraphy, the phonograph's immediate precursor, was motivated by Bell's and Edison's attempts to record and preserve messages from the dead in the form of sound vibrations transmitted from an invisible world. This was, as Palmié notes, after Sahlins (1981), a genuine "structure of the conjuncture" between two semiotic systems, Spiritism and sound recording.

Brian Brazeal's chapter in this volume reveals a different structure of the conjuncture, between technologies of authentication applied in gemstone mining and in verifying "real" spirit possession. The economies of mining and Candomblé are woven together in Bahia, Brazil, since both depend on claims of value that are difficult if not impossible to verify on the surface of things or the surfaces of bodies: "Just as a shell of mica schist can conceal a worthless rock or a brilliant gem, so too can the bodily hexis of spirit possession performance conceal a fraud or reveal a veritable god on earth." In these linked economies, accusations of fraud are chronic, only reinforcing the prestige of the authentic. (See also Romberg's chapter here and Wirtz 2007.) In both gemstone mining and Candomblé ritual practice in Bahia, Brazeal shows, "quick" advantage is readily available but also spiritually dangerous. Money made with bad stones or bad rituals can equally well turn against their users. What shines in Brazeal's work is how he demonstrates that spirit possession is read through and in relation to the hermeneutics of gemstone trade and vice versa: emeralds, like certain spirits, have the gleam of the Devil.[19]

The key point is not simply that gemstones and spirit possession are similar, or even contiguous, in that they both depend on semiotic castings of inner/outer and the crisis of representation caused by the boundary. It is rather that the economies of spirit possession and gemstone trade are inextricably intermediated. Spirit possession in the Bahian hinterland takes place not just in terms of but *in and through* gemstone trade, just as spirit possession in nineteenth-century US Spiritualism transpired in and through the theater (Polk) and emerging phonographic research (Palmié), and just as Holy Spirit possession in Brazil's United Church of the Kingdom of God happens in and through the prospect of cell phone and automobile acquisition (Selka). These material regimes outfit spirits with their signs and modes of being, their perceptibility (Wirtz) in the world. Without these things, spirits fail to become present at all.

Yet this not the same as familiar materialist translation of spirit possession either, because the intermediation also pushes in the other direction, toward a recognition of the spiriting of things and the ways their very thingness, or materiality, is remade: sound technologies leading to the phonograph became hybrid spirit-sound technologies; gemstones in Bahia are spirit stones; cars aspired to by Brazilian Pentecostals are spirit cars; Haitian soil is thickly sedimented in spirits (Richman) and for that reason also a territory of war between Vodouists and Pentecostals (McAlister); Spiritualism in the United States was "theatrical" in its deployments of blackface minstrel characters, but the genre of theater was also possessed by Spiritualism. These spirited things, things that are intercalated within the semiotic ideology of possession by spirits, gain extrautilitarian powers and autonomy of their own. The woman holding her spirit phone to her ear is a different person with this prosthetic, listening differently to the sounds it makes, attending to the communications it brokers, and choosing carefully the words she utters into it. The camera understood by Alfred Russell Wallace to demonstrate irrefutably the near presence of spirits of the dead in portraits is a different camera than the one alleged to show the hard durability of the "objective" natural world.[20] Such objects act and exert force; they constrain, enable, extend, or channel even allegedly individual self-possessed will. As spoken-through vessels, spirit things brush against the "the tyranny of the individual"[21] and the private ownership and occupation of allegedly empty things, lands, or bodies.

On the issue of land possessions and the emptiness or fullness of land,

Elizabeth McAlister's groundbreaking chapter in this volume explores how contemporary Pentecostal missions in Haiti regard the land as "demonically entrenched" because of the presence of ancestors resident in the soil. Pentecostals seek to "dispossess" the earth of such ancestral spirit forces in order to "repossess" territory for Christ. McAlister calls this kind of spiritual mapping a theo-geography, one in which the attempt to replace Vodou spirits by the Holy Spirit in certain ways recapitulates the French colonial possession of Haiti, even as it also indigenizes the Holy Spirit, endowing it with a specifically Haitian profile.

Stephen Selka's essay on rival neo-Pentecostal and Afro-Brazilian discourses of "spirit possession" suggests how the phrase pivots between contrasting ideas of spirits—the Afro-Brazilian orixás of Candomblé versus the neo-Pentecostal Holy Spirit of the Universal Church of the Kingdom of God—but also between notions of materiality and material acquisition. In Universal Church exhortations, it is precisely the liberation from Afro-Brazilian spirit possession that opens the path to material possessions—a new cell phone or a new car becomes the material index of the authentic work of the Holy Spirit, who desires congregants to assert their true God-given freedom to "take possession" rather than forfeiting their freedom by "being possessed." Selka's chapter is exemplary of an important focus of this volume, the boundary work done by the category of spirit possession in classifying and distinguishing between religious groups and the material effects of those classifications.

We explore, in short, the ritual production of spirits from a regime of things: the plantation; the Catholic church; the sea; nineteenth-century theater; gemstone mining; land called *eritaj*; the telegraph, the phonograph, and the emergence of new sound technologies; the languages of European masters; the Pentecostal church; and, not least, the human body. The point of attending to the spiriting of things as well as the thinging of spirits is to open the way to the study of reciprocal actions of spirits and things as they generate hybrid forms of possessive agency, where such possessions are morally neutral rather than marked as deviant.

Spirits in the Theater of History

Michael Lambek's afterword to the volume raises important critiques, none more fundamental than the question of whether the economy of slavery and the trope of persons as property figure as prominently in contemporary possession practices as is proposed in this introduction and in chapter 1. For, as he notes, those possessed are as much the "owners" of their spirits as vice versa (see also Lewis 1971: 55, 63). Likewise, in Brazilian Candomblé, as Stefania Capone has written, initiated spirit holders are possessed by, but are also understood to possess, the tutelary deities seated in their head, as in "João's Xangô," expressing the interdependency and reciprocity of human-divine relationships (Capone 2010: 20). If so, possession priests as often play the part of owners as they do of spirits' slaves. A possession priest may also assume the role of a parent in relation to her spirit, striving to properly civilize an unruly child, as when dealing with a *santo bruto*, a deity that manifests but does not yet know how to properly behave (Cossard-Binon 1970: 204). People are possessed by but also possess their spirits; they are ridden but also ride the spirits; they are corrected and disciplined by spirits but also correct and discipline their spirits. Furthermore, spirits, at least those Lambek describes in Madagascar, which may be differently constituted than those forged in the context of the plantation system of the Americas, act like familiar persons more than historical masters or slaves. It is, he argues, far from clear that the history of slavery and its conversion of persons into possessable things formed a determinative structure for the significations of spirit possession rites.

Lambek's corrective caution is important. Still, one can reject the notion that the history of slavery structures and determines Afro-Atlantic spirit possession performances without rejecting the hypothesis that such rituals are predicated on a series of semantic links between possession and historically constituted notions of property and servitude. Chapter 1 makes a strong argument for the central role of these ideas in the historical production of the comparative category "spirit possession" in the Atlantic world. Taken as a whole, though, the essays in this volume resist such a straightforward thesis and follow Lambek's recommendation to explore the mixed tropes of ownership, servitude, partnership, and family as diverse forms of relationship are enacted and played out through spirit possession events. "Being possessed" weaves a web of reciprocal relationships that together constitute a form of (putatively) agentless action, an ironic deferral, as Lambek argues, and a shifting of one's place in the world. If so, it is possible to imagine possession less as a "loss of self" than as a "widening" of self, to borrow William James's term ([1901] 1961: 398), into a multivocal or polyphonic being. Rather than a loss of agency, spirit possession may multiply possibilities of speech and act by expanding what Michel Leiris (1958) referred to as the vestiary of personalities. Rather than a decrease of moral accountability, as has been claimed for religions in which "individual accountability" is replaced by a plurality of personae, moral accountability may in certain cases be expanded through the multiplication of witnesses and of truth-saying voices that easily discredit narrowly self-interested discourse.

We hope that the chapters in this volume generate empirical responses to some of the criticisms presented by Lambek. If not, how might scholars constructively respond in future work? One response is to treat Afro-Atlantic ritual complexes formed within and on the margins of chattel slavery in their proper specificity rather than as typical of spirit possession tout court. The second response is to properly distinguish the formation of "spirit possession" as a generic comparative class in the gaze of Europeans—which in my view *must* be contextualized in relation to the Atlantic slave trade and other colonial ideas of the body as property—from spirit possession *practices*, which, as Lambek rightly notes, are far from determined by such frames. The third response is to observe that the figurations of "master" and "slave" activated in the idiom of spirit possession practices do not determine how these roles are played out, since these roles may be worked, inverted, redeemed, or transcended in their enactments. And the fourth response is to attend not only to spirit possession's scripts and historically determined inflections but also to the ways spirit possession opens out and can serve as a radical semiotic shifter, at times entirely bursting the Afro-Atlantic frame set out here.

Though the idea of spirit possession as a local, subaltern form of history making has been extraordinarily important, not all ancestral or divine returns are about tradition, history, or the past at all. Sometimes they are assertions of cosmopolitanism, playing on the image of the Other (Taussig 1992) to imagine different pasts and futures than those documented by historians. The possession model is extraordinarily flexible toward this end, as the Angolan and Caboclo nations of Candomblé in Brazil affirm every day with their cast of cowboys, prostitutes, racecar drivers, and "turks" (e.g., Boyer 1999; Dianteill 2008; Hayes 2011), as do the Brazilian Spiritists with their pantheon of impressionist painters, scientists, and presidents (Aubrée and Laplantine 1990; Hess 1991).[22] In these cases, maybe it isn't worth arguing for the deep Africanness or Afro-Brazilianness of Candomblé that the ancestors-as-lived-history idea seems to require. Half of the practitioners of Candomblé, after all, aren't of African descent at all, or at least don't identify themselves that way in any context other than in the terreiro (Pierruci and Prandi 2000; Silva 1995; Sansone 2003).[23] Saraiva (2010), describing Candomblé in Portugal, portrays its constituency as mostly middle-class Portuguese, since most Afro-Brazilian immigrants in Portugal embrace not Candomblé but Pentecostalism. When a Portuguese is possessed by an African king and speaks of maintaining "the tradition," what shall we take this to mean? *Tradition* in these cases works as a placeholder for something important, but it very likely is not enslavement or the body as property or memory or history. It shifts to mean something more like the other mimetic mode described above, that of the tableau vivant, a performance devoted to cultivating and amplifying a sensibility. But a sensibility of what? The meanings attributed to spirits in these multiply diasporic situations are open ended, brilliantly creative, and unburdened of any foundational past.

Nevertheless, noting the play of possession and its creative capacity to "open out" (Boddy 1994) does not relieve the burden of attempting to trace the histories of domination when they *are* worked—remembered, revisited, revised, reversed—in at least many possession events of the Americas. And it also does not lessen the import of discovering the genealogy of "spirit possession" as a lens of the European and Euro-American gaze, ground in the context of transatlantic slavery, as we apply that scratched and blurry lens to the close study of specifically situated possession events and practices.

Many of the chapters that follow show how spirit possession performances are mediated by late-modern technologies and materials—sound amplification, gemstone authentication, and digital maps of theo-geographies. Yet spirit possession was for most of its intellectual life studied as a theater of pasts only anachronically related to the present.[24] Scholars of religion during the nineteenth and much of the twentieth century used the category of spirit possession and the African and Afro-Atlantic religions to which it was firmly tied as stepping-stones on which to chart progress.[25] "Atavistic," for example, was a recurring descriptor for possession. It was the word Fernando Ortiz, the first anthropologist of Afro-Cuban religions, applied to the African *brujos* of 1905 Cuba during a nervous period of determining the civil place of Afro-Cuban religions in the newly independent nation, if any. But the word begs some obvious questions: If spirit possession is an atavism, "from the time beyond our grandfathers," when, and where, is it from? What traces of the time of manufacture does "it" retain?

To begin to answer this question, chapter 1 moves the lens back to an earlier strategic point of entry, to spirit possession's place and time of departure as a comparative descriptor and generic thing, formed in relation to a very specific imagination of modernity and the purified ideas of spirits, persons, and things it required and hailed. Chapters 2 and 3, by Palmié and Polk, are also historical chapters on the material regimes out of which spirits and possessions were composed. Chapters 4 and 5, by Wirtz and Brazeal, address semiotic processes and structures of exchange out of which ideas of spirits are made to appear, become perceptible, and to possess and be possessed by ritual practitioners. Chapters 6 and 7, by Selka and McAlister, deal with the interfaces of Afro-American spirit possessions and Christian Pentecostal practices of ongoing revelation, of "getting the Spirit," in Brazil and in Haiti. The chapters speak to the material domains that register successful spirit presence, money and land, and the ways these are also sites for making and marking religious difference. Chapters 8 and 9, by Richman and Romberg, present sophisticated interrogations and critiques of "spirit possession." Richman gives close attention to universalist claims embedded in the category, delineating both a genealogy of how they came into being in the study of Vodou and the specific ways they distort the actual practice of Vodou. Romberg offers a splendid exploration of the issues of mimesis and fakery as they have developed within and in relation to the category of spirit possession, drawing on her long-standing fieldwork in Puerto Rico. Finally, Chapter 10, by Michael Lambek, offers a careful response to the issues raised in the volume as a whole, penned by the scholar whose many books informed and stimulated all of the contributors' interest in the category of spirit possession.

ONE

Toward an Atlantic Genealogy of "Spirit Possession"

PAUL CHRISTOPHER JOHNSON

Discourses and legal actions naming and constraining "spirit possession" over the past four centuries were a lever creating the dual notions of the rational individual agent—one who possesses, rather than being possessed—and the civil subject of an emergent modern state. The silhouette of the propertied citizen and free individual took form between, on one hand, the specter of the automaton or zombie, a machine-body without will and, on the other hand, the threat of the primitive or animal, being ruled by passions (or the two merged, as in Descartes's "nature's automata," animals as machines [2003: 24, 29, 66]).[1]

The balance between the lack of will and its unchecked excess, especially in relation to governance, has been perceived through the prism of the dangers of spirits in relation to persons and objects at least from the mid-seventeenth century to the present. Often it has been thought of in relation to African religions, where the prospect of turning bodies into machines, as slaves, and Europeans' dread of unrestrained religious frenzy, often named as "possession," were conjoined, with the latter justifying the former.

This is not to suggest that the term "possession" first or solely emerged out of colonial processes. Possession is a very old Latin term derived from the roots of *potus*, to be able, and *sedere*, to sit. Though it has long been applied to the image of spirits' occupations of bodies, what is important for my purposes is simply the observation that notions of property preceded and guided notions of spirits' capacity to "sit" in flesh. I would like to consider how the terms of property, the place one can sit, were transferred to ideas about the human body, its ownership, and its volition.[2]

"Religion" was part and parcel of this project. As a freshly minted universal feature of the newborn universal man around the mid-seventeenth century, it emerged as a generic human class of thought and action through a process of purification, the exorcism of spirits to leave a properly buffered, impenetrable, self-possessed being (De Certeau 1975; Taylor 2007), one who could then *freely believe* in God, or at least in God's natural laws.[3] This purification harnessed the new anthropology of the savage to descriptions of classical antiquity—often, present West Africa to ancient Egypt—conjuring the category of "religion" from the comparison of present enactments with those of earlier stages and places. This was a story of progress rather than of declension as the savage had usually been narrated in the wake of the Columbian encounter. Thus by the time of Diderot and D'Alembert's *Encyclopédie*, to consider just one site of the making of a generic class, "religion," we find a squawking menagerie of all the savage things religion had allegedly superseded—"superstition," "magic," "fanaticism," "idolatry," "fetishism," and many others from before and abroad. By the time we arrive at "religion," there's little point in reading further; we know it will consist of the duly cleansed remainder. The new universal man was construed as a bearer of a new generic content, Religion, and this new being at once marked and helped create the conditions for concluding a century and a half of wars following the Reformation. But those conditions only came into being through the "whithering" of ecstasy (Heidegger 1962: 416), pushing it overseas to places that were chronotopes of the spatially distanced past of humankind.[4] Possession by spirits was circumscribed by a broad range of descriptors of boiling religious excess—passions, frenzy, enthusiasm and, sociologically, the "horde," or "la foule" (Le Bon 1894, 1895). Kant, to take one prominent example, derided practices of seeking direct divine inspiration with Martin Luther's dismissive word *Schwärmerei* (Hollywood 2011). Nested within a cluster of such terms, "possession" was rendered a stable concept in parallel with "religion." The mid-seventeenth-century category of religion, a properly *civil* religion of Jean Bodin, Hobbes, or Locke, was purified in dialogue with a protoanthropological notion of spirit possession as civil danger. "Bit by bit concepts are purified: a small part remains, while the rest is thrown away as rubbish" (Kant [1766] 2002: 45).

Via the labor of the negative, "spirit possession" defined the rational, autonomous, self-possessed individual imagined as the foundation of the modern state, in canonical texts from Hobbes, Locke, Charles de Brosses, Hume, Kant, and many others, as those texts constructed the free individual and citizen against a backdrop of emerging colonial horizons. It would be too simple to reduce the matter to "outing" the old gang by recounting Hobbes's stakes in the Virginia Company from 1622 to 1624 or Locke's role in the writing of the constitution of the Carolinas, where absolute power

Another complication of the conventional argument is that it isn't sufficient to suggest that spirit possession merely *derived* from (mis)translations of what missionaries and traders encountered, for those agents also created or at least accelerated what they "found" (Mayes 1995: 5). Spirit possession gained force and frequency in the African Americas under and after the regimes of slavery, even compared with Africa itself (Mattos 1986: 127), so much so that African-born slaves in Brazil were surprised at the prominence and frequency of possession in creole practices they in other ways found similar to those of the homeland (Nina Rodrigues 1935: 101; Harding 2000: 155). To take a contemporary example, "possession" befalls Haitian migrants in the United States like children who would never be legitimate candidates for being possessed at home (K. Brown 1991: 253; Richman 2005). In this sense, Sartre's intervention in his preface to Fanon's *Wretched of the Earth* has it wrong: "In certain districts they make use of that last resort—possession by spirits. Formerly this was a religious experience in all its simplicity, a certain communion of the faithful with sacred things; now they make of it a weapon against humiliation and despair." (1963: 19). Sartre was wrong in the sense that it was not just the *uses* of it, but the very "it" that was made and remade as social and economic relations changed in time and place. Without going so far as to reduce spirit possession to a ritual response to conditions of suffering—though that argument has been powerfully made, especially to assess the overwhelming frequency of women as its enactors (e.g., Lewis 1971; Caciola 2003)—there seems to be something about "possession" as at once the filling of and the mediating and reinstituting of diasporic and other kinds of absence.[9]

A third complication from the conventional narrative is that spirit possession's arc was not merely descriptive or theoretical but entailed dramatic practical effects on the ways formerly secret religions became public (P. Johnson 2002). Its anthropological canonization was enormously influential on the study of Afro-Atlantic religions. The first ethnographic descriptions of Afro-Brazilian and Afro-Cuban religions, by Raymundo Nina Rodrigues and Fernando Ortiz, respectively, were direct applications of Tylor's ideas. But these studies in turn also had far-reaching legal consequences. Spirit possession was a gatekeeping mechanism for constructing the good society and proper civil comportment, and its long-standing association with religions of African origin posed high legal, political, and social barriers to former slaves in the new republics of Brazil, Cuba, the United States, and elsewhere.

Finally, there is a fourth complication to the conventional narrative, and though I only have space to signal it here, the chapters that follow demonstrate it amply: as religious adepts themselves begin to adopt the moniker of "possession" as a first-order term in their own practices, this translated bodily phenomena previously described in manifold other ways into the terms of property and ownership, *potus sedere*. Learning to perform certain forms of ritual experience *as* "being possessed" transforms religious practice and experience itself.

Topography of the Possessed: From the Indian to the African

As spirit possession emerged as a generic comparative class in the seventeenth century, it served simultaneously as a medicalization of demonology and an engendering of a novel hermeneutics of the self. Determining who and what possesses who and what possesses a given body required an articulated system of interior life (Foucault (1962) 1999). But as that interior life was shaped in Europe, possession was increasingly "found" abroad, and the two processes were related. In the sixteenth and seventeenth centuries, the possessed were primarily "Indians." Recall the long trajectory of the Amerindians like the Brazilian Tupi in European thought—from Montaigne to Shakespeare to Rousseau.[10] All these citations hinged at their outset on the rival descriptions by the French Franciscan royal cosmographer André Thevet ([1575] 1986) and the Huguenot Jean de Léry ([1578] 1990). Cannibalism was the spectacular center of both descriptions, but possession was a near second. Thevet reported that more than one hundred times he seized the bodies of possessed Indians and, reciting the Gospel of Saint John and other texts, conquered every demon—all in ten weeks. These repeated possession events provided at once an alleged domain of religious intersubjectivity that linked Frenchman to Tupi—since they used an overlapping repertory of ideas and acts to communicate a body occupied by spirits (de Léry, to wit, found in Indians' possessions a soapbox from which to fulminate against what he called the atheist dogs of Europe)—and a graphic demonstration of religious hierarchy, Christians on top. The transfer of "possession" to the Americas and then Africa entailed the mapping of Christian demonic imagery and nomenclature onto the figure of the savage.

A century after Jean de Léry's and André Thevet's reports, possession began to be viewed less as the problem of the savage and more and more as a dangerous propensity generic to all humanity. The spectacle of victory over the spirits would become less that of Christian over savage and increasingly one of the civil over the mob. Indigenous religions continued to play the foil, but the geography of the possessed Other gradually shifted from the Americas to Africa and the Caribbean. By the 1700s, the possessed place was Africa and the African Americas.[11]

The key juncture in the shift to Africa was the publication of the Dutchman Willem Bosman's *A New and Accurate Description of the Coast of Guinea*. Composed as a series of twenty-two letters during 1701–2, it was published in Dutch in 1704, then translated into French and English in 1705 and into German in 1706. Bosman's was the definitive text about Africa of the age, but its wider significance lay in disseminating in print the word *fetiche*.[12] Bosman's report and the word *fetiche* were quickly picked up in the last version of Pierre Bayle's *Réponse aux questions d'un provincial* (1707, 4: 372), for example, where he placed African savages and ancient Greek temple priests within the same frame of comparison in a rhetorical move that thereafter became standard. Several decades later it became the primary source for Charles de Brosses's *Du culte de dieux fétiches* (1760). Though in Diderot's *Encyclopédie* it was awarded its own entry, it retained a stricter provenance, "nom que les peoples de Guinée en Afrique donnent à leurs divinité" (name that the people of Guinea give to their god).[13] It was de Brosses, in his 1760 *Du culte des dieux fétiches*, who applied the word for the first time as a much wider class, "La Religion du Fétichisme" (18).[14] De Brosses gave a distinctive meaning to fetishism, as the worship of objects themselves, a sub-process of "idolatry" (84). His ideas influenced Hume, who avidly read Bayle and exchanged letters and manuscripts with de Brosses. Thereafter, Kant used fetishism in his *Religion within the Limits of Reason Alone* ([1791] 1960a: 168), and Hegel invoked it in the *Philosophy of History* (1956: 94). Auguste Comte declared fetishism a universal stage of development—though with Africans as exemplary (e.g., 1891: 260)—on the ascent to theology, the metaphysical, and ultimately positive knowledge. Marx adopted it from his reading of de Brosses in 1842 but also through his readings of Hegel and, later, the anthropologist Sir John Lubbock's *The Origin of Civilisation* (1870), and Tylor's *Primitive Culture* (1871). Tylor subsumed fetishism within the still more encompassing category of animism.[15] Much of this is familiar terrain.

What hasn't been noted is how, in nearly all of these uses, possession (whether as that word itself, or using analogous descriptive terms like "frenzy," "madness," or "wild gesticulation") appears as fetishism's accomplice. In Hegel's *Philosophy of History*, to take just one instance, the two noted features of African magic are fetishism—objects indiscriminately endowed with independent agency—and "special ceremonies with all sorts of gesticulations, dances, uproar, and shouting" (1956: 94). The link between these was applied even to late nineteenth-century descriptions of African American Christianity, where "fetish dances" and "animal excitement" remained a tandem description (Chireau 2003: 125–26). The pioneering ethnographic books on Afro-Brazilian and Afro-Cuban religions likewise yoked fetishism and possession tightly together, even nominatively: Raymundo Nina Rodrigues referred to "fetishist possession" ([1896] 1935: 109), and Fernando Ortiz (1906: 84, 26) suggested "idol possession" (*posesión del ídolo*) and "fetichismo con manifestaciones animistas." These new theoretical hybrids joined the primitives' faulty ontology of objects to a loss of personhood in uncontrolled states.[16] Yet the whole artifice, the link between ideas about the misperception of things (fetishism), a mental state of indeterminate agency (possession), and a social quality (the frenzy of the horde, or *la foule*), was in certain ways an invention of Charles de Brosses. More specifically, it emerged from the gap between Bosman's text and de Brosses's later expansion of it into a second-order theory.

Willem Bosman's report had invoked the fetiche in his letters 6 and 10. The first is about gold and its sometime dilution into "fetiches," false gold; "fetiche" in this sense is a descriptive term applied as often by Europeans as by West Africans. Letter 10 promises to deal with "Religion" but in fact is mostly about rituals of personal luck, oath taking, and the establishment of binding contracts between persons by sealing them over a fetiche. John Atkins (1735) likewise (sometimes citing Bosman [Atkins 1735: 116, 123]), also called attention to the use of the fetish in business affairs and oath taking: the fetish is the thing contractors first see after determining upon an affair, or sometimes as "*that which determines them to that affair*" (119, italics mine). Here there is no talk of possession or ecstasy or any reference to dissociative states whatsoever. Phenomena we might describe in these terms appear only in letter 19, which addresses government, authority, and, again, "Religion," but now the religion of the royal serpent cult at the seat of power in Ouidah, where a snake in a sacred hut is consulted by priests as an oracle of national destiny. In letter 19, Bosman (1705) makes no mention of fetiche in the nearly twenty pages of description (367–86) but makes much of priestesses "seized by the snake" and entering a state of agitated fury.

Put schematically, Bosman's descriptions locate fetiche in relation to problems of contracts, especially in relation to dealing gold with Europeans; the royal cult's "idolatry," by contrast, calls up a "madness like that of the Bacchantes," on the one hand negotiating *things* of unknown content and, on the other, negotiating *persons* of unknown content; on one hand, the (mostly) economic problem of the fetish, on the other, the (mostly) religious problem of possession.

A half century later, Charles de Brosses made two key moves: One was in expanding the meaning of fetish to a generic thing, "La Religion du Fétichisme." The second lay in conflating two domains, and two regions that in Bosman had remained relatively distinct. The serpent became the fetish, and the cult at Ouidah became the exemplar of fetishism, synecdoche of "everything similar in the rest of Africa" ([1760] 1970: 18). Africa, in turn, as the "most superstitious nation in the universe" (18), made the serpent cult at Ouidah the chronotopic site of fetishism par excellence. Bosman's earlier chapters on gold trade, meanwhile, completely dropped out. In de Brosses, the economic sphere of contracts and its problematic of fetish were mostly absorbed into the public religious sphere of kingship and national destiny, the latter involving states of ecstasy, or what would come to be called spirit possession. Now the fetish was identified with the sacred serpent itself, contaminating those who touched it with possession crises: "several of them started right away to have their horrible crises when the Fetish touched them. . . . They become furious like the Pythonisses; they break anything that comes into their hand" (26).

In other words, de Brosses pulled what had been distinct issues of property and ecstasy—or gold contracts and serpent-cult madness, separated by some three hundred miles of distance—into a single frame. The conflation set the groundwork for Africa to be viewed as the model antimodern site of possession, a place where the inner content of objects and persons was misrecognized in similar ways and where economic and religious spheres of action were incorrigibly confounded. If this reading is correct, de Brosses's metacategory of fetishism was itself a hybrid of possessed persons and indiscriminately empowered things. It extended the problem of things to the problem of personhood and, even more, to the specter of an undifferentiated and savage society, a seething horde.[17]

But what *was* the proper view of things? What views of person and property was de Brosses engaging—even helping to construct, through the juxtaposition with the depiction of possessed things and persons—and why were Bosman's description and then de Brosses's theorization so resonant and compelling? Part of the answer lies in the fact that that African religions, and then the religions of Africans in the Americas, were inserted into a nexus of ideas about property, contracts, personhood, and society in which spirit possession was *already* featured in debates about the civil order required to end the era of the wars of religion and to undergird an expanding colonial economy. I'll briefly address each of these vectors—property, contracts, person, society—in turn.

"Possession" in Relation to Property, Person, and Society

Property

The prospect of "possession" by spirits, of being owned or occupied, was a metaphor lifted from descriptions of property and proprietorship and assigned as a general human propensity. Hobbes's *De Cive* (1642) and then *Leviathan* (1651) were the key texts in which possession by spirits was first given this generic, protoanthropological character.[18] For Hobbes, spirit possession posed a grave danger both individually and for the prospect of civil life under the sovereign. He described "spirits" as madness and lunacy; man is in truth possessed by none but his own "Corporeall Spirit" ([1651] 1985: 661), the spirit of him- or herself. Locke asserted something similar when he described man as "proprietor of his own person," the basic premise through which the foundations of property in general were laid ([1680] 2003: 119).[19] In this version of early modern political theory, persons were to be envisioned as "their own" property, owners of themselves. This was true only in ideal terms, of course, as Africa and the growing plantation system of the Americas provided the chiaroscuro backdrop for this portrait.

If questions about the place and actions of spirits were essential for defining the autonomous individual, that determination was in turn viewed as crucial for constructing a civil society, which depended on predictable and regulated rules of property ownership and exchange. Property was endowed by Hobbes with nothing less than the magic of social transformation: property is the reason for entering or becoming a society; it moves a person from abstract liberty to concrete political liberty; it saves humanity from the state of nature; it joins generation to generation, constructing temporal order; and it demarks slaves from nonslaves and so builds a meaningful social order.[20] The emerging civil society would be a relation of free individuals, an exchange between free *possessors* and that which they possess.[21] The semantics of possession were more than clever wordplay. Hobbes recognized and played on the dual meanings of possession—possession by spirits and material possessions—and the relations that linked them. Possession by the "wrong" spirits posed a risk to civil society because agency and will, expressed in acquisition, the freedom to *take possession*, were compromised (Hobbes [1651] 1985: 93, 236, 344, 366, 371).

These issues warrant further explication, but in this opening chapter I propose the following as an orienting overture: *Spirit possession is an occidental category predicated from its inception on the idea that persons are, or can be, a kind of property and an economic resource.*

Contracts

For Hobbes, the problem of contracts and of spirit possession were linked because contracts' authenticity, identity, and agreement as to mediating authority are all rendered uncertain by spirits' occupation of bodies. Civil society, he argued, depends on the recognized and legitimate transfer of rights to lands, goods, or labor. Contracts, in turn, require at least these three virtues: authenticity, the assurance that contracts in fact express the actual wills of contracting partners; identity, the assurance that contracts made today will still abide in the future; and authority, an agreement as to the common power compelling and ensuring the contract's fulfillment. Possession by spirits throws all of these, and thus the contract itself, into question.[22] Authenticity and identity are forfeit if a person is perceived as compromised by multiple, possibly conflicting agents in the space of a single body. "Passions" pose a similar, if lesser, risk (Hobbes [1651] 1985: 196), since the contractor may or not "be himself" at the moment an agreement is made (cf. Léry 1990: 138; Hegel 1956: 23, 27; cf. Lambek 1993: 312).[23] In short, contracts can only be assumed between agents who agree on the nature, and limits, of their agency. That is why no contract can be assumed, wrote Hobbes, with beasts, on the one hand, and God, on the other ([1651] 1985: 197).[24]

Consider Kant's later formulations on the principle of possession in his "Doctrine of Right" in *The Metaphysics of Morals* ([1797] 1996). Here, property was specified as being that "with which I am so connected that another's use of it without my consent would wrong me" (6: 245). Rightful possession must be possession of an object without holding it so that another's use of the object without my consent harms me even when I am not physically affected and not currently using the object. The spirit of possession circulates and binds citizens into a polity, premised on the omnipresence of a principle of ownership.[25] The spirit *of* possession is a part of the prioritization of public over private ends that Kant (1766) began to work out in his early text on the notorious mystic visionary, Swedenborg, *Dreams of a Spirit Seer*. To oversimplify, his complaint against Swedenborg focused on the risks of private interests acquired through special revelation. Kant's idea of a civil spirit, by contrast, was a social and moral force capable of elevating society above private interests: "A foreign will, as it were, is active in us, and thus our liking is subject to the condition of external consent. A secret power compels us to adapt our intention to the welfare of others" (in Zammito 2002: 205).

Similar to Hobbes, Kant proposed that particularist versions of illuminism, or "fancied occult *intercourse* with God" ([1791] 1960a: 189; italic in original) subverts the hope of a public religion and a shared standard of morality and truth ([1766] 2002: 29, 108). Leibniz's *Theodicy*, a text Kant followed closely, formulated the matter similarly. Morality depends on the firm status of the "I," grounded in free will. Free will, for Leibniz, included three features: the spontaneity of action, the assurance that action originates from the one who acts; the contingency of action, the fact that other courses not taken were possible; and the rationality of action, the guarantee that it follows from the deliberation of alternatives. Only the maintenance of these three qualities of action—spontaneity, contingency, rationality—could ensure the maintenance of law. "Law" in turn includes, most importantly, the law of eternal rewards and punishments, which requires a continuous accountable self. It was in this sense that Foucault ([1962] 1999) called attention to how possession hailed a new attentiveness to interiority, but we can say more. The "I" required an interiority continually gauged for its identity *over time*. This is what Locke meant by the "forensic" meaning of personhood: it is only by means of attributing actions to the same entity in time that [civil] concern and accountability are created ([1689] 1975: XXVII, pt. 26).

Measuring "identity" involved the weighing of eternal treasures but also of more immediately pressing issues of trust. The Atlantic world's emerging market economies entailed conducting business across increasing distances and numbers of mediators. This required, in turn, the production of trust, especially prior to the opening of the first national banks in England and the Netherlands at the close of the seventeenth century. Commercial trust was a political and social riddle to be solved, a confidence game, and so it remains today. It required, for example, the confidence that banknotes genuinely represented gold or silver money as they were claimed to do, that they were not, so to speak, mere fetishes. The agent of such belief was the banker. The solidity of money, or that solidity's persuasive representation, required a persuasively solid personality, an issue highlighted by, among others, Hume's loyal friend Adam Smith: "When the people of any particular country have such confidence in the fortune, probity, and prudence of a particular banker, as to believe that he is always ready to pay upon demand such of his promissory notes as are likely to be at any time presented to him; those notes come to have the same currency as gold and silver money, from the confidence that such money can at any time be had for them" ([1776] 1976: 292 [II.ii.28]). The key is that with the expansion of paper money's circulation, its value depended on its future redeemability for precious metals. But the promise of that future hinged, in turn, on the putative integrity—present and future—of the *person* issuing the paper bill. Paper money was a question of trust in the person, of his probity, prudence, and credit. The spirit-infused were the antithesis of such contract-worthy trust: "But thus far we do not see that those who, in their own opinion, are extraordinarily favored (the chosen ones) surpass in the very least the naturally honest man, *who can be relied upon in social intercourse, in business, or in trouble*." (Kant [1791] 1960a: 189–90; italics mine). Moreover, this was all radically complicated when Europeans began contracting business with partners of an entirely different and unknown religious formation. The idea of the fetish played across these domains, but so did possession. It undermined confidence by rendering transparency a rare achievement. On Africa's Gold Coast were encountered persons of unknown content, trading metals of unknown mix, and the twin problems of transparency and authentic interiority were interlocked.[26] Contracts required the production of equivalence, not only in the sense of exchange value between different currencies, but also an equivalence of persons, agents, and authorities.

At this juncture I propose a second orienting proposition: *Spirit possession, the ownership or occupation of the body by unseen agents, emerged out of an analogical relation with material possessions and lands, even as perceived possession by spirits also complicated the lawful exchange* of *possessions and lands.*

Person

Hobbes argued that contracting agents act on behalf of authors, or principals, across vast distances and across time. It is the guarantee of authorship, the trust that agents are in fact legitimately able to speak for transactions of which they are not the authors, that yields the notions of futures and of what Hobbes called "Suretyes," the legal ability to assume debt. The promise of the delivery of distant or future goods is quite different from the simple handing over a thing and requires the development of trust in a network of constant or enduring individuals.

Hobbes viewed spirit possession as a civil threat because, even if we grant the diversity of representation (what Hobbes called personating) required by contracts and other social transactions, an author is required. The particular authorship speaking through any specific body is all too often unclear and becomes far less clear when spirits enter the equation. The problems of spirit possession and material possessions are harnessed together in the idea of the transparently trustworthy, and contract-worthy, individual. How are "people of undoubted credit" to acquire such a reputation, and then circulate it? As Hume described himself in the *Treatise of Human Nature*, that sort of monumental, enduring "self" is at best slippery and elusive:

> For my part, when I enter most intimately into what I call *myself*, I always stumble on some particular perception or other, of heat or cold, light or shade, love or hatred, pain or pleasure. I never can catch *myself* at any time without a perception, and never can observe any thing but the perception. When my perceptions are remov'd for any time, as by sound-sleep; so long am I insensible of myself. . . . He [another person] may perhaps, perceive something simple and countinu'd, which he calls *himself*; tho' I am certain there is no such principle in me. ([1739] 2006a: I.iv.6)

The right sort of civil person could not simply be "found," Hume reminded readers; he had to be cultivated, and performed. And that principle of personhood—Locke's "Principium Individuationis"—was sought within bodies, bodies turned inside out in the quest after a weighty center heavy with identity, conscience, continuity, probity, and a series of other features hailed by the new ideal of civil society.

Descartes's first three meditations had begun to address this problem in relation to spirits and their occupation of the body. But the question of spirits is rendered far more complex in Locke's *An Essay Concerning Human Understanding*, especially in the chapter entitled "Of Identity and Diversity." For it was here that Locke presented a spirit possession thought-experiment: if the "soul" (and consciousness) of a prince were inserted into the body of a cobbler, after the cobbler's own soul deserted, would the resulting being be the prince or the cobbler? The answer for Locke was clear—the prince.[27] What makes the person is consciousness, not soul (thinking substance, or that which "thinks in us") or body. More specifically, it is consciousness over time, or memory, the series of actions reckoned in relation to their consequence, that defines rational awareness. This precise bounding of consciousness seemed crucial. "Soul," to Locke, was too fickle; one can't be sure she retains the same soul asleep or in a state of inebriation. Bodies, likewise, provide at best a shifting foundation—an infant becomes an elder, the slim fatten up, another loses a hand in an accident. The "self" that previously extended its sympathy to the fingertips now adjusts to end in a stump (Locke's example), and the consciousness occupying that changed body continues to accumulate memory and experience for which it is accountable in the future. This last seems to be the crucial point. Law, including the eternal law of rewards and punishments, depends on such precise accounting. Effective civil participation, requiring lawful behavior, must be anchored on the individual *person* rather than on soul or body.

Intriguing for my purposes is that this discussion wasn't just framed as a fable of a prince and a cobbler. Peter Walmsley (1995) notes that Locke responded to a problem articulated by Hobbes's contemporary Robert Boyle. Boyle had cast into doubt the doctrine of resurrection through the challenge of the cannibal. When an individual body is eaten by others, he asked, with the flesh of the first now reconstituted as the flesh of a whole series of others, in what form would the original body be resurrected? Boyle elsewhere extended the challenge of cannibalism much further, describing an infant's nursing, for example, as the ingestion of the "blanched blood" of the mother, such that so-called individual life is in fact a constant process of the cannibalizing and hybridizing of bodies.

Locke, like Boyle, drew on tropes and stories from the colonial world to compose his version of the rational person. In Locke's fourth edition of the *Essays* (1700), for example, he added the tale of a possessed Brazilian parrot.[28] The Dutch colonial governor of Pernambuco (the primary seventeenth-century sugar-producing region of Brazil), "Prince Maurice" (Johan Maurits van Nassau-Siegen) had heard about a famous talking parrot and asked to have it brought to him. Upon entering the chamber to be presented to the governor, the parrot first observed, "What a company of white men are here!" "Who is this prince?" the parrot was asked about the governor. "Some general or other," he replied. The parrot was then asked where he was from ("Marignan"), to whom he belonged ("a Portuguese") and what he did, "Je garde des poulles" (I take care of the chickens).

Locke quoted the story from William Temple, who had tendered it as nothing but a curiosity, an "idle question" that "came in his head." Locke in turn also used the story for amusement, a good story and a digression from a "busy scene." But he also had a purpose: could a parrot be possessed of personal identity? Locke seems to say no, for personal identity hinges on reason and reflection, the ability to consider itself as the same thinking thing across different times and places—hence a self that may "be continued in the same or divers substances." Locke seems to decide that a parrot is but a mimic, able to parrot rationality, so to speak, but not generate it.

Surely there is more to this digression than Locke concedes. The backstory hinges on the racial cue that initiates the parrot's speech, "What a company of white men are here!" The parrot is from Europe, Marignan, and while himself owned by a Portuguese, he is supervisor of "the chickens," which we can suppose to stand in for Africans. After all, Prince Maurits of Nassau not only ruled Pernambuco from 1637 to 1642, he led the mission to take control of Elmina Castle (São Jorge da Mina) on the Gold Coast of Africa, the very site from which another Dutchman, named Willem Bosman, already introduced above, composed his story of gold and slave trading several decades later. Though Locke didn't use the phrase, he seems to be writing about the prospect of fetish persons, persons who give the appearance of being an enduring individual or a genuinely rational parrot but are in fact entities unknown, like fetish gold that mimics the outer flash but is internally composed of copper and iron. Yet the parrot is hardly powerless in this negotiation, since he accuses the governor of being little more than a mime in his own right, playing an assigned role, as "some General or other."

In the exchange, Pernambuco, the Brazilian sugar colony, was made the site of a comic interlude. The joke lay in the animal personating the human, a being who can only be spoken through claiming to speak for itself, as author, or, perhaps, a slave "personating" a fully human being.

The *individual* person so carefully distilled by Locke through a series of possession thought-experiments—the possessed parrot, the body of a cobbler occupied by the soul of a prince—is measured against those lacking genuine internal credit. Such are those who are not self-possessed, who are mere parodies, or parrots. Religiously, they are like someone of "fetish-faith," as Kant put it ([1791] 1960a: 181), the enthusiast who "fanatically imagines that he feels special works of grace within himself," such that virtue comes to "arouse his loathing" (189). To return to Hobbes, when the religious idiom of command is overtaken by that of possession, civic virtue is dead ([1651] 1985: 144).

Society and the Specter of the Horde

Dangerous possession practices could lead to civil disorder. "In a little time, the inspired person comes to regard himself as a distinguished favourite of the Divinity; and when this *frenzy* once takes place, which is the summit of enthusiasm, every whimsy is consecrated," wrote Hume (2006b: 75; italics mine). Or as Spinoza wrote, "The mob is terrifying, if unafraid" (1996: 144). The prophets commended humility and repentance for the good of the "common advantage," argued Spinoza, which would lead all toward the blessings of reason. Sociologically, Kant's writing on Swedenborg and elsewhere had conveyed a similar concern with class distinctions; illuminism is attached to the danger of the masses, the crowd seething under a spell ([1791] 1960a: 168). This sociology came with a cartography, as the irrational possessed body shifted from the state of nature Hobbes had located in the savage Americas to new representations of African religions. Hume and Kant both adopted some of de Brosses's descriptions not only of individual irrationality but also of questionable social mores, where "every whimsy is consecrated." The frenzy of possession—the horde's swarming enthusiasm, *Schwärmerei* (Kant 1960b: 107, 123)—was projected as the sociological outcome of fetish faith in practice. Some sectors of Protestantism, of course, included an enthusiast dimension, and this was part of the problem; enthusiast forms of Protestantism risked confusing the Holy Spirit with other spirits. Hobbes hoped his idea of the Leviathan, the sovereign "mortall God" who is possessor of all his subjects, mirrored by a single divine God encompassing all rival spirits, would counter the religious and social cacophony. We should note that even this Sovereign and this God were premised on contract and the right to property, as Kant makes plain with his nomination of God as "First Possessor" in *Religion Within the Limits of Reason Alone* ([1791] 1960a: 74).[29] Even God was being made a proper, and propertied, individual.

In Hegel's writing , the swarming horde was given an anthropological frame, depicted most vividly in the African religion of fetishes, imagined to misrecognize random objects as containers of presence and elevate them for veneration. This became a standard refrain in the colonial period. "The fetich doctor and fetich belief were a *vis a tergo* with the native horde" (Nassau 1904: 127) goes one of the most widely read missionary accounts at the start of the twentieth century.

The confluence of possession by spirits with the dangerous force of the crowd reached its apex in texts like Gustave Le Bon's extremely influential 1895 *Psychologie des foules*. Le Bon's popular tract on "la foule" seems to have been influenced by Tocqueville, and it in turn drew responses from readers ranging from Freud to Mussolini.[30] What I find striking in Le Bon's work is the drawing together of vivid portraits of modern massification, and so-called primitive culture. In his scenario, modern humanity, under the force of the crowd, descends the evolutionary ladder to become a nonrational primitive, a role filled by "Ethiopians" and "negroes." Le Bon names the process by which this primitive "soul of the masses" becomes immanent in the individual, *religion* (book 1, chap. 4). Socialism and traditional religion are but two versions of the same phenomenon for Le Bon.

The man lost in the crowd, just like the primitive, is blindly obedient and incapable of exercising free will; he is possessed. Similarly to Hobbes and others, but with a different, evolutionary argument, Le Bon suggested that such possessions posed not just intellectual but political risks: "In this way the religious spirit replaces at one stroke the slow hereditary accumulation necessary to form the soul of a nation" (Le Bon 1898: 194). Possession religions, like the urban crowd, caused Europeans to descend the evolutionary ladder and become Africans. It is not surprising, then, that Le Bon paid close attention to the spiritualist movement that surrounded him in France, and included them in his studies.[31] The Spiritualists provided a perfect proof of his argument for the irrationality of the modern crowd, a primitive irrationality for which, however, "Ethiopians" remained the preeminent exemplar (1898: 100, 104, 109). Paradoxically, then, a new version of "African" possession was born of the sociological depiction of the French crowd.

Here I offer a third intervention: *Spirit possession indexed both the lack of a properly bounded self and an inadequately defined society. As possession's locus par excellence, Africa served as chronotope of the anticitizen and the ungoverned state, a place and time (the past in the present, the primitive) of frenzy and the horde, a socially undifferentiated and uncontrollable mob.*

Spirit Possession and Governance in the Twentieth-Century Americas

With the mutually constituting categories of civil man and possessed man in place, the civil risks of Afro-American possessions had to be controlled by colonies and then states, and they were, everywhere from Surinam in the 1770s to Brazil and Cuba in the 1890s to Trinidad in 1916. The issue of civil risk was quickened in the wake of slaves' emancipations in the Americas, and former slaves' religions were often interpolated in the terms of the literatures explored above. As noted, both Raymundo Nina Rodrigues's groundbreaking work on Afro-Brazilian religions of 1896, *O animismo fetichista dos negros bahianos*, and Fernando Ortiz's inaugural study of Afro-Cuban religiosity, *Los negros brujos* (1906), were extended engagements with Tylor's key idea of animism. The twin studies by these two pioneer criminologists, penned a decade apart in Brazil and Cuba, respectively, served as the gate of entry for the religious practices of former slaves into the civil religious union of the fledgling republics. This was a crucial moment, the rupture of hierarchic tranquility (Sodré 1988: 43) by a new social proximity, requiring a rethinking of the nation and its religious proxemics.[32]

For the early Ortiz, Cuba's turn-of-the-century "mala vida," the gray zone of prostitution, crime, and vice, defined in opposition to the "vida honrada" and the "vida buena" ([1906] 1916: 1), were direct consequences of lingering African spirits. Despite their being "every day more assimilable" (vii), the African remained "slave of his passions" (55), locked in his "atavismo moral" and "parasitismo social" (21), evidenced above all in rites of possession. Nina Rodrigues, for his part, cited the whole lineage from Bosman to de Brosses to Tylor in grappling with Brazil's republican problem and underscored multiple civil risks related to Afro-Brazilian Candomblé.

First, argued Nina Rodrigues, Afro-Brazilian religion interrupts the regularity of work and justifies vagrancy (*vadiagem*) ([1896] 1935: 18).[33] Second, Candomblé is in part inspired by Yoruba religion of West Africa and is a religion copied from a form of foreign civil government, where the king corresponds to the high god, mediating ranks of nobles correspond to the mediating deities called *orixás*, and so on. Therefore, he argued, Africans, criollos, and mestizos who practice Yoruba religion in Brazil are all already living within a rival political system. Nina Rodrigues declared that he had even heard of possession's power in motivating battle and sedition, thus (it was reported to him) the reason for prohibiting African immigration (112). He even noted in this context that the most famous community of runaway slaves in Brazil, Palmares, could easily have seeded a Haitian-like revolution that might have led to the very demise of Brazil, were it not for its prudent destruction in 1694 (124). Third, Afro-Brazilians are in a state of transition from fetishism to idolatry, and given their *hybrid* religion (15), as "mestizos of spirit" (*mestiços do espirito*, 28), not liable to conversion to a purified Catholicism. Because of their religion, he wrote, it is not clear that Afro-Brazilians are assimilable to the nation of Brazil whatsoever, at least in the near term. Fourth, the religion involves possession—the loss of individual personality, memory, and accountability (99, 116–17)—but even worse, involves the faking of possession (101–3, 130; see also Ortiz [1906] 1916: 84). Fifth, Candomblé has already taken possession of the country; it is embedded "no ânimo publico" (in the public spirit) and poses the danger of further expansion via contagion, as his dramatic story of a possessed white girl conveys (Nina Rodrigues [1896] 1935: 123–26; see also Ortiz [1906] 1916: 17).

The classifications afforded by "spirit possession" were not only an anthropological project but also a legal project applied and enforced in the making of nations according to preferred religious profiles and "civil religious" institutions. Nina Rodrigues's terminology, ranging from "possession" to "espirita sonâmbulo" (somnambulant spirit) appears in police reports of cases of illegal religion at the close of the nineteenth century and the first decades of the twentieth century, as republican Brazil took shape. His studies and their vocabulary provided the grammar for legal control of religion during the first decades after emancipation as slave religion was reformed as part and parcel of a civil religious project. It is in this light that we should read the new "public health" laws mobilized in 1890 Brazil, which declared it illegal to "captivate and subjugate the credulity of the public" (article 157, in Maggie 1992), and the 1930s efforts by the state to subject spirit mediums to psychological screening and licensing procedures.

During the same period, spirit possession began to occupy a central place in narratives of late modernity from Marx to Benjamin. The rational individual was turned inside out, exposed as possessed by the state, by social ideals, and by latent memories rising to incarnate form in moments of sudden arrest.[34] The social transformations of late modernity were routinely written of in the terms of spirit possession, as formulations by Marx, Morgan, Freud, and Durkheim about modern life were informed by and appealed to ethnographic accounts of "primitive" religions arriving en masse from the colonial world, a process that had begun already with de Brosses's notation of fetishism as a way of thinking (*façon de penser*, 52) that modern man never quite left behind. As Locke had put it, it described a person when "not himself" or "beside himself." To name the savagery of late modernity itself, the founding figures of the social sciences drew on the language of spirit possession as a critique of the rational citizen and self-possessed individual or, conversely, its celebration.[35] If in the earlier version spirit possession had served as a negative marker of free will, here it pointed to the inevitable vertigo experienced by the civilized but alienated new industrial man. We are all many, all possessed.[36]

As de Brosses had formulated fetishism, spirit possession emerged as a phenomenon general to all humanity but exemplified in Africa. One might say that it was redeemed from its marginalizing and locative power—that which is *over there*—through its becoming sedimented as a concept and circulated into wider use as it passed from local to universal significations, all the while never forgoing its chronotopic force. E. B. Tylor began *Primitive Culture* in 1871 with a dismissal of notions of free will from Aristotle to Leibniz ([1871] 1958: 2). The idea of free will is itself a kind of possession state: "This view of an anomalous action of the will, which it need hardly be said is incompatible with scientific argument, subsists as an opinion patent or latent in men's minds, and strongly affecting theoretic views of history." (3). The newest version of the "new man" was inhabited by regular laws instead of misty-eyed, gauzy notions of freedom; the history of mankind is to be seen as "part and parcel of the history of nature" (2). With this single move, Tylor inaugurates the social sciences in their recent incarnation. And yet the "early" part of this history is ruled by spirit possession and its various kin, and though its primary vector is temporal, time is riddled through and through by a geography that, over and over, returned spirit possession to Africa and the African Americas.

In spite of the habitual association of Africa and spirit possession, the category infiltrated the twentieth century anthropological production of "religion," and even religious practice itself, in paradoxical ways. First, ethnographers documenting spirit possession often use the phrase, and their engagement with the phenomena it describes, as a way of posing resistance, or at least alternatives, to the "possessive individualism" of the West (e.g., Miller 2001; Lambek 2002; Mosse 2006; Sharp 1993). Indeed, they themselves are nowadays often possessed, as at once a subversion of "objectivity," an expression of epistemic creativity, and a bid for bona fide ethnographic authenticity.[37] The first published account of the scholar possessed that I know came from the hand of Zora Neale Hurston in *Mules and Men* (1935), but if the move was initiated by Hurston, it was most notoriously applied in Maya Deren's description of "white darkness" in her 1953 *Divine Horsemen* (see Richman in this volume). Since then, the trend of narrating the ethnographer possessed has only expanded, and now it seems nearly a cliché in the anthropology of Afro-Atlantic religions. Though not all anthropologists make this ethnographic and rhetorical move, nearly all must at least address it, respond to it, in some fashion *account* for it, even apologize for it, as they construct their authorial position in relation to possession (Keller 2002: 23). The intertextuality that since Hobbes's *De Cive* (1641) has linked spirit possession to the diagnoses of society and the self has finally reached even the anthropologist, who had long remained safely cordoned off.

The ways in which the category of spirit possession serves as an avenue of critique for this particular set of issues (what is an integrated individual, what is pathology, what is a bounded, rational self)—at least sufficiently so to be able to interpret other selves—reveals how "spirit possession" remains haunted by early modernity's rattling ghosts.[38] Today, ethnographers of Afro-Atlantic religions, and many others as well, must locate themselves in relation to possession: whether they are in it, near it, avoiding it, rejecting it, they must in any case keep on saying why. No doubt the category says as much about those applying it as about the religious practices it is supposed to describe.

Back to Ethnography

With this genealogy of the material and political economic dimensions of spirit possession in view, let us return to questions of ritual practice itself. The question is how to trace the visitations of theory in ritual practice. It is not too far-fetched to claim that early modern philosophies of property and personhood inhabit not only the terminology but also the ritual enactments of so-called spirit possession, since those early modern philosophical formulations inhabited the institutions of the Atlantic slave trade. To crib from the opening lines of the Gospel of John, words may become flesh and dwell among us. Or, as I am arguing, ideas of personhood and property can be incarnated in the flesh of their enactors, whether masters or slaves. Do Hobbes and Locke somehow still live in the gods (orixás) of Candomblé when those gods arrive to possess their devotees? I think so. A new initiate of Candomblé whose head will be "ruled" by a West African god is "sold" at the end, in a mimesis of slave auctions; she must "pay for the floor" she occupied during the ritual process while she acquired a new "owner" of her head. The tropes of body as property, expressed in the absenting of will and the economic value of that evacuation, inflect the process throughout. To be possessed is in at least one sense to become a slave or contract laborer (Palmié 2002) or its inverse, as the spirit's master (Capone 2010: 20).[39] In Vodou, to take another contemporary example, the image of the zombie is precisely a reprise of the slave, a body owned and occupied yet simultaneously empty and agentless, movement minus will (McAlister 2002; Richman 2005). As an Umbanda priestess in Rio de Janeiro expressed it, "I don't have free choice, I don't have it. I don't have my own life: I am a slave" (Hayes 2011: 12).[40] If Afro-Brazilian religious practice presented in a certain sense, resistance to enslavement—at least by posing the oxymoron of the *slave at liberty* to engage in rituals that forged allegiances superseding that of slave to master (Reis 2011)—and in that sense a making of free bodies (Harding 2000: 158), this was a complex kind of regained autonomy—a rather Kantian autonomy, if you like: freedom as conformity to a rule. As the historian João Reis put it, in initiation to Candomblé "slaves had to learn to be slaves for a second time" (2011: 66).[41] To say this is not to reduce the ritual practices called spirit possession as a kind of false consciousness or misrecognition. To the contrary, it is to say that the powers of possession, at least in the Afro-Atlantic context, are unleashed by working in and through the history of slavery, sometimes consciously, though often not.

What I am suggesting, and what the rest of the chapters in this volume in different ways argue, is that our scholarly practices should try to mimic those of ritual actors at least in the modest sense of working through the genealogies of the category of spirit possession rather than around them.

Wrote Locke: "Thus in the beginning all the world was America, and more so than that is now; for no such thing as money was anywhere known. Find out something that hath the use and value of money amongst his neighbours, you shall see the same man will presently begin to enlarge his possessions" (Locke [1680] 2003: 121). My argument is that swirling ideas about persons as property and bodies without will provided the matrix out of which "possession" in its multiple valences emerged, already entwined. Spirit possession was a hybrid by which Europe interpolated and then was in turn infiltrated by fantastically phantasmic Others. It bridged notions of the person, religion, and the good society (*la vida honrada*). It lasted for centuries and expressed with increasing prominence the trajectory from Hobbes and Locke to de Brosses and Kant, from Hegel to Tylor and the founding of modern anthropology. The shadow of possession lengthened as the stakes of states increased, from brazilwood to sugar to coffee, and as lands without owner and bodies without will became more and more central to the economies of Europe. It should not surprise that the locus of the civil problem of spirit possession moved from the Americas to Africa and the places where enslaved Africans lived, to Brazil and the Caribbean.

Spirit possession describes the idea of being spoken through, but it has itself always been spoken through too, ventriloquizing a series of positions. I've tried to gloss some of them here, as a placeholder for the more detailed work that is to come in the chapters that follow. The trick will be to also hear who and what is speaking sideways and in translation—through parrots, zombies, the spirits; from the belly (ventriloquism); and in the language of "being possessed" itself. But this can only start by figuring out the mediating terms—the *facteurs* (agents) in the factory—with which the category of spirit possession was made whatsoever.

Looking with this sort of double vision, through what Freud called the demon optician's spectacles (see note 36), is the first step toward a reanimated program of thinking through spirits in the Afro-Atlantic world.

TWO

The Ejamba of North Fairmount Avenue, the Wizard of Menlo Park, and the Dialectics of Ensoniment: An Episode in the History of an Acoustic Mask

STEPHAN PALMIÉ

"Step into the second floor front room of 21[32] Fairmount avenue and get initiated into the strangest form of worship in Philadelphia." So begins an article featured prominently on page 1 of the *Philadelphia North American* of May 4, 1908. And indeed, its author describes what even by the standards of early twentieth-century Philadelphia's exuberantly diversified religious landscape must have been quite a remarkable scene:

> a wonderful place filled with altars, war drums, speaking tubes and trumpets. Over in one corner hangs a figure dressed in white satin and crowned with a garish crown of glittering imitation gems. That's the Queen of Ethiopia and she is worshipped with due solemnity.
>
> On the walls are robes of purple and yellow, masks of strange design, and brushes to sweep away the evil spirits. A battered photograph of the slain President Garfield, mounted on a stick, in the form of a cross, also figures in the ceremonies.

Speaking in near accent-free English, the journalist's interlocutor, a "powerfully built" black Cuban "of about 45 years" named Timothy Leay (as the article rendered his name) amiably explains: "I am Ejamba, the leader. I show the true way; our symbol is the rooster, and we pray to him and dance in his honor. How we worship is a secret, and only the initiated dare to join in. We also believe in the Great God, and we dance to please him. . . . I talk with the spirits. I talk with the spirits and they talk with me. See my echo?" This is something Timoteo Leal (which likely was his name) seems genuinely proud of. The journalist expresses amazement. "There's something worth the while that echo," he writes.

> It starts in the middle of the room in a sort of pagoda filled with water. Things that look like painted spools float around gaily. A tiny bell is suspended from the roof of the pagoda and when any spirits happen around they always notify Ejamba Leay by ringing this bell.
>
> From under the water a speaking tube stretches across the room to a converter. It is filled with wheels, has a glass front, and a bit of stovepipe sticks out the top. Leading into the converter, from the western end of the room, is another speaking tube. Still another tube finds its way into the converter from a kettle drum in the east. This kettle drum is made of a china washbowl covered with skin.
>
> A final tube is carried out into Fairmount Avenue. This has a megaphone exit, and it is from this megaphone that the people in the neighborhood get notice that the spirits are busy.

The unnamed journalist further tells us that the masks are made from jute. What at first glance seem to be feather dusters turn out, according to Leal, to be ceremonial staffs adorned with "the sacred feathers of the rooster which we sacrifice." A woman present reports having heard the drums "beating on their own accord" and that the "echo . . . made a noise like this—Whoo-o-o!" Leal further assures the writer that they pray not only to the plumed staffs but also "to the echo. We pray to the big drum in the corner. That represents the seven constellations. We pray to the bow and arrows. We pray to the sun." A group of women chime in assertively when Leal declares that "we have a beautiful and inspiring ceremony." "We have indeed," they declare. "Why, when the candles are lit and the men get on their robes and masks and the spirits commence talking, it's simply grand."

What I have just excerpted here is likely the only record we have on the "Temple of the Ancient Grace" that the two Afro-Cuban brothers "Timothy and Edward Leay" were operating in Philadelphia in the first decade of the twentieth century. I do not know how contemporary Philadelphians—particularly the residents of the 2100 block of North Fairmount Avenue—reacted to the sounds the Leal brothers and their flock broadcasted onto the street. But I do know what the pioneer of Afro-Cuban studies, Fernando Ortiz, made of a contemporary Cuban journalistic recension of this very article: he filed it away in what eventually became the folder entitled "Negros—ñáñigos" in his vast and sprawling archive—which is where I first encountered it in the late 1990s.

Clearly, what must have drawn Ortiz's interest was a number of intriguing features of the report—most prominently perhaps Leal's use of the term "Ejamba" to designate his ritual office. For it points to a connection between the Leal brothers' temple and an Afro-Cuban male esoteric sodality known as *abakuá* that emerged in Cuba in the 1830s and had by the early twentieth century become a vital force in Havana's dockside social worlds. To this day, the term *Illamba*[1] designates one of the four preeminent titles in abakuá, and one of the major ritual functions of the incumbent of this office lies in the activation and transmission of a numinous voice. As Ortiz knew, the social dislocations effected by the two Cuban wars of independence (1868–78, 1895–98) had led to a truly Atlantic dispersal of the form of association and ritual characteristic of abakuá. As I have argued elsewhere, by the time Ortiz clipped this article, not only had abakuá-inspired practices surfaced among Cuban deportees to Spanish presidios in North Africa and Fernando Po, they also seem to have taken hold among émigré tobacco workers in Key West, and it is not unreasonable to presume that the growing Cuban exile communities in the urban Northeast were harboring members of abakuá as well (Palmié 2008).

Surely, as Ortiz seems to have surmised in filing this clipping under "Negros—ñáñigos,"[2] at least some of the Leals' ritual practices might well have looked familiar, if perhaps somewhat heterodox, to members of Havana's abakuá lodges: the robes and jute masks thus might have turned out to be "*sacos*" or *afoíreme*, the characteristic body masks giving visual shape to spiritual presences known as *íreme* who are drawn into human life-worlds during abakuá *barocos* or *plantes* (large-scale public ceremonies). From such a perspective, the "feather dusters" would become readable as "plumeros" or *muñones*, plumed adornments that crown *Illamba*'s *iton*, or sacred staff, and also figure on the drums of the holders of the *Empegó* and *Ecueñón* titles and the mute ceremonial drum *sese eribó* wielded by the holder of the *Isué* title. Male initiatory esotericism fits such an interpretation, as do Leal's remarks about the symbolic centrality of the sun (*ebión*) and ritual designs resembling bows and arrows (*firmas*, *gandos*, or *anaforuana*). The article's photograph depicting a cross in the temple's window might be taken to evoke the high god *Abasí* (represented by the Christian crucifix in many contemporary abakuá temples). Leal's repeated mention of the rooster (*enquico*) as both object of worship and sacrificial victim would make good sense, as would his reference to "seven constellations," which might be taken to connote the seven ancestral personages involved in the discovery of the mystery from which abakuá was born and who subsequently transformed into the seven major titles integrating every abakuá "potencia" (chapter or lodge).[3]

Even such ostensibly peculiar objects as the figure glossed as "the Queen of Ethiopia" or the photo of the slain President Garfield mounted on a cruciform stick might be subjected to such interpretations. We know that even before the end of the Spanish colonial period, Cuban abakuá potencias had begun to incorporate political emblems into their altars (see Palmié 2002), and it is not unimaginable that the "Queen of Ethiopia" could have represented a visual rendering of *Sikan*, the woman who first encountered abakuá's central cult agency in the mythical time-space known as *Enllenisón*—embellished, whether for the reporter's benefit or the temple's Afro-North American adherents, by Ethiopianist references.

Such guesswork could be extended. Yet this is not what I am after in this essay.[4] Instead, I want to present one more tantalizing detail from the reporter's account and then proceed to a more theoretically focused discussion of the rather extraordinary technology that, in the Leals' temple, might have come to mediate what, following Edward Lifschitz (1988), I would call an "acoustic mask." In particular, I want to foreground what appears to be a remarkable convergence between the phonic and auditory ideologies underwriting the mediation of the divine in abakuá and the technologies of acoustic transmission across space and time that had begun to reconfigure Western auditory worlds since the second half of the nineteenth century. I argue that just as abakuá's sacramental technologies of sound transmission—activating the disembodied voice of the mystery—in real-world space and historical time generates numinous sound envelopes that defy precisely those time-space coordinates, so did the rational technologies of sound propagation and acoustic disembodiment of the mundane human voice that began to flourish in the second half of the nineteenth century engender their own numinous penumbra and sacramental logics.

If indeed the two did converge on Philadelphia's North Fairmount Avenue in 1908, this must surely be interpreted as sheer contingency. But that such convergence between the phonic ideologies of an African-derived esoteric sodality and those beginning to regiment the indexicalities of electroacoustic transmission and reproduction in North America would have occurred at all may not be much of a surprise. Such an argument, however, demands a discussion of both the conceptions of phonation and audition in contemporary abakuá ritual praxis and the mysteries of sound recording and reproduction in early twentieth-century America.[5]

Conceptio per Aurem: Phonation and Audition in Contemporary Abakuá

In several crucial respects, abakuá ritual shares in the anamnestic and iterative qualities of the Christian Eucharist. It is a rite of re-presentation in the literal rather than figurative sense. Its goal is to fuse the ritual present with a sacred past by weaving a notionally unbroken metonymical chain from an originary sequence of events that is both foundational and authorizing to their successive reinstantiations in increasingly distant time. Just like scripturally grounded charisma of office enables a Catholic priest to effect the *mysterium tremendum* of transubstantiation during the Mass, so do their offices enable abakuá titleholders to collectively bring into being a "real presence." What they re-presence in the course of a plante or baroco—ceremonies lasting upward of twelve hours—is the mystery of the voice of *Écue* that once hailed a set of human actors and subsequently transformed them into everlasting ritual personae. Such rituals unleash the mystery's transformative powers by once more hailing those within earshot in the instant in (linear, historical) time that has become an occasion for its sounding. Just as the Catholic Mass materializes the mystical body of the church by drawing the congregants into physical communion with Christ, so does the sounding of Écue's voice beckon its hearers to assist in and attest to the changes it is to effect within the present confines of a sonically delimited ritual space.

Much has been written about abakuá's founding myth. But for my present purposes the barest schematic account of its structure of eventuation will suffice. A good starting point may be to emphasize one more resonant parallel between contemporary ethnography and the 1908 *Philadelphia North American* report and note the stunning irony—for anyone familiar with contemporary abakuá lore and ritual praxis—in the fact that in the journalist's account it is a *woman* who gives an approximation of the phonetic qualities of what she and Leal call "the echo." "Do the spirits really talk?" asks the journalist. "Why," she answers, "I have been in there alone and the drums have started beating on their own account, and the echo made a noise like this—Whoo-o-o!—and then I got away." This, of course, is what the mythical woman Sikan failed to do when she first heard the voice of Tance, the piscine ancestral presence that she accidentally scooped up in her calabash when drawing water at the embankment of *Usagaré* from the river *Oldán* that bisects the territory of *Bekura Mendó* in the *Efó* region of abakuá's mythical homeland, Enllenisón.

It is the end of a starry night. Enquico, the rooster, sings on the hilltop where Ecueñón, the hunter, waits for his prey, bow and arrow poised for the kill. A caiman initially blocks Sikan's path to the river, but the man soon to experience transformation into the íreme *Eribangandó* clears her way with a ritual brush. She bows down and scoops up a calabash of water, but when she hoists it on her head, a tremendous roar issues forth from the container. It is *Obon Tance*—a numinous presence in the shape of a fish—who speaks to her in his otherworldly voice. Having been the first to hear Tance's awesome logos—described in much of the literature on abakuá as the growl of the leopard[6]—Sikan is variously said to have confided her terror to her father, *Mocongo*, or her husband, *Isunécue*. Either or both betray her to the supreme chief, Illamba, and the sorcerer *Nasacó*, who had been tracing Tance's movement and vocalizations—*camá ororó* (speaking in the center)—in the lagoon for days. *Ecueñón*, whose name is glossed as "slave to Écue," is ordered to kill her. However, even before Sikan meets her violent end, Tance is dead as well. His voice has fallen silent.

Horrified, Nasacó, Illamba, and the other *obones* (founding figures, soon to become titles) try to revive and recuperate its awesome, lawgiving sonic capacities. What ensues is a strangely phonocentric version of the search for a male social contract: Sikan is seated on three stones awaiting her immolation when she begins to menstruate, thus foreshadowing the feeding of the three-footed friction drum around which the ritual technos enabling men to cause other men to be "born over the drum skin" (*ecória ñene abakuá*) will soon congeal. Following Sikan's execution, Nasacó fuses her skin to that of Tance—to no avail. He and the other obones will sacrifice the snake (*ñangabión*) that had coiled itself around the palm tree that night; *erombe*, the Congo slave "captured by the sound of the voice"; *erón*, the ram, and *llebengó*, the tiger—also to no avail. Much blood (*efión*) is shed in vain in their frantic experiments. It is only when they resort to sacrificing *embori*—the goat—that "el parche" (the drumskin) eventually takes shape and, once fused to *ocanco*—the hollowed-out trunk of *úcano beconsí*, the ceiba tree—becomes operative as *nambe erí*, the "flesh of the voice." What results is a technology capable of transmitting "la voz" across time, materializing its awesome sound onward from baroco to baroco. This is the moment from whence, as contemporary Cuban *obonécues* envision it, an unbroken chain of "transmisiones" of the voice links the *cuarto fambá* (interior sanctum) of their temples and the ritual exterior spaces (*isaroco*)—often simple alleyways—to the primal "*embarcadero*" of Usagaré, where the sound approximated by the onomatopoetic phrase "*el uyó*" was first materialized in and mediated by an esoteric biotechnological phonic device, el Écue.

But Écue itself is only an agent within a larger network that forms as soon as the original thirteen obones of the "tierra *efó*"—now turned into ancestral personae with names designating their future offices ("plazas")—transact the secret of the voice across the river to a group of men soon to constitute the first potencia of the "tierra *efí*." Reviving the voice is only the first step in its reproduction. It now begins to spread in space and time. Here we can omit much of the mythological detail and switch to the sequence informing contemporary barocos in all their multimediated splendor. Hours of predawn work go into the "fabricación"—production, or perhaps better, assembly—of the conditions under which Écue's voice can be transferred to a medium that will carry it forward in time and social space by enabling men "born over the drumskin" to perform assisted reproduction in bringing into being other such men. Even before midnight, the titleholders of a potencia will assemble in the *fambá* (inner sanctum of an abakuá temple) to conduct a rigorous schedule of ritual work. Nasacó begins to concoct "la *wemba*" and the basic ingredients of "la *mocuba*," the former a cleansing fluid, the latter a liquid conducer of Écue's extrasonic powers; *Empegó* will begin to write authorizing glyphs ("firmas," or *anaforuana*) with yellow chalk on all major ritual implements as well as on the ground leading from the innermost sanctum (*fo Écue*, *iriongo*, or *famballín*) toward the door of the temple, charting the path the voice will travel hours from then.[7]

In all of this, as David Brown (2003: 58) notes, "the physical temple" is only a space through which Écue "maintains its relationship to the world." The voice itself "lives" in the waters from which it has to be summoned and to which it eventually returns. To this end, a potencia activates a ritual infrastructure composed of an elaborate network of human, man-made, and natural agents: a sacramental machinery designed to conduct or, perhaps better, *transduce*, a numinous energy into a variety of worldly forms available to the human sensorium. The altars, drums, staff, and insignia, the hieroglyphic writing, even its ritual personnel are mediators that need to be brought to a vanishing point of im-mediation that is reached when the "plazas" have once more become the ancestral presences who bring about the sounding of Écue's voice (Peters 1999; Sterne 2003; Mazzarella 2004). Once the "fabricación" nears its completion after hours of performing esoteric ritual "works" (*obras*), Nasacó will trace a line of gunpowder along the elaborate diagrammatic "firma" that will mark the path for Écue to once more emerge and sonically transform the world within its acoustic range—for those capable of heeding its call.[8] By then Ecueñón will step out into the first light of daybreak, announcing the impending sonic incarnation to the profane world. "*Jelley baribá, bencamá*" (Attention/admiration, I/it will speak)—so begins the lengthy chant he intones before Nasacó lights the gunpowder and the door of the sanctuary flings open in an explosive visual and auditory blast.

What emerges from the temple's door is the first stage of "la procession," the major "plazas" (titleholders) followed by a full drum orchestra; guided by the íreme Eribangandó, who once more clears the path, they go in search of the voice.[9] Only when they return will Illamba, who has stayed behind in the fo Écue (a corner of the fambá secluded by a curtain), begin to apply his fingers, moistened with drops of mocuba to the *llin*—a plumed piece of "caña brava" (bamboo)—poised on the resonant surface of a small, three-footed friction drum that is the source of Écue's vocalizations. But just as the procession is a mere effect of an as yet unrevealed cause, so is Illamba himself (or better perhaps the human body that has become his office) a mere instrumentality. Blindfolded, he himself only hears but does not see how the llin in his hands induces the vibrations on the drumskin that activates Écue's voice. "How is this possible," Ortiz (1952–55: 5:237) reports having asked an Illamba who agreed to cooperate with his research, "how can you deny that an initiate, namely you, passes the *yin* through his own fingers every time the *uyu* speaks?" His interlocutor replied, "Well, accepting that this may be so, who is it that inspires him who handles the *güín* but a mysterious being through an action of *Abasí* who is god?" Ortiz goes on to qualify his informant as a theologian. But the principle itself—transductive mediation from one form of energy into another—suffuses the entire event. Strictly speaking, the baroco is no "reproduction" of an originary moment of revelation. There is no later or earlier. It is an instantiation of presence beyond time. Illamba's fingers merely carry Écue's numinous energy over into the phenomenal (i.e., auditory) world, where it will pass through and bring into being further chains of transduction.

From the moment it begins to resonate from within the temple, the drone of Écue's vocalizations notionally both effects and directs every one of the twists and turns of the exoteric part of a plante that unfolds in the isaroco's public space over the next six to eight hours. What ensues is a synesthetic riot that involves elaborate "conversaciones" between Écue and "la música" (a five-piece drum orchestra), the íremes, who, though mute themselves, will react to modulation in Écue's volume and timbre in a gestural language of their own, and the officiating plazas who will judge from the sound emerging from the cuarto fambá whether or not the ritual steps they just executed were pleasing to "la voz." Even the movement of non-titled obonécues, who, during intervals between major phases of the ritual, line up in two rows ("la valla"), between which one after another of them displays his prowess at dancing, is inspired by Écue. They are said to be roused and energized by "the voice" which, emanating from the potencia's inner sanctum, envelops the exoteric space of the isaroco in a dense cloud of sound. Transmitted to nambe erí—the drumskin—by the motions of the llin in Illamba's hand, Écue's power shifts from numinous to auditory to kinetic and, as Ortiz (1952–55: 5:234) recognized, not just aesthetic but ethical modalities.

In a *baroco llansao* that involves the initiation and swearing in ("juramento") of new obonécues or plazas into an existing potencia, it is Écue who calls the íreme Aberisún to deal a deadly blow to the sacrificial goat embori, and it initially does so by deceiving the íreme: attracted to the scene of the ritual by the voice, *Aberisún* shrinks back in horror as he hears Écue's command and beholds embori, whose body has received the same chalk markings as the *indísime* (candidates for initiation). And just as Écue's voice will gain urgency every time Aberisún recoils until he finally strikes embori down with a cudgel, so will it rejoice when the goat's skin (*sucu bacariongo*) will be finally presented to the waning stars in the early morning hours as the potencia's banner ("estandarte"). Écue jubilates when the indísime, marked as "dead" by white rather than yellow chalk writings on their bodies, are lead into the fambá. And it will give birth to new ecória ñene abakuá (men born over the drumskin) soon after, when, in the course of a series of esoteric procedures, the head of a new initiate is placed on top of the sese eribó—the mute drum that only moments before supported the severed head of the sacrificial victim (embori)—and is "crowned" with the powerfully vibrating presence of Écue herself.

Conversely, during the type of funerary rite known as *enlloro* or *llanto* that marks the end of a period after the death of one of a potencia's members when the potencia is considered defiled ("sucio") and barred from any other ritual action, Écue's initial joyous vocalizations turn into lamentations when, in the course of the ritual's commencement, news of the death of one of her sons is relayed to her by the íreme of death, *Anamanguí*. Just as the powerful sound of Écue's voice was necessary to transform his body into a medium of her propagation—a *conceptio per aurem* if there ever was one—so can that body not be expedited to the grave without Écue's taking leave of him. Écue, in other words, has intentionality and sensory powers and is capable of expressing affect—all the while affecting ritual actors within its phonic reach, sacralizing and directing their actions. It is, in sum, a mask—just not a visual one that subsumes the body of its wearer under its power but an acoustic one whose sacralizing capacities extend to all who know how to experience and heed its call (Lifschitz 1988, Napier 1988, cf. D. Brown 2003: 37).

In this sense, the acoustic mask that is Écue is a complex assemblage of human and nonhuman agencies. And I think I am cleaving rather close to the views of contemporary ecória ñene abakuá when I qualify it as a biotechnology that, while capable of exerting powerful agency on its own, needs to enlist human actors not only to compose its material instrumentalities but to transduce its mystical energy from the numinous to the phenomenal realms, *thereby reproducing* its agency across secular space and time as well. This is even more obvious in some of the activities entailed in a *baroco ninllao*—that is, the type of ritual in the course of which not only individual members but new chapters of abakuá are "born." Here the challenge is not so much to reinstantiate the foundational conditions in Enllenisón under which Obon Tance's voice was first transferred to the technology composed from parts of Sikan's and embori's bodies and ocanco's wooden receptacle. It rather is to once more bring into being the moment when enslaved titleholders who had regrouped within Regla's "cabildo de los carabalí ápapa efí" (a voluntary association of Africans condoned by the Spanish colonial state) succeeded, in 1836, in achieving the first audible transduction on Cuban soil of Écue's numinous presence.[10]

Here is the barest account of what ecória ñene abakuá have been calling "la mecánica (de la transmisión)" since at least the 1950s when Cabrera (1969: 157) recorded that term in a comparable instance. Different from the "juramento" (swearing in) of individual new obonécues or even plazas in existing potencias whose Écue is already capacitated to extend itself in time and social space by birthing new members, the coming into being of a new potencia involves more than just the ritual work necessary to effect the vanishing of mediators and media into the message. It demands a different type of fabricación: one that involves recreating the mecánica originally deployed by the African slaves who found themselves "swaying back and forth like the waves" (*quende máriba quende*) upon disembarkation at the dockside of the town of Regla (*Itía Ororó Cande*) in the first decades of the nineteenth century. Few will venture to speculate on how this event actually occurred. But there is wide agreement that the original group of Cuban founders could not have been in possession of a consecrated Écue brought with them from Africa. How then to reactivate the voice? The solution was found in substituting the interior shell of a coconut now known as "el coco de *Efique Butón*" (named after the first potencia of abakuá, founded in Regla in 1836), and to this day, a coconut shell figures as the primary transmitter of el uyó to any new Écue drum and the "piezas" or "atributos" (staffs, drums, afoíreme, etc.) of a potencia *in statu nascendi*. Such transmission is (and is imagined to have originally been) a complex and protracted process during which a full set of seven different voices have to be brought into successive mystical resonance to prepare every single ritual implement for activation. In order to effect this, the "coco" is sounded as *if* it were Écue, while the functioning Écue drum of the potencia sponsoring the "birth" of a new one is suspended in a tub ("batea" or "palangana") of water from which the transfer is being effected by the phonic emissions of four further objects and two animals.[11] Lengthy *encames* (orations) accompany the process, but even though its details remain highly esoteric, it is once more clear that its goal consists in a form of mediation that results in "pure presence" or immediacy.

Yet while the baroco llansao could be viewed as repeating or even commemorating a foundational series of events (in this case the transmission of Écue's voice from Enllenisón into nineteenth-century Cuban geotemporality and so from "myth" into "history"), to call this a repetition would be as misguided as to view the Eucharist as mere commemoration. What strict adherence to the mecánica of "transmission" is supposed to ensure is no repetition at all. Or if it is, it is one where the copy proves the prior original—an event, in other words, that not only occurs *over and over again* but attains significance precisely in indexical iterations rather than in some form of iconic recall. If in the contemporary baroco llansao Cuban alleyways facing an abakuá temple collapse into a chronotope coextensive with the mythical embarcadero of Usagaré where Sikan first encountered the mystery, so the baroco ninllao collapses the historical distance between the founding of the first Cuban potencia Efique Buton and the present occasion of the birth of its latest progeny. In both cases, this is the result of extensive and highly methodical ritual mediation that involves the systematic erasure of its own traces: while genealogical relations between older and younger potencias are certainly recognized (Palmié 2006), they are modeled on godparenthood or perhaps midwifery, such as when obonécues speak of an older potencia that sponsored the inception of theirs as their "padrino," who "has pulled us out" ("nos ha sacado"). Their "nascimiento" (birth or, better, coming into the world), however, is unmediated—except in the sense that Écue itself has given birth to them, thus enlisting them as the human component of the media of its own propagation.

Ghosts in the Machine: Making Things Talk, ca. 1908

Was the "echo" at 2132 North Fairmount Avenue "el Écue"? Chances are good that the journalist simply misheard what Leal and the unnamed woman said. Clearly, under such a description even more details of the report seem to fall into place:[12] the drum in the corner, the washbasin, perhaps even the pagoda-like structure. Leal's remark "I talk with the spirits and they talk with me" would make perfect sense, as would his showing the journalist around in what might have been a curiously modified cuarto fambá. "See my Écue?" not "See my echo!" Or so he may have prodded the journalist who, of course, had no idea what he was seeing or what Leal was talking about.

Yet what about all the tubes, the aquatic "converter," the painted spools, the speaking trumpets, the megaphone? Hard as it is to tell from the journalist's account what exactly the Leals had set up at their Temple of the Ancient Grace and to what degree the "echo" was propagated by electroacoustic means, there clearly were forms of mediation involved in the Leals' temple that contemporary Cuban obonécues would regard as inappropriate, unacceptable, even potentially sacrilegious. Any attempt to assimilate these to contemporary Cuban ethnography will likely go nowhere. And that is as it should be. In fact, it might be as ostensibly preposterous to suggest that the contraptions at 2132 North Fairmount Avenue were a precursor to Caribbean sound-system technology as to regard them as an offshoot of abakuá. Ostensibly preposterous, for both contemporary Cuban abakuá and Jamaican sound systems, in fact, share the use of interfaces between humans and technologies to effect what Henriques (2003) calls "sonic dominance," that is, the creation of social contexts in which the sheer physical volume or the semiotic weight of sound begins to privilege audition as the preeminent sensory modality over and above other aspects of the sensorium. But this would have to be the subject of another publication.[13]

What interests me instead is the kind of cultural threshold the Leals and the unnamed *Philadelphia North American* journalist jointly inhabited at the beginning of the twentieth century. More specifically, how may this juncture—the dawn of electroacoustic analog media—have brought what one might call abakuá's sonic and auditory ideologies[14] into a momentary alignment with regimes of sonic semiosis that were then still far from becoming fully rationalized, let alone naturalized in the way contemporary Western hearers routinely consume mechanically reproduced sound? As Jonathan Sterne (2003: 2) so well puts it, just as "there was an Enlightenment, so too was there an 'Ensoniment'" that paralleled the rise of visualism in the "West" to a degree that has, until recently, largely remained unappreciated or has even been actively consigned to what Charles Hirschkind (2006) calls a "subterranean" status. Though one could debate Sterne's periodization, he is certainly right when he argues that "between about 1750 and 1925, sound itself became an object and a domain of thought and practice, where it had previously been conceptualized in particular idealized instances like voice or music. Hearing was reconstructed as a physiological process, a kind of receptivity and capacity based on physics, biology, and mechanics. Through techniques of listening, people harnessed, modified, and shaped their powers of auditory perception in the service of rationality" (2003: 2). By the same token, as Leigh Eric Schmidt (2000) has argued, the secularization of hearing that paralleled this process in the constitution of "modern subjects" disciplined into no longer "hearing things" (for which there was no rational explanation) not only remained woefully incomplete—as evidenced for example in nineteenth-century evangelical revivalism or contemporary Pentecostalism. Rather, as it turned out, Walter J. Ong's (1982) technologically induced "secondary orality" carried the day—if not exactly in the sense intended by him[15]—through a rather oddly Weberian enchantment of the very technological means of rational sound propagation and reproduction evolving in a curious "dialectic of ensoniment."

Attempts to control and manipulate sonation, of course, go back far beyond the threshold set by Sterne. When Athanasius Kircher and Samuel Morland fought over the precedent of developing devices of sound amplification in the second half of the seventeenth century, both referred back not only to supposedly ancient hermetic wisdom but to the practical knowledge that mariners, herdsmen, and soldiers had deployed for millennia to effect "action at a distance" through amplification and broadcasting of vocal utterances. Moreland (1671) intended his "Tuba Stentoro-Phonica or Speaking Trumpet" (a trumpet-shaped megaphone) mainly for nautical and military purposes. Yet Kircher's speaking trumpets and panacoustic technologies[16] were directly inspired by the baroque *magia naturalis* that informed his theories of cosmic harmonies. In line with his theories of the capability of *musica pathetica* to induce affective states, Kircher also designed hailing technologies in the form of giant speaking trumpets that, once projected from hillside shrines, would beckon the faithful to hear the word and the universal harmony projected by the divine organist (one of Kircher's favorite metaphors) and reverberating through his creation.[17]

Aside from studies of ecclesiastic acoustic architecture (Gouk 1999), a systematic history of the use of amplification in the production of what Hirschkind (2006) calls "pious soundscapes" in the West remains to be written.[18] We do know, however, that sonic technologies were contemplated for secular disciplinary purposes and forms of affective manipulation and control. Foucault's overinterpretation of its visual aspects notwithstanding,

Bentham's original plan for the panopticon included tin tubes connecting individual cells with the inspector's lodge to allow for both eavesdropping and targeted reprimands (Schmidt 2000: 117). Charles Babbage—ever ready to exploit a disciplinary technology when he saw its potential—also recommended the use of tin tubes in the implementation of industrial and even domestic command structures (Mills 2009). Yet prior to the development of electroacoustic technologies, these remained relatively isolated thought experiments (foiled by the then still insurmountable mutuality in audibility, as opposed to the engineerable unidirectionality of the "gaze"). By the eighteenth century, interest on the part of the emerging sciences of acoustics and phonology had come to focus not so much on the extension of sonic reach as on the artificial production of human vocalizations. This was the age of automata and speaking machines, which reached its height in the period between 1770 and 1790 when the Abbé Mical, Christian Gottlieb Kratzenstein, Wolfgang von Kempelen, and none other than Erasmus Darwin (afflicted as he was with a terrible stutter) constructed apparently working but rather cumbersome "speaking machines" modeled on the mechanics of the human vocal tract (Hankins and Silverman 1995: 186–98). Improvements in this genre of technologies modeled on the human larynx and mouth persisted throughout the nineteenth and even early twentieth centuries.[19] By the middle of the nineteenth century, however, a massive sea change in the conception of sound and practices of sonic manipulation was already well under way.

Though understandings of sound as oscillatory pulsations transmitted through media such as air can be traced back as far as Aristotle, the primary focus of post-Enlightenment acoustic and phonetic research had been on the production rather than reception of audible phonation—on the mouth rather than the ear, on the origins of sound rather than on its effect in the world. The reorientation of thought about sound and practices of its manipulation that made possible electroacoustic technologies that started to proliferate in the second half of the nineteenth century, was based on multiple transfers of knowledge between domains that had barely begun to differentiate institutionally—physics, physiology, and phonetics. And it was driven less by the system-building ambitions of the baroque than by the kind of experimental tinkering that led Volta to galvanize frogs' legs or Benjamin Franklin to ascend rooftops with metal rod in hand. The latter examples are not arbitrary. The gradual secularization of electricity (one recalls the elderly Franklin's role in Franz Mesmer's downfall), indeed the diffusion of practical knowledge about electromagnetism (as well as its popular display in electrical showmanship) paved the way for what, following

Sterne (2003), we might call a largely unheralded transductive revolution: a protracted, if eventually principled revaluation of sonation *and* audition as a *joint* phenomenon—and one that revolved around the transduction of one source of energy, sonic vibrations, into electromagnetic impulses and back into auditory frequencies. The key, as it turned out, lay not in the physiological mechanics of vocalization but in those of audition.

While Morse and his numerous precursors had certainly managed to reduce linguistic signage to a code of binary electrical impulses enabled by mechanical circuit breakers, telegraphy remained, despite its truly amazing—and amazingly rapid—impact on global information flows, just what its name suggested: writing at or across a distance.[20] To be sure, the truly dramatic departure telegraphy represented from older communication technologies aiming to supersede the limited capacities of speech and handwriting to bind time and space (such as the printing press and publishing networks) can hardly be overemphasized (e.g., Peters 1999: 138–43), and it may come as no surprise that the spirit rappings of Hydesville, New York, commenced a mere four years after Morse had successfully demonstrated that his system of transducing mechanical into electrical impulses could carry coherent semantic weight in nearby Rochester (Sollors 1983; Connor 1999; Stolow 1999; Sconce 2000).[21] Yet while the birth of Spiritualism from the technology of electromechanical telegraphy nicely exemplifies the convergence of a much older "electrical sublime" with a novel technological interface allowing for disembodied communication in (almost) real time, the birth of telephony from the spirit of anatomical praxis—though much less noticed publicly—already brings us closer to some of the mysteries that may have animated the voices emanating from the Temple of the Ancient Grace at 2132 North Fairmount Avenue.

As Alexander Graham Bell himself told the story in the massive transcript of the 1892 Massachusetts Circuit Court lawsuit threatening annulment of his patents, in the spring and summer of 1874, he had been intermittently working on devising a method of telegraphy capable of transmitting several sets of impulses at the same time (thus ideally enabling vocal rather than mere code transmission). But he was also experimenting with the phonautograph (an apparatus for translating sound waves into graphic traces invented in 1857 by Leon Scott) to further his goals in devising a pedagogical tool for the education of the deaf-mute.[22] "I was struck," says Bell (Bell Telephone Company 1908: 29), "by the likeness between the mechanism of the phonautograph and the mechanism of the human ear, the membrane of the one being loaded by a lever of wood, and the membrane of the other by levers of bone. It appeared to me that a phonautograph modeled after the pattern of the human ear would probably produce more accurate tracings of speech-vibrations than the imperfect instrument with which I was operating." "For this purpose," Bell continues, "I consulted a distinguished aurist," his friend Dr. Clarence J. Blake, a pioneer in American otology, then affiliated with the Massachusetts Charitable Eye and Ear Infirmary and Harvard Medical School (Snyder 1974). "He seemed much interested in my experiments," Bell states, "and suggested that, instead of trying to make a phonautograph modeled after the pattern of the human ear, I should attempt to use a human ear itself, taken from a dead subject, as a phonautograph" (Bell Telephone Company 1908: 29). And so they did. Well connected to the source of corpses at Harvard Medical School, made possible by the 1832 Massachusetts Anatomical Act, Blake supplied two middle ears—whose extraction and resection he describes in loving detail in his own publications on the matter (Blake 1878)—one for his own experiments, one for Bell to take to his summer home in Nova Scotia. For all we know, the results were eminently satisfying. Much as in the case of Nasacó's experiments with various membranes cut from sacrificial victims in his attempts to revive Tance's voice, the tympani of middle ears cut from the bodies of Harvard's dead paupers or criminals proved a breakthrough: once mounted on a microscope stand, moistened with glycerin and water, and outfitted with a stylus that transferred to a plate of smoked glass the vibrations registered by an eardrum no longer connected to a living human being but recruited into auditory science as an agent of what Sterne (2003) calls "tympanic transduction," Bell and Blake's so-called ear-phonautograph graphically rendered sound like no other device had ever done before.

Bell had earlier experimented with applying electricity to his own ears (Bell Telephone Company 1908: 45) and had been tinkering with electromagnetic devices for what he envisioned as a "harmonic" (i.e., multifrequency) conducting, and so potentially voice-conferring, telegraph. But it struck him that the disproportion between the eardrum's diaphragm and the bones moved by it suggested that "a larger and stouter membrane be capable to move a piece of steel" (ibid.: 39)—in other words, a conduit for electromagnetic "undulations": "At once the conception of a membrane speaking telephone became complete in my mind; for I saw that a similar instrument to that used as a transmitter could also be employed as a receiver" (ibid.). Emulation of the vocal tract in the reproduction of the human voice—which the youthful Bell had engaged in after seeing Charles Wheatstone's reconstruction of von Kempelen's speaking machine—had been obliterated as a viable principle of sonic propagation in an instant, the mouth forever displaced by the ear. Sound became an effect registered by the human sensorium rather that an independent cause in the world. It has remained so ever since.

Bell later repeatedly voiced regret over not having invented the phonograph at one and the same time as the telephone, leaving the former's—no less uncanny—inauguration to the future (self-promoted) Wizard of Menlo Park, Thomas Alva Edison. Edison's discovery of phonography has been described as involving a similar logic of human sacrifice, not of the ears of cadaveric organ donors but his own blood. The Count de Monceil (1879: 237), himself a pioneer of electrified communication, recounts the episode as follows:

> In the course of some experiments Mr. Edison was making with the telephone, a stylus attached to the diaphragm pierced his finger at the moment when the diaphragm began to vibrate under the influence of the voice, and the prick was enough to draw blood. It then occurred to him that if the vibrations of the diaphragm enabled the stylus to pierce his skin, they might produce on a flexible surface such distinct outlines as to represent all the undulations produced by the voice, and even that the same outlines might mechanically reproduce the vibrations which had caused them, by reacting on a plate capable of vibrating in the same way as that which he had already used for the reproduction of the Morse signals.

De Monceil himself expresses skepticism about this particular myth of origin (and there are indeed other versions). Yet the blood sacrifice occasioned by the transduction of sound to Edison's own flesh has its equivalent in Edison's physical engagement with the sonic technologies he was bringing into being. If Bell had inherited his father's lifelong concern with the hard of hearing, one reason Edison applied the stylus to his finger in the first place was that a childhood bout with scarlet fever[23] had left him partially deaf himself. As he himself publicly recounted on several occasions, it was his deafness that had led him to telegraphy, his fateful experiment with Bell's telephone, and the subsequent "perfection of the phonograph." This was so because his auditory disability forced him to analogize between different sensory modalities and their receptivity to sound waves as a form of energy (Edison 1948: 47–48, 53–54). A 1913 advertisement thus quotes him as saying, "I hear through my teeth . . . and through my skull. Ordinarily I merely place my head against the phonograph. But if there is some faint sound that I don't quite catch this way, I bite my teeth into the wood, and then I get it good and strong" (quoted in Peters 2004: 191).[24] The uncanny nature of such merging of body and machine into the conduit of an absent presence—previously recorded sound—was not lost on Edison's contemporaries.

As a reviewer of Edison's first phonograph noted in *Scientific American* ("Talking Phonograph" 1877: 385), it was "a little curious" that in the test recordings (of phrases such as "How do you do?" and "Do you like the phonograph?") the "machine pronounces its own name with especial clearness." But it wasn't just that the medium—"a little affair of a few pieces of metal, set up roughly on an iron stand about a foot square"—seemingly disappeared into a self-naming message that appears to hail the listener. Rather, "No matter how familiar a person will be with modern machinery and its wonderful performances, or how clear in his mind the principle underlying this strange device may be, it is impossible to listen to the mechanical speech without his experiencing the idea that his senses are deceiving him" (ibid.). Given its capacity to arrest time itself by capturing acoustic data flows in a series of mechanical traces—analog indexes of past sonic events—the phonograph's necromantic potential was immediately obvious. What particularly astonished the reviewer was "the startling possibility of the voices of the dead being reheard through this device," thus producing "the illusion of real presence" (ibid.)—the dream of transcendence and immediation come true in the human voice permanently separated from the speaking body.

In Edison's (1878: 530) own words, the "captivity of all manner of sound-waves hitherto designated as 'fugitive'"—including human vocalizations—"their permanent retention," and their "reproduction with all their original characteristics at will, without the presence or consent of the original source, and after any length of time" could now be considered as "*faits accomplis.*" While much of this was hyperbole, given the miserable sound quality of early tinfoil recordings and their rapid deterioration in the course of very few replays, Peters (1999: 160) is correct when he argues that, right from the start, the phonograph was "a more shocking emblem of modernity than the photograph," which, after all, recurred to realistic conventions of iconic representation reaching back at least to Renaissance perspectivism. If the telephone had seemed to cut distance out of communicative processes, as the *Scientific American* reviewer's evocation of Eucharistic language suggests, phonographic recording not only appeared to undermine time's status as an a priori dimension of human life, but to relativize mortality itself.

Though not—at least at the time—given to explicit statements about the spirit world, Edison more than hinted at this when, in response to the "abundance of conjectural and prophetic opinions which have been disseminated by the press," he outlined a series of rational uses of the phonograph that included, significantly, "preserving the sayings, the voices, and the last words of the dying member of the family—as of great men" or speeches by "our Washingtons, our Lincolns, our Gladstones" so as to have them once more "give us their 'greatest effort' in every town and hamlet of the country, upon our holidays" (Edison 1878: 533–34). Ten years later, he still spoke of "speeches of orators" and "discourses of clergymen" that could "be had 'on tap,' in every house that owns a phonograph." Yet venturing into what at the time was becoming known as psychophysics, he made an even more ominous comment about the subsumption of the original into—sublation by?—the copy. Whereas in his earlier essay he had hinted at future forensic uses of the phonograph, he now (1888: 649–50) argued that "the phonograph, in one sense, knows more than we do ourselves. For it will retain a perfect mechanical memory of many things which we may forget, even though we have said them." Edison's initial prosthetic device designed to overcome the temporally evanescent nature of the human voice had turned into a Derridean supplement to the kind of personhood that had hinged on the continuity of memory since Aristotle and had been hitched to forensic notions of individual accountability by John Locke. No doubt, biting into his phonograph, late in his life, would have confirmed Edison's sense of having changed the world of sonic communication. But the new regime of hearing his invention inaugurated spread across the globe as quickly as it began to reverberate through a whole variety of cultural domains. Some of them were highly receptive to the enchanted potentialities the phonograph helped usher in.

Phonurgia Pathetica: Mr. Edison's Transductive Cosmology

Ever since Edison's announcement of the "perfection" of the phonograph, much advertisement and newspaper copy was expended on extolling the magic worked by the transductive agency—a sympathy of vibrations from sound waves to electromagnetic impulses and back again—of the phonographic diaphragm, or the similarly magical hold the recorded trace seemed to exert in conjuring the original. In what may well be one of the most wildly enchanted, even spooky praises the phonograph ever received, the Reverend Horatio N. Powers thus rhapsodized after hearing Edison's original machine: "I seize the palpitating air. I hoard music and speech. All lips that speak are mine. I speak; and the inviolate word authenticates its origin and sign! I am a tomb, a paradise, a throne, and angel, prophet, slave, immortal friend! My living record in their native tone convicts the knaves and disputations end. In me are souls embalmed. I am an ear, flawless as truth, and truth's own tongue am I. I am a resurrection, and men hear the quick and the dead converse as I reply" (quoted in Hughbanks 1945: 13) If Powers did not go quite as far as to suggest a phonographic theogony, the ominously apocalyptic tone of his adoption of the phonograph's persona amply bears out how ghosts came rushing into the machine as soon as its perceived functions came to resonate with themes that had occupied Western thinkers from Plato and Aristotle to Saint Augustine (Peters 1999; Schmidt 2000) and had been all but effectively dispelled by the enlightened rationality that had brought forth the material technos that now spoke with the captured logos of its creator: a mechanical angel and slave, promising justice, redemption, and everlasting replication to those who entered into a covenant with the apparatus bodying forth the ear and tongue of truth.

Not infrequently, early writers on the wonders of phonography readily speculated that had Edison's invention occurred in less enlightened times, its simulacral work would have been perceived as witchcraft.[25] An equally popular topos was the displacement of self-consciously "modern" ambivalences toward electroacoustic technology not onto one's own unenlightened ancestors but on the primitive Other elsewhere. In what Pietz (1987a) aptly describes as a technocolonial fantasy, an 1885 *New York Times* article on two travelers' plan to embark to Africa equipped with the phonograph (to record African languages) thus mused that "not only would the native Kings have an unbounded respect for the proprietors of such a wonderful fetich [*sic*], but they could be induced or entrapped into making remarks in the presence of the phonograph which could afterward be reproduced with excellent effect. For example, no African would venture to disobey the voice of his King ordering him to 'bring the white men food,' and the fact of the voice issuing from the phonograph instead of the King's own lips would add, if anything, additional force to the order" (quoted in Pietz 1987a: 268). In an even more ingenuous political move, "the travelers could describe the phonograph as a new and improved portable speaking god, and call upon the native Kings to obey it. A god capable of speaking, and even of carrying on a conversation in the presence of swarms of hearers could be something entirely new in Central Africa, where the local gods are constructed of billets of wood, and are hopelessly dumb. There is not a Central African who would not obey the Phonograph god" (ibid.: 269). Of course, if anything, this was American, not African fetishism—"a fantasy about the capacity of modern language technology to acquire the power of the 'fetish' of primitives and despots without the need to participate in the forms of subjectivity imagined to be proper to pre-civilized 'fetishism' " (ibid.).

Indeed, as Taussig (1993) and Brady (1999) have noted, Western attempts to imbue the phonograph with mystical attributes deliberately played on acoustic sensibilities and semiotic ideologies characteristic of the Victorian world that tended to quickly break down into sheer fantasy when projected elsewhere. As Brady (1999: 46) puts it, that the voice of the phonograph would have initially been invested with "quasi-supernatural authority" was by no means an effect that exposure to this technology would have "naturally" produced among human listeners. Instead, it had everything to do with Western notions of the semiotics of sound and audition.[26] Indeed the phonograph often failed to elicit much wonderment among non-Westerners upon first exposure to the technology. Much to the surprise of Jesse Walter Fewkes, the first anthropologist to make use of Edisonian technology in the field, the Zuñi whom he exposed to this self-conscious marvel of modernity in 1890 not only failed to be impressed but promptly incorporated a parody of Fewkes and his recording apparatus in the ritual clowning of the Basket Dance (ibid.: 31). Frances Densmore similarly encountered not awestruck admiration but straightforward instrumentalism when in 1917, after considerable trouble, she managed to get the northern Ute chief Red Cap to sing into her phonograph tube. "After the recording was finished,' " she writes (quoted in ibid.: 93),

> Red Cap said, "I have done as you wished. Now I want to ask a favor. I do not sing, as I said, but I would like to talk into your phonograph. Will it record talking?" Guilelessly I said it would record any song.
>
> "Well" said the wily old chief, "Then I will talk and I want you to play the record for the Indian Commissioner in Washington. I want to tell him that we do not like this Agent. We want him sent somewhere else. We don't like the things he does. What we tell him does not get to the Commissioner but I want the Commissioner to hear my voice."[27]

But while the phonograph may not have made much of an impression on people accustomed to communicating with disembodied others—in vision quests, oracles, shamanistic trances, or spirit possession—it amply worked its magic upon the Western imagination. This was so not least because the phonograph raised what Engelke (2007) has called "the problem of presence" in a fashion that had hitherto been largely unthinkable but immediately seemed to resonate with long-standing metaphysical questions in Western religious as well as secular thought.

Foremost among these was the question of life after death. Perhaps not ironically, the time-transcendent epistemic superiority of the mechanical copy over the biotic original that Edison's 1888 remarks had aimed to convey was to take its recursive toll even on the creator himself.[28] Evidence for Edison's own curious electrobiotic monadology goes back to his brief collaboration with George Miller Beard, a physician, founding editor of the short-lived *Archives of Electrology and Neurology* and author of the massive tomes *American Nervousness* and *Sexual Neurasthenia*, who came to Edison's rescue in the course of the controversy over Edison's premature announcement of his discovery of an "etheric force" in 1875 (Wills 2009).[29] By 1878 Edison had taken up correspondence with Madame Blavatsky and become a member of the Theosophical Society. But it was not until a series of interviews he gave in 1910 and 1911 that the wider public seems to have become aware of Edison's own branch of enchanted hyper-Cartesian materialism.

The initial occasion, as the journalist Edward Marshall (Edison 1910) put it, was "the recent death of Prof. William James, Harvard's distinguished psychologist, and the alleged reappearance or 'manifestation' of Prof. James's soul on earth." "The newspapers have been teeming with the subject," Marshall wrote. "The psychic researchers are even now quarreling bitterly over it. The public is puzzled." Might the Wizard of Menlo Park have an answer? Edison did. Yet unlike Bell's assistant, Thomas Watson, who, in his autobiography, happily rambles on about asking the spirits for help in bringing Bell's telephonic experiments to a successful conclusion (Watson 1926: 100), Edison flatly (and scandalously) denied "immortality" as envisioned by contemporary "creedists." Instead, he offered his own biomechanistic vision of the universe. Like cities such as New York (Edison's favorite example), human individuals were really aggregates of myriads of life units, their bodies shedding cells just as social aggregates were shedding members upon the death of individuals. And just like memory in the individual brain ("a queer and wonderful machine") was "like the phonograph cylinder" in preserving "things which have been impressed upon it by the mysterious power that actuates it," the brain, like any machine, could not be conceived of as "immortal." Machines, after all, break down.

As Edison phrased the matter even more succinctly in an interview with the *Columbian Magazine* (Edison 1911) a year later,

> There is no dodging the plain fact that we are mere machines. . . . I used the term "mere meat machines" when we were talking on these lines before. I like the term. It is a good one. We are machines made up of an infinity of parts, each one made up of an infinity of cells. Life lies within the cells, and

> the cells are the real individuals. Our intelligence is the aggregate intelligence of the cells which make us up. There is no soul, distinct from mind, and what we speak of as the mind is just the aggregate intelligence of cells.

From such a perspective—one that Edison (much like Athanasius Kircher) thought capable of being scaled up or down from micro- to macrocosmic dimensions—death seemed to loose its sting. Just like the individual "meat machine" endowed with a mental phonograph that ensured the coherence of its mortal identity was a replaceable part in the New York City–like cosmos, so were its individual cell-borne "life units" part and parcel of a larger cosmic drama conceived of, in terms both strikingly Durkheimian and Spencerian at the same time, as unraveling under the impact of new technology impinging upon the human body and sensorium, challenging its "life units" to reaggregate in novel adaptations. The inventions produced by mortal "meat machines" like Thomas Edison himself, in other words, drove onward the perfection of the human race.

It was along such lines that, late in his life, Edison finally outed himself as a proponent of a rather more than casually spiritualized materialism. "I am working on the theory that our personality exists after what we call life leaves our present material bodies," he told Bertie C. Forbes (Edison 1920: 11): "Take our bodies. I believe they are composed of myriads and myriads of infinitesimally small individuals, each in itself a unit of life, and that these units work in squads—or swarms, as I prefer to call them, and that these infinitesimally small units live forever." Though "reluctant to discuss the machine he was reported to be building for the apprehension of messages from the dead," as the *New York Times'* A. D. Rothman (1921: 1) reported a few months later, Edison "did admit that he was engaged—had been engaged for a number of years—in the construction of such an apparatus." When a man dies, Edison told Rothman, "the life units which have formed that man do not die. They merely pass out of the unimportant mechanism which they have been inhabiting, which has been called a man and has been mistaken for an individual, and select some other habitat or habitats. . . . These little entities of personality which I hope to detect with my apparatus are still animal entities" (ibid.: 1, 6). Nor were these reports mere journalistic exaggeration. The excerpts from Edison's own notebooks, posthumously published in 1948, show that between 1920 and 1925, the aging Wizard of Menlo Park again and again returned to his swarming life units and the possibility of registering their energetic signatures by means of an apparatus "perhaps most readily . . . described as a sort of valve. In exactly the same way in which a megaphone increases many times the volume and carrying power of the human voice, so with my 'valve,' whatever original force is used upon it is increased enormously for purposes of registration of the phenomena behind it" (Edison 1948: 205). "If my theory is correct," he writes elsewhere (ibid.: 215–16), and if on the breakage of "the machine called man" the individual life units that had composed it "keep together, including those which have charge of memory (which is our personality)—then I think it is possible to devise apparatus [*sic*] to receive communications, if they desire to make them." Such an apparatus "would rid the world of harmful superstitions such as spiritualism" (ibid.: 224)—though we might add that it would have done so by proving them right.

Did Edison ever build such an apparatus? Wainwright Evans (1963) claims he did. Writing for *Fate* magazine, Evans recalled an interview he had with Edison's private secretary William A. Meadowcroft in 1921 in which Meadowcroft told him that "according to Edison's theory, what survived death would be an electronic replica, so to speak, of the body as it was in life—a sort of electronic ghost, made up of an aggregate of the 'entities' or 'electrons.'" As Evans explained, "This collective entity, Edison reasoned, would be able to put forth physical energy, and could presumably manifest its presence through a mechanism if one sufficiently sensitive were available. Therefore he set himself the problem of designing something that would respond to the wispy physical impulses such a very attenuated organism might provide" (ibid.). In the remainder of the article, Evans unravels an intricate story about how, in 1941 (ten years after Edison's death), J. Gilbert Wright, a General Electric researcher and inventor of silicone rubber, and his associate Harry C. Gardner received communications from Edison through a spirit medium, laboriously set about locating the blueprints for Edison's apparatus, and then tried to reconstruct it. It eventually took the form of an aluminum trumpet mounted on top of a microphone enclosed in a sound box and filled with a potassium permanganate solution that acted as an electrolyte once connected to an antenna, the base of which was submerged in the solution at one pole and connected to the microphone at the other. Alas, the contraption did not seem to successfully transmit any life units. And so, in a beautiful exemplification of the dialectics of ensoniment, Wright and Gardner eventually resorted to the by then rather old-fashioned solution of having a human medium project an ectoplasmic larynx into the sound box, through which spirits would speak into the microphone. Edison apparently "came through," and recommended the use of Wright's silicone putty as a lining for the sound box. But while one would doubt that he approved of such hybridization of his plan for what psychic researchers would nowadays call a "transcommunicative" device, his spirit remains active to this day in furthering the electromechanics of future telephonic communication between the living and the dead (Streiff 2009).[30]

The Phonograph Unmasked: High Fidelity

Edison's enchanted musings may appear to have come rather too late to give us a handle on how to judge the impact of late nineteenth- and early twentieth-century sonic technologies on the world the tenants at 2132 North Fairmount Avenue might have inhabited. But Edison's increasingly mystical pronouncements on the technologies he had helped bring into being were themselves only symptomatic of a larger dialectic that enchanted technology in the service of rationalizing the numinous. Ironically, it was precisely this moment that had already characterized, even driven, much of nineteenth-century Spiritualism. If Comte had suggested sociology as the religion to end all religions, his countryman Allan Kardec had thrown the afterlife open to positivistic investigation.[31] Indeed it should come as no surprise that the member lists of British and American Spiritualist societies soon featured the names of some of the most prominent scientists of the second half of the nineteenth century dedicating themselves to the rational pursuit of the irrational.[32] In turn, Spiritualism itself became a veritable vortex, sucking up new communication technologies almost as soon as their invention became public knowledge.[33]

If spirits somewhat belatedly appropriated photography as a medium for manifestation,[34] they began using Morse code shortly after the initial 1848 rappings at Hydesville. As Thomas Watson (1926: 42–43), Bell's assistant, spelled out the logic in his autobiography, "Mediums are endowed with the power to transform subtle, bodily radiation into a mechanical force that produces the raps, movements, and slate writings as a steam engine changes heat into mechanical motion or a telegraph transforms pulsations of electricity into the taps of the Morse code." Small wonder, then, that the spirits were eagerly poised to make themselves heard in what came to be known as "direct voice manifestations" once telephony and phonography made hearing disembodied speech a matter of increasingly common experience.

As Connor (1999: 212) describes the practice that appears to have originated in the 1850s (Schmidt 2000: 238) but attained its heyday just after the turn of the twentieth century, "direct voice" manifestations involved "a voice which speaks independently of the medium's vocal organs." As

Connor explains, "Often in 'direct voice' manifestations, the spirits would employ a trumpet (resembling a speaking trumpet or megaphone rather than the musical instrument), or even a series of trumpets, which might be placed in the room at a distance from the medium. The trumpet served both to amplify the voice, and to change its position: trumpets would be moved telekinetically through the air and around the room" (ibid.: 212–13). Electromagnetic transduction seems to have been a widespread model for direct voice mediumship. The Spiritualist W. W. Aber's instructions for producing trumpet manifestations thus recommend: "Place a trumpet in a basin of water in the center of the floor; form a circle around it, and connect the battery by touching feet all around the circle" (quoted in Enns 2005: 14). Trumpet medium Mrs. Cecil M. Cook likewise favored the use of electrolytes: "Somehow, the voices seem to come clearer when the trumpets are moist. There is something about the forces that resembles electrical energy" (quoted in ibid.: 14).

His frequent diatribes against Spiritualism notwithstanding, Edison could not but have agreed on matters of principle. After all, both he and Bell had experimented with placing induction coils over their heads to effect sound transference (Conot 1979: 428; Enns 2005). After sticking wires connected to an electromagnet in his water-filled ears, and experimenting with various substances to increase resistance ("water, especially when lightly acidulated . . . [r]etort carbon, plumbago, animal and vegetable tissues, and other substances . . . answer the purpose" [Bell Telephone Company 1908: 86]), Bell in 1876 invented the "Centennial Liquid Transmitter," a transductive device curiously akin to a speaking trumpet mounted on top of a liquid-filled vessel (ibid.: 99)—or, for that matter, to the central element of the Leal brothers' contraption: a speaking tube sticking out from a glass-encased container of liquid, stretching across to a converter, complete with a bit of stovepipe on the top, and another tube leading into the converter from a kettle drum made of a skin-covered china washbowl.[35]

Different from earlier, more agitated mediumistic performances such as those pioneered by the Fox sisters themselves, trumpet mediums were characteristically passive, their mouths closed, their bodies mere conduits (tympanic membranes?) for the transmission of spiritual emanations that would take on audible form in and through the trumpet. Connor suggests the switchboard operator as a social model (the passive female human element throwing switches within increasingly widening telephonic communication circuits). Yet while eminently plausible, this analogy may not go far enough. Instead, "direct voice" mediums became a human adjunct to what increasingly seems to have been envisioned as a technology very much akin to the transductive components of the telephone or phonograph—a membrane and electrolytic conduit of variable impedance connected to a battery-powered circuit rather than an operator in her own right. While spirit trumpets were manufactured in a variety of forms and designs (such as telescoping ones for busy traveling mediums), many of them bore more than incidental resemblance to the Victrola horn or, for that matter, the horns sticking out of the window of 2132 North Fairmount Avenue in 1908. Had Écue's voice and its material instrumentalities—nambe erí, "the flesh of the drum" and Illamba's llin—found a new medium for its sonic propagation? Might the Leals' contraption perhaps even have provided a worldly storage for its numinous energies?

If so, such convergences alone would tell us little. Surely ideas about the electroacoustic transduction of numinous energies into the sublunar phenomenal sphere were swirling around in the social worlds that the Ejamba of North Fairmount Avenue, to some degree, shared with the Wizard of Menlo Park. Still, as in phonography, so in spiritualism and abakuá: with Friedrich Kittler (1999: 55), we might say that "technological media guarantee the similarity of the dead to stored data by turning them into the latter's stored products." Yet such mediated guarantees are not technological but social outcomes. They are the result of variable social agreements about which sonic phenomena can be taken to indicate what forms of presence. In fact, they became thinkable *as* transparent technological achievements only *after* thorough social routinization had naturalized them as part of an auditory habitus. Initially, at least, such "guarantees" depended very much upon the growth and social diffusion of a technological imaginary concerning what machines could and could not do in the world (such as speak with the voices of the dead—or, for that matter, that of Écue). Put differently, perceptions of audio technologies as conduits for the numinous were contingent upon the increasing social pervasiveness of semiotic ideologies that metapragmatically regimented how specific types of mediated sonic data output could be indexically construed as iterable forms of collectively salient semiotic input—rather than sheer variations of meaningless noise or individual auditory hallucinations.[36] No matter the extent to which analog recordings—such as the traces left on wax cylinders by a stylus moved by electroacoustic transduction—do carry the material traces of an original event (Rothenbuhler and Peters 1997, Kittler 1999), indexical recognition, as we might say with Keane (2003: 419; cf. Keane 2008), comes at a price: it needs to be furnished with socially routinized instructions to occur at all.

Such rules of recognition for technologically mediated indexes of the numinous were, of course, proliferating in luxurious heterogeneity in late nineteenth-century urban America. By the time the *Philadelphia North American* journalist described the Leal brothers' curious apparatus, the use of speaking tubes for religious purposes was no longer particularly new. Already in 1860 the *New York Times* had reported on a local church's adoption of a megaphonic device involving tubes presumably much like those depicted in the photographs in the 1908 *Philadelphia North American*.[37] But while it is hard to guess from the journalist's account how exactly the Leal brothers' sound system functioned and to what degree it was electrified,[38] it is not at all unimaginable that the Leal brothers may have been engaging in their own brand of enchanted engineering. At the very least, they seem to have managed to convince a social collectivity (of what size we do not know) that their contraption activated "the echo"/el Écue in a way some of its hearers found convincing. In doing so, they might have fought to overcome the same barriers to the "willing suspension of disbelief" that early pioneers of electroacoustic media struggled with. Placing speaking trumpets or phonograph tubes to blare out of your window is one thing. Convincing others of the numinous immediacy of the sounds projected from them would have been another. After all, as Sterne (2003: 308) puts it, "Any medium requires a modicum of faith in the social relations that constitute it."

This is an issue that pertains to contemporary abakuá rituals just as much as it would have pertained to the Leals' contraption in 1908, precisely because it has bearing on any socially meaningful form of mediation. Could you or I, with a bit of practice, apply a piece of bamboo to a friction drum and make it emit sounds closely approximating Écue's awesome uyó? Of course we could. But would such exercises yield more than fairly meaningless, perhaps even debased replications of an "original" sound? Just as my singing of a Verdi aria, however well-executed, will not substitute for the scratchy excess of the best analog recordings of Caruso's voice from the turn of the twentieth century, the copy will remain haunted by the original or—and this is the crucial point—an *idea* of it. But this idea is one that, as Sterne (2003) persuasively argues, only became thinkable as the basis for an ontology of mediation once Western listeners became accustomed to the notion that there *could* be an "original sound" in the absence of the potential for its artificially mediated reproduction across space and time.[39] The very notion of sonic "fidelity" betrays a social absence of faith in the medium. And in this sense, the challenge the Leals might have faced was not whether their technology *faithfully rendered* the sound of Écue's voice or not. It was to ensure that their sacramental actions believably collapsed into each other what Charles Sanders Peirce might have called the "interpretant" with its "representamen": the idea of Écue's voice and the sonic vibrations emerging from the tubes, trumpets, and other gadgetry as they affect the human sensorium.

To reiterate Sterne's important point, just as the sonic impact of Écue's voice will register as a mere drone among uninitiated bystanders at contemporary abakuá rituals, so can early audio technologies in no way be said to have capitalized on *mere* technologically achievable mimesis. What people heard on Edison's tinfoil recordings or over Bell's first telephones was largely noise. That they actively forged a culture of hearing in which copy and original could become habitually understandable as "naturally" commensurate, even equivalent in the strong sense, has now been duly forgotten as history, as Bourdieu might have put it. But such forgetting was not a process of fading or attrition, nor was it a mere response to improved technological means. It was "cultural work."[40] What stands at the threshold of such forgetting are icons such as RCA's Nipper—the faithful dog not just listening for, but being hailed by, His (dead) Master's Voice emanating from a Victrola horn. Nipper's quizzical look notwithstanding, the very image reminds us just how much investment of belief was necessary to cross the threshold beyond which Edison's phonograph (or even its acoustically much improved successors) really *did* come to convey the recorded copy's permanent fidelity to the hitherto evanescent "original." What a triumph for a correspondence theory of representational truth this was. But at the same time, what a hollow victory.

If my conjectures are right, it is this very threshold at which the technology the Leal brothers installed at 2132 North Fairmount Avenue must be situated. The emerging American social faith in technological "fidelity" and the Leals' experiments with technologically enhancing what members of abakuá nowadays call "la fabricación" and potentially electrifying "la mecánica" of sounding Écue's voice would have been part and parcel of one and the same "structure of the conjuncture" (Sahlins 1981) between two different historical streams and semiotic systems. That early phonograph companies would have adorned their logos with recording angels (the Christian dream figure of communicative im-mediacy; see Peters 1999: 74–80) or faithful dogs listening to dead masters (Hegel's abject animal bondsman affirming his lord's mastery even beyond the grave) were part and parcel of a "dialectics of ensoniment"—and not just because capitalist entrepreneurs sought to foster the fetishization of a novel commodity. On the contrary, different from Marx's industrial machinery and dancing tables—dead labor acting upon the living—the phonographic machinery pressed the voices of the dead into the service of the living not by concealing a reality beyond appearances but by enveloping both in a cloud of paradoxical undecidability.

In this sense, the technology itself took on a good number of the ambiguities usually ascribed to ritual masks. Ever since Lévy Bruhl, the anthropology of ritual masking has uneasily (and often quite illogically) vacillated between suppositions either that the wearer of a mask is believed to undergo an actual transformation into the numinous presence the mask is supposed to bring into world or that maskers and their audiences are well aware that masquerades are based in histrionics and the kind of pious suspension of disbelief they maintain in the course of masked performances (Napier 1986; Pernet 1992). As Henry Pernet (1992) rightly argues, both horns of this somewhat artificial dilemma are ultimately traceable to modernistic Western imputations—namely, on the one hand, the kind of radical alterity of non-Western thought that Evans-Pritchard (1937) had sought to empirically refute and, on the other, the unwarrantedly charitable suggestion that at least the smarter natives are well aware of the symbolic or, at best, iconic nature of the performatively instantiated illusion. If so, however, might not the necromantic frisson cultivated in the writings of early commentators on and promoters of phonography bespeak exactly the same dilemma? Did American and European hearers of the phonograph really believe that they were hearing the dead, we might ask—or did they willingly collude in crafting a set of collective representations suggesting the equivalence of the audible copy to the absent original? Forever inscribed into and conjurable at will from the analog grooves cut into a wax cylinder by transductive force, had what Peirce (1940: 249) called "the man sign" become a function of the technical reproducibility of its traces left in a suitably pliable material? Was hearing believing? Was, to spell it out, early phonography a modernistic acoustic mask?

By the same token, might not Ejamba Leal have perfectly understood what was at stake in phonographic re-presentation? Different from their American contemporaries, the Leals—whether they had been exposed to phonographic technologies in Cuba or not—might have seen nothing intrinsically mysterious or surprising in "tympanic transduction" or analog recording. This would have been so precisely because abakuá ritual had revolved around this principle (or became understood in its terms) ever since the members of the "cabildo de los carabalí ápapa efí" managed to swear in the first Cuban chapter of abakuá in 1836. While they may well have come to appreciate and possibly capitalize on the mystical charge Edisonian technology had acquired within their American host society (and among contemporary Cuban elites back home as well), chances are that the Leals might have perceived analog sound technology as a fairly straightforwardly rational enhancement of the means to the end of sacred immediation.

If so, this would have been because the multiple human and material media activated, harnessed to, and fused with each other in the course of a baroco constitute what I have earlier called a complex biotechnology that does not *represent* but facilitates the emanation of pure presence. Transducing Écue's voice from one ontological sphere (the waters where it "lives") to another—the cuarto fambá from which it emerges, and the isaroco that it sonically envelops—so curiously parallels the telephonic and phonographic transduction of the human voice by electroacoustic means that the Leals may well have immediately grasped these technologies' "poietic" potential.[41]

If, to reiterate David Brown's (2003) felicitous phrase, the "physical space of the temple" and its ritual personnel is merely a conduit through which the voice "maintains its relationship to the world," and if it is Écue itself that enlists the agency of men born over the drumskin in order to give birth to new ecória ñene abakuá, then we arrive at a point where harnessing a "found" (but already amply enchanted) technology to the propagation of the acoustic mask that is Écue could have made eminent sense. Just as any contemporary alleyway in Havana is transformed into the embarcadero of Usagaré in the course of a baroco, so might the vicinity of 2132 North Fairmount Avenue have been enveloped and thus transformed into an instantiation of Enllenisón by "the echo's"/Écue's "Whoo-o-o!" (or uyó, depending upon interpretation) of the Leal brothers' sacred machinery.

Assuming that the Leals did employ electroacoustic technology to transduce Écue's voice, would they have shared in their American contemporaries' ambivalently reverent investments in Edisonian media? This, of course, is anyone's guess, and I have already indicated that I do not necessarily think so. Still, spinning my conjectures and this essay to a conclusion, it remains to be asked for what reasons they might have taken over elements of the sonic ideologies of their immediate social environment. Robert Lowie (quoted in Brady 1999: 31) offers an anecdote about the effects, or lack thereof, of Clark Wissler's paeans to Edisonian technology on the Blackfeet that may shed limited light on this final hypothetical question: "[Wissler] had procured some phonograph record from the lips of an aged Blackfoot, and by way of making conversation, enlarged on the wonderful ability of the man who invented this marvelous apparatus. The old man would have none of this; the inventor was not a whit abler than anyone else, he contended, he merely had the good fortune of having the machine, with all of its details, revealed to him by a supernatural being." Contrary to Wissler himself, his elderly informant, so it seems, felt no need to fetishize the mysteries of a "modernity" that neither dazzled nor impressed him much. If technological innovations are bestowed upon those who realize them by supernatural agencies through dreams or visions, for example, then that's how the phonograph he was asked to speak into had come into the world. Techne and poiesis collapse into each other. Means and ends have become coextensive. The mediator that refurnishes the world has vanished into the furniture.

Such may have been the case in the Leal brothers' Temple of the Ancient Grace. The medium would have been the message—and vice versa. But this is as far as my conjectures can take us. In the end, at any rate, the Leal brothers' technoreligious experiments remained fruitless, at least as far as I can tell. Nothing socially enduring ever came of their efforts. As everywhere else—except in the three Cuban port cities of Havana, Matanzas, and Cárdenas—attempts at transplanting abakuá's organizational format and mode of reproduction failed. As in Spain, North Africa, Fernando Po, South Florida, and other sites to which the political dislocations of the Cuban anticolonial struggle may have propelled late nineteenth-century obonécues, the Leals' Philadelphia potencia (if it was that) faded away, never achieving the stage where holding a baroco ninllao and so birthing and authorizing independent daughter cells became possible. But if I am right in surmising that their elaborate contraption fused abakuá ritualism with state-of-the-art electroacoustic technology, this may tell us quite a bit about the rationality, indeed modernity, of abakuá and the irrationality, indeed multiply enchanted nature, of the auditory regimes Bell, Edison, and others helped to usher in at the turn of the twentieth century.

If, for a time, Écue's voice did, in fact, ring out from the Leal's trumpets onto North Fairmount Avenue, perhaps we could do better than treat this as a curious episode in the history of the public reception of electroacoustic technology or, for that matter, in the history of the acoustic mask that is Écue. More could be said about the way in which electroacoustic technologies have changed the world since 1908. But the lasting irony, perhaps, is that while sonic-analog media have virtually vanished from the Western world at the beginning of the twenty-first century, the Leals' attempts at technoritual innovation never made a lasting impact on the "fabricación" and "mecánica" by which contemporary members of abakuá continue to transmit Écue's voice across space and time.

THREE

"Who's Dat Knocking at the Door?" A Tragicomic Ethiopian Spirit Delineation in Three Parts

PATRICK A. POLK

From barroom to barroom, an endless howl and endless smiling dance beneath a Venus ever rising. Mask of tragedy, mask of comedy, mask of blackface.

—Nick Tosches, *Where Dead Voices Gather* (2001: 139)

Both the supply of and demand for humor of a grotesque and exaggerated form are maintained by this increasing requirement for recreation; not the vulgar, the untrained alone, but the disciplined, the intellectual, the finely organized man and woman of position, dignity, responsibility and genius, of strong and solid acquisitions, enjoy and follow up and sustain those amusements which are in our land so very common, as American—such as the negro minstrels or experiments in induced or mesmeric trance.

—George M. Beard, *American Nervousness* (1881: 83)

Did you know that my mother married a spiritualist?
How are they getting on?
Oh, medium.

—H. H. Wheeler, *Up-to-Date Minstrel Jokes* (1902: 59)

Overture: Strange Relations in Boston, Massachusetts

It must have been a singularly rare piece of jewelry, the brilliant emerald stickpin that occasioned the untimely demise of so many eminent men of the nineteenth-century minstrel stage. Consider the fates of some whose soot-blackened and soon to be permanently clasped hands had caressed the deadly gem as reported by the Boston-based *Gleason's Monthly Companion* (1877: 400). Banjo master Luke West (née William Sheppard; see

Figure 3.1. Matt Peel and Luke West (ca. 1848). Harvard Theatre Collection, Houghton Library, Harvard University, TCS 38.

figure 3.1), it was stated, unwisely purchased the ornament from George Washington "Pony" Moore, who had performed with the Virginia Serenaders, Christy's Minstrels, and the Saint James Hall Minstrels before founding the Moore and Burgess Minstrels. Not long after acquiring the piece, West's excellent health inexplicably began to fail, and he soon gave up the ghost at the tender age of twenty-eight in Boston on May 26, 1854.

Sensing the Reaper's approach, Luke had bequeathed the precious stone to his stage partner Matt Peel (Matthew Flannery; see figure 3.1) in gratitude for care given during his final days. Only a short while after receiving the unfortunate gift (according to legend it was within a year), Peel too was gone from this world (died May 4, 1859, age twenty-nine). Eventually, the jewel came into the possession of blackface impresario George Christy, who didn't last long either (died May 12, 1868, age forty-one). Later, within a six-month span, it was said to have hastened the end of Sherwood Campbell (died November 26, 1874, age forty-five), Nelse Seymour (died February 2, 1875, age thirty-nine), James Unsworth (died February 21, 1875, age thirty-nine), and Dan Bryant (April 10, 1875, age forty-two), all giants of blackface. To put a stop to the curse, Seymour's surviving brother along with vaudeville pioneer Tony Pastor smashed the emerald into tiny pieces. Thus living actors could rest easy, and the hallowed dead of the stage could rest in peace. Perhaps.

In the spring of 1858, nearly two full decades before the so-called gravestone was finally destroyed, the renowned Boston trance medium Mrs. Frances "Fanny" Conant held a public séance that was attended by members of a blackface troupe.[1] A brief transcript presented in the April 3, 1858, edition of the Spiritualist newspaper *The Banner of Light* includes an interesting spirit dialogue reputedly given through (or better yet enacted by) Conant at that gathering. The record opens, appropriately enough, with the refrain "Oh, Jordan am a hard road to trabbel, I believe." As would soon be revealed, this snippet of dialect was not just an invocation of Dan Emmett's popular 1853 minstrel song of the same title but a rendition of it by a departed songster momentarily back from the other side. Unidentified, the voice teases the listeners: "Don't know me, do you?" It proposes to sing again but then declines, stating it did not have its whistle. Eventually, the ghost identifies himself as one Luke West. Obviously concerned with broader recognition of the visitant, an editorial comment informs readers: "Luke West was a negro minstrel, when on earth, one of West, Campbell and Peel's troupe."

This epitaph was something of an understatement. A genuine headliner, "the lamented Luke West" was later fondly remembered as "an accomplished comedian, dancer and banjoist" and was credited as the first in American minstrelsy to present a whistling solo (Rice 1911: 52). After the bit of play in the Conant's séance room, West offered his comrades in the flesh some practical advice on how to succeed in the theater business. It was a fairly straightforward recipe: stay away from rum, manage your own affairs, and generously support fellow actors in times of need. This having been said, the spirit made his exit. Stage left. No one-hit wonder of the invisible world, West's appearance was in fact a return engagement. As related in a November 21, 1857, *Banner of Light* account of a séance, the wandering minstrel tried to convince his audience that the living weren't the only ones who enjoyed a bit of entertainment. So he came back when he could through the agency of the Boston medium "partly to have a little fun, and partly to talk to my wife."

The gregarious West was also apparently not shy about switching psychics much as he did theatrical companies during his earthly career. In June 1854, the ethereal entertainer dropped in at a New York Spiritualist meeting where his spirit-controlled guitar deftly struck the chords of such minstrel standbys as "Old Dan Tucker," "Uncle Ned," "Lilly Dale," and "The Shaker Song" (Linton 1855: 50ff.). After the music died down, letters of the alphabet rapped out in ghostly fashion gave the introduction, "My name is Luke West, formerly of Christy's Minstrels." For those uncertain of West's status, someone in the room recollected that a touring performer of the same name had died in Boston just that week. The identity of the musician and the validity of the lively stringed spirit encounter were thereby confirmed. And undoubtedly encores were commanded.

In recounting the sad saga of the fatal gemstone and the after-death appearances of Luke West, it is not my intent to merely highlight the fact that actors such as he frequently died young or the reality that those left behind often sought signs of continued presence through the operations of mediums. Rather, I wish to illustrate how the personas shaped by Anglophone blackface performers served as rich grist for the mills of nineteenth- and early twentieth-century popular belief. With the rise of Anglo-American Spiritualism, a host of corporeal concerns were vividly expressed through the legions of restless ghosts who haunted public theaters and private homes throughout the United States, Great Britain, and elsewhere. In the context of a volume primarily dedicated to the work of possession in black Atlantic religions, my primary goal is to illuminate specific performative modes by which theatrical and spiritual actors (white folk in this case) took "possession" of blackness or were possessed by "blacks."

Given that connections between Anglo-American minstrel and Spiritualist practices remain largely unexplored, in this chapter I hope to raise the curtain just a bit on the shared scenery of stereotypical personifications as encountered in séances and the portrayals of black folk common to the minstrel stage. The formulaic impersonations of African Americans developed by "Ethiopian delineators" in bright concert halls also played well in darkened parlors. In each setting, their alternatingly plaintive and happy plantation melodies, comedic banter, and transgressive "Negro" tomfoolery struck audiences as both perfectly natural and delightfully unnatural. The act of a Luke West—whether live or dead—could not have been more perfectly crafted for his age's concerns with complexion. Continuing with the metaphor of staging "blackness," the discussion that follows is structured around an April 10, 1854, Broadway performance (poor Luke West had been in the grave but two weeks) by the Original George Christy and Wood's Minstrels.[2] Playing off of the roles acted by the legendary George Christy himself, I hope to delineate (admittedly in an abbreviated, rollicking sort of way) how thoroughly these types of racial representation informed one another.

Part the First: Back in Blackface

> No more this old darkey will hoe the corn,
> Or rise with the lark in the early morn,
> When o'er the plantation old massa's horn
> Calls me to till the soil.
> They were happy days, but they'll come no more,
> For old Sambo's journey is almost o'er,
> And soon he will be on that happy shore
> Where darkies do not toil. Then hush all your sighs,
> That this darkey dies,
> And goes to his home 'way up in the skies;
> For he'll work no more
> On that blissful shore,
> Where care and trouble are forever o'er.
>
> —*Christy's Plantation Melodies, "Old Sambo's Lament"* (1851: 45)

> The white folks, in fine, plagiarized the negro, body and soul; and the wandering "minstrels" of Christy, and a dozen other companies in our cities, are proofs that they have done a profitable thing.
>
> —Anonymous, *"A Talk about Popular Songs"* (1856: 413)

> The musical instruments of the dark séance have no more correspondence to the states of the spirits around than have the tambourines of the corner men at the Christy Minstrels.
>
> —Joseph Deans, *"Spiritism," Morning Light* (1883: 282)

Beginning in the early 1840s, companies led by George Christy (née George Harrington) and his stepfather, Edwin Pearce Christy (1815–62), set the standard for blackface theatrics and were widely credited with the development of the "classical" three-part format of the minstrel show.[3] So great was their influence that the name Christy became a generic label for the wildly successful "Negro" extravaganzas. As fine-tuned by this clan, a concert commenced with the entire troupe parading onto the stage, singing and dancing all the while. Once the actors had taken their prearranged seats in a semicircle facing the audience, the entertainment proper would begin. A cast member referred to as "Mr. Interlocutor" or "The Middle Man" always took center chair, as it was he who traditionally acted as host or master of ceremonies. In this position he served as the straight man for other stock characters such as "Tambo" and "Bones" who acted the lead comedic roles. These "Endmen" or "Cornermen" were named for the instruments they played, namely the tambourine and rattling rib bones. Collectively, Mr. Interlocutor, Tambo, Bones, and the rest of the ensemble would unleash a torrent of colloquial speech, picaresque jokes, quaint ditties, and "Negro" dances.

The audience seated in Broadway's Minstrel Hall on the evening of April 10, 1854, was greeted by the full Christy and Wood's company marching in to the melody "We Come." Among the standard tunes that followed were Stephen C. Foster's "Lilly Dear" performed by J. A. Herman, "Jolly Old Crow" sung by George Christy, "Cheer Boys for Old Virginia" by M. Campbell, "Hazel Dell" by C. Henry, "Camptown Races" by George Christy, and "Old Jaw Bone" by S. A. Wells. The players then shifted from vocal to instrumental pieces with dance accompaniment. P. H. Keenan strummed a banjo solo, J. T. Huntley offered a medley dance, George Christy and the drag prodigy Master Eugene (Eugene d'Amilie) performed "El Bolero," and so on. Here was a perfect expression of the essential minstrel trope of properly cultured and carefully controlled white bodies magically morphing into unrestrained and uncouth, if not grotesque, black personas.

Spiritualist enactments of blackface revenants, like blackface minstrelsy itself, depended on stark racial stereotypes and frequently gross physical caricature. Frances Conant, who ably conjured Luke West, claimed to have interacted with countless deceased African Americans during her long career. As described in *The Banner of Light*, her renderings mirrored prevailing stereotypes of "blackness": pious elders, jolly servants, faithful chattel, nurturing Mammy figures, impish children, tragic mulattos, and so on (see Polk 2010). The editorial preface to a message from a deceased slave named Aunt Judy, for example, asserts that readers "will recognize the true negro style in which this is spoken, which we defy Mrs. Conant to mimic in her natural state" (February 20, 1858). She was by no means alone in this. A New York medium consulted by publisher Isaac Funk frequently channeled an African American female "of the extreme Southern-plantation type" whose defining characteristics were that she "talked a broad negro dialect" and "was full of a very earthy negro humor" (1904: 45–46). Likewise, Mrs. C. J. Hunt reported to *Spiritual Magazine* that when "Negro Bill" manifested through a channeler, he "talked loud, laughed, whistled, danced," and engaged in many other "negro antics" (1875: 400).

And imagine how Victorian-era readers of James Connelly's theosophical fable "Calling Araminta Back" (1891) reacted to the trance-channeled voice of Her Highness Elizabeth I of England being suddenly muzzled by a boisterous otherworldly African. As the author tells it, the returned Virgin Queen "talked sentimentally of the sweetness and beauty of life in the summer-land, and, being asked who she was, replied that she was known on earth as Elizabeth, daughter of King Henry VIII of England. Mr. Blodgett, who was much astonished, wanted to converse with her a little, but she was shoved aside by a spirit who called himself 'Sambo,' chattered nonsense in a negro dialect, and laughed loudly, 'Yah! Yah! Yah!'" (Connelly 1891: 147). A progressively liberal mind of that era might have found it appropriately ironic that the monarch who served as midwife to the birth of England's Atlantic slave trade was so easily silenced by one who was surely a victim of that system. More likely, though, the tale's primary audience took it for granted that such was the way of Sambo and his kind.

The foregoing vignette most certainly owed much to minstrelsy, as visitants bearing the name of this stock character or eerily similarly ones were common. The celebrated British medium Annie Fairlamb Mellon channeled her own "Sambo" (Anonymous 1878: 533), as did the less-well-known Mr. Fogon (Dickson 1885: 762). The American Catherine Berry brought forth an "Ambo" (1876: 26) in her circles, and one Mrs. Olive embodied a mulatto spirit called "Hambo" (the Hambone of blackface and later vaudeville tradition?), "a joking, amusing sort of fellow, who poked his fun at all the sitters" (Marryat 1891: 198). Mrs. Wallis, yet another John Bull psychic, gave voice to "Morambo," a belligerent African who was said to have died somewhere in South America (Austen [1932] 2006: 128). Evidencing the close interplay of literary authorship and spiritual mediumship, her spirit companion bears more than a passing resemblance to the enslaved African chief Morambo featured in a sentimental work of abolitionist fiction entitled "The Slave Ship" who sacrifices his life and thereby gains eternal freedom during a shipboard slave revolt (Rose 1829).

Moving beyond character types and cognomens, let us consider more closely the musical components of the program presented by the Christy and Wood's players that night in April 1854. Without question, vocal and instrumental elements served as crucial bridges between minstrel and Spiritualist practice. Séance observers routinely marveled at the melodic skills of the dead as, time and time again, disembodied singers offered favorite tunes to the supernatural accompaniment of banjos, guitars, tambourines, horns, and whistles. These remarkable demonstrations of spirit power most typically occurred during "cabinet" or "curtain" séances where instruments set aside in apparently inaccessible spaces nonetheless issued forth harmonic sounds. Describing such manifestations at the Koons family farm in Ohio, for example, Charles Partridge wrote, "I have seen the tambourine players in the minstrel bands in New York; I have seen the best performers in the country; but they cannot perform equal to these spirits" (quoted in Daniels 1856: 25).

The potential appeal of the popular ditties offered up by Christy and his fellow delineators to Spiritualists is significant and obvious. Luke West knew well what was expected of him when he journeyed back to the place he had left behind. The imagined pasts explicit in the plantation melodies and paeans to old southern homes penned by the likes of Stephen C. Foster are all too easily haunted. There is, then, a deep sympathy embedded within the playlists of minstrelsy and Spiritualism, as so many of the songs speak directly to experiences of parting and yearning for the departed. Touching refrains from Foster's "Lilly Dear" (1851) evoke the sadness of one far from his family and native Tennessee:

> Oh! Lilly dear, 'tis mournful
> To leave you here alone,
> You'll smile before I leave you,
> And weep when I am gone.

In similar fashion, George Frederick Root's "The Hazel Dell" (1853) offers a heart-wrenching portrait of loss and longing:

> In the Hazel Dell my Nelly's sleeping,
> Nelly lov'd so long!
> And my lonely lonely watch I'm keeping,

Nellie lost and gone;
Here in moonlight often we have wander'd
Thro' the silent shade,
Now where leafy branches drooping downward,
Little Nelly's laid.

Given that reunification with the dead was the raison d'être of Spiritualism, one would expect that sentiments such as these struck a powerful chord with many spirit seekers.

And sing the revenants did. Many were represented as black, such as those of a cabinet medium patronized by Isabella Beecher Hooker (sister of Harriet Beecher Stowe), whose spirit control Rosa performed "darkey" songs (Beighle 1903: 218). On other occasions, such as the appearances of Luke West, vocalizations of "Negro" tunes were given by white visitants. Loren Albert Sherman testified that, through the agency of several different channelers, his drowned son, Willie, returned to belt out "Swanee River" and "Old Kentucky Home" (1895: 113). Recollecting an 1888 celebration marking the fortieth anniversary of the 1848 Rochester Spiritualist Awakening, Horace Lorenzo Hastings noted: "We saw perhaps a thousand or more persons who had paid their fee to obtain admission; while on the platform stood a little girl with a short dress; and spindle legs encased in white stockings, singing a negro song, which, if we remember correctly, told us something about 'the Swanee River.' And we thought as we passed on, if that was a specimen of what 'the spirits' had achieved for human advancement in forty years, it was hardly worth our while to stop to hear more" (Hastings 1890: 180–81). Both this well-attended spirit recital of Stephen C. Foster's grand opus and Hastings's subsequent mockery of it would likely have done George Christy proud had he not been twenty years dead. But then again, maybe that hardly mattered.

Part the Second: "Dat You Daddy?"

Bones: Den de spiritual orchestry started in.
Interlocutor: The leader that issued those notes—was he a medium?
Bones: Yes; he was a circulatin' medium, if you know what dat am. Well—findin' de spirits was rader shaky, tinks I, I'll bodder dem some, so I pulls de old pair of ivories from my pockets and sailed in wid an accompaniment. Dat 'peard to friten dem some, an dey all stop. De mejum he tought a real spirit had got in amongst 'em, and, says he, from out of de darkness, "De spirit of Daddy Rice hab

broke loose and wants to conwerse wid you. Dat you, Daddy?" "Dat's me," said I, gibin' him a thump on de head wid de bones."

—Orville A. Roorbach, *"Bones Attends a Spiritual Séance," Minstrel Gags and End-Men's Hand Book* (1875: 126)

There is something inexpressibly funny in seeing a sedate old man forget his sedateness, and make passionate avowals of affection to a supposed young lady (who is another man dressed up in a poke-bonnet and shawl), or becoming the end man for a troupe of Christy Minstrels.

—James Coates, *How to Mesmerize* (1897: 113)

Why is Rochester like a threepenny grocery? Because it keeps bad spirits on the tap.

—Anonymous, *"Bad Spirits on the Tap," The Literary World* (1850: 276)

Just months before Luke West was laid to rest, an anonymous critic for the *New York Musical Review* announced that "Negro Minstrelsy is dead" ([1854] 1858: 118). The eulogy called readers to "Draw around its *sable* bier in tearful groups, ye lovers of Ethiopian absurdities." The writer did not suggest that blackface had given up the ghost, so to speak, but instead pointed out that a significant shift in the nature of minstrel performance had recently taken place, moving it away from the straightforward presentation of down-home melodies thought to be rooted in the slave culture of southern plantations. The author testifies: "The truth is, genuine 'negro music' is no longer written; and if it were written, it could not be sold. People have grown tired of its burlesques upon a degraded race, of its vulgarity, its silliness, and its insipidity. Henceforth they will be satisfied only with something worthy of being called music. Taking advantage of this change in popular sentiment, Buckley's Minstrels, Wood's and Christy's have within eighteen months commenced the performance of burlesque operas and introduced travesties upon 'spirit knocking,' women's rights lectures, etc." (ibid.). While one may argue with the presumption that American audiences had become tired of mockingly stereotypical impersonations of the subaltern, it was quite true that leading minstrel companies had partly turned their attention to popular spiritual movements in their search for the next big hit. Fitting the bill nicely were the wide range of contemporary metaphysical or pseudoscientific traditions variously labeled as animal magnetism, electro-biology, hypnotism, mesmerism, somnambulism, trance mediumship, and so on.[4]

After the first intermission of Christy and Wood's April 10, 1854, presentation, the troupe returned with a variety-like segment, often referred to as the "olio," consisting of a concertina solo by A. Sedgwick, a "Highland Fling" by Master Eugene, and a skit entitled "Burlesque Rochester Knockings!" in which George Christy and S. A. Wells impersonated table-rapping psychics, probably the famed Fox sisters (Margaret and Kate), American Spiritualism's first luminaries. This last comedic piece focusing on the epicenter of the Spiritualist movement—Rochester, New York—was quite in keeping with the up-to-the moment social awareness and criticism that increasingly typified the olio. By this time, in fact, Christy specialized in send-ups of Spiritualists, mesmerists, and the like. It seems only fitting that one who made his living burlesquing (and thus reinforcing) the prevailing logics of corporeality and race should target other faddish practices that depended in part on the same sensibilities.

The developing strands of Anglo-American minstrelsy and spirit, of course, had become intertwined with one another well before George Christy darkened American and British stages. Contemplate, for example, one odd chapter among many from the strange career of "Jim Crow," the foundational minstrel archetype introduced by Thomas Dartmouth "T.D." Rice in the early 1830s, who became a veritable international craze (see Lhamon 1998). Not long after Rice brought his trademark stylings to London audiences in 1836, "jumping Jim Crow" took on a whole new set of meanings within the mesmeric experimentations of British physician John Elliotson (1791–1868).[5] A university professor and practicing physician, Elliotson was an ardent champion of avant-garde healing modalities, especially those associated with the supposedly untapped powers of the mind. Seeking a revolutionary advancement in surgical anesthesia, he promoted the utilization of "the mesmeric state," or hypnotically induced coma. Because of Elliotson's almost irreproachable institutional status, his experimentations offered a remarkable platform from which the utility or futility of such therapies could be debated. Enter Jim Crow. Laughing.

In 1837, Elliotson's highly theatrical demonstrations of mesmerism increasingly centered on the sisters Elizabeth and Jane O'Key, two teenage Irish servant girls. Each having been diagnosed with epilepsy and hysteria, among other things, they appeared the perfect subjects for the learned doctor's investigations into mesmeric diagnosis and cure. While literally under Elliotson's influence, the O'Keys began to exhibit odd and exciting behaviors, many of which seemed to have no scientific explanation at the time. Among these were the claim that a "black" or "Negro" spirit would sometimes appear to them and their propensity to sing and dance Jim Crow when entranced. An anonymous writer for the *Lancet* noted that during a treatment (performance) before a packed audience, one of the young women "whistled and sang in a sweet tone, with once very artist-like variations, evincing symptoms of a ripe faculty of music. Ending, at last with *Jim Crow*, she stopped in one verse to ask Dr. Elliotson if *he* also had 'come over from Kentucky,' like Mr. Crow, and then volunteered to 'wheel about, and turn about,' but was prevented, to the manifest disappointment of many spectators" (Anonymous 1838: 287). While such displays fueled the quickly mounting and ultimately crushing professional criticism of Elliotson and the authenticity of his trance subjects' behaviors, some colleagues did find it compelling, as is shown by one physician who reported that a youth under his mesmeric care also "commenced singing Jim Crow" (Elliotson 1846: 398).

Even as highly theatrical ecstatic states and psychical powers such as those purportedly displayed by the O'Keys were increasingly dismissed by mainstream medical faculties following repeated experimental failures and high-profile exposures of frauds, elements of minstrelsy nonetheless became entrenched in Anglo-American spirit channeling and kindred practices. By the late nineteenth century, British Spiritualist organizations routinely staged blackface performances as pleasant diversions, fundraisers, and such.[6] One society's Annual Tea Meeting at Hetton-Le-Hole on April 20, 1884, featured "a Christy-Minstrel Entertainment" that included no less than seventeen performers (J. Murray 1884: 271). More than mere frivolity, such acts could also serve as proofs of hypnotic skill, as evidenced by C. P. Christensen's claim that, when properly trained, a master can "make a half dozen subjects imagine themselves to be minstrels, and they will amuse you and entertain you with a hat for a base drum, a cane for a fife, a couple of tin plates for cymbals, etc. They will give your audience more delight than any minstrel show" (1915: 13). Indeed, what could be more indicative of effective personal transformation than a handful of prim and proper Anglo-Saxons who imagine themselves to be black(face) musicians and dutifully act out a ridiculous pantomime? To be sure, an unsuspecting white person who suddenly gained unprecedented banjo skills was long taken as a substantiation of paranormal activity.

And why not take the conceptual and performative merging of mesmerism and minstrelsy to its logical conclusion with a full-blown hypnosis-fueled musical program? An unnamed correspondent for the *Medium and Daybreak* offers a remarkable description of what was surely more than a one-night affair. Dropping in on a medical demonstration at the Blackburn Town Hall presented by the well-known "medical electrician" and traveling mesmerist Professor James Kershaw, the writer states: "When we arrived, the patients, men and women, under influence, were giving a negro minstrel entertainment, with 'end men,' bones, tambourine, triangles, bells, guitars, &c., one gentleman in the centre performing on the cornet" (Anonymous 1885: 163). Noting that the instrument-wielding subjects seemed to be entirely controlled by the stamping foot of the professor, the observer wondered if such musical ability as well as the "puns and colloquy given, and general comic 'business' " were innate and merely set free by mesmeric operations.

Whether these entertaining talents were instinctual or acquired through practice, it is clear that accomplished actor-musicians could readily move back and forth between the theaters of minstrelsy and those of popular medicine and spirituality. Evan Evans Horn (died January 3, 1877), who rose to fame as Eph. Horn, started his career in blackface after an apprenticeship of sorts as a professional mesmeric subject for one "Professor Rogers," an itinerant mesmerist and phrenologist (Scharf and Westcott 1884: 1091). More telling, though, is the reality that a number of leading mediums (especially women) first performed on the lighted stage before turning to the darkened room (see Lehman 2009). Even George Washington Dixon, to whom is credited the creation of the Zip Coon archetype and who was among the first American blackface minstrels of note, reportedly reinvented himself late in his career as a hypnotist and clairvoyant (Cockrell 1997: 137).

Part the Third: The Spirits in Uncle Tom's Cabinet

> I have long since come to the conclusion that the marvels of spiritualism are natural, and not supernatural phenomena—an uncommon working of natural laws. I believe that the door between those in the body and those out has never in any age been entirely closed, and that occasional perceptions within the veil are a part of the course of nature, and therefore not miraculous.
>
> —Harriet Beecher Stowe, as cited in Annie Fields, *Life and Letters of Harriet Beecher Stowe* (1897: 371)

> I don't see that it's any more easily credulous for one to believe in the reality of a fireside chat with the spirit of Little Eva or Chief Igloo than to believe in the miracle of walking on water or the loaves and fishes or the tuning of water into wine (though the last named would be a good trick if it could be worked).
>
> —E. Haldeman-Julius, *"Name Your Poison"* (1948:18)

> Then the tambourines, dolls, and whistles began again. They were being played with, carried from one end of the room to the other end, then up to the ceiling, banging themselves there, so that everybody could hear and have no doubt. . . . It was a mad frolic. One brought out a tambourine and began to play on my head. The force, gaining in power and audacity, played to time in my face and head and then came round and placed the tambourine on my knees. I fell into the spirit of the thing. I whistled the first bars of "Pop goes the weasel," and the tambourine finished the refrain in fine style.
>
> —Sydney A. Moseley, *An Amazing Séance and an Exposure* (1919: 46)

Following the rocking, mocking, and knocking olio, the Christy and Wood's Minstrels' last offering of the April 10, 1854, performance was a comic take on *Uncle Tom's Cabin* written and arranged by Nelson Kneass. In the standard minstrel program, the "Afterpiece" was typically a burlesque rendition of a classic drama or an au courant literary or stage production. Regardless of the source material, the piece was almost invariably set on a southern plantation with all the prerequisite character types pressed into theatrical service. On this evening, attendees were treated to Miss Annie Kneass as Little Eva, Nelson Kneass as Aunt Chloe, and S. A. Wells as Uncle Tom. George Christy played the role of Topsy, the undisputed star of the delineation. Consisting of three song-and-dance-filled tableaus that followed the general dramatic trajectory of Harriet Beecher Stowe's narrative, the skit climaxed with a rousing rendition of "Pop Goes the Weazel."

While the varied legacies of *Uncle Tom's Cabin* are far too broad to outline here, let me suggest something of its lasting Spiritualist implications. Viewed by some—then and now—as channeled material, Stowe's masterpiece became a wellspring of inspiration. Focusing as it does on the suffering of saintly spirits and the ultimate triumph of dearly departed souls, the work nicely jibed, even if not by explicit design, with the emergent principles of Spiritualism, so much so that when Josiah Henson (a reputed model for Uncle Tom) passed away, his ghost began to visit the Reverend John Lobb, a devoted Spiritualist who served as Henson's biographer and lecture-circuit manager (Lobb 1907: 32). The shade of Harriet Beecher Stowe, who not coincidentally had penned the introduction to *An Autobiography of the Rev. Josiah Henson* (1878) edited by Lobb, also turned up on occasion (ibid.: 33).

The melodramatic death of Little Eva in *Uncle Tom's Cabin*, which so powerfully affected readers and theatergoers worldwide, directly influenced the production of séance-related performances and texts. In *Religion as*

Revealed by the Material and Spiritual Universe, Edwin Dwight Babbitt proclaims that when one of Harriet's children begged her not to have Little Eva die at the end of the work, the author "answered that she had to write as she was guided to do" (1881: 262). Literary scholar Bridget Bennett (2007) argues that Stowe's noble waif has served as a paradigmatic model for the innumerable deceased and sanctified child spirits that have haunted séances from Spiritualism's very beginning. Eva's death, she states, showed Spiritualists "one way in which farewells could be conducted and could be rendered powerfully full of meaning and comfort for those left behind" (2007: 139). A character in *The Professor's Mystery,* an early twentieth-century novel by Wells Southworth Hastings and Brian Hooker, suggests as much when he describes New York séances in this way: "Hamlet's old grandfather comes in an' rough-houses the furniture, an' Little Eva says a lot more than her prayers, an' you sit in a circle holdin' hands to get a line on the higher life" (1911: 208).

Regardless of how integral the figure of Little Eva may have been to the development of seminal themes in Anglo-American mediumship, her black counterpart or alter ego, Topsy, may have more often been the object of spirit materialization. As described by Stowe in *Uncle Tom's Cabin,* the little slave girl was

> one of the blackest of her race; and her round, shining eyes, glittering as glass beads, moved with quick and restless glances over everything in the room. Her mouth half open with astonishment at the wonders of the new Mas'r's parlor, displayed a white and brilliant set of teeth. Her woolly hair was braided in sundry little tails, which stuck out in every direction. The expression of her face was an odd mixture of shrewdness and cunning, over which was oddly drawn, like a veil, an expression of the most doleful gravity and solemnity. She was dressed in a single filthy, ragged garment, made of bagging; and stood with her hands demurely folded in front of her. Altogether, there was something odd and goblin-like about her appearance—something as Miss Ophelia afterwards said, "so heathenish," as to inspire that good lady with utter dismay." (1852: 260)

A racial grotesque of the first order, the Topsy character practically leapt from page and stage into the séance circle. Amoral and militantly mischievous, she said of herself, "I's wicked,—I is. I's mighty wicked, any how. I can't help it" (ibid.: 267).

A number of Spiritualists (especially British ones) simply could not resist the temptations of Stowe's dark creation, particularly during the first half of the twentieth century. In the United Kingdom, from the 1920s through at least the 1950s (possibly still to this day), psychics such as Mrs. Ada Emma Deane, Mrs. Warren Elliott, and Mr. Hunter Selkirk regularly channeled child spirits bearing the name Topsy or Topsey. Mrs. Deane's Topsy was "a mischievous child-control" (Warrick 1939: 225), while Mrs. Elliot's "Topsy-persona" had a habit of saying things like "Does you know what Topsy means? Not small and smallerer but small and biggerer" (J. Thomas 1929: 46). Selkirk's Topsy, "a little coloured girl who is very witty," liked to sing, play the tambourine, and bring mirthful gaiety to his spirit cabinet sessions (Emerson 1946: 29). Who knows how many others came to life in a similar fashion? An anonymous entertainment writer for the *Clipper* (February 10, 1877) later commented that in the April 10, 1854, performance by George Christy the role of the "whimsical Topsy fell naturally to the share of George Christy." As Christy himself had passed away nearly a decade earlier, the author concluded that "it is, perhaps, needless to add that this particular Topsy is dead." Or was that actually the case?

Curtain Call

> If Eph Horn or Nelse Seymour could return to earth and see the way in which vaudeville artists—the variety man no longer exists—are patronized by the exclusives of Vanity Fair, he would curse the ill luck which put him on the earth a quarter of a century too soon.
>
> —Anonymous, *"The Stage," Munsey's Magazine* (1898: 625)

> In case I ever become a spirit, I trust I shall not be summoned into anybody's drawing-room and made to play the banjo and rap people's heads, in return for a fee of a guinea.
>
> —Richard Burton, *quoted in Horace Wyndham, Mr. Sludge, the Medium* (1937: 135)

> But now that ghosts in the form of souls are the most authentic of phenomena, now that thought-transference and the action of the mind on mind, and the appearance of phantasms are the most ordinary of occurrences, the old business of spirit-rapping, and low turned lights with waving of phosphorescent hands, the beating of heavenly cymbals and thrumming of earthly banjos, have become quite too stale. Every man his own ghost is the modern watchword.
>
> —John Dewey, *"The Revival of the Soul," The University* (1885: 6)

If minstrel styles were useful in creating racialized otherworldly experiences, imagine how effective could be the spirit of a professional Ethiopian delineator—or a professional delineator of Ethiopian spirits if one prefers. In general, Spiritualist practice relies on one or more controlling entities that regulate the arrival, departure, and order of appearance of other revenants, often entertaining attendees between visitations much like Mr. Interlocutor. As we have seen, Luke West was more than eager to come back. Or some were more than willing to bring him back. His was not a solitary fate. A British participant in a New York circle in the 1880s recounted that the medium in charge had two main "controls." One was an aged Native American woman, and the other was "Nelson Seymour," who, she writes, "appears to have belonged to a sort of Christy Minstrel company over here" (Bates 1887: 209). Indeed he had. One of the unlucky inheritors of Luke West's evil emerald, Nelse Seymour (Thomas N. Sanderson), had a celebrated (though possibly gem-shortened) career in blackface. Back for a reprise, he teased the living in a good-natured and perfectly undignified fashion.

If minstrels were truly drawn to the limelight after death, why not summon one of those listed at the very top of the April 10, 1854, playbill? Accordingly, at some point in the last decades of the nineteenth century, Pierre Louie Ormand Augustus Keeler (figure 3.2) resurrected George N. Christy himself and put the actor to work as his own guiding spirit or "control" (Lippitt 1888). A "materializing" and "slate-writing" medium who produced phenomena through musical instruments, chalk writing, and other means, Keeler was widely respected, frequently disrespected, and repeatedly investigated during a career that spanned more than fifty years. Discussing one of his slate sessions, in which messages from beyond were otherwise inexplicably graphed onto hidden surfaces, an attendee observed that "George Christy is constantly passing over writings of his own apropos of something that has just occurred or been said; thus carrying on an incessant conversation, as it were, with the circle, or some member of it" (ibid.: 63). A perfect Middle Man to the very end.

At a materializing séance Keeler conducted on May 27, 1885, an exhibition closely observed by members of the Seybert Commission for Investigating Modern Spiritualism sponsored by the University of Pennsylvania, Keeler trusted the returned minstrel to help put on a good a show. After the careful preparation of a convoluted multicurtained stage, "Raps indicated that the Spirit, George Christy, was present. As one of those present played on the piano, the tambourine was played in the curtained space

Figure 3.2. Portrait of P. L. O. A. Keeler with his "control," George Christy. From *Proceedings of the American Society for Psychical Research*, vol. 15 (New York: American Society for Psychical Research, 1921), 481.

and thrown over the curtain; bells were rung; the guitar was thrummed a little" (Seybert 1920: 85). For members of the Seybert Commission who suspected a sham, the layout, interlocutory structure, and central musicality of Keeler's performance all likely seemed too similar to Christy's earthly profession. Indeed, his masterful Christy-guided orchestration of "curtain séances" had more than just a passing similarity to minstrel shows. Following a séance conducted by Keeler in a Moravia, New York, farmhouse, George C. Bartlett related: "There were about ten of us, from different parts of the country. We sat in a semicircle, similar to a minstrel band. As the spirits were announced, and were supposed to appear at this aperture, we asked around, commencing with Bones at the end, 'Is it for me?' 'Is it for me?' and so on, until we came to the Tambourine end" (1891: 46). Bartlett likely did not realize just how apt was his comparison. Then as now, a medium's fame and effectiveness depended on talents ascribed to the hidden hands of his or her control. Supremely gifted psychic or outrageous fraud, Keeler certainly was an engaging amanuensis who made the best of the illustrious blackface showman's reputation.

In this chapter, though lacking a tambourine end, I have attempted to at least hint at the complex interplay of collective symbolism, individual fantasy or creativity, and ritualized enactment that has informed the production of blackness in Spiritualism and minstrelsy. Mediumship, I argue, was (and still remains) closely aligned with other textual, graphic, and theatrical modes of racial representation. Secular stage impersonations were easily and purposefully conjoined with acts of popular religiosity. They shared not only similar precepts and techniques but also surely sometimes the same performers. Were these fascinations often no more than jokes and gibes at the expense of others? Perhaps. Did they also enable the nonblack to either possess or be possessed by "blackness" and thereby express or negotiate coexisting fears, fetishes, and desires? It would seem likely. Could the performances help render the kingdoms of this world and the next more understandable and acceptable to some? Certainly. And clearly, more meaningful insights can be divined from data presented here. For now, though, I would have to respond to those seeking deeper or broader interpretations by invoking Mr. Keeler's irascible old thespian spirit guide who answered one overly pressing inquirer: "See some other medium—Damn it! George Christy" (W. Prince 1921: 481).

FOUR

Spiritual Agency, Materiality, and Knowledge in Cuba

KRISTINA WIRTZ

This essay explores the representational economy of spirit presence among practitioners of Cuban folk religion, in which spirit materializations in human bodies and other objects make objective sense. By "representational economy" I refer to the localized semiotic and ontological orders that inform how people take some things (objects and their objectifications in discourse) to stand for others—in short, how signs gain their indexical value as signs (Keane 2003). My project is in some ways an exercise in what Holbraad (2008) calls "infinition" or "inventive definition," in which the ethnographer attempts to understand an unfamiliar orientation to the world by accepting as valid its basic premises about the nature of evidence and truth. To this imaginative leap toward an alternate ontological grounding for rationality I would add the need for a certain phenomenological openness to the "feel" for a different experience of the world. As Stoller so eloquently argues in his study of Hauka spirit possession in Niger, "Anthropologists who have lost their senses often write ethnographies that are disconnected from the worlds they seek to portray. . . . That they have lost their senses of the smells, sounds, and tastes of the places they study is unfortunate" (1995: 15). My goal, then, is to weave together the semiotic and the sensuous with minimal distortion.

To begin, consider three moments of spirit presence I recorded on three different occasions, all involving the same Spiritist medium in Santiago de Cuba:

(1) As we talked, Josefina kept running her hands up and down her forearms, saying that she was feeling energy in her arms, signifying that the spirits were all around us. [At the end of the consultation] she pointed out that of the two candles I'd given her for the altars, the one for Eleggua [an *oricha*

of Santería] was still slowly burning and barely consumed, while the one for the spirits had been "eaten" by them and had gone out and melted all over the place. She explained: that's because that was where the spirits were working, so they "ate" the candle. Eleggua opens and closes the [ritual] way, and so his candle kept burning to show the way was still open. It was finally a stub, still burning, when I left at 3:50 p.m. (Field notes, July 2006, p. 14)

(2) Josefina [pointing to the plaster statue in figure 4.1]: La Gitana es mi espiritu guía que va delante de mi. (The gypsy woman is my spirit guide who goes before me.) (Field notes, May 2008, p. 25)

(3) La Gitana (speaking through Josefina about the author's deceased father): Hija, que linda, no sufras, no llores. Un camino amplio y ancho te espera. Este padre le acompaña de la mano, aquí está él. (My pretty child, don't suffer, don't cry. A wide, open path awaits you. This father accompanies you by hand, here he is.) (Video recording, Santiago de Cuba, May 11, 2007)

Across all of Cuban folk-religious practice, variations on moments such as these are commonplace because it is a well-established fact of religious life in Cuba that spirits are perceivable agencies in the world. In this essay, I seek to revisit the phenomenon of spirit possession in Cuba, not to repeat what is already well attested in the ethnographic literature, but to bring together scattered pieces that are not usually discussed together, in order to suggest three necessary angles on the representational economy of spirit presence, of which spirit possession is but one case: agency, materiality, and perspicience, or knowledgeable "seeing."

I choose these three focal points (to continue the visual metaphor) based on broad understandings in Cuba of spirits as immaterial, incorporeal agencies that nonetheless can infuse and saturate things, even bodies, without themselves being embodied things or having bodies. The agency of spirits and their amenability to the agency of people become evident through material relations. Spirits act in the world through materializations, and humans seek to capture the attention and power of spirits through complex manipulations of the material world. But to recognize the immaterial agency of spirits in the material world requires a special kind of sensory orientation, one I seek to describe with the archaic term perspicience. Perspicience, like perspicacity, carries a metaphor for vision in its etymology: it is indeed about seeing and by extension about sensing more generally. But perspicience also conveys the role of knowledge in sensory awareness: to discern spirits requires being inculcated into a culturally specific phenomenology in which the material effects of immaterial agencies become sensible experiences.

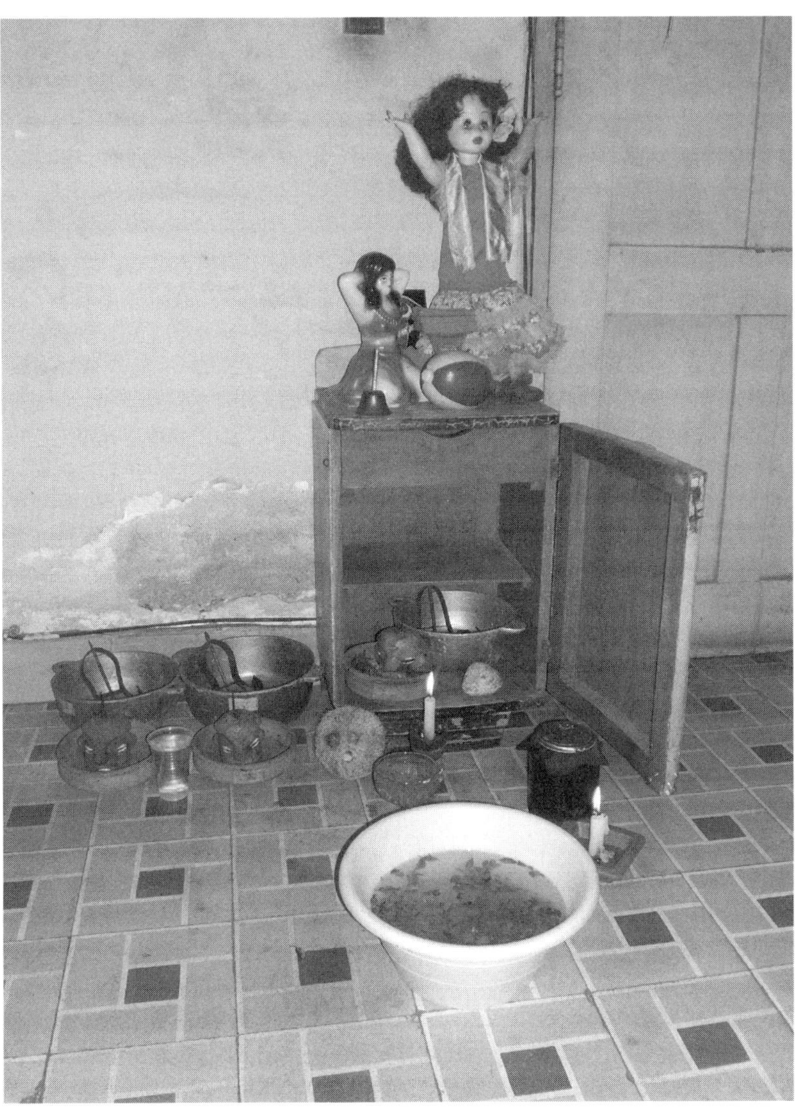

Figure 4.1. Two representations of the Gypsy, a common "ethnic" spirit, stand atop a box that houses Eleggua and other warrior orichas of Santería next to the front door. The white bowl and glass jar hold water consecrated with herbs. Santiago de Cuba, August 2008. Photograph by K. Wirtz.

My discussion begins by situating spirit possession within the larger ethnographic frame of spirit presence in Cuban folk religion. I also revisit that fundamental opposition between spirit and matter, which is commonly accepted by both Cuban religious practitioners and our own scholarly tradition, both of which are, after all, products of the West (Lambek 1998a; Palmié 2002). I then revisit the metaphysical first principles of Charles Sanders Peirce's semiotic: his notions of Firstness, Secondness, and Thirdness as metaphysical states describing pure existential being, dyadic relationships, and mediated being. Applying these to Cuban folk-religious notions of spirit presence highlights the need to consider spirit presence in light of what Webb Keane has called the "representational economy" or locally relevant semiotic regime through which signs gain their indexical values (2003: 410–11). The opposition of spirit and matter is part of the representational economy of Cuban folk religion, as are ideas about what constitutes evidence of spirit presence. Here I am interested in an emically relevant aesthetics of sensibility (or sense-ability, adapting from Desjarlais 1992) of spirits as signs and in signs of spirit presence in the material world.

It bears repeating that understanding spirit possession as an ethnographic fact in a particular place and time constitutes but part of a broader representational economy involving relationships among agencies (people, spirits) and materialities (bodies, things, the sensible world). But it is easy to get distracted by the spectacle of a person falling into possession trance, flailing about perhaps, or as in Josefina's case, stumbling backward and swooning with forearm over eyes, then manifesting the sometimes dramatic signs of another presence directing the body's actions and making pronouncements with the vocal instrument of the possessed person. But Josefina's well-developed relationship with identifiable spirits like La Gitana and with deceased family members like her father (and, more recently and disconcertingly for me, my deceased father) is part of what she would describe as her more general sensitivity to the spiritual, including that host of undifferentiated spiritual energies she can sometimes sense, like an electrical current. Her spiritual gifts may have emerged early and unbidden in her life—as she tells it, she was the daughter of a well-to-do doctor, and her family found her childhood episodes of trance disturbing enough to take her to doctors and psychiatrists, to no avail—but as an adult woman raising a family after the 1959 Cuban Revolution, she learned how to manipulate the material world of candles, altars, prayers, songs, dolls, and plaster icons like La Gitana and to train the sensitivities of her own body to effectively channel the spirits as a Spiritist medium and Santería practitioner (santera).

A Sensorium of Cuban Spirits

For more than a decade now I have been doing fieldwork in Santiago de Cuba with practitioners of Cuban folk religions such as Spiritism and Santería (also known as Ocha)—"folk" being my gloss of what Cuban scholars call "popular religion," as in "of the people." I have heard countless stories and seen wide-ranging practices involving the spirits. As Ochoa (2007) and others (e.g., Fuentes Guerra and Gómez Gómez 1994; James Figarola 1999; Palmié 2002) have described it, Cuban folk religion is populated with a diverse array of kinds of spirits and deities. By way of loosely introducing the ethnographic ground, here is a partial catalog of spirit beings recognized in Cuba: Spiritists tend to focus on "evolved" spirits seeking light and *burlones* causing trouble to get attention, and they recognize undifferentiated "commissions" of helping spirits, as well as fully biographical spirits of deceased relatives or unrelated spiritual helpers and protectors. These latter encompass the diversity of ethnic, racial, and national stereotypes recognized in Cuba, although subaltern spirit types such as Africans or Josefina's Gypsy protector are especially common. The *muertos*, or spirits of the dead, are recognized widely among religious practitioners of distinct traditions: practitioners of the Reglas de Palo, understood as Kongo-derived religion, work with what, in Kongo ritual jargon are called individualized *nfumbi* and the undifferentiated mass of *kalunga*, the dead. Practitioners of Ocha likewise describe the collective mass of the dead and particular spirits, such as ancestors, with the Yoruba-derived term *ikú*. Moreover, religious practitioners recognize the *santos* (saints) as both Catholic icons and orichas of Ocha, and the *mpungu*, or deities, of Reglas de Palo, also correspond to particular Catholic saints and orichas. And then there are what folk practitioners of all kinds may refer to as spirits or spiritual energies, which are seen to inhabit places, plants, stones, rivers, and other materials and locations (for example, crossroads, trees, mountains, as well as human-made objects including dolls and powders), where they must be contended with and appropriately handled. Such spiritual energies may be channeled as forces of good luck or *malas influencias*, bad influences, that may even emanate from human intentions (e.g., in witchcraft) and that may contaminate a person or place and need to be driven away through purifications.

The many contrasts among these classes of spirit, energy, and divinity and the combinations and juxtapositions religious practitioners create through ritual practice are dizzying indeed: consider, for example, figures 4.2 and 4.3, showing two views of a Spiritist's altar celebrating so many different spirits and saints that it has taken over an entire room that he dedicates to his spiritual practice and spilled out into other rooms. Multiple altars in the same home are common, even when a particular practitioner professes dedication to one particular religious tradition. The general view is that one can never have too much spiritual protection and aid and that different kinds of spiritual beings have different functions. In other work, I discuss processes of combining and differentiating among what practitioners and scholars conceptualize as distinct traditions (Wirtz 2007). I suggest, following Palmié (2002) and others, that folk-religious practices and identifications in Cuba form a system or complex of mutually constituting relationships that is much more dynamic, modern, and fluid than static typologies of "traditions" convey (cf. Argüelles Mederos and Hodge Limonta 1991; Dodson 2008; see Wirtz 2007). Here I will instead emphasize the common idioms that emerge in how folk practitioners of all affiliations sense and interact with this vast spiritual world interpenetrating the tangible world: energies, influences, vibrations, and even electrical currents signal spiritual presence in a diffuse way; plaster figurines, cloth dolls, and even the nonanthropomorphic stones, shells, bones, and other assemblages of Ocha santos (saints) and Palo *ngangas* (power objects) embody spirits in fully material form on altars; and transmissions, speech, and other practices including possession itself indicate the actions of specific spirits or deities in the tangible world.

My account thus far, and especially the illustrations, suggest that there are also more sociological dimensions informing the "identities" of Cuban spirits, as gendered, historically located entities that as often as not are also ascribed race, ethnicity, nationality, and even occupation according to stereotypes that shape religious practitioners' expectations regarding spirits' behavior: common types populating Spiritist altars include earthy African slaves, mystic Arab healers, flamboyant Gypsies, and stoic Plains Indians. The nfumbi captured in the ngangas, or vessels of ritual power owned by Palo practitioners, were often criminals or other marginal and troublesome (or, conversely, powerful but worldly) characters in life. And, of course, the correspondences made among Catholic saints, orichas of Santería, and mpungu of Palo often highlight characterological comparisons and overall contrasts pitting what practitioners understand to be European models of saintly morality against rather more amoral African models of divinity.

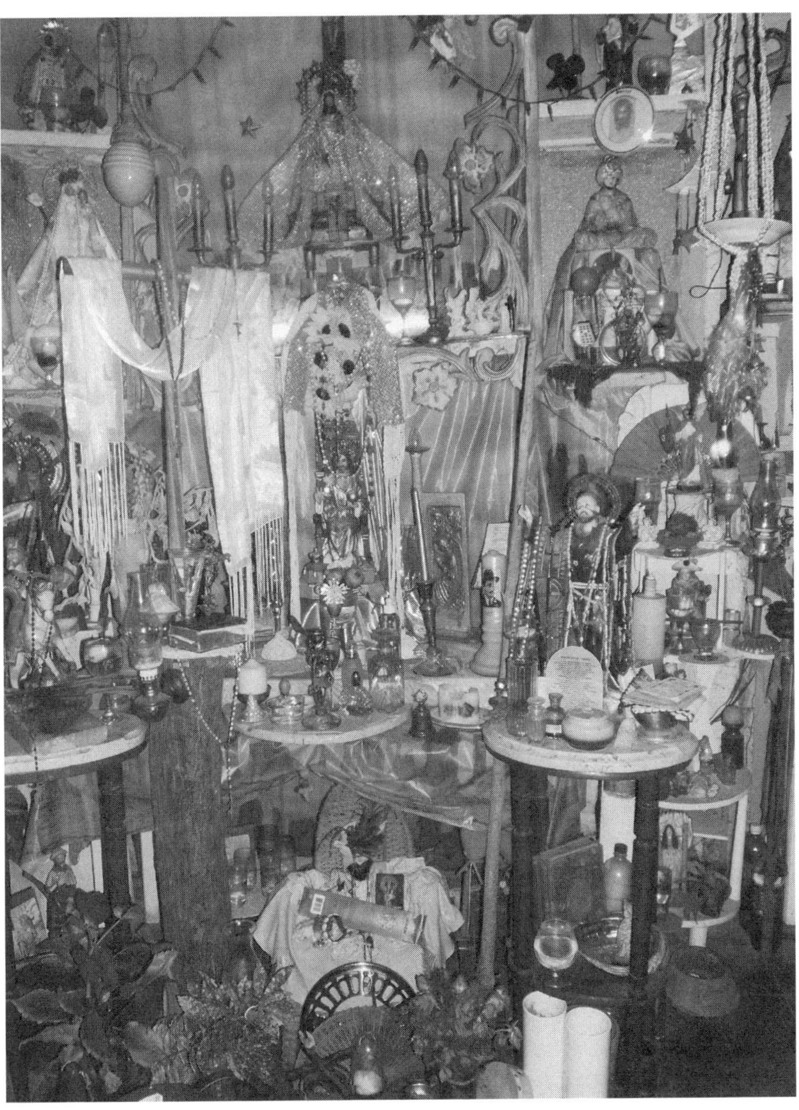

Figure 4.2. One view of a Spiritist's room dedicated to altars to various spirits and saints, which are represented by dolls, statues, colors, and other objects. Santiago de Cuba, August 2008. Photograph by K. Wirtz.

Figure 4.3. Another view of a Spiritist's room dedicated to altars to various spirits and saints, which are represented by dolls, statues, photographs of deceased family members, colors, and other objects. Santiago de Cuba, August 2008. Photograph by K. Wirtz.

There is much to unpack in these kinds of representations, especially in what they tell us about notions of historical consciousness and the roles spirits take in enacting narratives of nation, race, gender, and autobiography alike, making particular spatiotemporal frameworks of history and myth immanent and therefore immediately relevant (see Wirtz 2011, forthcoming). But my analytical goals here are somewhat different. For my current purposes, it will suffice to point out that the mobilization of social types in representing spirits of different kinds is one way religious practitioners develop the necessary familiarity to make sense of spiritual entities as agents in the material world.

Not all kinds of material instantiations are available to all categories of spirits cataloged above. Spiritual energies that are not anthropomorphized or individuated and that therefore do not manifest on altars or in spirit possessions may still become tangible and manipulable through the often-elaborate actions of purifications. Some households still toss a bucket of water out the front door at noon and roll a coconut around the corners of a room on special occasions like New Year's Eve in order to remove "bad (spiritual) influences." And many folk-religious rituals follow a similar procedure of brushing someone's body with a branch of *porsiana* (or some other purifying material—even a dove); of having the person pass perfumed hands over their head, neck, shoulders, arms, torso, behind, and legs, then shaking the droplets off the hands with a distinctive snap of the fingers; or of a medium, or *santero* grabbing a person's hands, spinning them first one way and then the other, as if dancing, then flinging their hands up into the air to shake the hands with that same sharp snapping of the fingers. With that motion, with the release of a dove or its sacrifice, or with the discarding of whatever material was used in the purification, away go the bad spiritual energies.

I suggest, then, that the agency of spirits (of all sorts) requires materialization to become manifest and that the material world is understood to be permeable to—indeed, animated by—spirits. The momentous and dramatic events of spirit possession thus must be situated in the larger context of (1) the interconnections between people and a wide variety of types of spirits and spirit collectivities and the saturation of people and things by spirits and (2) the ways in which the materiality of bodies and things serve as ground (in the Peircean sense) for spirit signifiers and signifieds (representamens and objects, in Peirce's terms) alike. More on this semiotic angle momentarily. My account of spirit and materiality intentionally resonates with how Cuban santeros and Yoruba oricha devotees alike conceptualize the interdependent relationship between people and spirits. What Barber (1981) argued for the latter relationship in "How Man Makes God in West Africa" also applies to the Cuban case: that humans and spirits are in a symbiotic relationship, each relying on the other to empower them for their mutual survival. Deities thrive or disappear depending on the attention or neglect of devotees, and such devotions are grounded in the social-political-historical realities of the human world.

A further resonance in this argument about spiritual presence and materiality is its instantiation of a basic duality for Western thought, that of body and spirit or of matter and energy, which can be expanded in various ways, some of which Kirsch (2008: 1–2) enumerates: "immanence/transcendence, materiality/immateriality, visibility/invisibility, presence/absence, this-worldliness/other-worldliness, and immediacy/eternity." Kirsch, in his study of an African Pentecostal church, goes on to suggest that each pair reflects a gap that is problematic for Christians and scholars alike, albeit for different reasons. Where for Christians the gap represents a "foundational" separation between humans and the divine, scholars face a different kind of challenge to demonstrate that our concern with, say, bridging between the material, visible world and the immaterial, invisible world, reflects ontological concerns held by those we study (even when, as in this case, the study site is Western). Holbraad (2012), however, challenges the anthropological projection of the Christian gap between transcendence and immanence to other cases, arguing that Cuban Ifá diviners (*babalawos*), for example, approach the spirit-materiality gap as a practical matter rather than an ontological problem. With this critique in mind, my goal is not to challenge the primacy of the spirit-matter dyad, since, like Lambek (1998b), I have concluded that there seems to be no getting away from it in interpreting my ethnographic material. Rather, I want to overtly describe the operation of the dyad in various kinds of accounts and enactments of spirit presence and possession, because it is so central to the varied representational economies we (and our religious Cuban interlocutors, among many others) bring to bear on the larger issue of spirit presence.

Representational Economies of Spirit Presence

Keane's notion of representational economies highlights how perception, even of the qualities of things, is culturally mediated. That is, we may think of material things as capable of transcending cultural context because of their durability and their material presence, which we imagine can be encountered directly. Objects are, as Keane says, "detachable" from particular contexts (1997: 92). At the same time, however, a long anthropological tradition pointing back to Marx also recognizes the integral way in which objects become vested with social value because things—property, products of labor, indeed, all "material conditions of life"—mediate agency, social relations, and entire political economies (see Patterson 2009: 138–40). The fact of objects' detachability allows them to be exchanged and to carry marks and erasures of their transactional histories to create what Appadurai (1986) has dubbed "the social life of things." Considering the intersection of social biographies of things and their detachable material presence, Keane identifies a "problem of representation" in the underdetermined meaning of material things, because of the "vicissitudes to which material signs are prone," attributable to "three things about objects as social media: that they are readily separated from the moment of transaction, and with it, the words, gestures, and other critical aspects of context; that they are available for multiple interpretations; and that, however semiotically we may treat them, they remain material objects and thus vulnerable to all that can happen to things" (1997: 31–32). Moreover, objects can have, or seem to have, their own agency by virtue of their material properties and social biographies—therein lies the definition of the "fetish"—and, as Keane points out, objects are capable of extending the agency of those who possess them, through exchange, for example (ibid.: 75). To explain how this happens, especially in light of the special vulnerability of objects to becoming separated from their transactional contexts, Keane argues: "The potential for expansive agency that exchange possesses is not found in the objects alone but in the repeated events wherein they are transacted, in the links forged among sequences of events, and in the words spoken as the objects move" (ibid.: 92). Words and things must travel together, in other words, so that things can in fact embody and extend the agency of people. Moreover, and more to my point here, the subject possessing an object and the object possessed must (and do) become identified with each other, although this ongoing process is not seamless: objects have to be "detachable" in order to "exteriorize and represent their possessors" (ibid.).

It is an interesting exercise to read this passage with spirit possession in mind, especially because putative spirit possessions do often trigger a crisis of representation, as other participants assess the material evidence of the possessed body to decide whether the possession is real and who the possessing agency is. Indeed, I have written elsewhere about Cuban santeros' near obsession with testing and proving spirit presence in ceremonies (Wirtz 2007). Moreover, santeros and other Cuban folk-religious practitioners envision spirit possession as one step in a complex series of exchanges between spirits and people: people make offerings or promise to make offerings to spirits, which serve to activate the spiritual potential of spirits, who reciprocate by manifesting their power through material interventions including spirit possession, and who are then thanked with further material offerings from people, in an ongoing cycle variously characterized as reciprocity or manipulation, depending on the particular tradition in question (see, for example, Espirito Santo 2010; Holbraad 2005; Routon 2008).

Within the representational economy that permits this cycle of coordinated action between people and spirits, material things stand in both for the otherwise intangible spirits themselves (however material their desires) and for the transactional glue of the human-spirit relationship. A plaster statue of Saint Lazarus (to take one example) iconically represents the salient characteristics of Saint Lazarus—his leprosy and mendicancy, the dogs that accompany him—which are also the sources of his power over infectious disease and ill fortune more generally. The vase of flowers and bowl of fruit put before the statue and the lavish gold cape draped over it, like the recorded music or live drums played before the altar, index the relationship between the human keeper of the altar and the deity lavished with these objects of devotion. Such relationships of similarity and contiguity—iconicity and indexicality—built as they are upon notions that fruit, flowers, fabric, and music are desirable to spirits and that a plaster statue can stand in to receive offerings for an otherwise intangible spirit, are meaningful only when taken up, processed, and framed by semiotic regimes that contribute social salience to those relationships.

To probe deeper into the role of things and their material properties in the workings of representational economies, we can draw upon C. S. Peirce's (1997) description of three metaphysical degrees of reality. Calling them Firstness, Secondness, and Thirdness, Peirce proposed that these principles shape our processes of perception and cognition as follows:

Firstness: an existential degree of reality involving the sensation of perceivable qualities inherent in things in themselves (e.g., hardness as a quality).

Secondness: a relational degree of reality in which we perceive things in contrast with other perceivable things (e.g., an object is recognizable as a rock by comparison with other examples of "rockness").

Thirdness: a mediated degree of reality, in which perceivable objects can be classified, defined, and interpreted in terms of laws and conventions, such that things with rockness can be called "rocks" and further classified as igneous, metamorphic, volcanic, and so forth.

All degrees of reality are simultaneously present, so that the Firstness of things, their directly felt qualities, provides the material for comparing them with other things and, ultimately, for imbuing them with social value. And likewise, our very perception of Firstness is always already saturated by relational and representational degrees because we are cultural beings. Having been socialized since birth into a world fully mediated by complex sign systems (such as language and culture), it might be hardest for us to appreciate the rawness of Firstness. As soon as we try to describe our perceptions, we invoke the categories and types of Thirdness. Recent anthropological treatments of phenomenology, such as Duranti's reconsideration of Husserl's work, make a similar philosophical argument without reference to Peirce. Duranti (2009), for example, adapts Husserl's notion of Einstellung, translatable as attitude or orientation, to argue that processes of socialization imbue our very encounter with the sensual world with culturally relevant categories. Sensory perception as we experience it, then, is never "raw" but in fact always "cooked." As Duranti says, perception is not natural but naturalized, via processes that modify our attention in order "to transform [our] social and natural environment into particular kinds of 'phenomena' " (2009: 206). Peircean relations of Secondness and Thirdness describe this "cooking" process.

Peirce developed a complex model of perception and cognition by applying the three degrees of reality to several parts of his model of the sign. His model of the sign is itself irreducibly triadic, built as it is out of the triad of metaphysical degrees of reality, and each of its parts can also be examined for their qualities, relationships, and mediation by other signs (Lee 1997: 95–134; Peirce 1997). The Peircean sign consists of an object and representamen, corresponding loosely to the more familiar Saussurean semiological terminology of signified and signifier. But Peirce gave a central role to mediation in this representational relationship: object and representamen come together only as mediated by the third part of the sign, the interpretant.

Firstness, Secondness, and Thirdness can be mapped onto the representamen and object as separate entities, or onto their relationship to one another and to the interpretant. Thinking in terms of these degrees of reality permits us to differentiate kinds of representamen-object linkages and different relationships between those and the interpretant. To very briefly review what is explained in detail in many other places, icons are signs where some similar qualities of the object and representamen create a link (as a portrait resembles its subject); indexes are signs where the object and representamen are linked because they co-occur (as smoke indexes fire);

and symbols are signs in which representamen and object are arbitrarily linked, as by social convention (as a grapheme like <t> represents a particular speech sound). But Firstness, Secondness, and Thirdness also allow further differentiations among kinds of icons, indexes, and symbols, such that each can undergo further degrees of social mediation: "woof" sounds like a dog (an iconic link) to English speakers because of social convention—a history of utterances that have created a durable indexical link between the token "woof" and its object, a dog's bark. This iconicity may not be apparent to speakers of other languages, however. It depends on a particular, locally relevant history of semiosis.

Without detailing Peirce's entire grid of possibilities (see Lee 1997: 118–26; Peirce 1997), some implications should be clear. Most important, to ask about the experience of spirit presence is not to make an inquiry into raw Firstness. There is no unmediated perception of spirits in themselves, nor is spirit Firstness in itself possible because of a basic understanding of spirits as "not matter." Spirits by definition have no material existence and thus no felt qualities of Firstness. Their presence in the material world is manifest through their agency, which is relational and thus already in the metaphysical realm of Secondness. When people describe the first-order signs of spirit presence, as in the examples from Josefina quoted above, they are actually describing the qualities of other things affected by spirits, even if some of those things seem quite ephemeral, energy more than matter: electricity, vibrations, shivers. This is also true, in a more obviously socially mediated way, when one is describing other kinds of spirit presence, such as when cowry shells "talk" or when a person "sees" images sent by the spirits or even when the spirits talk or act through someone's body. All of these, too, are things (sound waves, images, bodies), and it is qualities of those things (writhing bodies, embodied voices, sacred objects, even mental images) that are existentially perceived first, even if then interpreted as indexing spirit presence, in the realms of Secondness and Thirdness. Within the semiotic chains of interpretants that make up a Cuban folk-religious framework, the perceivable qualities of things—vibrations, voices, shivers, shells, bodily movements—can serve as indexes of spirit presence and agency. As ethnographers we seek to travel back up this chain of interpretants to arrive at some "feel" (in a relational and mediated sense) for the experience of spirit presence.

There are three points of entry into this "feel" for spirit presence that I would like to detail. Each is an important aspect of the representational economy of folk religiosity in Cuba. I begin by considering agency.

Agency

Spirit agency is most evidently on display during spirit possession trances, in which the devotee's body becomes the vehicle for a spirit that temporarily usurps the conscious control of the devotee. Erving Goffman's (1976) notion of participant footing, meaning the stances participants take during an interaction, is useful for understanding the interactional effects of spirit possession. Goffman's insight was that these footings are much more complex than suggested by the simple roles of speaker or hearer: consider a stage actor, who animates a role by uttering words authored by a playwright, and whose actions the theater audience agrees to accept as temporarily representing those of a character who is the "principal" bearing responsibility within the frame of the performance (see further elaborations in Irvine 1996). In spirit possession, too, the participant footing of the devotee shifts dramatically, even theatrically, from the normative, unmarked congruence between role fractions of author, animator, and principal of one's words and actions to being merely the animator—the bodily instrument—directed by a possessing spirit, who takes responsibility for authorship. Whether in spirit possession or on the stage, such footings can never be accomplished solely by the actor. Footings require ratification, such as appropriate audience reactions, to be accepted into the participant structure of the event. It is interesting, then, that the lines between religiously verifiable possession trances and theatrical enactments of trances are blurred indeed in Cuba. Not only does spirit possession enter the choreography of folklore shows. It sometimes happens that the performance of music and movements used to induce trance in folklore settings can accidentally bring down actual spirits, a situation understood as dangerously out of control by religious practitioners and folklore directors alike, albeit for differing reasons (Hagedorn 2001: 107–16).

For example, on the occasion of a lengthy outdoor event called the "ceremony to the cimarrón (maroon)," held in the small town of El Cobre during nearby Santiago de Cuba's annual Festival of the Caribbean, a locally well-known religious practitioner was possessed by his muerto, or spirit of a dead person. Amid the long afternoon's events, a number of amateur folklore groups had performed a mélange of Afro-Cuban folklore traditions, including a lengthy facsimile of a Spiritist and Palo ceremony in which performers became possessed (or acted out becoming possessed—it was never clear) by African slaves and maroons. Later, after a performance of Haitian dances in Cuba and a bonfire revealing sculptures under the flammable hay, a third folklore ensemble presented sacred dances of the orichas of Santería. It was during this final event that the muerto made an unscheduled appearance and then refused to depart his host. A santero acquaintance standing next to me explained that the muerto must have been attracted by the sacred songs played for the performance, an interpretation supported by several other religious practitioners who later watched my video recording or heard my description. The possessed man wandered around the edges of the performance space ringed by the crowd, alternately interacting with audience members and running out to disrupt the dancers, who gamely attempted to continue their choreography around him. This disruption finally attracted the attention of some of the religious practitioners and folklorists from the organization running the event, who came down off the small stage to the side of the dance event to attempt to take the possessed man around behind the stage and ritually send away his muerto. He emerged again, still possessed.

For the remainder of the event, one or two people kept a close eye on him, to keep the muerto from inadvertently endangering his host or harassing the audience too much. At one point, one person directly asked him what he wanted, receiving a hard stare in return. At other points, his self-appointed guardians stepped in to translate his highly marked speech when he gave impromptu consultations to a few audience members. An hour later, they were still at it: as my tour bus drove down the mountain road in the twilight, heading back through the town of El Cobre to return to Santiago, we saw the muerto leading his minders up a steep hillside path to visit the Monument to the Cimarrón high above where the event had been held. I turned to my santero companion for an explanation, and he shook his head and said that it seemed that no one had the skills needed to force the muerto to leave and that this was a risk of having a ceremony—or even a folkloric rendition of a ceremony—without proper religious supervision by experts. On this and other occasions I heard religious practitioners criticize such shows because those hosting them would be unprepared to properly handle an accidental spirit possession, a situation potentially dangerous (and certainly inconvenient and exhausting) for the possessed person if the spirit refused to leave.

With or without recognized religious expertise, the largely Cuban audience at the event, as well as its organizers and scheduled performers, accepted the man's behavior as a clear case of spirit possession and that his actions were undeniably under the control of the possessing muerto. As on any occasion of spirit possession, an accumulation of cues, from his brief "crisis" of falling into trance under the influence of the sacred music to his wide-open, staring eyes, stiff comportment, change of speaking register, and even his refusal to cooperate, cued the shift in footing to being possessed.

In Santería ceremonies, such signs of possession may not always be accepted at face value: santeros evince skepticism by "testing" a putative possession trance, usually to see whether the oricha responds appropriately to particular ritual songs, drum rhythms, or sung challenges (called *puyas*, or insults). Even when most participants seem to readily go along with the performance of a spirit possession, they may later voice suspicions. There is thus a widespread recognition among religious practitioners and folklore performers alike about possibilities for slippage between theatrical and religious frames (e.g., a "faker" performing for my camera at a religious ceremony or an actual spirit who gets attracted to a folklore performance).

We might also consider how people in a particular setting are socialized into becoming proper vehicles ("horses" in a widespread Caribbean metaphor) to be "mounted" by a spirit. Spiritists describe a spiritually gifted person's choice to "develop" their potential for mediumship by attending ceremonies and learning how to call upon their spirit or spirits in order to induce them to come. The initial episode of spirit possession may be quite dramatic: a good friend who is a santero in Santiago related how, as a child, he attended a *bembé*, or festive drumming ceremony, and was possessed by a muerto. Once possessed, he fled out of the bembé with other participants in pursuit, taking them to the nearby house of someone ill, where his possessing muerto called for particular herbs and did a purification then and there. In his account, the person was healed, and he discovered his spiritual abilities through his affinity with this one possessing spirit. This narrative, recounted years later, does not provide any specifics about this initial possession event; indeed, the santero only knew some of the events because someone had told him after he came out of possession.

Cuban santeros and most Spiritist mediums who "succumb" to possession describe the entranced state as one in which they have no conscious awareness or volition. Learning when and how to "let go" or not let go is key to developing as a *subidor*, or one who can readily undergo possession (*subir*, to rise, also means to be possessed). The possessing spirit, or oricha, too, must be developed if it is to speak and act coherently. Early attempts at possession trance often do not progress beyond the crisis of swooning and staggering around, making cases like the young child described above stand out for having a powerful spirit and being a spiritually talented "horse." How, then, does someone learn to undergo a dissociative state, especially when the sensations of that state are of losing consciousness and ceding control to another presence?

One striking scene from the documentary film *Yo Soy Hechicero*, produced by Iván Drufovka and directed by Ron Stanford in 1996 and filmed in Union City, New Jersey, exploring the ritual practice of a Cuban American folk-religious practitioner, shows one moment in a new initiate's socialization into feeling the presence of her saint. The priest in charge during the ceremony, who is himself possessed by his muerto at this moment, has just administered a very bitter drink to a client, who gags on it, then bows over and seems not at all herself. He and others gather around:

PRIEST TO FEMALE CLIENT: All in one swallow.
Don't taste it. [*No lo pruebes*, 2nd pers. informal]
[Client drinks, then swoons with her eyes closed, mouth open and raspy, heavy breathing]
WOMAN: Do you want [*quieres*, 2nd pers. informal] to vomit?
PRIEST: Take her outside.
It's the effect of the saint and the spirit.
[Client sways and almost loses her balance]
SEVERAL VOICES: No no no no.
PRIEST: No.
Do it [*hazlo*, 2nd pers. informal] like this, calmly.
Brother, if you (*usted*, 2nd pers. formal] are going to enter, enter.
If not, leave her in peace.[1]

It is noteworthy that the experienced santero guides the neophyte into experiencing the onset of spirit possession by first having her drink something that makes her gag—an involuntary bodily reaction. He then encourages her into a fuller trance state by marking a shift in her footing toward relinquishing consciousness and control to a spirit: he addresses a comment in her direction but not to her. Calling to his "Brother," using the second-person formal conjugation and pronoun, "usted," and referring to the client in the third person, "leave *her* in peace," suggests that another male participant has joined the interaction from within her. The santero explicitly makes a connection between her experience of gagging as a bodily loss of control and a more complete ceding of bodily control to a spiritual presence already within her: "It's the effect of the saint and the spirit." He calls upon this spiritual presence to either fully possess her or leave her alone. In directly addressing the entering spirit, he assigns agency to it instead of to the swooning, gagging woman primed to be possessed.

One final question in this consideration of the agency of spirits: since Cubans understand spirits to represent people who once lived and deities like orichas to be African in origin, we might ask how they align themselves relative to these beings of the past. What kind of historical subjectivity is invoked by such headstrong presences as muertos who refuse to be subdued and spirits who guide other spirits to enter into possession? As Routon (2008) has argued for the case of the Reglas de Palo, folk-religious practices like Palo that are rooted in Afro-Cuban experiences of slavery and oppression enact an "implicit knowledge about social relations and power" through which contemporary practitioners of all backgrounds can "fashion a kind of sorcery out of history" (638). As several recent ethnographies of spirit possession in Africa have pointed out, the violence of colonial and slave exploitation is remembered and channeled through the embodied experience of being "possessed," owned, and controlled by a powerful outside agency (Cole 2001; Lambek 1998b; Stoller 1995). And the orientation—Husserl's Einstellung—shaping this sensual experience requires material relationships: in the example above, a bitter, unpleasant liquid triggers bodily sensations that the accompanying talk dispossessing the woman of her own agency frames as cues of spirit possession.

Materiality

The foregoing examples illustrate how spirit possession as an interactional event involves a temporary shift in the footing of the possessed person from being an agent responsible for his or her actions to being an animated body directed by a possessing entity. Spirit possession thus highlights people's reducibility to the material presence of their bodies and their susceptibility to control by more powerful external agents. Even when characterized as benign, or even useful, as most spirit possessions in Cuba are, the spirits and saints are conceived to be pure agency that can trump the agency of their human hosts if not properly handled. That said, because Cuban folk-religious practitioners understand being possessed to require a natural spiritual talent and considerable practice, spirit possession is not seen as a sign of social marginality or as a last resort of the powerless in the way Boddy (1989) describes Sudanese Zar spirit possession. Rather, spirit possession follows the central Cuban folk-religious logic of using material things to constitute relationships with the spirit world, as a special case of having one's body serve that mediating role.

If spirit possession emphasizes the materiality of human bodies and their "permeability to some kind of Otherness" in Corin's (1998: 88) phrase, it is also indicative of how spirits saturate all manner of things, imbuing them with spiritual agency. For this reason, the ceding of control at the heart of spirit possession serves as a model for the susceptibility of the entire physical and human world to the influence of spirits, and hence the necessity to work with the spirits in order to receive their positive attention and assistance in matters of material existence. Working with the spirits and saints in turn requires the mediation of material things, which can even acquire an interactional footing not typical of our treatment of things in which the object comes to be regarded, at least temporarily and in strictly delimited ways, as having communicative agency in a person-like way. As Garoutte and Wambaugh (2007) describe religious practitioners in Santiago de Cuba, citing Maya Deren's work on Haitian Vodou, they enter into a triadic power relationship with the spirits and their material embodiments in sacred objects like the receptacles containing the *otánes*, or consecrated stones of the orichas; the ngangas, or ritual power objects, created by practitioners of Palo; the cowries through which saint and spirit "speak" in divination; and the ubiquitous plaster statues and cloth dolls (*chicherekú*) found on many altars. Whether in the practices of Santería, Palo, Spiritism, folk Catholicism, or some combination of these, all such sacred representations serve both as icons of spiritual beings and as indexes of their presence. They both stand for and, when activated, contain spirit presence. In many kinds of ritual work, religious practitioners treat these embodiments or representations directly, in Goffman's terms, as animators of the spiritual being itself. In feeding one's orichas or nganga, within Santería or Palo, one can directly spray rum, blow cigar smoke, pour animal blood, or add consecrated herbs and water onto the sacred vessel (see figure 4.4). Other offerings, from flowers to food to candles, are placed directly in front of the sacred vessels.

Practitioners of Santería and Palo agree that such offerings serve to energize the spirits and saints so that they can act in the world; santeros use the Lucumí word *aché* to describe this sacred energy that humans must provide through material offerings in order for the saints to act in the world. Cowry shells and amulets such as the beaded necklaces or bracelets many religious practitioners wear are activated in similar ways. Other religious practices may include not only feeding and venerating the embodied representations of spirits and saints but even punishing them, as when someone displaces his or her plaster statue of Saint Lazarus from the altar to the floor, promising to elevate the statue back to the altar and perhaps give it

Figure 4.4. Several sets of orichas of Santería that were "fed" offerings including several sacrificed doves and chickens as part of a ceremony for the oricha Olokun. The blue vessels in the foreground contain the oricha Yemayá, associated with Olokun; behind them, the metal poles with roosters represent the oricha Osun, and the plates and clay bowls contain the other warrior orichas Eleggua, Ogún, and Ochosí. Santiago de Cuba, February 2010. Photograph by K. Wirtz.

special offerings in return for having the saint intervene to solve a health, economic, legal, or personal problem. Notions of spiritual energy or force, then, point to a reliance of spirits on the material world, which must necessarily provide the physical medium for spiritual agency to be expressed.

Material offerings include not only the durable (and perishable) offerings of objects, animals, and foodstuffs but also the more ephemeral but equally material offerings of smoke, candlelight, and even music and speech (as seen in figure 4.5, for example). The sounds of drums, bells, and voices after all are physical phenomena in the form of acoustic waves, however briefly. Even giving praise to the saints serves as an offering. Describing the role of sacred songs called *suyeré* in Santería, a santero explained:

> If there is one important thing in the religion, it is the songs sung to the orichas. These are how one gives praise. This is what invokes the saint. For this reason, I told you just now that to accomplish any purification, to do

Figure 4.5. Offerings presented to the oricha Olokun during a ceremony to "feed" him include plates of chopped raw foods, sacrificed birds, burning candles, ringing bells, and songs. Santiago de Cuba, February 2010. Photograph by K. Wirtz.

> any spiritual work, to make the saint [initiate someone], one always has to invoke the saint. This has to be done with the prayers, this has to be done with the chants which are the suyeré. That is, one sings a story to the oricha so that the oricha can work in the space one creates. This is done within the ritual space. (Field notes, November 8, 1999)

While the santero emphasizes the importance of the song's referential content—in telling a story to the oricha, for example—it is equally important to realize that the lyrics of such songs are in a ritual register, Lucumí, that is often not fully intelligible to religious practitioners (Wirtz 2005). One effect of using this esoteric ritual register, then, is to shift the emphasis to the tangible qualities of the sound itself: the song as offering.

Moreover, offerings of prayer, song, and music usually accompany offerings of food and other perishable items (flowers, candles, sprays of alcohol, animal blood, or perfumed water) during ceremonies, serving to elaborate on and articulate the recipients and goals of offerings. All kinds of offerings serve to activate sacred energy, to attract the spirits and saints, and to elicit their cooperation in human projects. That said, what Espirito Santo characterizes as the "degree" or "density" of material mediators of spirits carries moral as well as practical connotations for religious practitioners (Espirito Santo 2010: 80).

Espirito Santo argues that religious practitioners situate themselves and carve out boundaries between different "traditions" across the spectrum of Cuban folk religion by distinguishing the kinds of spirits they work with and their goals in working with those spirits according to distinct regimes of material intervention. One often-invoked major divide is between "the spiritual" and the "the material" as two aspects of well-being that religious practices must attend to. While religious practitioners of any affiliation may discuss this distinction, even if only to make the point that tending to the spiritual side of things also brings material benefits, the discourse is perhaps best developed among Spiritists, as Espirito Santo (2010) documents. Spiritists, and especially those identifying with Scientific Spiritism, give priority to helping the "spirits of light" in their striving toward higher levels of spirituality that take them away from the material concerns of human lives they once lived. Such spirits are offered material things thought to have a more ephemeral, clear, cooling, or pure character: glasses of clear water, aromatic perfumes and flowers, candle flames to help them find light. Even the prayers and songs of spiritual masses, sung a cappella and without drums, have this thinner, more "heavenly" character, which Cubans readily identify with European as opposed to African spiritual traditions.

Compare this to the messy materiality of "feeding the saints" in Santería, a ceremony that may begin with a courtyard full of fowl and four-legged animals awaiting sacrifice to the saints, whose sacred vessels will be spiritually "charged" by receiving warm blood, plates of raw animal parts carrying spiritual energy, aché, and bowls of cooked meat that will also give spiritual blessings to the human participants who share it. Here, the transubstantiation of offerings into spiritual energy is intended to link humans and orichas and to activate the power of the orichas to intervene in the material world and improve the lives of their devotees. Santeros, in contradistinction to Scientific Spiritists concerned with spiritual purity, conceptualize spiritual power in terms of good relations with the world of spirits and deities that manifest as physical well-being and material progress (perhaps not unlike the good capitalists Protestants make, in Weber's classic analysis). But even in Scientific Spiritist practice, which takes greatest pains to distance itself from the materialistic spirits of even other kinds of Spiritism, there is still the need for spirits to materialize and for physical materials to mediate relations between humans and spirits.

Practitioners of Palo take "feeding the nganga" even further than santeros, emphasizing a sort of reversal in which spirits are compelled by offerings of food to do human bidding, even the bidding of someone other than the owner of their nganga, if their owner has neglected feeding them and made them vulnerable to outside coercion. Indeed, the bald reproduction of social relations between masters and slaves enacted by Palo practitioners may put the ethereal concerns of Scientific Spiritists, who understand their tradition to be "purely" European, into proper historical perspective as a sort of misrecognition of or refusal to wield white, elite power.

Thus the compositions of materials and the ways in which they constitute and mediate human-spirit relationships vary across different religious traditions and trajectories, often expressing the deeply felt tension between "the spiritual" and "the material" that creates potential for human knowledge of and relations with spirits. These dynamics were apparent on one occasion when the santera and Spiritist Josefina and I were planning a spiritual mass for my recently deceased father. The ceremony was an undertaking I viewed with trepidation, but Josefina was insistent that family spirits require this spiritual intervention on a regular basis, to ensure their acceptance of their death and their evolution toward a state of purity and grace.

Two days before the mass, we enumerated the items we would need to purchase for it and exactly where and how we would procure each item, in what quantity, and at what price—these are hardly trivial matters in a place with the material scarcities, daily hardships, and monetary complexities of Cuba. At one point, I pointed to a large, white plastic tub (like the one in figure 4.1) next to the central altar table, which was filled with water and herbs, and asked her its purpose. As she responded, she gestured to the tub and said:

JOSEFINA: ¿Qué quiero decir con esto? [What do I want to say with this?]
Esto es una composición de las dos cosas [This is a composition of the two things.]
De lo espiritual con el santo. [Of the spiritual with the saint.]
Porque el muerto parió al santo [Because the dead gave birth to the saint]
no hay santos sin muertos. [there are no saints without the dead.]
Estando aquí un diós y un espiritu [There being here a god and a spirit]
KW: Ikú lobí ocha (je-je-je-je). [The dead gave birth to the saint (ha-ha-ha-ha).]
JOSEFINA: Así es, así, así. [Yes, that's it, that's it, that's it.]

Here, Josefina explained that the tub contained herbs representing both the orichas of Santería and the muertos of Spiritism, repeating a common proverb describing the nature of the connection between muertos and santos: that the dead give birth to the saint. I repeated this proverb, but in its Lucumí form as I frequently heard it said among santeros in the city. Then, perhaps recalling that Josefina does not have much knowledge of Lucumí ritual speech, I went on (rather pedantically) to explain what each Lucumí word meant. When I had finished, Josefina responded as follows:

JOSEFINA: Ahora, cuando tú dijiste eso, has dicho eso, [Just now, when you said that, when you were saying that,]
y yo empecé a sentirme en los pies, en las piernas, [and I begin to feel in my feet, in my legs,]
en todo mi cuerpo, los brazos, y todo, [in all of my body, my arms, and everywhere,]
y la camisa . . . estoy [congelizada?] con esto, [and my shirt . . . I am [frozen?] with this,]
con la corriente, [with the current,]
con la práctica que cogiste eso solo por decir estas palabras [with the practice you achieved, that only in saying these words]
KW: (laughing)
JOSEFINA: y eso es verdad, [and that is true,]
y es verdad, sí [and it is true, yes]
KW: (laughing)
JOSEFINA: ¡Aaaaa! [marked rising then falling intonation like a siren]
¡Es la prueba! [It is the proof!]
KW: Sí. [Yes.]
JOSEFINA: La primera que decimos la prueba soy yo, [The first of us to state the proof is me,]
con lo que estabas diciendo, [with what you were saying,]
con nada más que decir estas palabras, [with nothing more than saying these words,]
y yo contestarle ¿a quién? [and I, to answer them, to whom?]
Y estoy, ya no, pero sentí una corriente [And I am, not right now, but I did feel a current]
que ahora me cogió [that just now seized me]
y eso es la verdad [and that's the truth]
KW: (laughing)
JOSEFINA: en todo mi cuerpo. [throughout my entire body.]

The blending of herbs in the plastic tub represented for Josefina an important religious principle about the primary role of spirits of the dead, and when I expressed the principle in Lucumí ritual speech, Josefina suddenly felt the presence of the spirits as a physical sensation in her body. Her description of that sensation as an electrical current invokes a metaphor I heard more than once when Cuban Spiritists in particular spoke of sensing the spirits. Religious practitioners understood their bodies to be the most sensitive instruments for detecting spirit presence, whether or not possession or even "spiritual transmissions" were occurring. Consider Ochoa's similar account of a practitioner of Palo's ability to sense the spirits, which were always present but sometimes required the stimulation of words or other things to become manifest, even in the barely susceptible sensations of goose bumps, stomach butterflies, and momentary vibrations: "The dead [Kalunga] appeared in her very sleeplessness and inhabited her body as the restlessness that woke her and drove her to get up, just as her dead (mis muertos) subsisted in encounters with old sayings and parables" (Ochoa 2007: 476, 482–83). The recognition of such bodily sensations as evidence of the spirits and, equally important, of a true connection with the spirits ("Proof!" as Josefina exclaimed) is a necessary step toward embracing the body's, and all matter's, permeability to spiritual Otherness.

Perspicience

As Josefina's talk of proof implies, agency and materiality together are essential to but not sufficient for an account of spirit presence as Cuban folk-religious practitioners understand it. Josefina's response to the sensation throughout her body suggests that the third, mediating piece of the puzzle involves a kind of experiential and ontological knowledge—Husserl's Einstellung—that permits the recognition of spirit presence. I suggest that "perspicience," a somewhat archaic word, might be dusted off and suited to the purpose. A near synonym of "discernment" and a cognate of the more familiar "perspicacity," perspicience expresses knowledge and knowingness, especially through the role of the intellect and the senses. According to the online *Oxford English Dictionary*, perspicience carries a connotation of being all-seeing, which nicely captures the connection between sensing and knowing, between sensory perception and ontological knowledge. If "perspicience" translates any particular emic term of Cuban religious practitioners, it would be *conocimiento*, knowledge, or better yet, knowing that comes from familiarity. Cuban religious practitioners use this word to refer to religious experience and understanding of the sort that comes from long practice but that can also be informed by (but emphatically not replaced by) academic study. Other emic candidates might be *claridad* and *clarividencia*, clarity and clairvoyance, as related to the sensible qualities of clear water offered to the spirits and used by some mediums for divination. Both terms describe spiritually developed minds attuned to the vibrations of the spirits. Perspicience partially captures the experiential and therefore sensory aspect of conocimiento and claridad, and it resonates with a Cuban folk-religious emphasis on tests, proofs, and confirmations as necessary aspects of religiosity and in particular of identifying and *discerning* the role of spirits in events of the material world. Josefina, speaking dramatically of her strong sensation of spiritual energies coursing across her body, repeats three times that she reports the truth, but what truth? The truth expressed by our utterance of a proverb that charges the very air with spiritual currents and the truth of the spirits, whose felt presence verifies that we are on a truly spiritual path together in our ritual plans. Indeed, Cuban religious practitioners frequently calibrate the veracity and potency of spirit presence according to the evidence of their senses, especially the senses of seeing and feeling.

Early in my dissertation fieldwork, and long before I had much understanding of Cuban religious life, I had the good fortune to be asked to interview an elderly gentleman, Bernardino Bidó y Borgoña, who was well known in religious and Carnival circles in Santiago. Together with his grown daughters and a few close neighbors, we sat in a circle in his living room as I asked my inexperienced questions about Spiritism. At my request, the group sang two or three Spiritist songs of the sort used to begin ceremonies. As they ended, Bernardino and his neighbor Isabel, both accomplished spiritual mediums, experienced spiritual transmissions. In the pause after the song, Bernardino began to speak:

BERNARDINO: Yo me quedé así [I was there like this]
entonces yo me quedé y vi a Santa Bárbara [so I was there and saw Saint Barbara]
ahí al lado de ella. [here at her side.]

Unsure what to make of this, I responded that I was not familiar with the saint, at which Bernardino commented: "She does not have knowledge" (*No tiene conocimiento*). Isabel then began to report a spiritual transmission in a rapid, low voice:

ISABEL: Pero dentro de la propia acción que ella está buscando no sé, [But within this same action that she is seeking I don't know,]
yo veo una acción de Elegguá [I see the influence of Eleggua]
como si le abriera un camino que usted está buscando. [as if he was opening a path that you (formal) are seeking]

And with this pronoun shift to the formal second person, the focus changed to conveying the transmission to me:

ISABEL: *Se me dejan ver distintas vistas y distintos lugares* [They are allowing me to see different scenes and different places]
pero también se me deja ver la acción de un espiritu de hombre blanco. [but also I am allowed to see the action of a spirit of a white man.]

As her transmission continued, Isabel, Bernardino, and others began to ask me questions, concerned to help me understand the message and interpret it in terms of my situation. As it dawned on me that I was no longer in control of the interview (if I had ever been) but instead was being subjected to a seeming spiritual event that put the focus on my personal life, the interaction devolved for a time into a comedy of cross-cultural misunderstanding (I inadvertently conveyed the false impression that the man I was living with in Cuba was not my American husband). The very cues of the spiritual transmission involve idioms of sensory perception, particularly vision: Bernardino describes having seen Saint Barbara as he sang, and Isabel reports seeing Eleggua's influence like an open path before her, then being allowed to see distant scenes and views from my exotic, foreign life, including the presence of the spirit of a white man.

Such idioms of seeing, but also of feeling and hearing, are common: some Spiritist friends have described giving a reading in terms of seeing an unfolding movie in their heads as they read the cards for someone, and others have described receiving these sorts of spiritual transmissions as akin to hearing a radio transmission or even feeling it in one's skin. Josefina frequently referred to feeling the spirits' vibrations and even pointed to a sputtering, fast-burning candle as further evidence of what the shivers up and down her arms told her about the presence of the spirits around us. Such signs simply escalate in cases of full possession, resulting in further sensible cues that other participants can also perceive when a possession is accepted as true. Perspicience, then, is related to the tangibility or sense-ability of spirits. The examples above show how in many cases the presence of spirits is hard to ignore, even when, strictly speaking, the moment for spirit presence is not entirely appropriate. Spirit presence begins with prickles and shivers and other perturbations of matter but ascends to the cinematics of spiritual transmission and the full dramatic spectacle of spirit possession. Each point on the continuum is linked and logically necessary to the next, as is the ever-present need for material mediation: it was, after all, the spiritual songs that brought on Bernardino's and Isabel's transmissions.

In reviewing Garoutte and Wambaugh's (2007) fine visual ethnography with the suggestive subtitle *A Photographic Path to the Afro-Cuban Spirit World*, Palmié poses a series of questions about what we are seeing in photographs of a Cuban religious practitioner possessed by his saint, his mpungu, or his muerto. He suggests: "What [their] images seem to ask of us is to make up our minds about who or what is looking at us from the eyes of the entranced bodies they so strikingly capture" (Palmié 2010: 92). One's answer, of course, depends upon the particular representational economy informing one's orientation toward spirit presence—and toward the visual evidence of photographic images as well. I witnessed a moment of clashing ontologies when the muerto who visited the folklore festival unbidden came face to face with an onlooker who neither looked nor backed away—a visiting Mexican tourist, I later learned—and the two locked gazes for what seemed minutes. The muerto never faltered in his bald, slightly bulging stare even in the face of the frank disbelief and curiosity of the tourist. Nor did the tourist acquiesce in accepting the veracity of the spirit possession, as he eventually shook his head dismissively and walked away. Looking from one to the other, through the lens of my video camera, I had the sensation of viewing a Gestalt-shifting image of the sort popular in introductory psychology textbooks.

Much as I have resisted acknowledging the perspicience of Cuban folk-religious practitioners and the representational economy that undergirds such discernment of the materialized agency of spirits, I have had moments of sensory immersion in it. Indeed, I find that I sometimes feel the charged atmosphere on my skin during festive ceremonies (or is that just the sweat, heat, and excitement?) and the sense of profound calm after a feeding of the saints or purification ceremony that I can best describe as feeling refreshed, an idiom I have been socialized into by my religious interlocutors, although knowing that does not diminish my *experience* of that feeling. And I developed a sudden new respect for Josefina's powers of careful observation, if not perspicience, when I realized in rereading forgotten field notes that she had astutely detected "possible circulation problems" in my legs during a spiritual consultation, pointing out a throbbing vein, a year (field notes, May 21, 2007) before this unexpected medical problem revealed itself to me or my doctor. Even as I wrote this, I found myself wondering what would have happened if I had taken her advice seriously and done the series of baths recommended by her spirit guide, La Gitana. While it is easy enough to explain her diagnosis in terms of Cubans' generally high level of medical knowledge and the fact that a member of her household is a cardiologist, the spiritually skeptical among us can still recognize her incredible sensitivity and insight—just the qualities I am suggesting Cuban religious practitioners find to be central to sensing spirit presence and knowing how to follow those inspired flashes of spiritual communication. Through the logic of infinition, it is "Proof!" as Josefina and other religious practitioners would put it.

The spectacle of spirit possession, then, is simply a more dramatic version of the same kinds of sensory signals that trigger knowing: the ordinary middle-aged man who, in a frenzy of possession by his muerto, somersaulted halfway across a cement-floored living room onto his back during a festive drumming ceremony, then drank most of a bottle of cane liquor, showing no ill affects of either. The medium who communicated someone's secret plan to leave Cuba out loud, demonstrating the veracity of the spiritual transmission but also necessitating an immediate response of "¡Luz!," "Light!," to keep the information from becoming public. The saint who dispensed advice in the special, barely understandable register of such spirit speech, and whose prognostications indeed came to pass. If there is a certain theatricality about all of this, one that in fact makes some participants dubious about spirit presence, it nonetheless makes sense as a way to socialize people into developing perspicience, or clarity, about what is being seen or felt and therefore what its significance is.

I have suggested that what the semiotician and philosopher C. S. Peirce called Firstness is not ever directly accessible to us but is always experienced through the mediation of additional metaphysical principles of relationality (Secondness) and mediation (Thirdness). Shivers are never just the raw physical sensation, but a sensation *of* something that itself represents a general type of thing, with all that the sensation indexes about its presumed causes. This principle is true of our encounters even with the most durable of objects (statues, stones) and obdurate experiences of events (unsolicited spiritual transmissions, dramatic spirit possessions). These are always already perceived through the "orientations" (Einstellung) provided by whatever representational economy we are working within. To apprehend and, better yet, to feel and understand the reality of (and through) a different representational economy requires a knowing shift to seeing things differently. I have suggested an approximation of spirit agency to Firstness—a quality of sensation we can never directly access, because the relational principles of Secondness in agency-materiality interconnections and the mediational principles of Thirdness in orientations of perspicience are also always operative. For those of us who approach phenomena such as spirit presence from across an ontological divide, perhaps a close examination of alternate conceptions of agency, materiality, and perspicience can provide a bridge of sorts.

FIVE

The Fetish and the Stone: A Moral Economy of Charlatans and Thieves

BRIAN BRAZEAL

Emeralds are like possessing spirits. They are beautiful but they can be dangerous. Like the *espíritos obsessores* of Kardecian mysticism, emeralds can take over the lives of well-meaning devotees and lead them down the road to perdition. Like Macumba, emeralds can bring comfort and solace, but they can also be a vice and an addiction. Like the *exús* of Candomblé, emeralds promise wealth to those who know how to deal with them, but the profits are fraught with peril. Dealers in emeralds, like those who earn their living purveying spiritual power, are not always to be trusted. The fact that charlatans and sharp dealers abound only augments the mystique of the reputedly authentic priestess and of the *pedra extra*, the fine stone hidden in mica schist that promises a life of leisure to the man who finds it.

This volume attempts an excavation of the relations between spirit possession and material possessions. Paul Johnson takes an ethnographic approach to the history of European philosophy to show how savage notions of things as possessors of men provided a foil against which modern notions of men as possessors of things could take shape. This chapter explores how perspectives derived from the study of Afro-Brazilian spirit possession religions might shed light on the mostly irreligious trade in emeralds in the Bahian backlands.

I ask questions that should probably be left alone. They concern religious charlatans who act in bad faith and deceive their clients by claiming powers that they will never have. They concern emerald thieves who steal with glib deceit rather than guns and knives. They concern the dangers of excessive profits garnered from saints and stones alike. They explore the inevitability of evil in the struggle to reproduce families and communities in a morally fraught economic milieu.

This chapter is the overripe fruit of an ethnographic project that is a decade old and the still-bitter pith of a study that is just beginning. I have been going to Bahia to investigate Afro-Brazilian religions since 2000 and have spent approximately three years living and working in backcountry religious communities. An otherwise unfortunate coincidence in 2004 led me to the Rat Market (Feira do Rato), where emeralds are traded in Campo Formoso. I've been back in the Rat Market every year since, but the visits have been too brief and too sporadic to constitute a conventional ethnographic engagement. A long fascination with the cultural determinants of economic value leads me to hope that I can build a bridge from the spirits to the stones. I explore the convoluted relations between trickery and authenticity negotiated every day by religious entrepreneurs and emerald dealers. I examine the consequences of immoderate profit earned from dealings with gods and emeralds alike.

There are adepts of Afro-Brazilian religions who work for evil. There are others who misrepresent their powers for pecuniary gain. Sometimes they are the same people. There are dealers in emeralds who willfully inflate the value of their merchandise to buyers and who lie to the people whose stones they sell about the money they received. There are workers in the bottoms of the mines who filch stones that should belong to the mines' owners. These are facts beyond dispute. Religious communities, like miners and traders, recognize the existence of thieves and charlatans. Adepts, miners, and dealers alike confront the image of the unscrupulous practitioners of their trades as they negotiate with their clients.

This does not mean that all priestesses practice fakery or that all emerald dealers always steal. I have witnessed innumerable demonstrations of sincere religious faith and healing ceremonies that might be described as miraculous in a less adamantly secular genre. I have also been party to honest and straightforward transactions for precious stones. But a careful exploration of the role of the unscrupulous adept and the dishonest dealer can illuminate the contours of the moral economies that bind communities of coreligionists and gem merchants together.

Priests and priestesses of Afro-Brazilian religions use the fruit of their spiritual labor to sustain large ritual families, to keep centenarian temples afloat, and to uphold the beautiful, multifaceted cult of their high gods. Many of these adepts find large followings and comfortable lives. But there are those for whom the wages of sorcery are poverty, insanity, and death. The remunerative rituals of Afro-Brazilian religions call upon deities whose cults carry a decidedly evil tinge. Those who do not reinvest their profits in more benevolent undertakings run the risk of divine retribution.

There are dealers in emeralds who plough their profits into the complex of overlapping credit relations that allow the trade to sustain itself. They use them to educate their children, to sustain their churches, and to better their community. But there are those who dissipate their wealth in games of chance, sumptuary consumption, and the easy but expensive virtue of the soiled doves who flit about the mining camps. A lapidary put it succinctly: "Garimpeiro tem uma vantagem, quando tem dinheiro, é cachaça, puta e carro novo" (Miners have one advantage; when they have money it's booze, whores, and a new car).

My argument unfolds as follows: ritual services and uncut emeralds are both commodities in that both condense labor into highly desired forms that can be exchanged for money. The prices of these commodities are subject to intricate and uncertain negotiations because their value rests on qualities that are hidden, ineffable, and numinous. The difficulties in determining the value of stones and ceremonies leave the clients of Afro-Brazilian religious adepts and emerald dealers uniquely open to fraud. Fraud is an openly acknowledged and even celebrated aspect of religious and mineral commerce alike. The existence of deceivers in both of these realms of exchange does not undercut but rather reinforces the value of the putatively genuine article. The genuine articles are efficacious ceremonies and elusive *pedras extras*, or gem-quality stones. Dishonesty and greed carry their own punishments in the form of divine retribution, alcoholism, and poverty. In order to avoid such dire consequences, spiritual and mineral merchants must reinvest the profits accrued in plying their trades into the communities that encompass them. These might be ritual or temporal families, networks of credit and trust, or even Protestant religious congregations. Those who would enjoy their wealth alone will suffer.

Thus we see a moral economy that functions with a logic alien to the self-maximizing impulse to truck and barter described by classical economics. Personal profit beyond what is necessary to sustain one's self is anathema. The maintenance of community takes precedence over individual gain. The thief, the sorcerer, and the charlatan are not deviant elements to be expunged. They are the lynchpins that allow the moral economies to sustain themselves.

The City of Witchcraft and the City of Gunpowder

This story takes place between Bahia's arid backlands and its fertile littoral. Cachoeira is a colonial coastal town known throughout Bahia as the Cidade da Macumba, the City of Witchcraft. Campo Formoso, where emeralds are traded, is the oldest city in the Bahian west. It is situated in a fertile valley in an otherwise harsh and famous region known as the *sertão*. Most of the emeralds in Campo Formoso come from the nearby settlement of Carnaiba, a small town with the improvised and impermanent feel of a mining camp. Both Cachoeira and Campo Formoso were once flourishing hubs of regional and international commerce. However, both towns are well past their prime, having ceded their pride of place to larger cities situated along Brazil's national highway network.

In Cachoeira, the religion of Candomblé holds out the promise of prestige and economic opportunity to a large Afro-Brazilian population that has never known prosperity. However, Candomblé's promise is tinged with danger. The most profitable spiritual services are those that call upon diabolical exús and fearsome spirits of the dead. Work with these pantheons can prove perilous. Tales of sorcerers' downfalls into misery and death provide a check on the ambitions of Candomblé adepts. In Campo Formoso the mining and marketing of emeralds provides the material for the innumerable rags-to-riches stories told in the Rat Market and the mining camps. Riches-to-rags stories circulate with almost equal currency. Bars, brothels, and purveyors of recreational alkaloids abound. Fortunes in emeralds are drunk, snorted, and fucked out of existence.

Thick historical connections link the two cities. The expeditions to subdue the native peoples of what is now Campo Formoso began and ended in Cachoeira (Freitas 2004). The search for the *Itaberaba-acú*, a mythical mountain of emeralds, was part and parcel of these expeditions (Buarque de Holanda 1968). However, it was not emeralds but gunpowder that first brought riches to Campo Formoso and cemented its connection to Cachoeira. The mule trains that brought the saltpeter from Campo Formoso's Rio Salitre to the Campo da Pólvora (Field of Gunpowder) in the Bahian capital passed through Cachoeira on Brazil's Royal Road.[1] The equipment and supplies that sustained the mines were disembarked from ships in Cachoeira to begin their overland journey into the sertão. Through the nineteenth and most of the twentieth century the two cities were linked by Bahia's railroad network, the Viação Ferrioviária do Leste (Zorzo 2001). Campo Formoso's mineral commodities went through Cachoeira on their way to the coast and the capital.

Today, however, these connections have lapsed. Highways have eclipsed railroads and waterways as the main means of moving goods and people through the interior. Cachoeira is no longer a hub of international commerce, but it remains a hub of a spiritual commerce that follows the routes traced by gunpowder. This commerce has taken a form that few could have predicted.

Nowadays, when the name of Cachoeira is heard in Campo Formoso, it is usually on the radio. Itinerant practitioners of Afro-Brazilian religions arrive in Campo Formoso or a nearby city and buy advertisements. Sonorous voice-overs promise potential clients that they can heal their struggling marriages, that they can reel in would-be lovers and straying husbands, that they can cure intractable diseases, break addictions, or ensure commercial success. New Age synthesizer music meanders in the background. Hard-bitten stone traders chuckle. If Macumba could really help you make money, then the *macumbeiros* would all be rich. Clearly they are not.

Many, perhaps most of the ads invoke Cachoeira: "Brother Cachoeira is consulting on Mondays and Thursdays in Senhor do Bomfim." "Sister Jurema from Cachoeira de São Félix has the solution to your love problems." Cachoeira is famous, and its fame is worth money in this context. It is the Cidade da Macumba, and people from the sertão have been going there to solve their spiritual problems for generations. Now Cachoeira comes to the sertão to save the *sertanejos* (backlanders) the trouble and expense of the journey.

The trouble is that these media-savvy healers are usually not from Cachoeira at all, nor are they adepts of Cachoeira's Candomblé. They practice a homegrown bricolage of palmistry, cartomancy, crystal-ball readings, and cowry-shell divinations. They prescribe ritual treatments that can be performed by the priest alone or even by the client herself with materials readily available from the local *loja de ervas*, or herb store. They charge for their divinations. They also charge for the rituals that those divinations reveal as necessary to cure the client's ills. Their diviners' fees are reasonable, but from the perspective of Cachoeira's Candomblé temples, the services they provide are not reasonable at all.

This is not to say that they don't work. Orthopraxis is by no means the sole determinant of ritual efficacy. Clients must believe that these traveling salesmen of the spirit can solve their problems; otherwise why would they pay them? Their faith, measured by the money they spend, can work wonders. However, to someone who has gone through the arduous initiation to Cachoeira's Candomblé and who has earned the right to work for clients through years of hard spiritual labor and the slow accumulation of ritual expertise, the ministrations of these itinerant magi are so much legerdemain and incoherent nonsense.

This perspective may not be available to sertanejo clients, and it might not matter if it were. These clients have no interest in maintaining the integrity of the initiatic system of Cachoeira's Candomblé or the ritual families it establishes. They have problems that they want to solve. If, during the process of their consultation, the priest or priestess can establish their authenticity, legitimacy, and efficacy to their clients, then the clients will contract their services, and those services will probably be effective. If the priest fails in this delicate act of self-presentation, the client will pay the fee for the initial consultation and go on her way.

Traveling healers are not the only ritual adepts who must argue for their authenticity. Respected priestesses in established Cachoeira cult houses undertake the same delicate negotiations, and they often fail. This in turn requires that the returns from successful spiritual transactions be high enough to maintain the priestess through the long dry spells that inevitably await. The shadow of the charlatan raises the prices for spiritual services across the entire Afro-Brazilian ritual continuum.

Prospective clients believe that some healers are effective and others are frauds. Stories of wondrous cures and money spent in vain on bogus rituals are equally easy to elicit in any backland Bahian town. They bubble up unbidden at any mention of Cachoeira in the sertão. The stakes are high. The clients are concerned with love and money, life and death. The prices for ritual services in Cachoeira and Campo Formoso alike can quickly exceed a month's wages. But there is no definitive way to distinguish the wheat from the chaff. True priests and gay deceivers alike draw on a common bank of symbols, techniques, and linguistic formulae. Authenticity is in the eye of the beholder, and the proof of efficacy is firmly in the pudding.

The value of a ritual service depends on its efficacy. However, it is impossible to determine the efficacy of a ritual in advance. This makes negotiations over the price of that ritual especially problematic. A ritual that is sold too cheap probably won't work. Simmel has it that money measures the desire of the individual to make use of a commodity. It is the objectification of the subjective value of that commodity (Simmel 1990; Deflem 2003). If the price of a ritual is set too low, it shortchanges the client's desire to see her problem resolved. It undercuts the subjective value and thus the ultimate efficacy of the ritual.

On the other hand, if a ritual is sold too dear, it leaves the priest open to the suspicion of fraud and thus undercuts the claims to authenticity on which the efficacy of the ritual is founded. This is particularly true of itinerant adepts. Does the radio priest want to make a killing and leave town before his ministrations are revealed as ackamarackus? Healers must make a living, but if they are gouging their clients, then their benevolence and thus their ability to heal becomes suspect.

Adam Smith's labor theory of value brings us to similar conclusions by a different path. "The real price of every thing, what every thing really costs to the man who wants to acquire it, is the toil and trouble of acquiring it" ([1776] 1976: 34). Spiritual power is won through long service to the *santos*, a toilsome and troublesome process by any measure.[2] Ritual efficacy is the fruit of that labor. A low-cost ritual would suggest that its purveyor had not worked long or hard enough to make that service truly effective. But a healing priced too high would make the client reflect on his own toil and trouble and measure it against a ceremony that is always potentially worthless.

The delicacy of negotiations over the price of a ritual ensures that many prescribed ceremonies go unperformed. They are commodities whose value is impossible to determine until after the transaction has been completed. Furthermore, they are sold by a group of people with a long-standing reputation for trickery. The immense potential value of a healing ceremony must be weighed against the possibility that the client's time and money will be spent in vain. Much the same is true of uncut emeralds.

All the Science in the World

Emeralds belong to the beryl family of minerals. Beryls form hexagonal crystals of varying clarity. Pure beryl is clear, but admixtures of other minerals give it various colors. When the aluminum ion in beryl is substituted for chrome, the crystals take on a distinctive and bewitching green hue. They are emeralds (Martins dos Santos 2009). The beryl family also includes aquamarine, heliodor, and other less-well-known gems. But emeralds alone have achieved the contentious and coveted title of precious stone.

The emeralds mined near Campo Formoso are found in a matrix of biotite schist, a crumbly black rock. They have formed through metasomatic processes at points of contact between layers of serpentine and layers of granite and quartz. They are also found in the faults and fractures in the rock near the contact points. In the early 1970s deposits of emeralds were found very near the earth's surface in the outlying district of Carnaiba. Today miners go more than two hundred meters into the ground in search of the green beryls.

What they find does not look like the emeralds in a jeweler's display case. When workers hit productive veins in the bottoms of the mines, they extract fist-sized lumps of black schist with beryl crystals inside them. Many of these emerald-bearing rocks find their way into mine workers' pockets and the tops of their heavy rubber gum boots, unbeknownst to the managers and owners of the small mines. Many more are carted out with the slag only to be discovered (and often secreted away) at the surface. This small-scale filching is universally recognized. It is considered a roguish and clever way to supplement a mine worker's meager salary. A man in Carnaiba who often deals in such stolen stones explained that you can't expect a worker to go underground all day for seventy or a hundred reais a month and be content with it.[3] If he sees something, he's going to take it. If the owner or the manager sees him doing it, he'll make him put it back in the sack, but he won't necessarily fire him for it. More stones are discarded in slag heaps only to be found by the *quijilas*, women who sift through mineralogical refuse looking for stray emeralds and molybdenum ore.

The stones that are not pilfered or thrown away are carried out in sacks by mine owners and the managers they employ. They then begin the laborious process of preparing them for sale. The outer layers of schist are chipped off with heavy pliers to reveal glimpses of the flat green crystal beneath. They are washed an oiled to provide potential buyers with a glimpse of the gems that they might contain. The stones then enter a series of complex and overlapping circuits of exchange.

Some buyers wait by the mouths of the mines to purchase the low-grade stones discovered by the quijilas. Others sit at the white tables that line the main street of Carnaiba de Cima, the hilltop settlement around the mines. Each one looks for lots of a particular kind of stone, large or small, potentially valuable or practically worthless. Buyers from Campo Formoso prowl the streets looking for stones to add to the lots that they will sell to the Rajasthani traders who cycle through the city. *Faisqueiros* (or sparkers) carry stones from their owners to potential buyers in hopes of miniscule commissions. *Corretores* (correctors, or sales agents) do much the same thing on a larger scale. The finest stones may never see the light of a Bahian day. They are quietly whisked off to the lapidaries who cut them and from there to international buyers who sell them in Asia, Europe, the Middle East, and North America or to the large jewelry firms in Rio de Janeiro and São Paulo.

Stones pass through dozens of hands before they find their way into a golden setting or a North Indian emerald workshop. My focus is on the negotiations that accompany each of these transactions. These negotiations are animated and complex, with sellers' asking prices and buyers' offers differing by orders of magnitude. Take this relatively simple example extracted from my field notes from August 6–8, 2009:

> I asked Xuxa what he was after. He wanted stones to sell to the Indians, but at the high end: big stuff in the neighborhood of ten reais per gram. The first

> thing that caught his eye came soon after we got out of the car. It was a huge pedra. He peered at it and cupped his hands around it to catch the light, but it was heavily overcast and not very good for looking at big stones. He asked the weight, and the seller told him that it was over seventy-five grams. [The rough is measured in grams vs. the cut, which comes in carats.][4] So we took it into a café where an incandescent lamp was screwed to the wall expressly for the purpose of peering at big stones. Xuxa was very impressed but was doing his best not to look excited. The seller brought us coffee, bread, and butter. They both hemmed and hawed before anyone was willing to name a price. Eventually it came out that the seller was asking 1,500. Xuxa offered 750. The seller looked crushed and walked away. We had another cup of coffee and went after him. After about an hour of wheedling each other in the streets and shops of Carnaiba, they settled on 850. Xuxa paid in cash in another café up the street. He chortled over his purchase and received the adulations of his colleagues all the way down the hill on our way back to Campo Formoso. They figured that he must have paid at least 1,500 for it.
>
> The next day, Xuxa took the stones that I watched him buy and put them into a lot that weighs 2 kilos. The lot is all made up of stones of that type, big and reasonably good. The lot is lacrado [closed and labeled] in the Indian's office while they work on a price. Xuxa's asking price was 32,000 reais. He said that he'd be willing to go down to 28,000. He paid an average of 6.69 r$ per gram for what I saw. If he got 28,000 for 2,000 grams, that would be 14R$ a gram, better than double what he paid. Nicely done, Xuxa.

These transactions are far simpler than the bulk of the emerald deals that happen in Campo Formoso. Xuxa bought the stone from its owner, added it to a lot that he owned free and clear, and brought it to the Indian buyers to negotiate with them himself. Most transactions would involve a much longer series of middlemen and professional negotiators, successful and failed deals, and a seemingly endless process of aggregation, separation, and improvement of larger lots of smaller stones. But even in this straightforward transaction we can see that the prices of the stones themselves are by no means fixed. The price of the seventy-five-gram rough pedra ranged from 750 to 1,500 reais. The price of the two-kilogram lot would be between 28,000 and 32,000 reais.

The prices ranged so widely because it is impossible to guess what sort of cut emerald the rough stone will yield. The seventy-five-gram pedra might yield a giant gem that was clear and richly colored and worth tens of thousands of reais. But it might just as likely be shot through with inclusions and imperfections. Its color might be dull and inconsistent. It might contain some hidden flaw that would cause it to turn to dust on the cutter's wheel.

Buyers can and do scrutinize the stones to their hearts' content, but the emeralds they contain will not reveal themselves until they are cut and polished by a lapidary. The balletic ritual of pouring over rough stones and the verbal performance of negotiating their price have far more to do with establishing the credentials and the savvy of the buyer and seller than with the characteristics of the stones at issue. These characteristics that differentiate a pearl beyond price from a piece of refuse are largely impossible to distinguish. One lapidary told me, "Pra comprar pedra bruta, toda ciência é pouca" (All the science in the world is not enough to buy rough stones).

The Art of Hammering a Nail

Emeralds are not like other mineral commodities. Gold, diamonds, and oil (all of which are mined in Bahia) are valued according to a fixed set of measurable characteristics. These characteristics are internationally recognized. The markets in these commodities are therefore far more efficient. A gram of gold or a round one-carat diamond graded G, VS1, or a barrel of light sweet crude will command much the same price in Rio de Janeiro, Amsterdam, or Istanbul.[5] This is not the case for emeralds. Their price and value defy international standardization. The qualities that make one emerald more desirable than another are beyond words and numbers. No international cartel controls their trade. No stock market determines their price. The value of the gems is an outcome of negotiations between miners, brokers, and traders.

The impossibility of determining the value of the cut emerald that a raw stone will yield makes the range in the price of a rough stone very wide. The indeterminacy of the price of raw stones makes transactions for emeralds uniquely liable to fraud. The most common form deception takes in the emerald market is known locally as *"batendo prego,"* or hammering a nail.

Nails are hammered when the owner of a stone or a lot of stones employs a professional negotiator to find a buyer for his merchandise. These negotiators are known as *corretores*, or correctors. Corretores know potential buyers, the sort of merchandise they prefer, and their bargaining styles. They are willing to perform the tiresome and occasionally vexing task of finding a buyer and negotiating a mutually acceptable price. The owner of the stones gives the corretor his merchandise and the range of prices that he will accept. Corretores either assess a flat fee or else take a percentage of the total transaction for their services.

Corretores will occasionally find a buyer who is willing to pay a price at the high end of the seller's acceptable range. The corretor will contact the seller and tell him that he has found a buyer but that the buyer is only willing to pay less than the owner is willing to accept. If the owner of the stones agrees to accept the price, the corretor hands the merchandise over to the buyer, gives the putative sale price to the seller and accepts his commission. Since the buyer in fact paid a much higher price than the corretor led the seller to believe, the negotiator can pocket the difference. He has hammered a nail into the owner of the stones.

Batendo prego is a universally recognized feature of dealings in the Rat Market. Sellers can expect that some of the corretores they employ will do their best to hammer them full of nails. This is not necessarily held to be a bad thing. The *prego* is evidence of the sort of roguish quick-wittedness that is essential to success in the emerald trade. Some dealers even claim to refuse to do business with corretores who do not *bater prego* because their lack of self-interest makes them worthless as negotiators.

Xuxa and his colleagues had a long conversation about pregos hammered on them as we returned from our trip to the mouth of the mines. It was as though the wily corretores, who are their colleagues and competitors at the same time, had beaten them at their own game, fair and square. In these stories the hero was clearly the corretor.

It is expected that *garimpeiros*, or mine workers, will steal any emeralds that present themselves in unguarded moments. It is equally expected that corretores will exploit the indeterminacy in the value of emeralds to dupe their owners into parting with their merchandise for far less than their clients are willing to pay. These two streams of deception often cross. The pilfering garimpeiros are particularly apt targets for the corretores' wiles, since they are not experienced traders and they would like to get rid of their merchandise quickly.

Deception and thievery are rife in the emerald business. The nimble-fingered garimpeiro and the sharp-dealing corretor are recognized and even celebrated by the very people whom their actions would seem to exploit. Labor relations in the emerald mines and the indeterminacy of the value of rough emeralds furnish the opportunities for pilfering and lies. But how are we to account for owners' complicity and even exultation in their trickery?

Perhaps it is because the ever-present possibility of self-interested deception brings into sharper relief the promise of the well-struck deal. When the corretor pockets the proceeds due to the stones' owner, he highlights the potential for those who have stones to sell them for ever-higher profits. Dealers often tell stories of the pregos they have received. They tell stories of buyers who paid ten times what they would have accepted just as often and with equal relish. The sneaky corretor reminds them that the indeterminacy of the value of raw stones can also work in their favor if only they can find the right buyer. They pursue their trade with renewed vigor in the hope of striking the deal that will change their lives. By the same token, when the mine worker filches a stone and turns a tidy profit, the owner realizes how much more wealth lies in the productive veins of his mine. Stealing is not a threat to his profits; it is their harbinger.

The specters of deception and thievery increase the allure of the rich vein and the profitable deal. So, too, does the ever-present shadow of the charlatan serve to underscore the value of the services of the authentic purveyor of magical services. Bad faith increases the value of the stones and ceremonies that are held to be good and true. This would seem to contradict classical economic and philosophical notions about the rational individual agent entering into exchanges with the totality of information available to him.

Saints of Lies, Saints of Liquor

The knowledge of the existence of charlatans is not the only factor that throws the value of Afro-Brazilian ritual services into question. Just as a shell of mica schist can conceal a worthless rock or a brilliant gem, so too can the bodily hexis of spirit possession performance conceal a fraud or reveal a veritable god on earth. With rough emeralds, as with saints incarnate, one can never be completely sure. The gods of Afro-Brazilian religions behave in stereotyped fashions during their sojourns on earth. These stereotypical performances vary among pantheons and regions. But they are recognizable and therefore imitable by those who are not actually possessed.

The caboclos are spirits of wild cowboys and Indians. When they come to earth in Cachoeira, they clench one fist behind their back and pace, their eyes bulging. They speak a distorted but conventionalized version of backland Portuguese and address their interlocutors as *Seu Moço* (Sir Youth) regardless of their age or sex. They dance a histrionic samba, kicking their legs toward the drummers. The *orixás* are more serene. They keep their eyes closed and do not speak or sing. They keep both hands behind their arched backs and sway gently as they wait for the drums to call them. Their dances are tightly choreographed. Even their characteristic screams (*ilá*) are somehow dignified and predictable.

Children in Cachoeira's poor neighborhoods grow up alongside its Candomblé temples. They delight in imitating the gods they see. Boys beat out the sacred rhythms on tin cans. Girls mime the behavior and the dances of orixás and caboclos. They mimic the screams of the saints that possess their neighbors, aunts, and grandmothers.

Tour groups and the occasional film crew come to Cachoeira to experience and record its Candomblé. But Candomblé ceremonies often take place at inconvenient times and with inadequate lighting. So tourists and videographers will sometimes contract a *folklore*. "Folklore" in the local parlance refers to a staged ceremony. Real adepts of Candomblé don the sacred wardrobe and dance the dances as *santos de mentira*, saints of lies. Observers who are not intimately acquainted with the participants in such performances may not be able to distinguish them from the real thing.

Such saints of lies appear for the amusement of the Candomblé faithful as well. Initiated members of Candomblé temples who do not become possessed will sometimes parody the possession behavior of the gods in informal ritual contexts. These are often the occasion of great drunken hilarity. I am often egged into adopting the role of Caboclo Gringo for the amusement of my Cachoeira coreligionists.

Children imitate the gods, drummers parody them, and tourists pay to see convincing simulacra. *Santos de mentira* are well ensconced in Cachoeira's streets and temples. The existence of saints of lies is fully accepted as a source of amusement or revenue. However, they become problematic when they seem to appear in actual Candomblé festivals, where divine visitations should be strictly authentic. This happens when those who are initiated to incarnate the orixás and caboclos fake their possessions for attention, for alcohol, or to conform to the expectations of the crowd.

Accusations of this sort of fakery are rarely made outright. But as members of other temples walk home, they begin a brutally critical *resenha*, or recounting, of the night's happenings. This resenha often includes speculations on the veracity of the possessions they witnessed. The next day, as the night's events are retold to friends and members of ritual families, accusations are amplified. The dances and actions of the saints of lies are mimicked to the cackles and guffaws of listeners.

The problem of fakery is especially acute in ceremonies for the caboclos. Drink flows freely at caboclo festivals. The gods themselves may demand or simply take it at any time. Spectators must wait for a divine invitation or accept it when it is proffered by the mistress of the house. After caboclo parties the alleged gods are often accused of being mere humans feigning possession for access to alcohol or reeling from the fumes of the booze that they had already consumed. Such false gods bear the name *santos de cachaça,* or saints of liquor.

The ubiquity of such counterfeit saints throws yet another wrench into negotiations over the efficacy and value of the ritual services sold by Candomblé adepts. If so much fakery abounds, how can a client be assured of the veracity of the saints whose powers she pays for? How can a priestess be sure that her children are bringing the gods she serves to earth and not merely imitating them for her benefit? These questions cannot be definitively answered. But the shadow of the false god makes the light of the putatively true orixá shine all the brighter. The successful priestess defines herself in explicit contradistinction to the charlatan and defines the gods whom she possesses and who possess her as true saints and not hollow, earthly imitations. If she can do so convincingly, the value of the services she provides will rise. Indeed they will rise all the higher for the knowledge that others are certainly faking it.

Marmots, Jelly, and Potatoes

As if that were not enough, perfectly respectable priestesses at the helms of centenarian temples are well known to stray from their own orthopractical canons. Goaded by necessity or by the demands of exigent clients, they mix elements of disparate traditions or perform ceremonies without the proper preparations to ensure their success. Thus wealthy clients on tight schedules may undergo a drastically abbreviated version of the initiation process but still consider themselves *feita,* fully "made" members of Candomblé houses.

One morning, five years ago, I was walking through a Saturday market with a Candomblé devotee. We spied an *iyawô,* a recent Candomblé initiate, walking with a member of her temple. She was tall, dark, and very beautiful. She had been born in Bahia but had married a foreigner and moved abroad. She had returned to be initiated and had undergone the ceremonies, but she still had a thick mane of curly hair. Initiates in the tradition of that temple should be shaven from head to toe with a straight razor. She was wearing colored clothes, while iyawôs are supposed to spend a year in pure white. She did not wear the *kelê,* a thick braided raffia cord, or the *chocalho,* a rattle worn at the ankle, that denotes her subordination to her initiating priestess. She did not wear the beaded necklaces that mark her subservience to the orixás.

I pointed her out to my companion. "Marmotagem," she scoffed. *Marmotagem* (literally translated as marmotry, the behavior of a marmot) is the defiance of Candomblé convention for fun or profit. But how could she do it, I asked. That priestess is one of the most respected religious leaders in town and is known all over the country. "She is a *marmoteira* and one of the finest," my friend responded. "She is the one who brought marmotagem to the city." I saw that priestess do wonderful work in Candomblé on many occasions, but she was not above exploiting her wealthy clients to sustain her temple.

Priestesses are often accused of using their divination ceremonies (*jogos de búzio*) to "discover" problems that clients do not actually have. They find dead relatives haunting the clients' lives and closing their roads to romantic and financial success. They discover jealous neighbors and rivals scattering sorcery powder at their homes and places of business. The clients must then decide whether or not to contract the expensive ceremonies that would remedy these ills. But it is impossible to know whether these malignant spirits and poisoning neighbors actually exist. A savvy and unscrupulous priestess with a convincing patter to go with her cowry-shell oracle can quickly make marmots of her troubled and unsuspecting clients.

By the same token, priestesses may take money for ritual sacrifices but skimp on the necessary supplies and pocket the difference. They may ignore the ritual prohibitions on drink, sex, and certain foods called *resguardos* that are necessary to ensure that ceremonies will succeed. They may put on lavish public ceremonies without performing the series of private oblations that ought to underlie them. They may borrow elements from multiple traditions and mix them indiscriminately while still claiming an orthodox adherence to one of Candomblé's denominations (*nações*). They may invent new traditions or new ritual actions while boasting of their fidelity to the ways of their ancestors. They may learn songs, ceremonies, or ritual formulae from books, even books published by anthropologists, but claim that they had learned them through oral transmission or divine revelation. This sort of self-interested, showy spirit-mongering is reviled in the community of Candomblé practitioners as *gelaba com batata*, or jelly with potatoes, the pernicious mixing of things that should be kept separate.

Along with marmotism and the saints of lies and liquor, the possibility that a priestess might be mixing jelly with her potatoes complicates the negotiation of her religious legitimacy and the efficacy of the ritual services that she provides. Clients can never know for sure. Neither can anyone else. A caboclo could be a true saint one day and an ethanol-fueled delusion the next. Two observers of the same god at the same time might disagree as to his veracity. A priestess might conduct a ceremony for one client with loving care and for another with greedy deceit and deeply cut corners. She might adhere to putatively pure traditions on one occasion and invent incoherent mixtures on another. There are no external means by which her conduct may be judged. There is only the encounter with the client over the divining table and the momentous decision as to whether or not to contract her services.

Profit and the Problem of Evil

The indeterminacy of the value of rough emeralds and the ritual services sold by adepts of Afro-Brazilian religions makes these two forms of commerce especially liable to fraud. Clients and buyers cannot know what they are getting ahead of time. They enter into negotiations with priestesses and sellers knowing that they run the risk of buying substandard stones or contracting worthless ceremonies. These same negotiations are fraught with peril for the sellers and priestesses as well. They work in a morally ambivalent arena, dealing in valuable and troublesome commodities and trafficking with powers that can defy their control. The money that they gain from these transactions can be dangerous and must be spent with circumspection. Otherwise the stones and the spirits may get the best of their purveyors and lead them down the road to perdition. The money becomes dangerous to the people who make it.

The dangers associated with earning a living from sorcery or from the emerald trade can be ameliorated if the money is used in the service of moral causes. Successful traders and priestesses alike must not grow too rich from their occupations. They must funnel the profits back into their communities lest they get the better of them. This popularly held belief is reinforced by numerous stories recounted in Cachoeira and Campo Formoso alike.

Perhaps the most famous and the most tragic tale of the dangers that attend on success in the emerald trade is the story of Gupta. I heard it on my first trip to the Rat Market and many times since. In its broadest outlines, it goes something like this.

Gupta was the first of the Indian traders to come to Campo Formoso. He bought vast amounts of emeralds of all qualities and took them back to Rajasthan. He was well loved by miners and traders for his open disposition. However, he was the only buyer capable of dealing in large quantities of low-grade stones. He was therefore able to exert great control over the prices. He prospered. He founded a firm in India and built a huge home in

Campo Formoso. One day he became embroiled in a dispute over money with one of his Brazilian partners. Heated words and accusations of thievery were exchanged. The Brazilian left, procured a gun, and then shot and killed Gupta. Gupta's wife, distraught, would never return to Campo Formoso. She donated their home to the city, and it is now a clinic for the aged and disabled.

Gupta's story is only one of the many that remind emerald dealers of the dangers of immoderate profit. An affable trader told me how he had made more than a million reais after being granted the exclusive right to scavenge the slag heaps of a famous mine at its productive peak. He married the beautiful daughter of a local landowner. Then he lost his millions at a poker table. He is respected and well loved in the Rat Market for his openhanded generosity and his breadth of experience. But he is reviled by his in-laws for his relative penury. His taste for strong drink and extramarital dalliance does little to raise him in the estimation of his Presbyterian relatives by marriage. Today he tries to raise capital to make his next big score, and he swears that he'll never go near a poker table again.

Dona Gracina is a widow who could have been rich many times over. Her now deceased husband extracted millions of reais worth of emeralds from their mine. He also gave her twelve children, who have given her sixty grandchildren. Her sons, like their father before them, are able miners and ardent procreators but not astute managers of their personal finances. In tunnels hundreds of feet underground they told me stories of designer shoes and old scotch whiskey; of cars and motorcycles bought, totaled, and replaced; of women in the once resplendent brothels of Carnaiba's salad days. But their tales of luxury stood in sharp contrast to the torn and faded dresses of their wives and the bare feet of their children who gathered around Gracina at the mouth of the mine. They were looking for the sparkle of *estanho* in a rusted sieve. This molybdenum ore sustains many owners of unproductive emerald mines. They needed to find enough for their weekly trip to the market, and there were many mouths to feed.

Josana works underground in Gracina's mine and as a corretora in Carnaiba's stone markets, runs a bar on weekends, and raises the daughter that she bore to her now estranged husband. He was a miner but was ruined by his own success. He abandoned his wife and their child in the first flush of prosperity. Now that he is broke and an alcoholic, he is too ashamed to return. Today he raises some skinny cows and stunted crops on a small patch of toxic earth. Emeralds form in the fissures of serpentine rock. But serpentine poisons soil (and miner's lungs), and it makes a mockery of farmers' attempts at agriculture. It is a humiliating fate to go from mineral riches to manual agricultural labor. Josana's husband won't speak to her, and a cloud passes over her proud face at the mention of his name.

These sorts of stories abound. People whisper about the once great fortunes of the drunken bums who beg them for change or cadge drinks and cigarettes. The outlines of such tales are always the same: someone strikes it big through lucky mining or smart trading. They spend their money on intoxication, adornment, automobiles, lavish entertainments for their many new friends, and extravagant expenditures on ladies of the night. They are ruined or killed, or they find themselves back in the bottom of a mine looking for the next big strike. Local lore once had it that the only way to ensure that one would find more emeralds was to spend the money earned on parties and prostitutes. Profits gained through the emerald trade ruined so many lives and families that they seem immoral even to the people who are chasing them. An aging woman pouring over the slag heaps told me that "esmeralda é do diabo" (emeralds are from the devil).

Profits from sorcery are at least as dangerous as those from emeralds, and their diabolical origin is much more in evidence. Even ritual healing carries significant risks. All sorts of instrumental magic in Candomblé and its associated Afro-Brazilian religious traditions call upon pantheons of exús and *egúns*. Exús are amoral and occasionally diabolical demons, pimps and tricksters. Their imagery abounds with horns, skulls, pitchforks, and engorged phalli. Their songs are replete with references to Lucifer and the gates of hell. Egúns are the much more dangerous spirits of the dead. They are treated with much greater care and circumspection than the rowdy and companionable exús. Witchcraft that calls upon their powers is especially feared, and healing clients of such witchcraft is especially dangerous to the clients and the adepts alike.

In healing ceremonies, priestesses and their congregations seek to propitiate these troublesome spirits with song and sacrifice so that they will leave their clients in peace. In magic rituals with specific earthly ends, they render offerings to these demons to work on clients' behalf. In the case of sorcery proper, by which I mean rituals with specifically malignant intent, they render similar offerings with an eye toward harming the client's enemies. Adepts may also manufacture magical poisons called *pemba preta*, infused with the power of these spirits, and sprinkle them on the home, the possessions, or the person of the intended victim.

In each case the adept is taking a calculated risk. Popular wisdom holds that "o feitiço vira contra o feiticeiro" (the sorcery can turn against the sorcerer). Too intimate relations with such powerful and problematic entities can jeopardize the life and the livelihood of the practitioner. But a Candomblé adept in Cachoeira can no more live without magic than an emerald miner can live without emeralds. Exú and egún are their stock-in-trade. Clients may come to consult caboclos incarnate, they may pay *promessas* (ritual debts for divine services rendered) to the orixás, or they may orient their lives on the basis of cowry-shell divination. But for the most part they come to be healed of the supernatural malice inflicted on them by their enemies, to inflict their enemies some supernatural malice of their own, or to advance some earthly scheme using the power of exú. They pay handsomely for these services. Their payments sustain priests and priestesses as religious professionals.

Sorcery is a dangerous means of production. Those who succeed too well may pay the ultimate price. One night in 2004 I heard an unfamiliar name in a litany of egúns who were called upon in a healing ceremony. The singer was invoking powerful deceased priests and priestesses to expel the spirits of the dead from the body of his client. I knew most of the names from my genealogies, but one stood out. When the work was done, I elicited his story. His name was Adalho. He was a priest with no temple but a great reputation. He had engaged in magical duels with another famous sorcerer of yore. But what killed him in the end was his own witchcraft. He used it to kill the wrong person. His tutelary gods withdrew the mantle of their protection. He was left exposed to attack. He joined the egúns, still powerful, but now unquestionably dead.

Nicolau was a sorcerer who never charged in advance.[6] He never needed to. He would tell his clients that if their enemy was not brought low within twenty-one days, his services would be free. But if the sorcery worked, they would have to pay him immediately, or else they would be next. He did his work possessed, consulting his clients and performing the services they required while incarnating exú. His exú, like so many others, had a taste for cane liquor and cheap cigars. As Nicolau's fame spread and his clientele increased, he earned more money, but he also spent more and more time possessed. His own personality merged with that of the demon whom he was supposed to command. The slave god came to own his putative master. Alcohol, tobacco, and a life of unalloyed malice killed Nicolau. In spite of his hundreds of paying clients, he received a pauper's funeral with no one to mourn his untimely passing.

Stories like these highlight the dangers associated with success in emerald dealing and in magic, healing, and witchcraft. But it is not as though these dangers overtake every dealer, priest, and priestess. Many of them manage to counterbalance their participation in these risky trades with a steady stream of payments to the people in their community and to the gods or god whom they serve. These remittances ameliorate the perils of personal success in these troublesome trades. They allow adepts, miners, and dealers to sustain themselves and their families and to support their communities even as they work against the untrammeled aggregation of individual wealth. The section that follows shows how moral community can be born from such morally fraught enterprises as the selling of emeralds and spiritual services.

Laying Up Treasures in Heaven

In spite of their often unsavory reputations, emerald dealing and Afro-Brazilian religion can both be eminently moral occupations. Both provide paths by which perennially impoverished and disenfranchised people from backland towns can prosper in the economic milieus that were built on their exploitation. This prosperity depends on the restraint of individual avarice with all of its attendant risks. In order to avoid the twin jeopardies of divine revenge and sumptuous self-destruction, those who ply these risky trades must plough their profits back into enterprises that are unequivocally good. For Afro-Brazilian adepts this means investing in the cult of the orixás and in their own ritual families. For emerald miners and dealers it means lending money to fellow traders in tight straits or subsidizing the Protestant congregations that have been evangelizing the backcountry for more than a century.

There is much more to Candomblé and its cognate Afro-Brazilian religious traditions than the healing, sorcery, and magic discussed above. The profits from these instrumental ceremonies underwrite a complex and beautiful cult of orixás, caboclos, ancestors, and the saints of popular Catholicism. Healing and witchcraft are most often done for clients who seek out adepts, contract their services, pay them, and go on their ways. Ceremonies for orixás and caboclos, on the other hand, anchor large ritual families into webs of obligation to each other and to the gods they serve.

The high gods of Candomblé are very demanding of their devotees. They require lavish parties replete with the finest raiment, delicate cuisine, and sumptuous decorations. They also require untold gallons of sacrificial blood to cement their relationships to their initiatic children. While the blood feeds the gods, the meat from the sacrificial animals feeds the hundreds of attendees at parties in honor of the orixás. Animals, lace, liquor, brocade, beans, honey, oil, and the rest of the supplies necessary to honor the orixás do not come cheap. Some of these expenses are defrayed through the mundane day jobs of devout practitioners. But day jobs are hard to come by in rural Bahia. Even the most exacting economies might not satisfy the demands of the gods and the desires of the practitioners to fête their tutelary deities in regal style. Some of these expenses are defrayed by the wealthy (and often white) patrons of Candomblé temples. This fact has been frequently cited by anthropologists who have fallen into this role (for example Ramos [1934] 1988). But such patrons can be hard to find, and anthropologists (though they are not in short supply) may not have the resources or the inclination to assume the role of religious benefactor.

Priests and priestesses have a revenue stream that does not depend on mundane work or on the largesse of local whites and foreigners. The work that they do with exús and egúns sustains their cult of the orixás. It also sustains many of the initiatic obligations of their ritual children. If work with exús and egúns is morally problematic, the worship of the orixás is held to be unequivocally good. If the orixás are properly propitiated, they can shield their followers from the potentially negative consequences of working too closely with exús and egúns. The constant demands of the orixás, coupled with the need to care for the spiritual and physical needs of large ritual families ensure that priestesses who uphold their obligations will not grow rich. However, with some luck and some astute dealings with their clients, most of them can at least get by. Exús are the slaves of the orixás, and if devotees pay the requisite homage to the high gods, they can be assured of their ability to appropriate the labor of their slaves on earth.

In addition to these strictly religious duties, priestesses have a host of mundane obligations. Their temple compounds often house members of their extended families and local communities whose religious faith is surpassed only by their poverty. Such indigent acolytes live in the temple's rooms and sup at its table until marriage, success, or interpersonal strife leads them to seek a house of their own. Many priestesses raise the children born of evanescent unions in the backcountry. Their impecunious mothers know that adepts of Candomblé have a stream of income and a strong religious sensibility. All priestesses raise large families of initiatic children, who often lack the means to fund their own devotions. Priestesses are often pillars of communities, even in matters that are not strictly religious. Many temples hold secular entertainments at which they provide music, food, and drink to the members of their communities. The sacred and profane demands on a priestess's largesse only increase with her income. If she fulfills them, she will not run much risk of becoming wealthy.

Emerald miners and traders may have a slightly easier time of it, but there are plenty of claims on their mineral wealth as well. Stones can be very expensive, and local traders might not have the capital necessary to buy the large lots that the Rajasthani traders demand. The cost of Xuxa's transaction described above was more than triple the annual municipal GDP per capita in Campo Formoso in 2007.[7] In order to defray these costs, miners borrow from their colleagues. Upon the successful completion of a lucrative transaction, they pay off their debts and loan out their profits through an elaborate system of postdated checks, promissory notes, and hastily negotiated handshake agreements. Some of these agreements include a provision for interest, but many more do not. These overlapping credit relationships allow the traders to sustain their enterprise without the vast sums that would be required to go it alone. Banks are understandably unwilling to make loans to participants in this gray-market economy. The traders provide for one another. If they do so conscientiously, they can avoid the pitfalls of unrestrained consumption and be assured of the largesse of their colleagues in the inevitable hard times to come.

The mundane necessity to lend out money to ensure access to capital in the future might seem like a self-interested and even rational capitalist endeavor. However, there are sacred claims on miners' profits as well. These often come from the Protestant churches that dot the Bahian backcountry. The ethic that they inculcate seems to have little to do with the worldly asceticism of Weber's ([1904] 2003) sturdy Puritans. It does protect miners and traders from the potentially negative consequences of their own success.

I was surprised by the profusion of Protestant churches of all stripes in Campo Formoso and Carnaiba. One finds North American missionary denominations alongside Pentecostal and neo-Pentecostal congregations, Seventh-Day Adventists, and more. Towns that once echoed with gunplay and the music of the brothels now echo with the amplified voices of pastors overtaken by the Holy Spirit. Men who once destroyed great fortunes in orgies of sumptuary consumption now invest in their homes, their families, their churches, and the education of their children. An ethic of character development and moral improvement has begun to replace an ethic in which men were judged by their liberality in consumption and entertainment. A network of Pentecostal miners and traders now extends throughout Brazil and connects Brazilian gemstone dealers to their church brethren in the United States and across the world. This network, anchored in religious faith, has temporal dimensions as *irmãos em Cristo* (brothers in Christ) enter into reciprocal relationships of trust and credit.

The trader Daniel exemplifies this trend. Daniel is a lifelong Seventh-Day Adventist. He regaled me with stories of great strikes, vast profits, trips to the United States, Mercedes-Benzes bought and sold. But his house was that of a comfortable but humble workingman. We were sitting in the living room. "Garimpeiros are supposed spend all their money on liquor and prostitutes," I said, "but you don't even eat meat. If you've made all this money, why aren't your rich?"

He opened his Bible (though he didn't really need to) and quoted me some verses about treasures in heaven (that he had clearly memorized long ago). He explained that he had used his money to build churches. He had already built six Adventist churches in Brazil, and if God continued to bless him with prosperity, he would build one for every year that he lived on earth.

By expending the profits from emeralds on religious obligations and supporting the efforts of fellow traders, emerald dealers avoid the dangers associated with excessive consumption. These dangers are real. Drugs, alcohol, gambling, and prostitution have destroyed many families in Carnaiba and Campo Formoso. Evangelical miners may not save and accumulate as Weber's Protestant ethic would prescribe. They do, however, manage to keep their businesses afloat and even reasonably prosperous. If emeralds are from the devil, at least some of the miners have managed to marshal their profits in the service of God.

The Fetish and the Stone

Candomblé was born in the maw of one of the most brutal labor regimes that has ever existed: the Atlantic system of slavery, sugar, and tobacco. The emerald trade in Campo Formoso arose from the expeditions that sought to evangelize or exterminate the native peoples of Brazil. Adepts of Afro-Brazilian religions took the phantoms that haunted the nightmares of the people who enslaved them—their devils, demons, and evil spirits—and turned them into sources of power and profit on earth. The miners of the sertão catered to the baser desires of their colonizers. They provided the gunpowder that fueled their wars. They provided the gold, diamonds, amethysts, and emeralds that stimulated their vanity.

Bahia's interpolation into world economies has rarely been beneficial to its inhabitants. Yet the same people whose labor was exploited carved out a few niches for themselves at the interstices of this economy, and some even found a modicum of prosperity. They struggle to sustain and reinvigorate their communities in contexts where the decks have always been stacked against them. They exploit the evils and the ambiguities in the system that encompasses them. In doing so, they transform both moral and economic values. The malice inherent in sorcery and even healing underwrites the families that are united in the worship of the benevolent and beautiful orixás. The vanity of women from Jaipur to Manhattan who want to deck themselves in precious stones funds the propagation of Protestant asceticism in the Bahian backlands.

These processes are not straightforward by any means, but this is perhaps for the best. If sorcery and ritual healing and the mining and marketing of emeralds were susceptible to capitalist rationalization, then the capitalists probably would have rationalized them long ago. Instead they depend on ambiguity and unpredictability. Values can never be precisely calculated. Profits can never be accurately predicted. Fraud is omnipresent and ineradicable.

Deception is not anathema in this system, and neither is transparency necessarily valued. Adepts of Afro-Brazilian religions and traders in emeralds alike thrive on the ambiguities inherent in their professions. The ever-present possibilities of hucksterism and sharp dealing enhances the values of the commodities that they provide. In order to prosper, these entrepreneurs of stones and spirits must present themselves and their wares as authentic in their negotiations with their clients. The value of the goods that they purvey comes to depend on interpersonal relationships formed through intricate negotiations. The knowledge that these negotiations can and usually do fail only raises the stakes.

Perhaps this perspective derived from the ethnographic study of charlatanism and thievery could be applied to other, more familiar spheres of economic action. Perhaps the apparently rational, mathematical calculations of profit and loss in other industries shrouds a confidence game in which authenticity and morality are really at issue. Perhaps the invisible hand that guides the market is more akin exú's deceptions than God's providence. Perhaps the commodities transacted in stock markets are no more subject to exact valuation than the rough emeralds in the Rat Market. But perhaps these depths are better left unplumbed.[8]

SIX

Demons and Money: Possessions in Brazilian Pentecostalism

STEPHEN SELKA

The Universal Church of the Kingdom of God (or IURD, Igreja Universal do Reino de Deus) is often cited as the fastest-growing church in Brazil. The IURD's impressive growth stems from its bold promises of material prosperity and relief from demonic afflictions. Here I focus on this juxtaposition of a central concern with material prosperity and a strong emphasis on exorcism[1] and on how spiritual and material possession are related and opposed in the IURD. This chapter is based on ethnographic fieldwork I have been conducting in the town of Cachoeira, a small town in the interior of the state of Bahia, since 1999. Cachoeira is both a center of Afro-Brazilian Candomblé and home to a wide array of Pentecostal churches. Here concerns about possession by spirits and of resources permeate everyday life.

On a Friday afternoon in late August 2009, I headed to the branch of the IURD in Cachoeira. The service I attended was sparsely attended; there were only seven of us in the pews. I was the only man in the church except for the pastor, a tall, prematurely bald man in his thirties. Throughout the service he darted back and forth in front of the altar, his robe flowing behind him as his voice boomed from the loudspeakers.

Soon after the service began, the pastor asked us to put our hands on top of our heads and pray. The women around me spoke in tongues as the pastor approached one of them who was standing in the front row. He placed his large hands on her head and asked that she be liberated from the *macumba* [a generally negative term for Candomblé] work, from the cemetery dirt, from the *pemba* [a substance, usually a powder, used in Candomblé work]." His voice rose as he asked that she be liberated "from the work done by spirits who are fed at the beach on at the banks of the river." He commanded the spirit to leave the woman's body in the name of Jesus.

For a moment her body shook and swayed like that of someone being possessed in Candomblé. Then it was over; the woman, her face drained but calm, plopped down in her seat.

After the rest of us sat down, the pastor began to preach. He complained that the media had been attacking the IURD for the last two weeks because Edir Macedo, the founder and leader of the IURD, had been accused of money laundering. The scandal was covered in the international news, as in this article in the *Guardian*: "Following an investigation into 10 years of the church's financial activities, prosecutors accused church leaders of illegally channeling donations from their largely impoverished flock into overseas accounts and businesses before returning the money to Brazil where it was allegedly used to invest in media outlets and property." ("Brazilian Evangelical Leader Charged with Fraud," *Guardian*, August 13, 2009). This was not the first time that Macedo had been charged with malfeasance. In 1991, the former leader of the Universal Church of the Kingdom of God in northeast Brazil, Carlos Magno de Miranda, accused Macedo of "tax evasion, involvement with drug trafficking and sending dollars overseas illegally" (Mariano 2004: 126; translation mine). Here is a description of some of the events surrounding the scandal:

> On May 24, 1992, accused of committing the crimes of charlatanism, shamanism and embezzlement, Macedo was imprisoned in the 91st precinct of the São Paulo police, where he remained incarcerated in a special cell for twelve days until released by habeas corpus. On Christmas Eve of 1995, Carlos Magno began the charge again by making public an unedited video, recorded in 1990, in which Edir Macedo appeared laughing while counting money in a temple in New York, having fun on a yacht in Angra dos Reis, and instructing the pastors, during the break in the middle of a football game, to be more effective in collecting tithes and offerings. (Mariano 2004: 126; translation mine)

These accusations prompted a government investigation of the church and its media holdings. In response, the IURD complained of religious persecution and media bias. From the late 1990s until 2009, however, the church managed to stay out of the headlines and continued to flourish in Brazil and beyond.

Not surprisingly, the pastor in Cachoeira raised the same objections against the media as his predecessors had during earlier scandals involving the IURD. He argued that the media only presented the church in a negative light: "Do they show the good that Universal does? No! Do they show the delinquents and gangsters that Universal has liberated? No!" He returned to the press coverage several more times during his sermon on the liberating power of Jesus, at one point asking rhetorically: "Where does this coverage come from? Satan!" Even with the recent attention to the IURD's questionable finances hanging over the service, the pastor was not at all shy about asking us to come up to the front of the church to give whatever money we could before we left. As in the other examples I explore below, this service brought together two of the foundational concerns of neo-Pentecostalism in addition to healing: demons and money.

With this in mind, this chapter explores interrelated understandings of spiritual and material possession—"possession by" and "possession of"—in the IURD and similar neo-Pentecostal churches. Spirit possession is central to Afro-Brazilian religions such as Candomblé and Umbanda. Yet many Pentecostal Christians believe that the spirits that possess the practitioners of these religions are demons, and the practices of the IURD in particular focus on liberating people from demonic influence. This influence is seen as the cause of afflictions ranging from physical illness to depression and of misfortunes such as divorce or unemployment.

In addition, some Pentecostal churches, especially third-wave or neo-Pentecostal ones, espouse what is often referred to derisively as the "theology of prosperity." Also known as the "health and wealth" gospel in North America, its proponents preach that the acquisition of material possessions is possible through faith.[2] The IURD and similar neo-Pentecostal churches combine their promises of prosperity with an emphasis on deliverance from demons. At first glance the relationship between these two kinds of possession might seem spurious, but they are closely connected. In the most explicit formulation of this connection, as we see in the IURD, liberation from spiritual possession opens the way for the accumulation of material possessions. That is, demonic control (possession by) impedes our realization of the prosperity (possession of) that God desires for human beings.

Most observers agree that it is no coincidence that Pentecostals are among the most visible and fastest-growing religious groups in Brazil, a country that has one of the largest and most rapidly growing consumer economies in Latin America—but also a high rate of poverty-related sicknesses (Chesnut 1997, 2007). In fact, the IURD in particular is now a global phenomenon; today it has churches throughout Latin America and Africa, as well as in North America and Europe. With respect to this global reach, many observers have emphasized the affinity between the IURD and neoliberal capitalism (Comaroff and Comaroff 2002; E. Kramer 1999; Campos

1997; Oro 1996; Mariano 1996). Jean and John Comaroff, for example, view the IURD in Africa as a vehicle for ordinary people befuddled by the global economy to seek immediate material gains via occult forces. These "occult economies" obscure the relationship between means and ends, generating "disturbing caricatures of market enterprise in motion" (Comaroff and Comaroff 2002: 786). In the theology of prosperity, for example, material gain comes not through labor but through sacrifices of money. As the Comaroffs write: "Highly controversial in its country of origin, this new Protestant denomination—which is rumored to issue charmed credit cards that register no debt—promises instant goods and gratification to those who embrace Christ and denounce Satan; but, as the local pastor put it, believers have also to 'make their faith practical' by publicly "sacrificing" as much cash as they can to the movement. Here Pentecostalism meets neoliberal enterprise: the chapel is, literally, a storefront in a shopping precinct" (1999: 291). In this view, the IURD appears somewhere between a pyramid scheme and a cargo cult.

Other observers of the IURD have focused more on rationalization than enchantment, however. Oro (2001), for example, argues that sacrifices of money in the IURD (more commonly known as the *dizimo*, or tithe) combine the logic of the gift with the logic of the market. From this perspective the dizimo is a quantified gift, and the fact that tithers expect a greater return for a greater donation suggests a certain kind of rationalized calculation. As Sansi points out, viewing the IURD in terms of occult economies "underestimates the rationalization and strategic planning of these churches" (2007: 320). That is, the IURD that has spread across the globe has followed the pattern of the expansion of a multinational corporation, and thus it represents less a caricature of market enterprise than the very embodiment of it. Indeed, the IURD thrives by bringing together seemingly antagonistic forces: rationalizing bureaucracy, consumer capitalism, and popular religiosity (cf. Semán 2001). At the same time, such combinations are not entirely new. Although some have stressed that the IURD is a religion of money (Campos 1997; Guareschi 1995; Jardilino 1994; Mariano 1996), Sansi reminds us that money and the market "are present in everyday religion in Brazil from its very origins" (2007: 334; cf. Baptista 2007). The exchange of money and the use of coins in ritual have long been central to Candomblé, for example (Brazeal, this volume).

The IURD is a global religious franchise whose growth stems not simply from its promises of prosperity but from its uncanny ability to engage local forms of religiosity. In Brazil, the IURD is keyed to Candomblé, a religion with which it shares a cosmological vision and ritual logic. The spirits from which one is delivered in the IURD, for example, are the very ones that are venerated in Candomblé. Indeed, the fact that residents of a place are befuddled by global economic forces is not enough for the IURD to thrive there; it is most successful where anxiety about demons and witchcraft already exists. As Oro (2004) argues, the IURD's concern with Satan is universal; what varies is the local form of religious practice that is taken to embody the satanic. The IURD engages such local practices in a way that sets up a complementary opposition similar to that between sorcerer and healer in African diaspora religions, thereby absorbing and reflecting that which it opposes along the way.[3] Yet this absorptive or reflective tendency involves more than the appropriation of selected elements. I argue that in Brazil neo-Pentecostal churches like the IURD and Afro-Brazilian religions such as Candomblé form complementary aspects of a single ritual network.

At the same time, I am not suggesting that evangelicals are simply practicing Candomblé under a different name. Here I echo others who have emphasized the ways that Pentecostalism differentiates itself from local religions in local terms, thereby indigenizing difference and managing to embody continuity and rupture at the same time (Robbins 2004, 2003; Coleman 2010). Without a doubt, many people dabble in Pentecostalism for various reasons that have nothing to do with earnest conversion. But for a considerable number of followers, the material prosperity that the IURD and similar churches promise is deeply intertwined with fears of demonic possession and hopes of the fulfillment of divine promises. In this context we see a shift of orientation through the polarization of spiritual agents who are identified with clear moral stances. What is continuous with the logic of Candomblé (and Umbanda, as we will see) here is the idea that sacrifice leads to remuneration; what is discontinuous is the emphasis on deliverance in order to take advantage of what is freely given by God. That is, the neo-Pentecostal repudiation of spirit possession in the name of autonomy (deliverance from possession by spirits) and accumulation (taking possession of material goods) casts the agents of attainment in Candomblé as agents of affliction and introduces a moral critique of certain paths to prosperity, thereby diverging in significant ways from the logic of both Candomblé and the market.

Ethnographic Setting

This chapter focuses on the Bahian Recôncavo, a center of Afro-Brazilian culture. The Recôncavo encompasses Salvador, the urban capital of Bahia situated on the coast, and the rural town of Cachoeira located in the interior. With a population of about 31,000 (Instituto Brasileiro Geográfica e Estadística 2005), Cachoeira is located about 110 kilometers inland from coastal Salvador and sits in a valley on the banks of the Paraguaçu River. The local economy is largely geared toward agriculture, and many of the businesses in town provide farming products or equipment repairs to the residents of the surrounding rural areas. Recently, however, an Italian-owned leather factory opened nearby, and several public works projects were initiated in Cachoeira, providing other sources of employment. The town also supports a modest tourist traffic that focuses on its colonial architecture and Afro-Brazilian traditions, including Candomblé.

The Candomblé that is practiced in Brazil today is a complex, hierarchical religion derived from a variety of practices that Africans brought to Brazil. The initiates are predominantly women, ranked by degree of initiation and ceremonial function. Candomblé practice revolves around the pantheon of African *orixás* and other spirits who possess their devotees in public ceremonies and to whom offerings are made in both public and private rituals. Candomblé *terreiros* are found in cities throughout Brazil, yet the oldest and most famous of them were established in the Recôncavo.

Around thirty regularly functioning terreiros exist in Cachoeira, several of which have histories that can be traced back to the nineteenth century. Day-to-day life at terreiros includes fulfilling *obrigações* (ritual obligations) to the orixás and other entities, such as animal sacrifices, food offerings, and other such rituals. These obligations are due on days that are dedicated to particular entities, before public celebrations, and as part of the requirements of initiation. Other kinds of spiritual work, including *limpezas* (cleanings) and *ebós* (offerings), are performed for paying clients. These may be aimed at healing, causing a person to fall in love, or harming someone, among other purposes.

According to research on the nationwide census, about 1.3 percent of the Brazilian population reports being involved with Candomblé (Prandi 1995). This modest statistic, however, probably reflects only the formally initiated. Initiation is a lengthy and expensive process, so few participate in the daily activities of the terreiro, most of which are not open to the public. A significantly larger number of people attend or have attended public Candomblé ceremonies or have consulted with a Candomblé practitioner for a number of possible reasons, including problems with health, money, or relationships. Judging from questionnaires I distributed and conversations with people in the field, I estimate that somewhere between one-third and one-half of Bahians living in Cachoeira had visited a terreiro at some point in their lives.

A large percentage of the town's population, however—somewhere between a fifth and a third—identify themselves as evangelical Christian. Groups of evangelicals heading to or from church, dressed in pressed shirts and long dresses with Bibles tucked under their arms, are as much a part of Cachoeiran street life as the ubiquitous vendors of *acarajé* (a fritter made from black-eyed peas and cooked in palm oil). Every evening one can hear amplified prayers reverberating through the streets Cachoeira, and every year I return, I find several new storefront churches open in the town center.

Nationwide, approximately 20 percent of Brazilians are evangelical Christians (Prandi 1995; Freston 1994). Generally speaking, evangelical churches differ from historical or mainstream Protestant denominations in their emphasis on the literal interpretation of the scriptures, the imminent second coming of Christ, and the separation of the faithful from the ways of this world (Freston 1994; Novaes and Floriano 1985; Costa 1979). In addition, Pentecostals, who make up about two-thirds of all evangelicals, emphasize the expression of certain "gifts of the Holy Spirit" such as speaking in tongues and faith healing by the laying on of hands. Moreover, many historically evangelical but non-Pentecostal churches, particularly Baptist ones, have become increasingly Pentecostal in their practices.

While evangelical churches in Cachoeira vary in many details, common elements include a relatively simple, if not spartan, church design in comparison to some of the elaborately baroque Catholic churches in town. Formal evangelical worship takes place in services that are held from several times a week to several times a day, depending on the church, as well as in weekly prayer meetings held in members' homes. Church services are typically quite vibrant and noisy; the sounds of hymns and praise usually echo well beyond the walls of the church. Visitors are almost always invited to come to the front of the church to accept Jesus Christ as their savior, and often healing services are conducted during which the pastor anoints or "lays hands" on the sick. Prayer meetings in people's homes involve Bible study and sometimes intense prayer and healing sessions in which believers manifest the gifts of the Holy Spirit.

Two of the most popular denominations in Cachoeira, Batista Betel (Bethel Baptist) and Assembleia de Deus (Assembly of God), have deep roots in Brazil. Baptist missionaries arrived in Brazil in the nineteenth century, and missionaries from the Assembly of God arrived in the early twentieth. Accordingly, the Assembly of God was part of the "first wave" of Pentecostal churches that arrived in Brazil (Mariano 1999). Around the middle of the twentieth century, a second wave of Pentecostalism emerged that was made up of homegrown churches such as Brasil Para Cristo (Brazil for Christ) and Deus é Amor (God is Love). A distinctive feature of these churches is that they stress divine healing even more than their first-wave predecessors.

In the past few decades, a third wave of "neo-Pentecostal" churches has emerged that are distinctive in the way they relate both to "the world" and to African-derived religions such as Candomblé. Neo-Pentecostals generally place less emphasis on separation from the world than other kinds of Pentecostals. The IURD, for example, provides relatively lax behavioral precepts; unlike in the Assembly of God,[4] for example, women are not prohibited from wearing pants or makeup. Furthermore, the IURD's heavy emphasis on material prosperity brings the instrumental orientation of the second wave of Pentecostals to a new level. Most important for the purposes of this chapter, another distinguishing feature of the IURD is its central focus on Afro-Brazilian religions. Pentecostals in general view Candomblé as demonic, but as I illustrate below, the IURD invites demons into its churches to be exorcised.

Exorcism

The most vivid examples of the central role that Candomblé plays in evangelical discourse come from the IURD. The popularity of the IURD is partly due to its appropriation, to a greater extent than most evangelical churches, of elements from Candomblé (Giumbelli 2007; Oro 1997; Mariz 1994). The IURD's message often focuses on how believers can be freed from poverty, sickness, and relationship problems by ridding themselves of the evil spirits—who are often identified with the entities of the Candomblé pantheon—who cause these misfortunes. In fact, some Cachoeirans, even members of other evangelical churches, claim that the IURD is obsessed with the devil and evil spirits. "All they talk about is demons and money," one resident with whom I spoke complained.

A clear example of the IURD's focus on demons is the *culto de libertação* (worship for liberation) held on Fridays to rid people of evil spirits. One Friday afternoon a friend and I attended such a service at the IURD church in Cachoeira. We arrived to find the spacious church full of people, and soon the pastor invited us all to stand up and sing. After the hymns, however, the pastor asked us to place our hands on our heads and instructed us to walk to the front of the church as he led the congregation in a prayer. Several *obreiros* anointed the palms of our hands with warm oil. The pastor stepped down from the podium, and he and his helpers began to "lay on hands." They placed one hand at the back of the neck and another on the forehead and then prayed to God and commanded the evil spirits to leave their hosts. Meanwhile, one of the obreiros paced back and forth in front of us, preaching into a microphone. Then spirits began to manifest in several members of the congregation; their bodies shook as they let loose plaintive cries that welled up from deep in their throats.

A couple of the obreiros herded the possessed to the front of the crowd, where they stood with their hands behind their backs, their eyes shut, and their bodies swaying back and forth exactly as they would if they had been possessed in a Candomblé terreiro. The pastor and his helpers continued the laying on of hands as the possessed stood in front. Eventually we went back to our seats, leaving only the possessed, all three of them women, standing in front of the church.

The pastor proceeded to interview the possessed women, asking each spirit for its name, what it had done to its host, and why it had come into the person's life. They answered that they had made their hosts lose cars, houses, spouses, jobs, and money and that they had come out of greed for obrigações. One of the possessed women nearly became violent; when the pastor attempted to speak with her, she pulled away from him and ran around the front of the church. Eventually the obreiros secured the woman, but she put up quite a struggle before she returned to her subdued stance in the front of the church.

As the pastor railed against the demons, everyone raised his or her arms and made pushing motions as if ordering the spirits to leave. "*Sai!*" (Leave!) they yelled over and over again as they pushed the air (in fact, Cachoeirans often dramatize this chant and the accompanying gesture to mock members of the IURD). Eventually the possessed women were taken away to rooms in the back of the church. Then one by one they came out to sit with the congregation. They appeared relieved, except for the unruly one, who kept getting up from the pews and wandering around the front of the church. Yet by the end of the service she seemed to return to her everyday demeanor.

After the women settled down, the pastor retook the podium and preached about evil spirits and what they do to a person's life. The equation was simple: if you are having problems—marital, financial, and so on—these troubles are caused by demons. Likewise, if you get involved with evil spirits, they will cause problems in your life. Furthermore, only

God can deliver you from these demons and relieve your suffering. Jesus provides the only way out for people who are trapped by evil spirits.

At the end of the sermon the pastor held up the IURD's newsletter and instructed the congregation to take a copy and place it on the floor under the feet of someone doing evil. He explained that the evil of the person would seep into the newsletter, which should then be folded and brought to the church, where the evil could be burned away through prayer. The IURD's strong emphasis on evil spirits, the manifestation of Candomblé spirits during its services, and its view of good and evil as forces or substances that can permeate materials highlight the extent to which this evangelical denomination draws upon the common denominators of Brazilian popular religion, including imagery from Candomblé. In general terms, these common denominators include a focus on spirits as well as on material prosperity (Chesnut 2007).

Yet the similarities between neo-Pentecostalism and Afro-Brazilian religions are more than abstract; again, neo-Pentecostalism and Afro-Brazilian religions often appear to constitute two aspects of a single ritual system. Spirits from the Afro-Brazilian pantheon, for example, regularly appear in evangelical churches. Although they are called demons in this context, they are also often identified by their Yoruba names. Furthermore, as anthropologist Vagner Gonçalves da Silva (2007) points out, the ritual calendars of IURD churches and Afro-Brazilian religious groups have come to parallel each other. On the same days and at the same times that are set aside for *exús*. and *pombagiras* to be received in Umbanda centers, for example, these same entities are exorcised from congregants in neo-Pentecostal churches.

Moreover, the rites and rituals of neo-Pentecostalism and Afro-Brazilian religions do not simply parallel each other; they are closely intertwined. On one of my visits to the IURD in Cachoeira, for example, during which the pastor invited the congregation to huddle around the altar, I glanced down at the pastor's podium to find his notes for his sermon. He had printed out a list of places where Candomblé work is done, which I provide an example of here:

> Places where one does witchcraft [*feitiços*]
>
> BEACH/SEA—Because of the waves, he comes and goes, goes up and down and never stays stable. Human beings don't tolerate this for very long and give up on their goals.

This cryptic note is a striking testament to the prominent role that discourses about specific Afro-Brazilian practices play in IURD churches.

Silva's (2007) discussion of ex-*pais de santos* (former Candomblé priests) who appear on evangelical television programs to provide consultations to victims of Candomblé work further emphasizes the central role that knowledge of Afro-Brazilian religion plays in neo-Pentecostalism. In fact, neo-Pentecostalism and the IURD in particular appear specifically keyed to Candomblé. Afro-Brazilian religion and the spirits venerated within it are the source of the afflictions that the IURD aims to cure. In a sense, then, Afro-Brazilian religion appears to provide its reason for being. As I explore below, however, despite the fact that their religious practices are so clearly enmeshed with each other, it is important to acknowledge the different terms in which evangelicals and *povo de santo* (Candomblé practitioners) view the relationship between spirits and prosperity.

Evangelicals' Views of Candomblé

Along with evangelical Christians, another group that has been central to my research in Cachoeira is the Sisterhood of Our Lady of Good Death (Boa Morte), an Afro-Catholic devotional group made up of women of African descent. Boa Morte's yearly celebration, which takes place in August around the Feast of the Assumption, attracts a wide array of visitors, including a large number of African American tourists from the United States who have provided financial assistance to Boa Morte (see Selka 2008). Although Boa Morte is a formally Catholic organization, all of its members also participate in Candomblé. Nearly all of the sisters are fully initiated and some of them are prominent *mães de santo* (Candomblé priestesses, literally "mother of saint") in town. The sisters openly discuss their involvement with Candomblé, but at least in public they tend to be evasive when answering questions about the place of Candomblé ritual in the sisterhood of Boa Morte. Most often, the sisters insist that these religious practices are separate from one another. Nevertheless, many povo de santo and evangelicals alike speculate about the *fundamentos* (secret knowledge and practices only available to initiates) derived from Candomblé that are at the center of the sisterhood. Most claim that these fundamentos have to do with the spirits of the dead, who are considered especially powerful and dangerous. The sisters themselves are understandably cagey about this issue, yet in informal conversations away from the cameras and microphones that are ubiquitous at the festival of Boa Morte, they are more likely to talk about the ways that Candomblé is interwoven into their practices. In fact, these connections are clearly visible in many ways. The sisters wear elaborate Candomblé necklaces during their processions through the streets of

Cachoeira, for example, and each year the festival is overseen by a different orixá.

Not surprisingly, most evangelicals view Boa Morte as a haven for macumba. Pedro, for example, who is an obreiro of the Bethel Baptist Church, claims that the food served at Boa Morte's festival is made of children's fingers and snails. Pedro explained that the food served during the festival is first offered to demons and then given preferentially to foreigners, while locals are pushed aside. In this way the food provides "a gateway for wicked spirits to enter other nations." Indeed, food is a common vector for certain kinds of Candomblé work. According to Pedro, the tainted food compels many foreign tourists, some of whom become initiated into Candomblé, to return year after year. Similarly, an evangelical man who attends the Assembly of God Church, Raimundo, emphasized that the sisters summon Americans to Cachoeira through secret rituals. Raimundo compared Boa Morte to the Freemasons in their restrictive membership, closed ceremonies, and association with wealth in the form of tourism dollars. Like the Masons, whom evangelicals frequently classify as devil worshipers, Boa Morte attracts wealth through demonic pacts. As I explore below, although evangelicals blame demons for misfortune, demons can also provide prosperity; yet evangelicals claim that this prosperity ultimately comes at the cost of one's soul.

Even though many evangelicals with whom I spoke hesitated to speak disparagingly of particular Candomblé practitioners, nearly all of the evangelical pastors and obreiros with whom I spoke characterized Candomblé as the antithesis of Christianity. "Instead of invoking Jesus or God, macumbeiros call on Satan and demons," the pastor of the Bethel Baptist Church explained. He insisted that people who become involved in Candomblé are afraid to leave. He told me the story of a young girl who confessed to him that she knew that Candomblé is the "wrong way," for example, but her ties to her orixá kept her bound. Those who try to leave Candomblé often end up sick or crazy, the pastor said. I knew a woman in Cachoeira who was involved with Candomblé for many years, for example, who spent most of her days lying on a cot in her son-in-law's house taking medicine for the various illnesses that her son-in-law, a former obreiro of the IURD, says she incurred when she abandoned the service of her orixá. The common saying "Quem está dentro não sai e quem está fora não entra" (Those on the inside don't leave, and those who are on the outside don't enter) succinctly expresses the idea that consequences follow those who leave Candomblé, and most Cachoeirans I know can cite cautionary tales about relatives and neighbors that corroborate this adage. For evangelicals especially, these tales illustrate how the Candomblé practitioner's will is not his own.

As Pedro the obreiro explains, however, there is a way out for those involved in Candomblé:

> They have this idea that once you are involved, you can no longer go back, you can no longer leave. They have a saying that "he who is outside does not enter and he who is inside does not leave." Actually, in our evangelical churches, for the honor and glory of God, we have many pais de santo [Candomblé priests, literally "fathers of saint"], many ogans [male members of a Candomblé temple who do not become possessed], many people who used to work with Candomblé and who today are liberated, proving that this notion that they have is as much a lie as their religiosity.

Pedro refers to leaving Candomblé as liberation, an important concept that recurs in evangelical discourses about Candomblé and mediates between possession and accumulation—if not of material goods specifically, of the good life that God desires for all of us (Oro 1997; Mariz 1994). At the same time, Pedro warns that how one leaves Candomblé is critical:

> When they leave in a rebellious way, in a way that does not lead to the evangelical church, they tend to go crazy, they tend to die or some kind of accident happens because the guides, the orixás, the caboclos, the preto velhos, the exús [these are all different kinds of spirits in the Candomblé pantheon], they act in the life of this person by bringing madness, by bringing death or putting him in a hospital bed. The candomblezeiro, the Spiritist, or whatever other religion, they only have victory and remain standing when they convert to Jesus, otherwise no.

Leaving Candomblé is fraught with danger. This theme is echoed in the following excerpt from an interview with Maria, a woman who left Candomblé for the Assembly of God Church:

S: Was it difficult to leave Candomblé?

M: It was, because twelve years [the length of time she was involved with Candomblé] is a lifetime, isn't it? But I had a lot of willpower and courage.

S: Are there many people who don't have the courage to leave Candomblé?

M: They are afraid.

S: Afraid of what?

M: Because we get sick, the santo [Candomblé spirit] can grab up right in the church and take to Candomblé again, there are even people who die. But I think that everything comes from faith and that God has power, and if he has the power, then nothing can contaminate, right?

S: And the santos won't . . .

M: No. Because He is stronger!

S: Deus é mais? [literally "God is more," a popular saying that refers to God's power over all circumstances]

M: Even if the santo tries more, when he gets close to God's power, he goes back.

S: There are many people who try to leave Candomblé, but they leave it for a while, then they come back.

M: That happens because they leave with vengeance, you understand? They say: "Ah, I'm going to leave Candomblé." So they leave. But they go with their minds, they don't go with faith, they don't give everything up and renew themselves as a new person and go to church. They go with thoughts about Candomblé, and the santo gets them again.

Pedro and Maria stress that if a person leaves Candomblé out of spite, they become vulnerable to possession, sickness, and even death. In fact, according to Maria and many others with whom I spoke, a person's santo can grab hold of her right in the middle of church. As we have seen, these "church possessions" are routinized in the IURD during the cultos de libertação such as the one I described above. These church possessions enact a battle of wills among the potential convert, the spirit, the pastor, and the divine. These events are indeterminate: sometimes they end with conversion, sometimes with people returning to Candomblé. They are dramatizations of a convergence of forces that shape people's spiritual paths and have material effects in people's lives. Along these lines, Faustian themes of struggles and pitfalls of spiritual servitude are prominent in popular conversion testimonies, such as one that I learned about in 2009.

The Testimony of the Ex-Bruxo Tio Chico

One August morning I went to visit my friend José, a painter who was born and raised in Cachoeira. When I first met him in 1999, José was selling paintings of the sisters of Boa Morte to American tourists. He has family connections to the sisterhood and to Candomblé: his aunt was a member of Boa Morte, and a number of his family members are povo de santo. Although José and I have visited Candomblé terreiros together, he claims that he has never been directly involved in the religion. In fact, over the years he gravitated toward evangelical Christianity, and he has been a member of the Bethel Baptist Church for several years. Consequently, he no longer paints pictures of the sisters of Boa Morte for tourists because of their involvement with Candomblé. Instead, he now paints stylized portraits of nondescript *baianas* (Afro-Bahian women dressed in traditional garb).

When I arrived at José's makeshift studio that morning, he was chatting with an evangelical friend about church, but the conversation soon shifted to Candomblé. As the years go by and as José becomes more devout, he criticizes Candomblé more stridently whenever I visit him. That morning, for example, José asked rhetorically: "Do you see these families that are all involved with Candomblé? What for? They have no kind of prosperity—they are all unemployed!" Pointing to me, he said, "If you were a pai de santo, I'd ask you, 'How come none of your initiates have jobs?' " José's friend asked me if I had heard the testimony of a pastor formerly known as Tio Chico. "Tio Chico has revealed things that no one else has talked openly about," he claimed, including the nefarious Candomblé rituals he conducted in order to gain power and wealth. I was intrigued; José said that he had the testimony on DVD and that he would copy it for me. Here I include a summary and some highlights from Tio Chico's testimony, which provides a dramatic illustration of evangelical discourses about prosperity.[5]

In his public testimonies that he shares at evangelical churches throughout Brazil, Pastor Vieira, a.k.a. *ex-bruxo* (ex-sorcerer) Tio Chico, tells of his former life involved in Masonry, Spiritism, Candomblé, diabolical pacts, and various illegal activities:

> My name is Pastor Franscisco Vieira. I am ex-bruxo Tio Chico, the ex-bruxo of many famous men, politicians, and businessmen. I worked for 680 companies, was involved with 28 Spiritist centers. I have been involved in Spiritism since I was a child. When I was ten years old I already was a pai de santo. . . . I walked this whole country, I walked through 68 countries doing macumba, doing nasty stuff. I was a gunman, a robber, a thief, a homosexual. I was everything. But today I am different, I am a new person.

Since he left his service, however, the devil has been trying to prevent him from prospering. Vieira explains:

> [The devil] appeared to me, saying: "Do you know what I'm doing to you? When you go to these churches for offerings of love, I won't let the crentes [literally "believers," a common term for evangelicals] give offerings to you.

You were born with a silver spoon in your mouth, and so you won't be able to stand it. I won't let the crentes buy your materials so you won't prosper. You were born with a silver spoon in your mouth. You're from a rich family with a name and with money. You studied and you're educated. [But] nothing will work out for you, and you'll come back to me."

Here, early in Vieira's narrative, we see that the devil is cast as an agent of both prosperity and misfortune.

Vieira reached a critical juncture in his religious biography while he was attempting to do Candomblé work in a cemetery in Bahia. Vieira claims to have been initiated into Candomblé in Bahia with Mãe Menínina of Gantois, one of the oldest and most prestigious Candomblé houses in Brazil. He explains:

In Salvador da Bahia I did twenty-one raspagens de cabeca [literally "head shavings," referring to the process of initiation] for Satan, and it was there that he started to use me to do absurd things worse than I have ever done. I got to the point of going to the cemetery at midnight to work with bodies. A young woman died, she was buried. After four days, I went to the cemetery. I already had an agreement with the gravedigger, and after midnight, I went up to the tomb . . . to the coffin to do my rituals. But there is a "however," friends. When I went up to the tomb . . . I saw at the gate of the cemetery a ball of fire [moving] at high speed. A demon materialized in the form of a giant bat, two meters high. It pointed to the tomb and said: "You cannot touch this here because she does not belong to us."

In the various versions of his testimony available online, Vieira tells at least two stories in which he is blocked from doing sorcery against persons who "belonged to Jesus." The turning point in his narrative comes when eventually he realizes that this means that Jesus is more powerful than the devil and comes to the following conclusion:

I said, "I'm following the wrong God. . . . I'm going to follow the God of the crentes." When I mentioned the crentes, he [the devil] was not happy, he didn't like that. And so, a little shaken, he said that you are not going because I hate the crentes and the God of the crentes. . . . He said to me that "you are not going to serve another God. I'm going to kill you in an accident."

Vieira goes on to describe his accident, beginning with the car in which it happened:[6]

> This BMW was all black, all dark, and people didn't approach it because they were afraid. I consecrated this car to the devil. On the dash of my car was written "Satan's Throne" and on the back bumper "The Devil's Gang." I did black-magic rituals in that car. . . . [On the day of the accident] I was going about ninety kilometers per hour, so it wasn't that fast. There weren't any holes in the road, no animal crossed in front of me, I didn't cross into the side of another car. I felt a heavy cloud, a dark wind. I looked in my rearview mirror, and behind me the devil materialized behind my car. Suddenly he struck my car eight times. Dear brothers and sisters, I was hospitalized for three years, in a coma for six months in the intensive care unit. I had twenty-one surgeries on my head, two on my throat, and two on my leg. . . . I went crazy and was tied to a bed in a hospital for one year and two months. . . . But Jesus, who is the doctor of doctors, transformed me. Just see the change: from [having to take] twenty-one prescription medicines per night, today . . . I take one prescription medicine per month. If I don't take it, I don't have spiritual peace. If I don't take it, I can't walk, I'm not happy, I don't have the will to live. This medicine is the supper of Lord Jesus Christ.

Although Vieira survived the devil's attempt on his life, he lost his wealth:

> And there in the hospital, where I spent three years and six months in the intensive care unit, I sold all of the material goods I acquired in the past doing rituals to pay for those three years in a private hospital. Dear ones, I had so much wealth, so much executive power, mansions, a new car, lots of money . . . [but] I became a beggar.

But then Vieira accepted Jesus, and his situation changed:

> In the hospital . . . I accepted Jesus. . . . One year and eight months later, the Lord restored my life. Lord Jesus furnished a house, he gave me a furnished house, a conventional telephone landline; Lord Jesus gave me a cell phone, he gave me a new car . . . because he is marvelous.

Here the emphasis on prosperity is laid out in the barest of terms: Vieira concludes his testimony by telling us that Jesus gave him a cell phone and a new car.

Despite Jesus's generosity, of course, the devil had already provided Vieira with these consumer items and more. The association between the accumulation of wealth and diabolical pacts is a familiar theme in Latin America, particularly in communities where capitalism is new and the social inequalities it produces are unfamiliar and disruptive (e.g., Foster 1987; Taussig [1980] 1983). The IURD has emerged in quite a different context, however: that of communities, especially urban ones, where consumer capitalism is already well entrenched. Here, accumulation is something to which to aspire, not something inherently antisocial or exclusively diabolical. Nevertheless, the high-profile scandals mentioned above illustrate that there are limits to acceptable accumulation. Moreover, the practices of tithing (dizimo) and monetary "sacrifices" do not necessarily indicate greed or an obsession with monetary accumulation among the followers of neo-Pentecostalism. As Premawardhana (2012) argues, these practices help to build community, strengthen personal relationships, and aim at the promotion of well-being rather than greed (Premawardhana 2012; see also Apgaua 1999).

At first glance Vieira's story seems fairly straightforward. He seems to tell us that the most compelling reason to follow Jesus is that he is more powerful than the devil and that he provides his followers houses, telephones, and cars. Despite scattered references to "spiritual peace" in his testimonies, Vieira does not appeal to the threat of damnation, obedience to one's creator, or any kind of moral principle; he appeals to desire. Furthermore, as Mariz argues: "The religious struggle in this field is in general a competition between leaders who try to show greater power" (1997: 99; translation mine). What we see here appears to be a battle of efficacy.

On the other hand, as Mariz points out and as I explore elsewhere (Selka 2010), the religious field also has a moral dimension that is closely intertwined with discourses about prosperity. From the evangelical perspective, for example, prosperity grounded in a relationship with Jesus is clearly something quite different from the prosperity that comes from involvement with diabolical forces. In the latter context, accumulation often comes from performing evil acts (e.g., digging up bodies in a cemetery). Furthermore, relationships between humans and demons are defined by negative reciprocity (Sansi 2007). There are always strings attached to these relationships, and those who do not live up to their end of the bargain will suffer the consequences. On the other hand, relationships with Jesus are characterized by generalized reciprocity, at least from Jesus's side; a simple affirmation and a small offering open the way for the bounty that God wants for all people.

Critics of neo-Pentecostalism often accuse churches such as the IURD of cynically taking money from the poor through the threat of withdrawing divine favor. I cannot deny that this kind of greed motivates some church leaders. Nevertheless, according to the logic that guides many churchgoers, prosperity is understood not in relation to the market but in relation to God's will, which demons are attempting to subvert. As Montero explains: "Prosperity, health, and love are a human destiny by the will of God; accordingly, 'to take possession' [*tomar posse*] means to make real that for which one is destined. The church makes viable the reintegration of the possession of what men have a right to by untying those who are deprived of divine blessings because of disruptive action of demons" (2006: 60; translation mine). Thus neo-Pentecostalism offers liberation from demonic interference, and this liberation opens the way for material accumulation—or for one to take possession rather than to be possessed—through a relationship with the divine. As Mariz (1994) argues, liberation in the neo-Pentecostal context aims at restoring one's autonomy or more specifically, freeing a person to be able to choose the life that God wants for us. From this perspective, liberation is just a first step; the liberated person must make an autonomous choice, signified by monetary offerings, in order for biblical promises of prosperity to be fulfilled. As Mariano explains: "As tithers and offerers, the faithful acquire and exercise the right to call upon God himself for the swift fulfillment of his biblical promises: healthy, prosperous, happy, and victorious life" (2004: 129; translation mine). Put this way, there seems to be something quite instrumental about these offerings. They appear to be transactions in which one demands something from God to which one is entitled.

Yet one of the keys to the success of neo-Pentecostalism is the way in which it articulates popular and divine desire. Understood this way, these offerings do not so much demand something from God as bring the person giving the offering into harmony with what God desires. In the discourse of the IURD in particular, for example, conversion is linked more to accumulation than renunciation; prosperity is part of God's plan, much like it was for Weber's aesthetic Protestant. In neo-Pentecostalism, however, the emphasis on the relationship between a particular work ethic and material prosperity is lacking; again, we find the path to prosperity begins with the elimination of demonic impediments to the fulfillment of biblical promises of prosperity.

One of the primary aims of neo-Pentecostal practice is material well-being, and this pragmatic orientation—enmeshed, of course, in a complex spiritual cosmology—is something that neo-Pentecostalism shares with Candomblé and Umbanda. In this context, neo-Pentecostal promises of prosperity often directly respond to those made by Afro-Brazilian religions. Neo-Pentecostal discourse casts the entities who are the agents of possession and accumulation in Candomblé as primary sources of affliction and misfortune, for example. Yet even here, neo-Pentecostalism overlaps and shares the logic with that which it condemns: Afro-Brazilian religions and Kardecist Spiritism are also centrally concerned with the ways that certain dangerous or "inferior" spirits can do harm and compromise a person's free will (Silva 2007; for an excellent ethnography of these issues in the context of Umbanda, see Hayes 2011). In the neo-Pentecostal frame of reference, however, the entire pantheon of spirits, and not just specific kinds of entities, is malevolent. It is nothing new, of course, for a proselytizing religion to cast its "competitors" as deficient and dangerous. It is also nothing new for an expanding religion to engage and absorb aspects of the cosmologies of the other traditions it encounters. What is striking about neo-Pentecostalism and the IURD in particular, however, is the intimate, even symbiotic connection of its ritual practices with those of Candomblé and Umbanda alongside its virulent opposition to these religions.

We have seen that there are two paths to prosperity. The first involves reciprocal relationship with spirits who possess their devotees. For neo-Pentecostals, this path is false: the spirits venerated in Afro-Brazilian religions are demons who rob individuals of the ability to make an autonomous decision to accept Jesus and to "take possession" of biblical promises of prosperity. Being possessed entails the loss of the capacity to exercise free will that is a prerequisite for making the decision to follow the "right" path. In addition, a person's autonomy is compromised by the weight of the spiritual and material obligations involved in serving these spirits. The common saying "Those on the inside don't leave," so dramatically illustrated in Vieira's testimony, captures this idea very succinctly.

The path that the IURD offers cannot be understood in isolation from the path of Candomblé; it represents a direct response to it. Critics have argued that the IURD calls on the poor to give what little they have in hopes of material gain, contradicting the teaching of the sanctity of poverty and recapitulating the logic of the casino to which contemporary capitalist speculation has often been compared. Indeed, we cannot understand the brand of neo-Pentecostalism that the IURD represents and its distinctive focus on deliverance and prosperity without reference to the wider context of neoliberal globalization. Yet I have emphasized that the IURD's emphasis on accumulation must be understood against the backdrop of moral polarization grounded in local religious idioms; Tio Chico's story, for example, seems to suggest a link between excessive riches and malevolent forces. From this perspective, we see that the IURD promises prosperity not simply by means of magic but through deliverance from demons, thereby integrating a moral distinction into a mode of accumulation that diverges from the logics of Candomblé and the market alike.

SEVEN

Possessing the Land for Jesus

ELIZABETH McALISTER

> Therefore shall ye keep all the commandments which I command you this day, that ye may be strong, and go in and possess the land, whither ye go to possess it.
>
> —Deuteronomy 11:8

For thirty seconds an enormous roar filled the air. The ground shook, and buildings split open and crumbled. Roofs fell onto floors and crushed thousands of people. Bidonvilles on hilltops slid into ravines and buried thousands more alive. The palace roof fell in on itself, and the Grand National Cathedral collapsed. A great cloud of white dust rose over the city of Port-au-Prince. In less than one minute, hundreds of thousands of people were dead, buried alive, or injured badly. Millions were traumatized.

The worst natural disaster in the history of the Americas struck the capital city of Haiti and paralyzed the nation on January 12, 2010. There were few trained emergency workers to respond. The quake killed so many that bodies were dumped into mass graves outside the city, and two million people were left homeless.

One month later, it would have been, and should have been, Carnival. Instead, it was all the government could do to organize an official day of mourning. In an ecumenical national ceremony, the president, the prime minister, dignitaries, and surviving leaders of the three main religious groups in the country (Catholics, Protestants, and Vodouists) came together to mark the one-month anniversary of the quake.

A woman in the Haitian diaspora received a revelation from God about his plan for Haiti. Born in the slum of Cité Soleil, Sister Ginom had become a successful businesswoman in Orlando, Florida. God told her that for the three days starting on February 12, evangelicals were to organize a revival in the Champ de Mars park downtown next to the National Palace. A transnational network of Haitian, Haitian American, US, and Latin American evangelicals gathered for a massive three-day prayer and fast in downtown Port-au-Prince. People came in droves. The spectacular revival was broadcast live on Télévision Nationale d'Haïti, and millions throughout the diaspora watched over the Internet or listened on the radio.

In the course of these three days, evangelicals, neo-Pentecostals, and charismatic Catholics came together to recast rhetorically and ritually the space of death into a space of rebirth. Drawing on biblical images and stories, they reimagined Haitian geography as the landscape of the Bible. The Haitian story became a biblical story. "Every time the Bible says Israel, we will say Haiti," said a pastor to the crowd on the first day of prayer. "God wants to give Haiti a second chance," another said. "God wants to save you and make you the light of the world." One pastor cited Matthew 24:7–8, which says: "Nation will rise against nation, and kingdom against kingdom. There will be famines and earthquakes in various places. All these are the beginning of birth pains." Drawing on Pauline images of birth pangs giving forth early Christianity, the speakers returned to a common refrain: the earthquake was the labor pains of a new Haiti.[1] *"We don't need a cesarean because Jesus is the doctor," declared one pastor. On the third day the pastors declared Haiti reborn. Sister Ginom returned to the stage to deliver the nation in a grand speech act: "In the name of Jesus I rebuke all evil spirits that want to stand as a barrier to the glory of God. Jesus is delivering Haiti."*

The longtime Anglo-American missionary Reverend J. L. Williams stood before the microphone and summed up God's connection to the broken land. "On January the 12th a great tragedy happened. But on February 12th a great triumph has begun. You are God's people. And here is a principle I want you to remember: God is healing his people today. And when God heals his people, his people heal their land. Glory be to God."

At the end of the third day, which would have been, and should have been, Dimanche Gras (Fat Sunday of Carnival), the crowd sang exuberantly and jumped up and down: "Jericho, miray-la kraze" *(Jericho, the walls are crashing down). Using this hymn from the Haitian Protestant repertoire, the masses of earthquake survivors sang the biblical city of Jericho into the devastation of Port-au-Prince. "There is nothing Jesus cannot break," said the verses. "Poverty, hunger. . . ." And then came the names of the Afro-Creole spirits:* "Ezili Freda . . . Pitit Lakwa . . ." "N'ap bay yo wosh" *(We'll stone them). As peaceful biblical images mixed with violent ones, a designated number of three hundred people attended to the most important piece of the spiritual business of the third day. They were dispatched to perform a "Jericho march," a ritual technique of evangelical "spiritual warfare." Moving slowly through the crowd of at least one hundred thousand, the prayer warriors sang and walked around the collapsed National Palace seven times. As various pastors took the stage, they painted their vision for the future. This powerful Jericho march would remove demonic spirits and free the land from "the enemy." The three-day revival, praying, fasting, and final prayer march would deliver Haiti and bring Haiti to its rightful place as a chosen nation of God. Jesus would possess the land.*

Since the 1970s, a fully global evangelical movement of charismatic Christian renewalism has expanded, in which flows of information, capital, media, people, and theologies have reached across national boundaries.[2] One branch of renewalism adopts a proactive stance on the question that followers of Jesus have posed since the time of Paul about whether they can help bring about the return of Christ and the end of history. Its leaders teach that the contemporary period is a new season in which "the Spirit of God is restoring the true apostle and prophet foundations of His '*ekklesia*,' meaning 'the called out ones.' He is also literally transforming the Church to become the expression of the Kingdom of God on Earth" (Chosa and Chosa 2004: 5). This form of millenarianism holds that true Christian believers can pray, live righteously, unify, and, through "intercessory prayer," "take dominion of the Earth." Then paradise can be restored as it was in the Garden of Eden and as it will be in the future Kingdom of God. The movement's overlapping substrands are variously named the Kingdom Now movement, the New Apostolic Reformation, third-wave evangelicalism, and the strategic-level spiritual warfare, spiritual mapping, or prayer warrior movement, titles I use interchangeably throughout this chapter.

These branches of thought and practice consist of loosely organized international networks of theologians, thinkers, pastors, apostles, prophets, organizations, churches, and prayer groups. They espouse a variety of creeds and so may differ on theological specifics, but they appeal across denominations by virtue of affinities based on belief in the immanence of the end times and in intercessory prayer and a "spirit-filled" sensibility (Connolly 2005). Their leaders head ministries, give sermons, write books, maintain websites and listservs, produce documentaries, and offer local, regional, and international conferences and webinars. In turn, lay consumers form mission teams and prayer groups and transform themselves into intercessors who receive "assignments" from the Holy Spirit.[3] In what follows, I examine the thought of published thinkers, unpublished leaders, and lay religious actors alike in the New Apostolic Reformation in the United States and in Haiti. I access their ideas through books and tracts as well as through interviews and fieldwork with American missionaries in Haiti, at their conferences, at revivals, in church sermons, and in small prayer groups. I select recurring discursive strands and logics (most succinctly expressed in books by American and Haitian thinkers) to compile a composite rendering of this new Protestant understanding of space, time, and law.[4]

This essay traces the transnational production of an evolving spiritual geography and argues that theologians, together with ordinary people, are developing a corresponding new legal imaginary.[5] This legal imaginary draws most of its material from the Bible and hinges on logics of possession and law on the one hand and spatial imagery on the other. In animating global evangelical renewalist networks, this imaginary is a variation on what Jean and John Comaroff describe as "a dialectic of law and dis/order" that is emerging as part of neoliberal deregulation, especially in postcolonial countries. In Haiti, even before the quake but certainly after, the state was weak and predatory, the legal system dysfunctional, and the overpopulated capital city known for its weak police capacity against high levels of crime, narco-trafficking, kidnapping, rape, and general lawlessness. The Comaroffs stress that "both the anxiety about and the fascination [with the law] point to a very general preoccupation in the postcolonial world with 'the law' and the citizen as *legal* subject, a preoccupation growing in counterpoint to, and deeply entailed in, the rise of the felonious state, private indirect government, and endemic cultures of illegality" (Comaroff and Comaroff 2006: 20). They compare criminal institutions and communities that establish "simulacra of social order" complete with modes of governance and taxation in an appropriation of forms of law. Here I am similarly interested in a religious movement whose members live in conditions of uncertainty and economic decline in the United States and in profound lawlessness and dispossession in Haiti and establish a hyperlegalistic imaginary with corresponding discourse and ritual modes of engagement with an absolute cosmic sovereign. This transnational circuit shows how a focus on the postcolony may occlude our understanding of the ways religious actors in the modern nation-states of the developed world coproduce the dialectic of law and disorder, with intriguing results. In the case I consider here, it is North American evangelicals who advocate privileging of *indigenous* "spiritual legal authority" over *ancestral* homelands. This means that Haitian Christians have the legal right to possess Haitian land. Renewalists in the spiritual warfare movement in both the United States and in the postcolony, then, are elaborating the theological-legal standing of individuals as well as of ethnic, racial, and religious groups.

In the ethnographic sections framing the essay I show how this spatial and legal imaginary informs and inspires Haitian neo-Pentecostals to reconcile their faith in God with their displacement and dispossession after the earthquake. The pastors and prophets from various places in the Americas who assembled outside the Palais Nationale the month after the Haiti quake show us that spiritual warfare Christians are together engaged in a global production of religious thought and practice concerning space, law, and logics of ownership and possession that are animating new collective identities. While most scholars of the evangelical expansion have been interested in the movement's resonance with capitalism, the juridical logics and diplomatic rhetoric that underpin the New Apostolic movement that I discuss here have not yet been examined.

Key to understanding the juridical logic of this third-wave movement is that its members believe that, as prophets and apostles of a new age, they have been given a divine mandate to possess the land in the name of Jesus. They seek to heal, cleanse, and dispossess "ancestral spiritual forces" that are not godly and therefore must be demonic. The "spirit of Freemasonry" is an American ancestral demonic "stronghold." The "spirit of apartheid" in South Africa was discerned to be a demonic force driving apartheid's political injustice (Wagner 1992: 170). For Native Americans and their allies in the third wave, the broken covenants and treaties that characterize the US government's dealings with Native tribes—and a crisis of dispossession—are a deep source of iniquity that has created demonic strongholds. In Haiti, ancestral demons consist of the inherited spirits of its traditional Afro-Creole religion called Vodou.

Haitians who appropriate third-wave thought, like those engaged in the three-day revival calling for Jesus to possess the land, form new identities through a process of repudiating traditional culture and elaborating new subjectivities. Central to this process is cultivating obedient submission to a God who has promised his people land, "a spot on this earth." Through this double logic, prayer warriors seek discursively to "cast out territorial spirits" and "posses the land," even, and especially, in the face of the traumatic displacement and dispossession of the 2010 quake.[6] Hence a dialectic of dispossession and possession unfolds in the Haitian circuits of the New Apostolic Reformation. The profound violence of the destruction of the capital city and the ensuing insecurity of life and desperation in the tent camps fueled a militaristic drive to "repossess" the country under the auspices of the ultimate sovereign, God himself.

Dispossession in Haiti

It is important to ground this discussion about the role of religion in the dialectics of law and disorder, possession and dispossession, in the contemporary context characterized by neocolonial and neoliberal economic conditions. These realities produced the racialized geography of poverty, and now disaster, so apparent in Haiti after the earthquake. The Inter-American Development Bank called the recent Haiti earthquake "the most destructive disaster in modern history." It is telling that the two indicators used to measure the destruction were the loss of more than 250,000 lives and the estimated $14 billion in damage. Under the present system of neoliberalism, value is most often measured in economic terms. The rising charismatic renewalist movement in the Americas is successful partly because its social structures and thought processes mesh so smoothly with the neoliberal economic system, even as its theology places preeminent value on the intangible saving of souls and on the unseen world of "the eternals."

Neoliberal economic policies, which privilege national production in underdeveloped countries toward the export market and free trade within the domestic market, were implemented throughout the Americas beginning in the 1970s by the major international financial institutions (the World Bank, the International Monetary Fund, etc.) together with USAID. As Alex Dupuy points out, "Their objectives have never been to promote meaningful and sustainable development of peripheral capitalist countries like Haiti. . . . Rather, their aim has always been to create outlets for the products of the core countries and sources of cheap labor for their manufacturers" (Dupuy 2010). Domestic structural adjustments made in response to pressures to keep wages low, discourage unions, and eliminate health and safety standards have all had a detrimental effect on farmers, the urban working class, and poor populations—or the majority in Haiti (Dupuy 1997: 22–23).

One of the corollaries of neoliberal structural adjustment coupled with large amounts of food aid entering Haiti in the 1990s was the virtual collapse of domestic agriculture, including rice farming. As a result, huge sections of the rural population moved to the cities, especially the capital, Port-au-Prince, which grew with virtually no city planning from a city of 150,000 in 1950 to one of 3 million in 2008 (Dupuy 2010: 17). Precariously situated and overpopulated shantytowns were ravaged by the quake. Millions who were already internal migrants were displaced for a second time from their homes in the city. At the time of this writing, some thirteen hundred tent encampments sheltered an estimated 2 million people, but land rights for tent camps were heavily disputed. Several camps have been subject to violent forced evictions by landowners seeking to reclaim their lands, citing legal rights to private property (Goodman 2010). Questions of legal ownership of land and rights to land possession came to the forefront as a national crisis.

Land tenure in general has long been a charged issue in Haiti, where elites and military officers frequently stole land from the majority nonliterate population. Multiple, often fraudulent land titles exist for the same property, and now many records have been destroyed in the quake, threatening further dispossession of lands. In Port-au-Prince, where up to 85 percent of residents do not own their own homes and where rents for undamaged houses after the quake went up 300 percent (Schuller 2010), tents, tarps, and bedsheets became the only option for the majority of the internally displaced population.

Analysts in the wake of the quake in Haiti pointed out that while many events are "natural disasters," they are sometimes preceded and followed by "second disasters" caused by inequality, vulnerability, and politicized responses (Schuller 2007). The quake in Haiti made visible a racialized geography of marginalization and structural violence similar to that revealed in the aftermath of Hurricane Katrina. Social geographers Katherine McKittrick and Clyde Woods write, "Hurricane Katrina was deemed a 'natural disaster,' but the language that propped up this supposed naturalness only served to naturalize poor and black agony, distress and death" (McKittrick and Woods 2007, 7). The same could be said of the quake in Haiti: "The storm also brought into clear focus, at least momentarily, a legacy of uneven geographies, of those locations long occupied by les damnés de la terre/the wretched of the earth: the geographies of the homeless, the jobless . . . the unescaped"(ibid., 2).

Disaster relief for those unable to flee and left vulnerable after the quake, as well as Haiti's social services in general, falls under the privatized auspices of charity and humanitarian assistance, as is becoming the case in the United States as social services shift to the purview of faith-based initiatives, including Katrina relief (Gunewardena 2008). Critics of the privatization of humanitarian recovery projects label the process "disaster capitalism" and point out the ways in which "assistance strategies rooted in neoliberal policy frameworks channel recovery through private corporate interests and entities (e.g., consulting firms, engineering companies, and developers) more interested in profiteering than a purely humanitarian motive"(Gunewardena 2008: 4) Some displaced persons living in tents who were members of the New Apostolic movement watched the unfolding of the profit-making process, which was often legal though sometimes not; this was not usually clear to them. As I have written elsewhere, they became disillusioned about the Haitian government, the UN peacekeeping mission to preserve law, order, and security, and even international humanitarian aid, and worked to cultivate a stance and practice of Christian self-sufficiency (McAlister 2013).

The American and Haitian religious actors I follow here are not part of the vast nongovernmental organization complex that has made Port-au-Prince a "Republic of NGOs." Rather, I am interested in independent missions and congregations that are also linked in global networks. North American evangelicals, including Haitian Americans in the diaspora, form relationships with Haitian church congregations precisely in the sphere of privatized humanitarian assistance that neoliberal economic policies have created as the primary theater of operations for aid, relief, recovery, rebuilding, and development. After the quake in Haiti, biblical quotations about land resonated with conflicts over land occupied by tent encampments, competition for international relief monies, and discussions about the best way to rebuild the nation. It was in this context that dispossessed Pentecostals began to think, speak, and strategize about "God's people possessing the land." On the radio, in churches, and in outdoor crusades and revivals, Haitian pastors used the language of the spiritual warfare movement to cast the quake as a form of God's divine love shaking the nation into obedience. During visits from pastors from the United States and elsewhere, Haitian evangelicals shaped a spiritual warfare interpretation that the quake was an invitation from the Holy Spirit to take dominion over the land.

Spiritual Mapping and Its Cosmology

The spiritual mapping theology and practice that informs the spiritual warfare movement is a fluid constellation of thought and ritual, with no single orthodoxy. In general, revelation from the Holy Spirit is understood to be the driving force of the movement. Difference and change in Holy Spirit revelation are embraced because, as part of the condition of the "last days," God is said to be working in new ways toward the fulfillment of prophecy and the ultimate victory over evil. The one foundational, indispensible, authoritative, and sacred text, of course, is the Bible. Spiritual mappers, like other evangelicals, consider the Bible the inerrant word of God, the ultimate truth, and a text applicable to every dimension of human life. The most prominent theologian of spiritual warfare, C. Peter Wagner, held a faculty position at Fuller Theological Seminary in Pasadena, California, and developed his teachings in courses on missiology and the special challenge of "reaching the unreached." Missionaries to Haiti have brought New Apostolic thought and practices to Haiti, and Haitian pastors and seminarians have likewise traveled to the United States as well as to Argentina and as far as Korea to attend workshops on spiritual mapping and other movement techniques (McAlister 2012).

Spiritual warfare renewalists picture the whole of human history as a consequence and effect of the cosmic battle of Satan against God. Although God's plan for humans is one of deliverance and salvation, Satan and his demons work to thwart that plan. This overarching Manichean battle between good and evil informs readings of history, current events, family life and personal life, law, and geography.

A story about the origin of law drawn from the Bible underlies and authorizes the cosmic order and all of reality for third-wave evangelicals. God created heaven and the earth and is ultimate sovereign over all creation. He gave earthly dominion to Adam and Eve in Genesis 1:28, and great emphasis is placed on the idea of legal authority and the rights that accompany dominion. When Satan's temptation of Eve in Genesis 3 leads to the Fall of Man, legal authority extends to Satan and explains why life on earth, even for Christians, is fraught with pain and suffering. Legally, Satan gained the right to be "prince of this world" (John 12:31) and to command an army of demons who maintain "strongholds"—geographic and spiritual bases of demonic power—throughout the world (Kraft 1994: 19). After Christ was crucified in payment for the sins of Adam and Eve and all of humankind, Satan was legally dispossessed of his dominion on earth. In this Christian legal economy, Christ paid for humanity's sins and bought creation back. However, spiritual warfare adherents believe that Satan's "strongholds" did not melt away. Instead, Satan and his demonic army hold on to what power they have cultivated through social vice and sin: sowing the seeds of war and violence, people's worship of idols, poverty, addiction, etc.[7] As in the Old Testament, "The purity of the land is determined by its people following all the laws, especially the law of fidelity to one deity. When Israel is not monotheistic, it is filthy and it pollutes the land" (Schwartz 1997: 63). War-torn countries, violence- and drug-plagued cities, farmlands suffering from drought, and certainly places where pagan gods are worshipped are potential material evidence of problems in the spiritual realm, with Satan's possession of a stronghold at their root.

Sin operates legally as an active invitation to Satan to establish himself and grow, and as a result, Satan gains legal rights over particular domains in the cosmos. The central text informing these prayer warriors is Ephesians 6:12: "For we wrestle not against flesh and blood, but against principalities, against powers, against the rulers of the darkness of this world, against spiritual wickedness in high places." One of the most frequently discussed domains is "demonic territory," spaces where Satan's army has created aggressive outposts of "wickedness in high places" and where his unseen "dignitaries" have seized spiritual dominion and sow disorder.

The task of third-wave evangelicals is to act as intercessors and prayer warriors to stage a "power encounter" that will bring about territorial deliverance in what C. Peter Wagner terms "strategic-level warfare" (Wagner 1991). It is the prayer warrior's job to "stand in the gap" and actively roll back Satan's grip on people and their land. This phrase is taken from Ezekiel 22:30: "And I sought for a man among them, that should make up the hedge, and stand in the gap before me for the land, that I should not destroy it; but I found none." The idea is that in this new age, Christian spiritual warriors will not disappoint God (who once could not find a man to stand in the gap) but rather can be key players in a cosmic battle in which they take orders directly from heaven and work according to God's legal principles to restore God's Kingdom.

Third-wave adherents interpret the Bible in a way that produces a spatial reorientation placing born-again Christians in a privileged relationship to the center of cosmic reality, truth, and power. They are consciously oriented toward the spatiotemporal notion of God's eternal Kingdom. God's Heavenly Kingdom is Christians' longed-for, true home and the subject of tremendous rhetorical focus. It is both a spiritual realm "out there"—a temporal condition of permanence—and a spiritual condition in which a believing Christian lives.

While the movement holds a common, if not orthodox, Christian understanding of God's Heavenly Kingdom, it refines and hyperlegalizes the concept. Members stress that those who are born again hold a "legal" status of belonging in heaven, pointing to the passage "We are citizens of the state which is in heaven" (Philippians 3:20–21). For some Haitian renewalists I have interviewed, the Haitian state is illegitimate by virtue of its history of corruption and exploitation of its people. Heavenly citizenship is far more important than national citizenship. Said one young woman to another researcher: "I am Christian. I am first and foremost a citizen of God the Father's kingdom, adopted into his family through Jesus Christ, whose ambassador I am to his honor and glory, in the power of the Holy Spirit" (Harkins-Pierre 2005: 33).[8]

The Heavenly Kingdom is accessible to the individual believer through a direct line to his or her body. This is because the "spiritual heart," which is superimposed upon the natural heart (just as the spiritual realm is superimposed on the natural realm), serves as "the hidden door of the kingdom of heaven" (Chosa and Chosa 2004: 9). Discourses of diplomacy provide the logic: once a believer invites Jesus into her heart, she is saved, eligible for citizenship in the Kingdom of God, and subject to God's rule and God's law. As a citizen of God's Kingdom, she is his "ambassador" and holds authority over Satan's "dignitaries." Spiritual warriors cite Luke 10:19, where Jesus says: "Behold, I give you authority to tread on serpents and scorpions, and over all the power of the enemy, and nothing shall by any means hurt you." However, spiritual warriors perceive their salvation to be always under attack by Satan, who seeks to tempt them away from God. Demons can possess humans "legally" when humans commit sin and thereby allow them in. Therefore, salvation is a state or condition that must be protected and guarded, similar to the seventeenth-century Quaker Richard Vickers's discussion of how to acquire and keep the "Heavenly Possession" (see Johnson, "Genealogy," this volume, n. 20).

This cosmic order that connects individuals to eternal time and space intersects seamlessly with a developing renewalist vision of the global order. Since the 1970s, South and North American third-wave evangelicals have produced what they term a global spiritual mapping of the "gaps" or territories that are ruled by "spiritual wickedness." In the 1990s, Argentinean-born pastor Luis Bush further developed this discourse with the image of a "Resistance belt," an area of the globe presenting a challenge to spreading the gospel in the world. (Bush n.d.) He and others mapped the territories reached and unreached by Christianity around the globe and concluded that "successful church planting in the Pacific, Africa and Latin America has largely reduced the world's prime evangelistic real estate to a swath of territory from 10 degrees to 40 degrees north latitude, running through Northern Africa and Asia known as the 10/40 Window." Not coincidentally, the parameters of the 10/40 Window include the Middle East and encompass "the core of the Islamic religion."[9] Because the Bible says that the gospel must be preached to the "ends of the earth" (Acts 13:47) in order for Jesus to return, these unevangelized places of "demonic entrenchment" are particularly important to missionaries who see themselves as actors in the drama of God's plan for world redemption.[10]

Spiritual warriors believe that Christianity cannot spread in the "resistance belt" because the ancient peoples there transacted pacts with un-Christian powers, usually territorial spirits and deities associated with rocks, trees, and rivers. These non-Christian religious practices resulted in, and were, effectively, covenants with demonic forces ceding territory for possession by Satan. According to biblical diplomatic law, these were "legal" although evil deals. In other parts of the world, like Haiti, which has received the word of Christ but has yet to realize Christ's blessings, pacts with ancestral demonic forces explain instability. In underdeveloped parts of the world, demonic territorial spirits may be holding "people groups" in a form of spiritual slavery.

Spiritual mapmakers are careful to study the spiritual legalities at work in these cases. In Haiti, for example, the long-standing traditional Afro-

Creole religion, which anthropologists call Vodou and that evangelicals usually misrecognize as "witchcraft," is interpreted in terms of ongoing "diplomatic relationships" with demons. Explains one evangelist, "The devil and his principalities have been *defeated* by Jesus on the cross, and they would not be able to stay on unless they were relying on old invitations that have never been cancelled" (Sjöberg 1993: 109). Says another, "In return for a particular deity's consent to resolve their immediate traumas, they have offered up their singular and ongoing allegiance. It is through the placement of these ancient welcome mats, then, that demonic territorial strongholds are established" (Otis 1993: 30). In such cases, the demon has a legal right to stay. American and Haitian evangelicals took up the question of demonic influence in Haiti in the 1980s, and a vocal minority became convinced that "a host of territorial demons was let loose in Haiti that . . . created for it the ecological, economic, moral and political disasters it is infamous for around the globe today" (McAlister 2012: 203).

Haitian theologians and pastors have since worked at spiritual mapping to fill in the details specific to their country. Pastor Gregory Toussaint, for example, writes that a demonic Jezebel spirit possessed one of the founders of the nation at a crucial moment in its development. "At the ceremony of Bois Caiman, it was Erzulie Dantò (i.e., Jezebel), who got the pioneer of the nation to . . . make a blood covenant with that spirit" (Toussaint 2009: 83). The "blood covenant," elaborated below, is an example of a spatiotemporal "time gate" when the nation was "given" legally to Satan, who now controls it. The character of this chronotype serves to explain why Haiti is chronically impoverished and politically instable; demons love sowing disorder, pain, and suffering throughout God's creation.

New Apostolic theology, with its hyperlegalistic elaboration of demonology, frames a dialectic of law and disorder that responds to the crisis of evangelical Christianity in the underdeveloped world. Evangelicals must cope with the dilemma that Christianity does not always bring the promised abundance, healing, justice, and peace that the gospel foretells. The same crises that social scientists blame on colonialism, neoimperialism, and neoliberal capitalism is for spiritual warfare intercessors a matter of biblical legality, ancestral sin, and Satan's work, which continues to affect present populations. The solution, they believe, is to cast out the demons from the space in the name of Jesus. In the legal diplomacy of spiritual warfare, Jesus gave all Christians authority over demons in Matthew 10:1: "And when he had called unto him his twelve disciples, he gave them power against unclean spirits, to cast them out, and to heal all manner of sickness and all manner of disease."[11] By dispossessing demonic forces, even problems that are national in scope can be resolved.

Militaristic imagery characterizes the theology of spiritual warfare, as a "prayer team" of "prayer warriors" come together for a given "prophetic prayer action" on the "spiritual battlefield." But the warfare does not entail physical aggression. Spiritual warfare theologians teach that man's dominion is over Satan's forces, not over other people. The battling consists of round-the-clock intercessory prayer, as experienced prayer warriors prepare and fast. Drawing on Ephesians 6:11, they "put on the whole armour of God, that [they] may be able to stand against the wiles of the devil." They gird their loins with truth and don the breastplate of righteousness. They take up the shield of faith, the helmet of salvation, and the sword of the spirit and mount "Jericho marches," walking around demonic spots in rebuking and prayer, just as the Haitian prayer warriors did on the one-month anniversary of the quake. Demons are cast out by name, and because they are cast out by a faithful, "blood-covered" Christian standing under the authority of Christ, the demon legally must flee. Christ's spirit and healing grace can enter the space and transform it.

This legalistic narrative of demonic entrenchment in Haiti is currently unfolding on the ground and in the global Christian renewalist public sphere. It has intensified a dialectic of possession and dispossession in Haiti since the quake. The catastrophe that displaced millions was read by some evangelicals as a call from God to bring Haiti to revival and rebirth and by others as a punishment for the ancestral sin of worshipping demons through "witchcraft." Of course, the demonic entrenchment that is figured as endemic to Haiti consists of the Afro-Creole spirits inherited through family lines by the majority of Haitians. Living in cemeteries, natural sites, and elsewhere in the unseen world, the spirits of Vodou are translated as demonic "welcome mats" that are legally holding Haiti back from development and prosperity.

The Spiritual Geography of Haiti

> To be God's rescue agents to a nation given to Satan.
>
> —In God's Heart Ministry

Haiti has long been figured by both Roman Catholic and Protestant thinkers as a land infused with sorcery and magic (see Ramsey 2011). Its majority religion of Vodou is a blend of various West and Central African religions, healing, divination, and juridical traditions, creolized together under forced Roman Catholic conversion during and after slavery. The Afro-Creole religious, political, legal, and familial complex assumes a remote-creator God, under whom exist multiple branches of deities called "*lwa*," or "spirits." Spirits are inherited through family lines, as Karen Richman elaborates in this volume. Vodou practices are oral, not scripture based, and are transmitted within an ethos of secrecy through initiation or family tradition. Only since the 1990s has there been an attempt to form a centralized hierarchy of officeholders or spokespeople. Although Vodou is very much creolized with Roman Catholicism, the servants of the spirits do not hold a biblical, millennial spatiotemporality. Rather, time is cyclical, and space is potentially inhabited by spiritual energies and entities. Third-wave evangelism shares with Vodou ontologies of spiritual reality and agency. But since the ancestral spirits are not the Holy Spirit, this is taken as (biblical) proof that the spirits are demons.

Most of the spirits are thought to rest in Ginen, a mythic Africa (sometimes said to be under the sea), and they can come to "ride" or "dance in the head" of their "servants" during prayer ceremonies. Spirits can also "own" and "live in" trees, lakes, and rivers, in cemeteries or in gates and intersections of paths or streets. They are thought to both afflict and protect family members. Karen Richman (this volume) explains how people inherit protection from their spirits, as well as corresponding obligations to the spirits, from the ancestor who founded their extended family homestead, or *eritaj* (from French *héritage*). The extended-family members descended from this ancestor by definition also make up the eritaj. They are called through spiritual messages from time to time to gather on the land and perform religious "work" requested by the family spirits. The spirit might negatively affect a family member (with recurring dreams, sickness, bad luck, or an accident), and then the work of "serving" and "feeding" must be done to assuage the spirit and set the relationship back into a state of balance and protection (Richman 2005).

Richman shows how the eritaj signifies both the land and the descent group, or family. She reveals how spirit possession "is a corporeal performance of interdependence between living members of a descent group, deceased members, and their spirits. . . . Connecting the living in a deeply embodied way to their ancestors, their lineal history, and their family land is an overlooked aspect of Haitians' experience of possession" (Richman, this volume). The religious life of long-standing families living in the eritaj system is connected and rooted in the soil, in the trees, rocks, rivers, cemeteries, and mountains where they live. Ideally, religious work would take place on the family land. Because family spirits "own" the land, ritual work done on land founded by an ancestor can produce results that are not possible anywhere else. However, as a result of mass migration since the 1970s, much religious work has been displaced from inherited land, and families have had to adapt ritual practice considerably.

As Richman points out, the idea of a person experiencing individual, "personal," spiritual transformation through the instrumental use of spirit possession is immoral in Afro-Creole tradition. Yet this is just how Jesus is said to affect Christians when they are born again or sanctified through indwelling by the Holy Spirit. Although each system contains elements the other would proclaim immoral, it is the evangelicals who loudly judge and condemn the Vodouists. Here we see in microcosm an example of the large-scale conversion described by Johnson as constitutive of the European modern, namely, the purification of spirits and possession by spirits in order to produce the properly bounded, accountable, and contract-worthy "individual" (Johnson, this volume).

Following the imperative of the Great Commission to spread Christianity to the nations and the New Apostolic mandate to exercise dominion over their God-given "spot of land," evangelicals proselytize, maintain they hold the only truth, and seek to expand their territory as part of their holy mission from God. Their goal is to convert the entire nation and "win Haiti for Jesus." Not incidentally, this also entails "winning Haiti" for a particular vision of economic development based on individual ownership and proprietary law.

For spiritual warfare adherents, the Haitian nation fits perfectly into the pattern they discern all over the globe. Haiti's downward political and economic spiral is evidence, proof, and result of deep demonic entrenchment. As we learn from Richman, spirits and land are intimately related in Haiti's indigenous religion, and spirits do in some sense dwell in and "own" family land. But third-wave evangelicals interpret the inherited spirits of extended families as demons in Satan's army. Each time a family gathers on its land to "serve" their spirits, they are renewing covenants with devilish forces and strengthening demonic entrenchment. In the legal diplomacy of the spirit world, the routine practices of Vodou allow the devil to stay, grow, and hold Haiti hostage, thereby standing in the way of God's plan for world redemption.

In the 1990s, American evangelicals worked out the spiritual mapping of Haiti and produced a new *theological* interpretation of Haitian national origins. It began with a sin—the French enslavement of Africans in the colony. New Apostolic thought teaches emphatically that racism is a sin against God and enslavement is its demonic fruit. It was only natural that the African and creole enslaved population would rise up to fight for their independence, which they did in 1791 in the world's only successful slave revolution. However, spiritual mappers stress a particular mythic event in Haitian nationalist history: Several weeks before the slave uprising, a military leader named Boukman Dutty held a political and religious rally on the outskirts of the northern capital in a place called Bois Caïman. Boukman and an African priestess named Cécile Fatima sacrificed a wild boar in order to propitiate and strengthen their ancestral spirits. In the ritual logic of the Afro-Creole system, the life force contained in the animal's blood was given to spirits as a form of "feeding" in return for strength and protection in battle. In many accounts, the revolutionaries also embraced the African gods and rejected the Christian god.

The story of this foundational political and religious gathering has been the subject of numerous tales, speeches, and writings by Haitian and other intellectuals. Some embroider the slaves' call for vengeance, while others argue that the event was apocryphal or that there were many such religio-political gatherings throughout the North, where the revolution began. Spiritual warfare evangelicals, as we might imagine, interpreted the details of the story in terms of their developing legal religious logic. In their view, the slaves of San Domingue were the triple victims of sin and iniquity. Not having had the benefit of the gospel, they were unsaved sinners by birth and fell victim to French iniquity and enslavement. Slavery was so terrible it created "welcome mats" for more sin and for demonic infestation. So in their desperation, and without the benefit of Christ's salvation, they had very little choice than to turn to whatever force would aid them—namely, their demonic ancestral spirits. For spiritual mappers, the sacrifice of the boar at Bois Caïman was nothing less than a "blood pact" with demons, legally sealing the fate of the new nation. Haitians freed themselves from French slavery only to sell themselves as slaves to Satan (McAlister 2012).

This evangelical legal mythography (see Masquelier 2002) of demonic possession has circulated throughout the Americas in media productions and sermons, and many evangelicals began to read current events in Haiti through the lens of this "blood pact." Contemporary occasions were viewed as "time gates" in spiritual diplomacy when the Haitian government—wittingly or unwittingly—participated in renewing old demonic pacts under the auspices of new bills and national commemorations. One such "time gate" was the April 2003 decree by President Aristide that made Vodou an official religion in Haiti for the first time in its two-hundred-year history. This law enfranchised Vodou priests and priestesses with the legal authority to officiate at baptisms and marriages and to operate in public with full legal rights.

The president's decree infuriated evangelicals throughout the Americas, who considered it a spiritual ratification of the colonial covenant with Satan. A few months later, on the 2003 anniversary of the ceremony for example, a Bahamian minister took out an ad in the *Nassau Guardian* for a "prayer warrior alert." Rife with territorial, legal, and military discourse, the Bahamian ad read:

> This bold stand taken by the Haitian President calls for action by the believers in the Body of Christ. It calls for us to fight against what is obviously a plan of the enemy to control the inhabitants of that nation and to take it as its own. . . . We must stand in the gap for the nation of Haiti. . . . As warriors and watchmen of the city, we must protect our borders through spiritual warfare. We must unite our efforts with the Christian Haitians whose earnest prayers are that their homeland will become a true Christian nation. . . . We must decree and declare salvation, deliverance, restoration and a new Godly governmental order within the nation. . . . My fellow prayer warriors, Let us war a good warfare! (*Nassau Guardian* 2003)[12]

When the earthquake hit Haiti in January of 2010, evangelicals in churches and newspapers and on television, radio, and the Internet strained to discern what the quake might have to do with God's plan. Two days later, Pat Robertson made a statement on the Christian Broadcasting Network saying: "They were under the heel of the French, uh, you know, Napoleon the third and whatever . . . and they got together and swore a pact to the devil. They said, "We will serve you, if you get us free from the prince." True story." A media storm surrounded Robertson's remarks because it seemed so outrageous that he would be blaming a Haitian pact with the devil for the quake. Very few media commentators were able to connect Robertson's statement with spiritual warfare theology. Yet for many evangelical and Pentecostal viewers, the quake's devastation made legal theological sense. The principalities and powers of darkness that rule Haiti were doing their devilish mischief to the extent that even God had lifted his protection from Haiti.

While third-wave evangelicals discern specific spaces to be demonic strongholds and declare certain cities, towns, and areas under attack from "the enemy," it seems that Haiti is the only *nation* in the Americas thought to be "given to Satan." Spiritual mapping is an enchantment of what Michael Shapiro calls "moral geography, a set of silent ethical assertions that preorganize explicit ethico-political discourses" and are produced and legitimated through "uncritical historical narratives" (1994: 482). Contemporary spiritual mapping discourse extends these moral geographies and maps space into unambiguous *theological* geographies. This geography is an enchantment of previously colonial geographies and demonizes racialized human geographies. The *damnés de la terre* are literally damned unless and until they engage Christian salvation, repentance, deliverance, and unity (McAlister 2005: 252). Then they can legally overthrow their subjection to the "prince of this earth" and become legal citizens of the Kingdom of God.

The Possession of God's Possession

The New Apostolic Reformation lays claim to a set of rights understood to be biblical and founded on God's spiritual laws by which he governs the universe. This means that true and real law at work in the cosmos derives from God's pleasure, from sovereign will alone. However, since the biblical law believers invoke and long for is not in fact the law of the land, spirit-filled Christians live in multiple relationships to legal regimes. They must imaginatively shift frames between God's law, state law, international law, and, in the Haitian context, traditional law (of rural juridical "secret societies" such as the Bizango) and the de facto lawlessness and unpredictable insecurity that so often characterizes life.

After the earthquake in Haiti, when millions of people were displaced from their homes, the legalities of landownership became a more charged issue than ever and intensified the dialectic of possession and dispossession. New Apostolic disciples believe that Christians are the rightful owners, stewards, and tenants of the earth, the nations, and the land. For them, once Christians realize the extent of their legal, God-given authority, the battles over land in the spiritual realm will be easier to fight, and transformation can occur. "The land of planet Earth is forever legally included in the long-term plan of God for man," writes third-wave apostle Jim Chosa. "Because Christ was the Father's only begotten son, He inherited all that the Father owned, which included the copyright ownership of the entire planet called Earth. To think otherwise, greatly limits the ministry of the Church in these last days against the forces of wickedness encamped as trespassers in the land" (Chosa and Chosa 2004: 90). In the United States the trespassers are the demons of neopagan communities, demons of addiction, and the spirit of Freemasonry, among other forces. In Haiti, these forces are exacerbated by the Vodou spirits, who are believed to be soldiers in Satan's army.

An oft-reiterated theme for evangelicals is "possession of the land." The word "possession" appears 244 times in the King James Bible, and in almost half, 111 of those instances, the word is used in connection with "the land." All but one of these iterations are from the Old Testament, which is, among other things, the story of the people of Israel, their exile, and their return to possess their divinely promised homeland.

To possess is "to hold as property; to inhabit and take up a space; to dominate and take control of." From the Latin *potus*, to be able, and *sedere*, to sit, etymologically possession has to do with an actualization, realization, or completing of two terms. The two parts of the term recall the situation of the Israelites, when for so much of their story, God has given (promised) them their land but they have yet to possess it. As Paul Johnson notes, "There seems to be something about 'possession' as at once the filling of but also the mediating and reinstituting of diasporic and other kinds of absence" (Johnson, this volume). Much of New Apostolic thought is concerned with the completing of these two terms, with Christians' new, God-given agency to bring about the *potential* ("potus") to control ("be seated"). God has promised victory over evil and the salvation of the world, but the redemption has yet to materialize fully. God has instructed his people to possess the land, but the land is unclean and full of illegal encampments.

The Old Testament is full of legal agreements, covenants with God, and the people breaking the covenants. The story of the Israelites is, in a sense, a dialectic of law and lawbreaking. In the context of the lawlessness of Haiti, the tension of laws given and covenants broken holds special interest. (In the United States, Native Americans in the movement have focused on the government's breaking of treaties as a sinful past that hurts the nation as a whole.) New Apostolics place emphasis on a diplomatic rhetoric about Christians' true authority over demons, land, and all of earth's creation. The only catch is the obligation of full obedience to the living spirit of God. Idolatry is the biblical sin most often responsible for the Israelites losing their land or failing to repossess it. It is also the sin thought by American and Haitian third-wave evangelicals to have been the root cause of Haiti's problems and its compromised sovereignty. Schwartz (1997: 54) writes of how in the Old Testament, the property rights of humans is contingent upon their obedience: "A self-enclosed circular system is thereby instituted: to be 'a people' is to be God's people is to inherit his land, and if they are not the people of God, they will not be a people, and they will lose the land. . . . In this formulation, identity is wholly dependent upon the notion of possessing the land—whether in promise, in realization, or in memory." Third-wave evangelicals are passionate in their belief that when Christians understand the legal authority they have been given by God, they then can work in the spiritual realm as intercessors to help bring about the Kingdom of Heaven on this earth by possessing the land. In 1 Peter 2:9, they read the (ostensible) Apostle Peter to be referencing this passage from Exodus: "Now therefore, if you will obey My voice in truth and keep My covenant, then you shall be My own peculiar *possession and treasure* from among and above all peoples; *for all the earth is Mine*. And you shall be to Me a *kingdom* of priests, a holy nation" (Exodus 19:5–6, quoted in Chosa and Chosa 2004: 97; their emphasis). Chosa and Chosa argue that land belongs to Christians as the possession's possession—the possession of the possession of God. They write: "If we are God's possession as an offspring, we are an heir of God and a joint-heir with Jesus, the Son of God (Rom 8:17). Since God owns the Earth, then the Earth is ours in joint-heir ship with Christ. . . . Both elements of our identity link us to God as King and grant to us legal authority as kings in the Kingdom of God, to release the authority and power of the Kingdom of Heaven into our earthly spot or territory" (Chosa and Chosa 2004: 97).

Through these logics of legally inherited rights to land, New Apostolic Reformation thinkers create a geography of sovereignty, imagined to be at once specifically ethnic (our earthly spot of land) and Christian/universal (as joint heirs with Christ). This is especially important to third-wave evangelization and provides the principal spiritual-legal reasoning for a recent paradigm shift in new missions. According to many mission groups, evangelists will be most effective working legally under the authority of God in the territory where they and their ancestors have dwelled the longest. Those believers who are native and indigenous to a territory have a privileged legal authority to "possess" or "sit in" the land. Just as each individual person has biological DNA, so does DNA contain a spiritual dimension, encoding a person's entire lineage with regard to his or her ancestors' relationships with spiritual forces or salvific relationship to Christ. In Acts 17:26, God assigns some people to precise earthly territory: he "hath made of one blood all nations of men for to dwell on all the face of the earth, and hath determined the times before appointed, and the bounds of their habitation." This inspired Chosa to write: "All members of the current population of Earth have an earthly indigenous identity that connects them through their ancestors to the geographical land of some nation or nations on the Earth. This we call national identity, and it is a key part of God's plan for man to exercise effective dominion on some spot of land in the Earth" (Chosa and Chosa 2004: 92).

Following this new trend in missionary thought, European American missionaries no longer envision long-term careers living in "the mission field." Rather, this new paradigm takes into account anthropological scholarship, postcolonial critiques of imperialism, and New Apostolic understandings of God's law. The proper way to evangelize is to "encourage, equip and empower" local pastors and missionaries, because they are more effective culturally and spiritually. Foreign aid for third-wave evangelism means supporting, equipping, and providing capital and entrepreneurial mentorship for local pastors and their business enterprises. Rev. J. L. Williams (who spoke at the revival one month after the quake), writes that, in much of the history of missions, "the local nationals never had 'ownership' of the mission or ministry from the very inception. At best they only had a 'passive partnership.' But true *ownership* was never theirs. . . . Therefore, when it comes to leadership in the Body of Christ—the best leaders are always 'local leaders'—people who are the 'native sons'—the 'sons of the soil.' In the final analysis, no foreign ex-patriot [*sic*] ever can lastingly take the place of the national" (J. Williams 2011; emphasis in original).

Following this philosophy, Reverend Williams frequently brings small teams of short-term missionaries to Haiti. In his view, church property and ministries rightfully belong to Haitians—provided they are Christian. Haitian prayer warriors enact this "right" when they deploy missions throughout Haiti. This complicates the accusation that this transnational evangelical form is neocolonial and American imposed. Still, while recent mission practice stresses the ownership of ministries by the "sons of the soil," the dominant Western legal scheme of "possession" is still in place, where ownership of property includes the right to both use and alienate the property. But Richman (this volume) has shown that in the context of the complex system of rights to land that exists in traditional rural Haitian culture, the eritaj is collectively possessed, and according to Afro-Creole spiritual realities, or laws, the family compound cannot be alienated—at least not without retributive spiritual repercussion. Thus, the evangelical possession of the land amounts to a spiritual coup d'état against the inherited Afro-Creole spirits.

Images of freeing captives from bondage are rife. Satan is pictured as the ultimate usurper of land and enslaver and "possessor" of souls. C. Peter Wagner quotes biblical scholar Susan Garrett to argue the links between Satan and his possessions, which in this case refer both to his spatial realm and to the humans he enslaves: "The dark regions are the realm of Satan, the ruler of this world, who for eons has set entrenched and well-guarded, his many possessions gathered like trophies around him. The sick and possessed are held captive by his demons" (Garrett 1989: 101; quoted in Wagner 1992: 67). This language of (demonic) captivity and (salvific) freedom for the nation is tremendously powerful in Haiti, a country whose national pride is directly connected to winning its revolutionary war against France and its subsequent abolition of slavery. It is also a resonant discourse for a culture in which traditions include the practice of being possessed, or "mounted by spirits." For Haitian spiritual warriors, the first political revolution can only be successful with the second, spiritual revolution, entailing what they term "Christian revival." Further, on the individual level, possession by Vodou spirits will in turn be supplanted by the indwelling of the Holy Spirit.[13]

The Lausanne Committee for World Evangelization emphasized the privileged authority of local pastors in its 1993 statement on spiritual warfare in writing that "it was necessary for the encounter with the powers of darkness to be undertaken by Christian people within the culture and in a way that is sensitive in applying biblical truth to their context" (LCWE: 1993). Spiritual warfare images about releasing Haitian land from the demons who "infest" it include, interestingly, ones that mirror techniques of Vodou spiritual "work." However, they are expressed in a Christian register. Binding and tying in the Holy Spirit is one such spiritual warfare method. In this imaginary, the godly "son of the soil" works "under the authority of the Holy Spirit" to paralyze and dispossess the Vodou spirit, analogized as "the strong man." In the legal and military imagination, spiritual warfare proponents say that Jesus gave his disciples the authority to "bind the strongman," quoting Matthew 12:29: "Or how can one enter into a strong man's house and spoil his goods, except he first bind the strong man?" and Matthew 16:19: "Whatsoever thou shalt bind on earth shall be bound in heaven: and whatsoever thou shalt loose on earth shall be loosed in heaven." In intense prayer sessions, teams of prayer warriors work "in the spirit" and "bind the strongman" and his dignitaries in speech acts of deliverance. It is words alone, uttered by a "possession of God's possession," that activates the power of the Holy Spirit to accomplish this metaphysical feat of restoring creation to its rightful owner.

Spiritual warfare is more powerful than Vodou because it beats Vodou at its own game. For example, the image of tying and binding in spiritual warfare transposes seamlessly into the idiom of Afro-Creole traditions, since images of "tying" and "wrapping" are central in Vodou spiritual work. Ritual experts in Vodou commonly construct physical objects whose elements semiotically instruct the spirits to address and direct a difficult situation (Rey and Richman 2010; McAlister 1995). Tying and wrapping have a number of effects: tying an adulterous husband spiritually to a chair in miniature prevents him from visiting his mistress; wrapping an object in certain colors calls and "heats up" the spirit being asked to bring about particular changes or events. Tying colored rope around the waist of a pilgrim to a shrine consolidates the power being engaged and directed. When preachers and prophets announce that they will "mare demon" (tie up the demon) in the name of Jesus, they exert their superior capacity to control the supernatural world. While the Vodouist operates within a scheme of ritual reciprocity, where the spirits act because they are being "fed" (by energy such as prayer, dance, flowers, food, or animal blood), the pastor's efficacy stems from his use of the diplomatic authority of the Holy Spirit, who, in turn, is God acting in history.

What renewalist Christians long for is complete and total transformation. As Rafael Sanchez (2008) notes regarding Spiritualism in Venezuela, where, unlike in Haiti, squatters have begun to appropriate city spaces for Jesus: "The Holy Ghost's ongoing, active reclamation, for and on behalf of God, of the spaces of His own creation may be characterized as limitless. . . . Spirit cannot but intervene in the world or, what comes to the same, in the spatiotemporal manifold so as to constantly reclaim and return it to its originating source and foundation" (272). When power is understood to be transcendent, it is elusive, absolute, and inviolate (Schwartz 1997: 12).

Prayer warriors are convinced of their possession of the right, true, and legal mission from God. They are not only at liberty to but mandated to take possession of all earthly territory on behalf of God. Unlike the traditional system in Haiti, where, as Richman argues, family members in some sense share a permeable identity, evangelicals focus on the individual saved soul. Yet each individual draws on the strength of his or her church, always mindful that he or she is part of the Body of Christ.

Dispossession and Possession in a Haitian Refugee Camp

I visited Haiti six months after the quake to spend time with a renewalist congregation that had "possessed the land" for its tent encampment in Port-au-Prince. Under the authority of a powerful leader, through the language of faith and practices of cooperation, and bolstered by transnational circuits of evangelical support, this group was surviving horrific catastrophe by fashioning themselves self-consciously as prophets and apostles living as citizens in the Kingdom of God. I was introduced to the congregation by Pastor John, an Anglo-American apostle from Illinois who preached a New Apostolic Reformation message of unifying the church to bring about the coming revival in Haiti. An unrelated medical team of four Americans from Chicago spent two weeks treating the camp's sick. With a daughter married and studying in Venezuela, the church leader, Pastor Yvette, maintained numerous transnational connections throughout the Americas. Pastor Yvette's house did not sustain damage, but she secured a tent from a relief organization and slept each night in the field with about five hundred members of her congregation. They were in tents close together and made up about half of an internally displaced persons encampment under the auspices of the Haitian Red Cross. (See also McAlister 2013.)

The camp seemed typical of Haiti's internally displaced persons encampments, set out in rows consisting of different-sized tents, tarp-covered wooden structures, and bedsheet awnings broiling under the hot Caribbean sun. The site was shielded from the busy road beyond by a tall cement wall. Along the front wall was a huge water bladder from which the camp residents pumped washing water. Along the side wall were two Red Cross latrines servicing the entire camp of fifteen hundred people.

Working according to New Apostolic theology, Pastor Yvette used spiritual warfare techniques to cleanse the soccer field of demonic forces. God told the church to walk the perimeter of the area where they had settled and to rebuke Satan in all his manifestations. With her team of twelve prophets, the pastor woke up each morning before sunrise for three days to perform a prayer walk on the modest patch of land. They spoke directly to the demonic spirits they discerned there and ordered them to flee to the bottom of the ocean. (This is where the spirits of ancestors are imagined to reside in the Vodou cosmology, although Pastor Yvette did not seem to think this significant.) The prophets declared the land their own "*au nom de Jesus*" (in the name of Jesus) and in this ritual way they *netwaye* (purified) the land and *pran'l* (took it). Pastor Yvette explained that God led them directly to that land and gave it to them for the time they were tenting there. She told me that the land was rightfully theirs as a gift from God and echoed Apostle Chosa's belief that "the real trespassers are the forces of wickedness encamped as trespassers in the land" (Chosa and Chosa 2004: 90). In the midst of the citywide contest over land rights and the violent eviction of other tent encampments by their putative landowners, Pastor Yvette ritually enacted the dialectic of dispossession and possession in the legal terms of the New Apostolics.

As soon as God helped them repossess a patch of the soccer field, he found them a set of wooden posts and crossbeams that they used for a church, and they set the congregation's tents in a square around this relatively large worship area. Gravel lined the ground, tarps formed a roof, and pews and chairs from the collapsed church building furnished the space. Next to the church area was a large tent serving as a clinic. A trained nurse, Sister Nadine, treated people, availing herself of a stockpile of medicine she rescued from the dispensary established by the church (but lost during the quake). With tents, church sanctuary, and clinic in place, they were planning to reopen their school for the children in the fall.

During my visits with the church, members insisted that despite living in tents they were fine and that God, who had not forsaken them, was leading them. They shared what resources they had, and they formed their own *brigad de vijilans* (vigilance brigade) to patrol the camp after dark. They related to me several accounts describing attacks they had endured at night in which someone or something had tried to steal children. Although they came in the guise of men, the church members believed the attackers to be *lougawou*, female mystical spirits who typically steal or afflict children as a way to "feed" their spiritual strength. As spiritual warriors they expected demonic attacks by such trespassers, and they were fully confident in their own power over evil. All the attacks had been thwarted by the vigilance brigade and, ultimately, by the warfare prayer of the church. The congregation was a tight-knit group who considered themselves a spiritual family and clearly supported one another.

Pastor Yvette's congregation, the "unescaped" and dispossessed, had carved out a space in which they lived not as God's damned but as God's blessed. They engendered certitude and deep strength through the language of faith. At the end of my conversations with every person in Pastor Yvette's camp, we exchanged encouragement through a kind of discursive triangulation with God. "Thank you for coming to see us, and may God protect you and lead you." "May God bless you and walk with you," I would reply. Invoking God, Jesus, or the Holy Spirit in every conversation was a powerful way to be centered and oriented toward sacred geography. Faith in the context of dispossession can be understood as an active mode of being and acting in the world. As Bornstein notes, "As a discourse, faith is much more than a mere description of an act. Faith is not a reflection of power relations; faith is itself a form of power" (2003: 59). The language and stance of faith made it possible for Pastor Yvette's congregation to declare that God was judging Haiti through the earthquake, that he had spared them for his special purpose, had allowed them to possess the soccer field as their own, and was leading them to build a new Haiti.

Just after daybreak each Friday morning, it was time for a direct connection to God. Pastor Yvette's congregation included a circle of twelve prophets—eleven women and one man—who prayed and prophesied together for several meetings each week. One Friday morning in July, a young woman "in the spirit" spent more than an hour speaking prophetically to each person gathered there, including Pastor John from Illinois and myself. Making pronouncements in the first person, much as an Afro-Creole spirit might, the Holy Spirit spoke of the earthquake as God's judgment on a disobedient nation. But the church here in the camp would be safe and protected. "I alone am keeping you alive and I am leading you," said the Holy Spirit–prophet. Despite the collapse of their church and homes, despite devastating losses of life and limb in their city, they maintained the goal of total obedience to God. These Haitian believers fought the most profound and abject dispossession with the most direct form of possession, by the Holy Spirit itself (see also Sanchez 2008: 295).

During that Friday's prayer session, Pastor John sat with a bowed head as a humble recipient of the prophetic word of the Holy Spirit. Although days before he had taken a leadership role in delivering a sermon to the church, now he submitted himself to the authority of this (financially) impoverished refugee woman, Pastor Yvette, to deliver the Word of God. Their mutually recognized "gifts of the spirit" made them brother and sister in the Kingdom, which for that moment was made spiritually manifest through the obedient holiness and chosen status of those gathered there. In praise songs, prayers, and prophecy, the Kingdom was dawning through the dust and stench of the camp. Not at all the displaced, unescaped victims of the devastating earthquake and a dysfunctional government, these brothers and sisters were God's blessed warriors following his law and citizens of the Eternal Kingdom who would permanently join the King of Kings as his court of heaven.

Notwithstanding the humility of Pastor John in joining in fellowship with the "body of Christ" in the Haitian tent camp, it cannot be denied that the expansionist drive of this form of evangelicalism, whose practitioners seek ultimately to (re)take Christian possession of the entire earth, reproduces colonial geographies of advanced (most blessed) and primitive (most demonic) nations. These theo-geographies are articulated with racialized processes of political economy, such that the most demonic nations are also those with populations that are non-Christian and nonwhite. As part and parcel of the neoliberal economic conditions that structure Haiti's relationship to international institutions, third-wave evangelicals are a passionate force within the privatized sphere of humanitarian aid. This movement superimposes a new legal imaginary and new theological geographies onto old moral geographies—but with a twist. It is the "sons of the soil," the "native nationals" who must now "own" Christian ministries and do the hard work of spiritual warfare and church growth that will usher in the Kingdom.

Even as structural readjustment policies and then the earthquake have resulted in the displacement of huge numbers of Haitians from family land and urban housing alike, the New Apostolic discourse of Christian dominion and "possession of the land" has circulated through transnational communication and partnership. Americans and Haitians—and Haitian Americans—together have worked out the legal logics of spiritual mapping for Haiti. Haitian pastors and prophets "on the ground" reached with a special urgency for this logic in the aftermath of the quake. The movement combines an Old Testament ethos about land with a neo-Pentecostal emphasis on intersession through the Holy Spirit. Like the biblical narratives from which this imaginary is drawn, congregations appropriate the message that a defining feature of God's chosen people is their divinely ordained right to (specific) land. It makes sense that in their most profound condition of traumatic displacement, insecurity, and lawlessness, Haitian believers would find special significance in biblical narratives about rights to land. After all, the Bible "records the wish of a people in exile to be landed, of a homeless people to have a home, and it depicts their aspiration as synonymous with the very will of God" (Schwartz 1997: 42). When God himself as the Holy Spirit lets the Body of Christ know that a particular section of a soccer field is given to them specifically, their certitude and collective identity are both strengthened. In turn, it is in these enclaved spaces that brothers and sisters in Christ draw on Christian structures of thought to create holiness, form alliances, minister to one another, speak against traditional religion, and imagine the new spaces and the new legal order and forms of governance that they expect will be formed when God creates the new heaven and the new earth. As the state continues to dissolve under the weight of NGOs, UN peacekeeping mandates, and dysfunction, New Apostolic legal imaginary provides a rich field of images and rituals with which to create an attentive (if punitive) sovereign and theory of justice. Through ritual practices (that often use the same vocabularies, logics, and techniques as those of Vodou) renewalists create a legal order and a moral community that functions as an alternative structure of governance even in the context of unlawfulness in post-quake Haiti.

I have shown how, based on Old Testament tropes, and projected by the third wave into the present, the Holy Spirit's possession of the people and the people's possession of the land are related in a legal logic that can be extrapolated by spiritual warriors to fit their own circumstances. God and the church belong to one another and to the land. But the price for disobedience is the punishment of dispossession. "If you go and serve the other gods and bow down before them, then Yahweh's anger will be roused against you and you will quickly vanish from the good land that he has given you" (Joshua 23:16; quoted in Schwartz 1997: 48). The nation of Haiti displeased God, and the result was the earthquake and its massive displacement. So the soccer field that God gives Pastor Yvette's church—like the land Yahweh gives to Israel—is always threatened by the same God's displeasure.

For countries such as Haiti with strong "territorial spirits," the existence of the "pagan" Afro-Creole gods still "served" by their families on *their* lands (and elsewhere) is thought to pose a serious threat to the whole nation. Evangelicals see the threat Vodou poses to the monotheistic imperative as equivalent to the threat of divine dispossession. Possession of humans by the wrong spirits can only be remedied by possession by the legitimate authority over creation, the Holy Spirit. For third-wave prayer warriors the only possible "legal" solution lies in submitting one's identity to the violent and absolute transformation in which one is open to the ongoing possession by Holy Spirit, to the reality that one is "the possession of God's possession," to become subject and captive of divine will.

In early winter of 2011 as I was finishing this essay, I used Skype to reach Pastor Yvette. I wanted to send my greetings as I sometimes did and to let her know that I had not forgotten her. She answered her cell phone from her home near the soccer field. "Tout moun tre byen," *she assured me cheerfully. She said God had found housing for most of the congregation and that he had told the rest of the families to move to tents in the courtyard of their collapsed church building, which they were now repairing. "You are like Moses," I told the pastor. "You led your people back home." She chuckled and agreed that God was leading them forward, and that* "nou viv nan men Jezi." *We live in Jesus' hands. Sister Nadine, the nurse, took the phone and said that she was still running their small tent clinic each week but also had a new assignment from God: to remove to the Central Plateau in the countryside to bring medicine and nursing there. My goodness, I thought, a displaced tent-camp refugee going to help somebody else in need. Incredible. The end of our call, as good-byes do among Haitian Pentecostals, took several minutes. Pastor Yvette and Sister Nadine spoke words of encouragement and blessing "over me": "May God help you write your paper; may he walk with you and inspire you to say everything he wants you to say. May God bless you and keep you close, protect you from evil, hide you from anybody seeking to harm you and render you invisible from evildoers. May God put his hands on you for protection and health and give you success, abundance, and strength." "I accept," I said, in the ritual answer I learned from them. Now I wanted to reciprocate. I stuttered a similar benediction: "May God bless you and walk with you and hold you in his hands. May he, um, help the sister go to the Central Plateau and succeed in, eh, bringing medicine there. May he, ummm, strengthen your gifts and protect you from anything that might harm you." Sister Nadine's calm and strong voice replied,* "M'aksepte." *"Tell everybody I said hello," I said. "Thank you for not forgetting us," said Pastor Yvette, returning to the line. "Go with God," I said. "May God bless you," she said, and we hung up.*

EIGHT

Possession and Attachment: Notes on Moral Ritual Communication among Haitian Descent Groups

KAREN RICHMAN

Fascination with the sensational imagery of possession by seemingly sympathetic observers of Vodou has obscured appreciation of some of the unremarkable aspects of Haitians' embodied communication with spirits. Modern narratives of Vodou have reproduced the unsubstantiated concepts of Haitian spirits as abstract, universalistic gods. Access to these archetypal spirits, called *lwa,* is theoretically open to anyone who chooses to serve them. The most profound mode of individual access—possession—is viewed as a transformative experience, the consummation of a quest for a pure self, unfettered by a crisis-ridden society and at one with a good and peaceful universe. This self-centered use of possession informs the practices of converts to invented Vodou traditions but would be immoral in the ordinary ritual communications of Haitian descent groups.[1]

Drawing upon ethnographic research over the past three decades on ritual practices in a transnational community anchored in the Léogane Plain of western Haiti, this chapter argues to the contrary that possession is a corporeal performance of interdependence between living members of a descent group, deceased members, and their spirits. Studies of Haitian possession performance assume that the ritual practice is a powerful communal expression of the bonds between the spirit and the assembled participants. But few studies have recognized how this practice brings ancestors back to life as well. Connecting the living and spirits in a deeply embodied way to their ancestors, their lineal history, and their family land is an overlooked aspect of Haitians' experience of possession. The intimacy and physicality of this mode of symbolizing interdependence and indirectly motivating recollection of the dead reveal the stirring power of possession.

Possession Terminology

Possession opens a somatic, interactive channel through which surge claims, accusations, promises, and critiques. "Possession is a form of communication; it has a rhetorical force, that is, it speaks and people listen" (Ward 2003: 194). Spirits may not only speak but also sing, mime, or dance out what their ordinary human "horses" may not, fulfilling a communicative role widely reported in comparative case studies of possession (Bourguignon 1973; Lewis 1971; Sered 1994; Crapanzano and Garrison 1977). The contents of spirits' messages are contextual, and the contexts may involve interpersonal, local, regional, or global processes and powers (Boddy 1989; Masquelier 2001).

Because of the widespread practices of embodied ritual communication, use of the Latin-derived term "possession" in the semiotic system linked to a mode of commodity production imposes a heavy rhetorical burden on the project of understanding the purpose and meaning of the subject at hand. The common sense of the English noun is "private property owned or occupied," that is, a unilinear taking and controlling of clearly demarcated and discrete material (Adorno 2008). Private, individual ownership is not merely the goal of modern culture; it is a way of knowing. Moreover, the materials known are imagined as discrete things unattached both from other things and from the persons who make and hold them. A more promising approach would entail the interpretation of the term in a premodern or nonalienated sense to mean intersubjective exchange between person and thing. Marcel Mauss ([1924] 2000) likened this idea to "the gift" in modernity because entities are conceived therein to be inherently unbounded or porous.[2]

Efforts to shape Haitians'—and so many other peoples'—experience of embodied communication to our definition of possession are bound to mislead scholarship more often than illuminate it. Neither of the two main senses of the term "possession" shed light on the Haitian case. Insofar as possession denotes "domination of a person's heart, mind, or soul by a person or other agent," the term does not reflect the Haitian principle of communication with spirits for the benefit of the group, including the person who momentarily "has" the lwa. Indeed the latter expression, as in "so and so has a lwa (in her head)" might imply that it is the person rather than the spirit who has the upper hand. Scholars have not, however, refrained from trying to shape the Haitian mode of communication between persons and spirits to this definition. Joan Dayan (1992), for example, queried why Haitians who freed themselves from plantation slavery would see fit to invent a religion with a pantheon of spiritual masters who symbolically possess (dominate and control) them.

The only valid point of departure for analyzing Haitians' ideas of possession is to begin with the Kreyòl words uttered to identify and describe them. Spirits, who are called lwa (pronounced like the French term *loi*), make themselves known to members of their descent groups by "speaking" (*pale*) or "dancing in/through the head" (*danse nan tèt*) of select members. These metaphors point to communication in its embodied modes. Through speech and gestures, lwa, who wield a social license granting them ample latitude, bless, warn, protect, cajole, and chastise others (K. Brown 1991). As Michael Lambek (1981: 83) has explained, the "minimal structure" required for the exchange of meaningful sounds and movements is a "triad" involving three selves (and at least two bodies) whose individual boundaries are fluid and porous. These forms of communication serve a communal purpose. Vivid illustrations of the belief in this function were provided in narratives of the devastating earthquake that occurred on January 12, 2010. Several survivors in Léogane, the epicenter of the seismic shocks, told me that lwa came to warn their community of a massive cataclysm. The spirits communicated these messages in the dreams and "heads"—possession performance—of certain persons. Several people I spoke to in July 2010 credited their survival to the spirits' alerts (Richman 2010).

In the particular social and cultural context described here, to direct spirit possession inwardly toward individual transcendent ends is immoral. Analysis of context is essential to a methodology of researching possession. Erika Bourguignon emphasizes the necessity of explaining the cultural (and moral) context as a point of departure in any study of possession:.

> We must not merely observe the subject or note how the (dissociated person's) state was induced; we must *ask* . . . how they explain the individual's transformation. We must note the cultural context in which the observed event occurs. Only in this way can we discover whether we are, in fact, dealing with *an individual, private*, perhaps deviant event or a patterned and institutionalized (read: communal) one; whether we are dealing with a profane or secular phenomenon; one that is positively evaluated and desired or one that is negatively evaluated and feared. (1973: 13; emphasis mine)

Yet the authorized discourse of well-meaning and sympathetic observers continues to reproduce just such decontextualized and immoral interpretations of Haitian "possession."

The notion that the possession experience can and should be a means to inner transcendence is deeply embedded in the literature on Haitian religion. The modern subject searches for the self in others—in peoples and places whose modern domination paradoxically makes them appear more authentic, quaint, or natural, fixed as moving statues on par with the flora and the fauna. Judith Williamson (1978) writes that "travel is an idea wide open for appropriation in terms of traversing the distance between you and the 'real you'—actually going off, spatially, to find the 'lost' Self." Selden Rodman asked, "What is (it) that we are all seeking and that we find in Haiti?" (quoted in Plummer 1992: 132). Since Rodman played an instrumental role in developing the tourist market for Haitian Vodou art, he was all too happy to both shape and satisfy this psychosocial quest (Richman 2008; Goldberg 1981; Plummer 1990).

This psychospatial substitution is possible in the first instance because the ideal self is imagined in isolation, free of the fetters of any particular social or historical context. As Bellah et al. (1985: 81) observe in their comprehensive study of American understandings of the individual, "External authority, cultural tradition and social institutions are all eschewed (and) the self in its pristine purity is affirmed . . . at one with the universe." The extraction of context permits one to imagine possession as a journey into one's pristine self.

Dance, Ethnography, and Possession

Professional women dancers who went to Haiti to study and record ritual dance wrote the canonical texts for this self-fulfilling project and eventually engaged in ethnography without sustained engagement with anthropological theory and debate. Maya Deren's *Divine Horsemen: The Living Gods of Haiti* ([1953] 1983) is the foundational text of the genre. Lauded by the author of *Best Nightmare on Earth* as "the first intimate study of the cult" (Gold 1991: 226), which covers the "golden age of Haitian (or Vodou) tourism" (Plummer 1990), Deren's text is so well known that it is commonly referred to as "*Horsemen.*" *Divine Horsemen* became a model for using an "intimate" study of Vodou for the modern quest of the self. Such intimacy required the ethnographer not only to witness ceremonies involving possession and animal sacrifice whose degree of excitement hinged on their putatively secret, spontaneous, and chaotic character but also to consummate the quest through total submission to another state of consciousness. In the last chapter of *Horsemen*, Deren confesses her final submission to trance. Through the pertinently titled "White Darkness," Deren ([1953] 1983: 247–62) offers extra support for the role of racial difference in leaving home to find oneself over or through another nation. Deren recounts how, while attending a ritual dance, she staves off several impulses to fall into trance before finally succumbing. When she does yield, though, she identifies neither with Haitians nor with particular Haitian spirits but with the whole cosmos, and she offers a prayer to the earth. (The sacred character of her prayer is reinforced by its separation from the rest of the prose and presentation in a different font.)

The late Katherine Dunham, was, like her mentor, Maya Deren, a dancer who became an ethnographer (Ramsey 2000). Dunham's (1969) account of her quest for self through Haitian Vodou in *Island Possessed*, for example, tenuously straddles the edge of self-control. Reviewing the book, Bourguignon (1970: 1133) notes that it is "sensationalist, full of clairvoyance and telepathy, ectoplasms and haunted places, and spirits that must be sent to their rest; the author is not quite sure about zombies or even human sacrifice."

A recent contribution to this ethnographic genre that uses Haitian religion as a voyage into the self is Yvonne Daniel's *Dancing Wisdom: Embodied Knowledge in Haitian Vodou, Cuban Yoruba, and Brazilian Condomblé* (2005). The author identifies herself as a dancer first and an ethnographer second. Daniel's repeated statements rejecting Western hegemonic epistemology notwithstanding, she stays loyal to its key social and cultural category, the individual, whose primary objective is finding the self independently of community. The author's analysis of Haitian, Cuban, and Brazilian ritual bypasses the members of those communities on the way to locating the endeavor in a universal "human condition." Reproducing the approach established by Deren, Daniel's perspective oscillates between her interior, self-absorbed world and a nonspecific, decontextualized African diaspora unencumbered by the voices and knowing bodies of particular believers and dancers.

The similarities between these three texts and the biographies of the female dancer-ethnographer authors would seem to suggest an additional explanation. Did immersion in the ritual and expressive practices of Haitians, the quintessential primitive and savage Other in North American racist consciousness, partially assuage the authors' own statuses as Others in the United States as women, minorities (Deren was Jewish; Dunham and Daniels were African American), and practitioners of exotic forms of dance, as opposed to the authorized European styles of ballet? Is it possible that early modern dance itself played a role, since two of the most influential founding schools, Denishawn (Ruth St. Denis and Ted Shawn) and Martha Graham (Terry [1956] 1971) reproduced grand visual narratives of modernity that reinforced in dramatic fashion both individualism and decontextualized stereotypes of primitive Others? Evidence against the inevitability of these coincidences is the life and work of Zora Neale Hurston, the first North American black woman anthropologist to go to Haiti to study Haitian religion. It is not a coincidence that she has been ignored as the apical ancestor to this methodological line, even though she, too, studied dance styles of the cultures she immersed herself in and incorporated these forms in her choreography (Kraut 2008).

Hurston's irrelevance to this "school" may be related to her utter disinterest in taking advantage of research for the private purpose of a liberating journey into the deep regions of her self. One critic of Hurston's restraint is Joyce Aschenbrenner, author of a fawning biography of Katherine Dunham. To build up her subject, the biographer first belittles Hurston's methodology as "brief and bare of affect." Dunham, by contrast "penetrated very deeply" (2002: 54).

Frustration with Hurston is no doubt related to her self-control, even while describing the rare opportunity to undergo an initiation, which involves substantial physical deprivation, meant to induce an altered state of consciousness. In *Mules and Men* ([1935] 1968), her first ethnographic work, Hurston provides a detailed account of her initiation as a hoodoo "worker" in New Orleans under the tutelage of a formidable specialist named Turner. In meticulous detail covering five pages of text, Hurston ([1935] 1968: 208–12) describes the visual, spatial, temporal, and physical elements of the difficult rite of passage whose ritual death and rebirth required her to fast and lie naked in seclusion for several days. Obviously aware that her own psychic journey is of little import, Hurston relegates her dissociative experience to a single passing reference to "five psychic experiences" (209). This straightforward, intimate retelling of her entrée into the secret powers of conjure is followed by an account of a series of instances of her mentor demonstrating how to put her newfound powers to work, manipulating the tools of a "science of the concrete" (Lévi-Strauss 1966) on behalf of clients who come seeking therapy for their "dis-eased" relationships.

Cheryl Wall (1989) interprets Hurston's apparent lack of indulgent self-expression as the burden of the female writer in a patriarchal world—social, literary, scholarly. According to Wall, Hurston's text shows "the ways in which women are relegated to subordinate roles in the culture she otherwise celebrates and, second, the means by which women in that culture gain access to creative expression and power" (661). Wall's thesis is that even though Hurston obediently silences herself throughout the text, in the end she comes "in possession of the word." Hurston allegedly gains that power through spirit possession. Wall never actually describes how Hurston's possession is a "journey back and the voyage within" that "empowered the anthropologist (Hurston) to tell her story to the world" (676). Confronted with the contradiction that Hurston does not manage to "tell her [uncensored] story" anywhere in the text of *Mules and Men*, Wall asserts that Hurston realizes the delayed personal and spiritual emancipation in her first novel, *Their Eyes Were Watching God* ([1937] 2006), in which she gives voice to a female protagonist who then becomes a model for subsequent protagonists, including Avey Johnson in Paule Marshall's *Praisesong for the Widow* (1983).

The Individual, Nature, and Possession in Modernity

The representation of Haitians' religion as the purest remnant of Africa in the New World is essential to its exotic appeal as a site for journey into the deepest regions of the self. Even though many key ritual elements derive from European practices, if they seem odd to outsiders, they are conveniently cast as African (Rey and Richman 2010). The imagination of African authenticity is more legible to modernity's discourses of history and "primitives." Rijk van Dijk (1998: 155) has argued with regard to discourses on tradition in Africa that "we have to shift our perspective from nostalgic theory to a theory of nostalgia." The nostalgic use of Haitian religion as a blank canvas through which to find the modern self is reinscribed in the application of outsiders' name for the religion, Vodou. Even today, some rural dwellers are confused when outsiders misuse this specific ritual term to indicate a broad and coherent set of beliefs and practices. Neither do they recognize its contents as assimilable in the same category. The creole term *vodou* refers to a genre of sacred music and dance performed in worship of a particular pantheon. The congregational forms and practices authorized as Vodou were not the authentic African religion of the peasants (as if there ever were one) but rather conventions of an evolving peri-urban institution (Richman 2005, 2007).

In the early decades of the twentieth century, the capital city of Port-au-Prince swelled with displaced rural migrants; their temples became anchors for a new congregational structure based on individual voluntary association unrelated to kinship (though kinship terms of address were used), elaborate and expensive rituals carried out by female initiates, and a separation between the roles of performer and spectator. In contrast to more egalitarian, particularistic, and local domestic practices associated with family-based worship, what came to be known as Vodou involved codification, homogenization, and monetization. Having been abstracted from their cumbersome and particularistic social, moral, and economic contexts, these elements were accessible to the adventurous tourist or ethnographer, even allowing one to delve into the deepest reaches—possession. Professional priests, as brokers of a new religious tradition welcomed converts, foreigners, and members of the Haitian elite or middle classes who were actively searching for meaning within modernity and who could join a reinvented Vodou, which had selectively appropriated aspects of the religion, rendered them harmless and offered them up as authentic African forms (cf. Peel 1994: 163). Central to these nostalgic Vodou ideas is the tenet that the spirits are universal nature gods.

Since the 1953 publication of *Horsemen*, at least, it has been taken for granted in the literature on Vodou that the lwa are universal. The common assumption in the ethnographic and popular literature is that anyone with the proper training and knowledge can worship Danbala Wedo, Ogou, or any other spirit. Haitians' use of a common nomenclature for their pantheons in asserting the universality of the lwa has no doubt confirmed the biases of researchers viewing Haitian cosmology through a lens foregrounding abstract individualism and universality. They wrongly concluded from evidence of widespread worship of Ogou that all of the devotees were worshipping one and the same Ogou as opposed to distinct spirits who share the same name. (The idea that there is only one Ogou would be similar to assuming that there is only one person named Smith or Jones.)

The assumption of the spirits' universality is the corollary of the modern notion of the abstract, equivalent individual. This notion is a requisite of capitalist culture because it allows all human labor to be reduced to the same essence in order for their different labor to be exchanged for varying quantities a uniform quality—money. This "magical" transformation is the basis of commodity fetishism (Marx 1977: 165). (Protestantism takes the homogenizing process a democratic step further by installing a direct line of communication from any person to the deity for instant messaging.) The application of the concept of the individual to experiencing Vodou is that, since all persons are free and equivalent, any person (and ultimately the researcher her- or himself) can have access to any spirit; there are no ontological barriers preventing communication. This communication is then focused inwardly on self-knowledge rather than communal interaction.

Though the Haitian peasantry emerged in and against a wholly modern system, as Sidney Mintz (1971: 37) has been at pains to point out, their descendants in places like Ti Rivyè have yet to countenance the notion of the abstract individual. As if in defense of their moral economy of difference and hierarchy, a creole proverb says: "Tout moun se moun men tout moun pa menm" (Everybody is a person but not all persons are equivalent). This adage does not make sense in North American morality, but if we were to invert the creole terms, we could crystallize contemporary North American morality and demonstrate how opposed it is to creole values. It would say, "Every person is the same, but not everyone is a (valid) person" (*Tout moun se menm, men tout moun pa moun*). My invented adage, which is absurd in a creole context, describes a system that professes equivalence at the same time as it creates and dehumanizes others and blames victims who fail at self-reliance.

Linked to the misleading impression of lwa as universal is the notion that they are nature spirits. Ritual discourse, mainly in song texts, and visual imagery often compare spirits to aspects or forces of nature, linking, for example, Danbala Wedo's energy with that of a water snake and Ogou's anger with thunder. It does not follow, however, that Danbala is an actual water snake or that Ogou in fact controls storms. This "denotative" reduction of Haitians' analogical classification (Lévi-Strauss 1966) continues largely unchallenged, despite the correction first tendered by Gerald Murray (1980). Unfortunately (perhaps for the lwa), Haitians do not think they wield powers to control air, land, or water. The powers of lwa are far more circumscribed. Their command is primarily confined to afflicting and protecting the health and labor power of members of descent groups to whom they belong. Yet they are also distinct from ancestors, who are worshipped in their own right and whose primary role, by virtue of their proximity to the other world, is to mediate relations between members of cognatic descent groups and their inherited lwa.

The *Eritaj*, Interdependence, and Possession

The interdependence among members of descent groups, namely, the living, the dead, and the lwa, has been largely overlooked by students of Haitian ritual communication in favor of a tendency to see Haitian persons as independent individuals who engage in dyadic relations with other autonomous actors (Mintz 1961). Anthropologists researching peasantries in Haiti and elsewhere in the Caribbean have assumed that slavery and migration have rendered marriages "fragile" and kinship "shallow" (Besson 2002: 290). Without evidence of lineages, it was thought that Caribbean peasants' primary social relations were through dyadic interpersonal networks. Researchers in fact overlooked evidence of the central foundation of rural social structure because they were searching for restricted, unilineal descent groups. Two ethnographic studies in the 1980s, one in Haiti and the other in Jamaica, independently compelled the long-overdue recognition of descent groups in the Caribbean. Ira Lowenthal (1987) and Jean Besson (1984, 2002) each found evidence of land-based cognatic descent groups tracing their beginnings to the early mid-nineteenth century and maintaining their identity and claims through rules about inalienable family land, land use, kinship terminology, and, of explicit relevance for this discussion, religious beliefs and practices involving invisible members of the group, the ancestors and the spirits.

A single word in creole signifies this mutually reinforcing and substantializing web of relations among living, deceased, and spiritual members of landholding descent groups: *eritaj*. From the French word *héritage*, the Kreyòl term both means and makes indivisible the cognatic descent group and the land left by the founding ancestor for all of his or her heirs (the founder could be male or female). This heroic ancestor is addressed by the title Prenmye Mèt Bitasyon (First Owner of the Estate), in recognition of his or her connection to the slave revolution of 1804 and the establishment of the material resource that symbolized resistance to plantation slavery. Veneration of the First Owner of the Estate further rests on the belief that he or she directly links the descent group to Ginen, the ancestral African homeland where ancestors' souls must return and the habitat of the lwa.

Not only do members of the eritaj inherit the family land left by the First Owner of the Estate, but, according the same principles of bilaterality and partible inheritance, they also come to the lwa served by the first owner and all of the ancestors. These spirits are "specific" and "exclusive" to particular eritaj regardless of their commonly used names. When eritaj members assemble, it is for the purpose of collectively propitiating their indivisible lwa. They gather on the sacred, reserved portion of the land, which usually consists of a homestead (*lakou*), often contiguous with the original homestead of the founder, a shrine housing the vessels containing the spirits of the founder and the ancestors, and various other landmarks personifying eritaj identity—the ruins of the foundation of the founder's house or well, certain trees, or a cemetery. At the beginning of each ritual on the family land, the descent group meticulously recites the entire genealogy of the spirits and the ancestors who belong to the eritaj and whose souls are believed to have returned to Ginen.

The lwa's powerful sway over the heirs derives from their inclination to afflict or "hold" (*kenbe*) members. Careful reckoning of this genealogy is critical to any diagnosis and cure of a lwa-caused illness. When a member falls sick, the medium, interceding on behalf of the family, typically summons discrete ancestors to find out the identity of the lwa who is now holding hostage the contemporary heir. Especially if the lwa has not been present to the members in recent memory, the ancestor will be asked to advise the appellants further on how to serve the spirit. The rhetorical framing of the finding about the etiology of the affliction is significant; it is said that the offender is a spirit inherited along a particular line of descent, for example, "a lwa Ogoun on the side of my mother's father is holding her."

Ira Lowenthal (1987) clarified the role of the ancestors in the course of discovering the central institution of the eritaj in rural Haitian society and economy. Ancestors bequeath rights and obligations in land and spirits to their heirs. Their main role in the complex of affliction and healing is to mediate communication between the living and the lwa (whom the same ancestors served). For members of the eritaj to stay on the right side of their lwa, they have to keep the names of their ancestors alive. They do so by reciting the names of ancestors at the rituals, carrying out regular ritual acts of remembrance and performing the more substantial annual rituals for the dead in November. Ancestors may not be want or be able to discipline heirs, but the belief that they alone hold the keys to knowledge about avenging spirits serves to keep their memories alive.

Lwa are, in effect, the protagonists of a cult of affliction and healing. When lwa feel neglected or ignored by the heirs, as they often do in their remote home in Ginen, they retaliate by sending affliction, "seizing" heirs with somatic illness, misfortune, and property loss. Worship by the kin group is a collective effort to ward off illness by enticing the avenging spirits to "release" their victims and to prevent future attacks. Such worship typically begins with substantial Catholic prayer, led in French by a lay priest, followed by drumming, singing in Kreyòl; dancing; visual art; parading; offerings of food, drink, and toiletries; animal sacrifice; and arrival of the spirit protagonist(s) "speaking" or "dancing in the head" of an heir (or heirs), a "personification" that signals that the intense multimedia ritual labor has successfully achieved its goal.

The symbolism of feeding encompasses all collective healing and ritual discourse and performance. Significantly, the very term for worship is "to serve" (*sèvi*), as in to serve food. The personalities of lwa are differentiated by their particular tastes in food and drink. Additionally, a lwa's displeasure is cast as hunger, and a ceremony is called a "feeding of the lwa." A successful "feeding" occurs when the spirit, having been enticed to journey all the way from Ginen, arrives personally to "party" with the family and to accept the lavish and copious offerings. The spirit's enjoyment of the music, dance, and food is an implicit signal that she or he has "let go" of the victim and/or agrees not to "take hold" of others, at least not in the immediate future.

Migrating members of descent groups do not escape the orbits of the mobile lwa served by their founding ancestors. Indeed they are prime "choices" of avenging spirits and primary sponsors of rites taking place back home. Elsewhere I have documented how transnational communities in Ti Rivyè appropriated audio and videocassette recording in order to perpetuate—and revitalize—the ritual communication practices of their land-based descent groups (Richman 2005). Members of these groups deem important religious rituals to be immobile, in the sense that they can only be performed on family land. Thus when migrants cannot personally attend the services, they participate in a delayed fashion by listening to cassette tapes of the rituals. On these tapes the migrants hear not only the sounds of the performance itself—drumming, singing, prayers, and chatter—but also the voices of narrators describing what the listener cannot see, including the climactic arrival of the spirit protagonist to "party" with the hosts both immediate and at a distance.[3]

A lwa who comes in "person" to "his" or "her" family party can be expected to indicate the speedy healing (or release) of the afflicted heir (whose physical presence is not required for efficacy), to heal tense relationships by objectifying them in humorous words and pantomime, and to offer blessings to the assembled. A less spectacular but no less palpable outcome is for the embodied spirit to serve as a physical conduit to the departed. The spirit's present manifestation simultaneously recollects the deceased person(s) whom the spirit "claimed" before. The "dissociation" of the consciousness of one person makes possible the reconnection with others. Michael Lambek (2003) found this reciprocity between dissociation and connection to be an important (if unspectacular) feature of Malagasy possession:

> Among Malagasy speakers, to gain (most kinds of) spirits is also to become increasingly connected to others. While relative to their hosts spirits are in one sense originally alien beings, non-selves, they are also social persons, and as such they carry with them the prior histories of their relations with humans. To become impassioned by a spirit is to interject aspects of this history. A woman who becomes possessed by a spirit who previously possessed and spoke through her mother or grandmother is identifying deeply with them, not only acknowledging her prior identification but also interjecting another aspect of their persons. (41)

Haitians' understanding of this deeply corporeal performance of interdependence between living members of a descent group, deceased members, and their spirits is informed by beliefs about the transmission of a spirit's unique "love" for one, and only one, member at a time and about how a spirit can mingle in human form with the group (though each unit does have enough lwa to furnish everyone with plenty of "love"). Until the chosen heir dies, the lwa cannot "love" another. And after the heir dies, a generation or more may pass before the lwa communicates her or his "love" for another heir through media of dreams, divination, or possession, often in the context of affliction. Until the lwa claims a new heir, the entire kin group loses touch with this source of support, connection with the past, and, not to be understated, means of entertainment.[4]

Spirits, Ancestors, and the Mediation of Transnational Affliction

The power of embodied communion with lwa to redeem and intensify connections with departed kin was made manifest to me during an episode involving the spiritual affliction and communal ritual healing of a man named Gérard. Not only did the ancestor help the eritaj members identify which lwa was "holding" their kinsman (and economic emissary); the lwa, in performance at the appointed time in the ritual, helped the members recollect the migrant's departed mother and cousin. I was living with the emigrant's family in Ti Rivyè when he became ill abroad and petitioned his relatives (living and deceased) to intervene.

Gérard was working in Delray Beach, Florida, at the time of his accident. Gérard fell from the second floor while working at a construction site. When the family got news of his accident, they went to the shrine on their mother's paternal estate. Ilavert, the resident *gangan ason*, a third-generation descendant of the founder and their maternal aunt's husband, summoned the lwa. Speaking through Ilavert from behind the door of the altar room, a lwa, Gede Nibo, or Guardian of the Yard (*Jeran Lakou*), claimed that he had protected Gérard from more serious injury. Gérard's father and sisters then promised Grandfather Gede / the Guardian that they would feed him.

According to Gérard's older sister, "They had been anticipating the funds to take care of the lwa for him" (*nou tap tann kòb la rantre pou nou kapab okipe lwa pou li*) when they received an urgent message from Gérard. The family and I assembled in the yard to listen to the cassette tape. Gérard was anxious. He complained that the spot where he bruised himself in the fall the previous year was eating him up inside (*manje 1andan*). He wanted his family to proceed with fulfillment of his obligation to the Guardian.

He told his aunt Filoza to take the funds necessary for a ritual feeding from the money he had sent her for the construction of his house.

That evening, Gérard's father and two sisters returned to the shrine. Ilavert "called the lwa." Grandfather Gede/the Guardian of the Yard and their mother's "dead" spirit gave instructions for the ritual offerings. The Guardian told them that he desired only a modest feast without drumming or dancing and that he expected only their branch of the descent group to be present (that is, Gérard's mother's siblings and his mother's and father's descendants). (The Guardian was being pragmatic; Gérard could not afford a more spectacular "feeding of the gods," nor the costs of providing many more guests with food and beverages.) Grandmother (Grann) Ezili, a lwa inherited through his father's mother, also spoke. She requested that Toro, Gérard's younger brother, who was also Outside, working in Florida, present her with her own "dessert" upon her altar place inside Toro's house. At about 8:00 one morning the next week, the family gathered inside and around Gérard's partially finished house. Gérard's sisters and their children and spouses, his father, and two of his maternal aunts and uncles and some of the latter's children and I were present. A tape recorder (in addition to my own) was also present. In a few days, Gérard would listen to the recording of the rite he sponsored.

While we were waiting for Ilavert to begin the ritual, I talked to Tenten, Gérard's maternal uncle, about the Guardian. The Guardian's wooden cross was planted at the boundary of his great-grandfather's estate. He described the Guardian as an "enormous protective force" (*gwo pwotèj*), "a good lwa" (*yon bon lwa*) who "stands up for us" (*kanpe pou nou*). Tenten went on in this tender tone to describe how the Guardian personified himself to family members, at once affirming the person's unique qualities and linking the individual to the "generation to generation" (*pitit an pitit*, literally, "child to child") continuity of the whole descent group. He described how when he was young, this "good lwa" used to "mount" his cousin Caridad, and after she died, the Guardian chose Lina, Gérard's mother, who was also an *ounsi*. (Lina died when Gérard and Toro were children.)

Thus the lwa had visited the family only once since Lina's death twenty-five years before, and Tenten regretted not being there. He had heard that a sorcerer had also stolen the lwa out of Filoza's head during the possession and had kept it away from the descent group. Tenten wondered if the Guardian would come to the service to accept Gérard's offering that morning and, if he did appear, whom the lwa would mount. So when, during the ritual bathing of the Guardian's sacrificial goat, the spirit suddenly mounted Filoza, Tenten and everyone else were profoundly moved and satisfied. Seeing the lwa proclaim his "love" for this worthy new "horse" in possession performance dramatized the continuity of substance from one generation to the next, even as it evoked memories of the Guardian's performances in Caridad and Lina, heirs who were no longer living.

I was the first to notice the onset of Filoza's possession, and I grabbed her arm to keep her from falling hard to the ground. The lwa swung the horse around and we supported "them" until "he" gained enough composure to stand by himself. His eyes finally focused straight forward after having been rolled hideously up and backward into his horse's head. The Guardian was a somber, gentle old man. He lovingly greeted and blessed each member one by one, drawing the person close, taking their hands in his and then extending their arms straight out to the side as he pressed his forehead solidly to theirs. Their adjoined foreheads became an axis fixing the slow rotation of two moving as one, side to side. The Guardian also blessed the fetus growing inside Fifi, Filoza's daughter-in-law, with a tender massage of her round belly and full breasts.

The lwa was mute; he signed messages by pointing his fingers, patting his fists, and thrusting his whole body in one direction or another. Ilavert, the *gangan ason,* interpreted the mime for the others. He indicated his satisfaction with the offering and chose Filoza's brother to sacrifice it. He told Filoza's other brother to drop out of a sorcerer's society in Archaie and to join the local one.

The lwa went away after the sacrifice, crossing the yard and dropping into a chair on Filoza's porch. Filoza awoke a few minutes later showing no signs of being aware of what had just happened to her. The goat and chickens were killed above a hole in the ground between the two emigrant brothers' houses into which their blood was allowed to drip. Gérard's sisters and their daughters then started cooking the ritual meal. To meet Toro's obligation to their Ezili, they laid a "dessert" table with a pink frosted cake and sweet drinks in the altar room (*ogatwa*) inside Toro's house. A plateful of cooked food was also placed upon the shrine. The goat's skull was later hung from a rafter in Gérard's house. That afternoon and evening everyone ate extremely well. The next morning, Gérard's fifteen-year-old niece, who had never before eaten so much meat, complained that she had suffered all night with a stomachache. Her mother and sister were already off serving bread and coffee to beggars at the local church, as the lwa had instructed them to do.

Communication by the spirit "in person" aids in the recollection of departed lineal kin who were once "loved" by the spirit, bringing back memories of how they uniquely interacted with the sprits now before them in a different body. As Tenten and his relatives demonstrated, this embodied mode of remembrance of lineal kin is profoundly satisfying. Possession offers the rare and precious occasion for members of the eritaj to contact not only the spirit but also the irreplaceable person (or persons) whom that spirit "loved." Writers obsessed with the spectacular features of possession in Haitian "voodoo" inevitably fail to perceive how possession can be a deeply felt mode of historical memory.

Rhetorical and scholarly biases have combined to blind researchers to the meanings of Haitians' embodied communication with spirits. Modern narratives of Vodou have reproduced the erroneous concepts of Haitian spirits, or lwa, as universalistic nature gods. Possession by one of these archetypal spirits has been viewed as a transformative experience for the individual, the consummation of a quest for an abstract self outside of a moral community but at one with the cosmos. The focus on auto communication was reinforced by the rhetorical burden of the term "possession" itself, meaning private ownership and unilateral control. This self-centered view of possession continues to inform the work of enthusiastic promoters of invented Vodou traditions but would be immoral in the ordinary ritual communications of Haitian descent groups. Attention to the Kreyòl metaphors that shape Haitians' perceptions of spirit and worship reveals that spirits are only known in and through family lines and that the purpose of possession is communication through performance of "speech" or "dance."

Belated scholarly recognition of the social institution of the eritaj—the cognatic descent group and the land settled in the defiant creation of a freeholding peasantry—enabled subsequent scholars finally to understand the role of ancestors in Haitian peasant belief and practice. The deceased are needed to mediate communication with lwa, who can willfully "hold" or "protect" members, no matter where they reside. My fieldwork detailing the everyday ritual practices of eritaj based in Ti Rivyè and stretching to Florida stumbled upon a corollary discovery: lwa, in turn, connect living members with their ancestors.

When they speak or dance "in person," they resuscitate the names and memories of the ones in whose bodies they celebrated in the past. If a triad is the minimum structure for possession to work as moral communication (Lambek 1981: 73), in the ritual practices of Haitian descent groups the implicit structure is often quadrangular. Four selves collaborate in this production of meaningful possession: the spirit, his or her present person (host), the assembled members of the kin group, and the departed ones through whom the same spirit once spoke and danced. The physicality of this quadrangular mode of symbolizing the interdependence of the descent group and recollection of the dead is the stirring power of Haitians' embodied communication. By speaking and dancing in person, spirits connect the living in a deeply embodied and intimate way to their ancestors, their lineal history, and their family land.

NINE

Mimetic Corporeality, Discourse, and Indeterminacy in Spirit Possession

RAQUEL ROMBERG

The Politics of Mimetic Corporeality and Alterity

Highly emotional and vivid, if mostly controversial, descriptions and evaluations of spirit possession have been produced by outsiders—from missionaries, travelers, and literati in colonial times to social scientists and artists in contemporary times. Rather than providing insights about their significance from the practitioners' perspective (unthinkable then), colonial representations of possession cults have been assessed by postcolonial scholars as reflections of colonialist and primitivist discourses about Others (see Dayan 1995). Another, more challenging perspective on colonial discourses about possession rituals takes into consideration the *dialogic* nature of colonial encounters: far from being the exclusive domain of Europeans, the reciprocal fascination with and fear of difference (Others) defines contact (F. Kramer 1993; Taussig 1993, 1997, 1999; Stoller 1989, 1995). Further, the exoticism of Europeans, as perceived by non-Europeans, is evidenced in ecstatic cults in which non-Europeans become possessed by European entities. In all cases of contact, the potential transformative power of exoticism transcends the merely obvious. Non-European exoticism, for example, may have done more than mediate transcultural contact and inform local forms of knowledge. It may have fed into mimetic performances such as, but not limited to, those of possession by means of which the powers of powerful Others could be invoked, channeled, and transgressed (Taussig 1993, 1999; Stoller 1995; Romberg 2003b, 2005, 2011).[1]

In an evocative rendition of the reality of possession, Paul Stoller (1995: 90) shows that the enactment of white colonial agents during Hauka spirit possession rituals, which are both frightening and funny, served the purpose of mastering whiteness through mimesis, of tapping into circuits of colonial and postcolonial power.[2] Referring to Hauka spirit possession as "horrific comedy," he further suggests that the embodiments of the Hauka were meant not only to evoke the colonial past but also to "manipulate the present, and provoke the future" (7).

Could a similar argument be made for Europeans embodying non-European alters in colonial and postcolonial contexts?[3] Drawing on Fritz Kramer's (1993) discussion of the mutual mimetic fascination of Europeans and non-Europeans, Irene Albers (2008) attempts to exorcise the morally accusative inferences made by postcolonial commentators about European misrepresentations of possession rituals, reframing them instead as evidence of *the reciprocal emotional shock of encountering others*. Disregarding the social and political effects that different kinds of emotional contact-shock might have unleashed, Albers argues that the "distortion and typification of the object—of which European exoticism is often accused—here serves the precise function of marking the state of being 'deeply moved' or 'possessed' by that which is represented in ecstatic cults" (2008: 274). Against both denunciations about false representations of Others and the possibility of neutral representations, Albers proposes "exoticism" as a medium of nonscientific knowledge, as a liberating form of visceral communication between cultures—not unlike the embodiment of Europeans in ecstatic cults of non-Europeans.

If one merely considers the differential effects that such "communication" has produced historically, this postulation appears to be amazingly naïve. Although the mimetic faculty of possession cults might be thought of as connecting self and alters by means of the ability to "yield into and become Other" (Taussig 1993: xiii), mimetic forms of "exoticism" or emotional transcultural knowledge—historical records teach us—have had deadly consequences. It has unleashed nightmares of representation and persecution. The life and memories of Médard (a Martiniquean artist/convict/legend), exquisitely articulated by Richard Price (1998: 157), illustrate the dangers of "knowing" or "possessing" the colonial masters via mimesis. Médard was imprisoned and exiled many times for "stealing" from the masters: not only did he steal food and commodities à la Robin Hood from Colonel Coppens's cane fields at Dizac to give to the poor, he also "stole" his image by means of a not-so-perfect carving of his image. In spite of living as a wild hermit in a cave, Médard was fascinated by the "exotic" world of French colonists, their dancing parties, pomp, and military parades; he made exact "photos" or carvings of colonial symbols of power and status such as ships, clocks, and musical instruments (70), as well as the French colonel in the area. For some unknown reason, the "photo" Médard made of the colonel was borne aloft by the crowd during the elections of 1925, which ended in a massacre. This unfortunate coincidence hurled Médard into exile as a convict. Pointing to the shared belief in the power of copies among both French colonial government agents and Martiniquean rebels, as well as Médard—one of Price's informants reminisced that when he was young, people used to tell the following story: " 'There was a general who came here. Méda drew him exactly. It was too true-to-life.' That's why they put him in prison, that's why they sent him to the *bagne* [penal colony]" (58).

As this and other colonial nightmares of illicit imitation and persecution show, the mimetic fascination with the symbols of colonial power had lethal consequences, particularly when the copying was made by polluting, wild alters who were both revered and feared for their assumed magical powers (Taussig [1980] 1983, 1987). Left at the moment of fascination and terror with the culture of oppressors, mimicry, or rather the production of imperfect copies of powerful "originals," has emerged as a tragic outcome of colonization, forever entangling any possible authentic expression of identity and real transformation.[4] But this impossibility acquires a different meaning within magic, the very imperfection of copies being constitutive of the technologies and excesses of magic, of its "wicked" side. Elsewhere I develop this idea further, linking the technologies of magic to "ritual piracy," or the strategic, unauthorized appropriation of symbols of power of powerful others for purposes other than those intended by them, and which become empowering because of this very transgression (Romberg 2005, 2011). Those who persecuted witches, sorcerers, and wild alters must have "known" that magic worked through copies, even imperfect ones.[5]

Reports by colonial agents and missionaries about what they wrongly perceived as primitive, devilish rituals of slaves morally justified their oppression and exploitation as well as forced conversion and regeneration. Numerous church edicts (in colonial times) and state laws (in postemancipation and postindependence periods) attest to the constant threat that alleged sorcerers posed to the social order (Romberg 2003a, 2003b). Joan Dayan (1995) and Sidney Mintz and Michel-Rolph Trouillot (1995) show, for instance, that the turbulence of Haitian political history is inseparable from the tribulations of Vodou, its wars, persecutions, gods, and fictions.[6] Tales of terror and cannibalism associated with the "magic" and "superstitions" of enslaved Africans fueled the urgent implementation and execution of laws that persecuted practitioners—depending on the historical period—for their alleged demonic and primitive or antimodern cults as heretics and charlatans, respectively (see Romberg 2003a). If during colonial times practitioners were persecuted for their devilish nature, during the postindependence state-building processes they would be persecuted for their alleged pathological and criminal behaviors—a common trend in Luso-Spanish-French colonial and postcolonial societies in the Americas and the Caribbean. For example, before shifting his professional persona from criminal lawyer to folklorist-ethnographer, Fernando Ortiz described the religious practices of Afro-Cubans (just four years after independence) in *La hampa Afrocubana* (1906) within a medico-criminal rhetoric as an "epidemic." In a tone completely opposed to his later work on Afro-Cuban religions, he suggested implementing a two-pronged campaign of "sanitation" directed against Afro-Cubans with the purpose of "eradicating infectious centers of worship" and "disinfecting the environment in order to prevent the persistence and reproduction of this disease" (374).[7]

In contrast, celebratory depictions of spirit possession rituals by artists, folklorists, and ethnographers driven by romanticizing quests for authentic ecstatic experiences have highlighted, only a couple of decades later, the esthetic-ethnic—not macabre or threatening—aspects of African-based spirit possession, drumming, and dance.[8] This esthetic-ethnic revaluation of possession provided state-sponsored cultural programs with folkloric evidence for asserting, in cultural terms, the African components of newly created postcolonial creole nations (Hagedorn 2001; Romberg 2007). Without question, the laudatory folklorization of spirit possession has contributed little if any to the improvement of the socioeconomic status and mobility of its practitioners (except, of course, those who were able to profit directly from this revalorization).[9]

The Reality of Spirit Possession and Spirit Presence

Although the historical assessment of spirit possession in colonial contexts is fundamental in order to address the tension between the creative powers of mimetic corporeality and its dangers (P. Johnson 2011), a more comparative (and less historical) exploration may help unravel another kind of tension, in this case from the practitioners' perspective between the mimetic corporeality of possession and the ritual effects of its discourse. In contrast to colonial and postcolonial regimes of social value, the evaluation and interpretation of possession rituals by practitioners and participants are more ambiguous and, in my view, more in need of further exploration. Drawing on specific cross-cultural instances in which the authenticity of possession is relentlessly questioned and tested by participants and proven by the possessed, this essay aims at illuminating their shared (should I say universal?) significance in shaping the drama and poetics of spirit presence. How is the reality of spirit possession accomplished? How is the mystery of the uncanny nature of spirit possession deferred? How do participants express their doubts about the veracity of possession events without endangering their very existence?

A brief excursus into the specific content of suspicions of fake spirit possession, even if beyond the focus of this essay, can tell a great deal about the sociohistorical context in which practitioners live and worship as well as make judgments about conditions and forms of authentic spirit presence. Stephan Palmié (2004), for example, discusses the content of suspicions of fake possession within the broader cash practices of a specific period in Cuba. In this context, the customary ritual conversion of commodities into spiritual gifts is further complicated by the moral and ritual consequences of paying a *derecho* (ritual fee) in either (devalued) pesos or (valued) dollars. During a *tambor* (a Santería celebration) Palmié attended with some friends in one of the problematic zones of Centro Havana in 1994, a medium incorporating Yemayá (the orisha owner of the sea) refused to accept the *derecho* offered by the anthropologist in the form of a peso because it was in the wrong currency. One of the intriguing explanations offered by Palmié's friends was that the possession of the medium was not actually "fake"; rather, it was a "fake deity"—a "*santo jinetero*" (hustling spirit)—not Yemayá, the one who possessed the horse and solicited "real money" (dollars) from the anthropologist, but "a recognizable stranger" who might have "turned into the trick of a divine prostitute" (a *santo jinetero*) or even perhaps of its impostor (256). Another explanation offered by Palmié in a footnote is that Yemayá herself might have demanded a more valuable gift—in dollars—than the devalued peso. A third plausible explanation is that the medium could have been faking possession altogether—that is, that the "horse was without a jockey," and thus it was the medium, not the deity, who was asking for dollars.[10]

All three scenarios are compelling for my purposes here; rather than threatening the possibility of spirit possession or its "reality" altogether, these kinds of suspicions of "fake" possession point to the insurmountable indeterminacy of its manifestation or its "reality effect." If spirits are whimsical and may choose to appear and deliver their messages in unprecedented ways, the ways in which they may appear are also capricious (Romberg 2012a, 2012b). Furthermore, if mimetic corporeality explains the manifestation of spirits in this world, who could set the limits to the mimetic resemblance manifested by "horses"? What is the significance of suspicions and explanations of "fake" possession, then? After all, who can determine the proper ways of the spirits, and who can then determine that the possession was feigned? Skepticism, rather than certainty, seems to be the sole intrinsic feature of spirit possession rituals. As illustrated below, the relentless cross-cultural attention to performances that aims at testing and proving the authentic (mimetic) nature of spirit manifestations suggests that doubt is an integral aspect of the technologies of presence in spirit possession rituals.[11] Perhaps the ever-present doubt before making a leap of faith is what makes the leap all the more dramatic for participants of spirit possession rituals.

As an ethnographer, I was always puzzled by the spontaneous comments participants in spirit possession rituals made to me and others present—never to the possessed individual—after or even during possession about their quality and authenticity.[12] At that time, these comments made me feel quite uncomfortable, especially when I knew well the person who was the object of such criticism; I interpreted them as evidence of the competition that I have noted existed among healers. Retrospectively, however, I see these critical remarks as constitutive elements of spirit possession rituals, as judgments of the level of mimetic resemblance of spirit manifestation, and my own reluctance to ask more about them at that time as less the result of a devoted form of cultural relativism and more an intuitive form of compliance with the "public secret" of spirit possession (Taussig 1992: 130–33). Everybody (myself and the possessed included) knew that such remarks were integral to the experience of spirit possession but also knew that these comments should not be articulated publicly. Michael Taussig's (1999: 5) definition of the public secret as "*that which is generally known, but cannot be articulated*" is relevant here. Rather than taking the secret at face value—that there is indeed a secret—the idea of "public secret" suggests that there are no secrets, because everybody knows that others know that they know, but nobody speaks openly about what they know others know. In a similar vein, Foucault's exploration of the history of sexuality suggests, among other things, that during the Victorian era, sexual repression produced just the opposite: relentless speech about sex. The power of the public secret therefore lies in that everybody talks about the secret and by doing so keeps the public secret—sexual repression, in the Victorians' case—alive, refueling its social power by negating its very existence. Stressing the power of negation, Taussig (1992: 133) poignantly notes that the public secret takes on the burden of protecting not only a possible deceit (of the possessed mediums) but most essentially "of protecting a great epistemology of appearance and reality . . . in which appearance is thought to shroud a concealed truth—but not the truth that there is none."

The Power of Spirit Possession: Mimetic Corporeality and Its Discourse

More than in other types of ritual performance, the reality of spirit possession depends on its emergent quality, on the participants' ability to summon and establish communication with the spirits through drumming, dancing, and sacrifices and the readiness of some to offer their bodies as hosts for the spirits. The risks of a failed ritual are therefore countless. By means of group-specific discourses that describe, evaluate, and control the manifestation of spirits during ritual possession, I suggest, participants implicitly address the otherwise elusively emergent and expressly indeterminate reality of spirit possession rituals. Rather than questioning the possibility of spirit possession, critical comments by participants about the possessed and the likelihood of their "faked" possession in fact re-create the assumed sacredness of spirit possession in roundabout ways—via an array of dramas of revelation that constantly conceal that which they reveal: the *"secretly familiar"* (Taussig 1999: 51) nature of spirit presence.

The ambiguity that informs what is dramatically performed and what is dramatically silenced (or what is visibly and invisibly present) during spirit possession rituals poses intriguing questions as to the kinds of emergent, indeterminate experiences this ambiguity engineers. In his analysis of Kaluli spirit séances, Edward Schieffelin characterizes emergence as that which happens *"by virtue of* performance" (1996: 64). "All conversation with the spirits, engrossment with them, anxiety and thrill over the information they impart, indeed the whole forward motion of the performance builds upon the successful creation of *the reality of spirit presence"* (64–54; my emphasis). In effect, as in many other cross-cultural phenomena, the convincing presence of spirits is dependent upon the unpredictable, unscripted, improvisational ways in which spirits manifest themselves (Romberg 2012b). And yet it seems the reality of spirit presence is equally dependent on the ability of mediums to make that presence compellingly felt (recognized) among participants. Thus the social evaluation of a good or bad séance or spirit possession, of whether the presence of the spirits has been perceived or felt as authentic or simulated reflects not on the assumed authenticity of visiting spirits but on the dexterity (excellence and authenticity) of mediums ("horses"). What is being judged in private and occa-

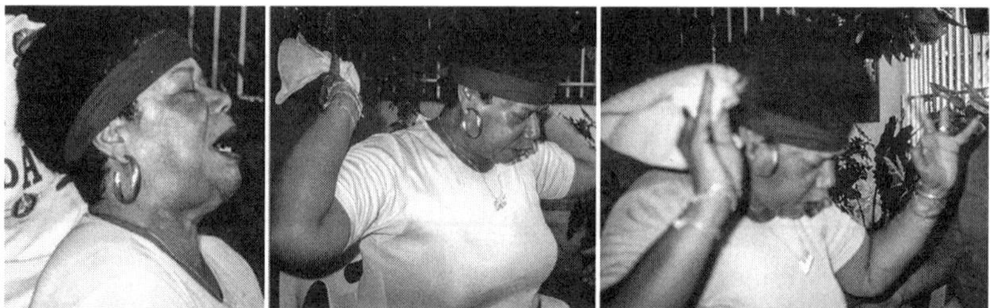

Figure 9.1. Haydée unexpectedly possessed in her waiting room by the Indio. Photograph by R. Romberg.

sionally in public is thereby the overall deftness of mediums, the accuracy of their gestures with regard to how well they embody the spirits' voices, how indistinguishable their movements are from those of the spirits, how unpredictably and succinctly they are able to convey the spirits' messages and raise the emotional engagement of participants.[13] This was the case every time Haydée— the *bruja* (witch healer I worked with for more than a year)—unexpectedly entered a state of trance in the middle of a consultation (see figure 9.1).

This points to a remarkable paradox about spirit possession rituals. While they are experienced as spirit-guided mimetic corporeal events outside of any form of human control and hence of any discourse, they are in fact ruled by particular, if implicit, hidden group-specific discourses about what constitutes successful, authentic spirit possession.[14] The recurring risks of failure, of spirit possession rituals not "working," of not being credible, pose fascinating questions about the technologies of presence, which are publicly performed, recognized, and commented upon but most crucially also stubbornly denied.

Emanating from apparently contradictory group-specific forms of explicit and implicit modes of somatic and discursive attention, these technologies of presence are partly responsible for the power and efficacy of spirit possession rituals.[15] In addition to participants' commentaries and gossip about the quality of the spirit possession event, they include all sorts of proving and testing performances whose sole purpose is to dispel suspicions that possession might have been fake. For example, writing about the proofs of authentic spirit possession, medical anthropologist Daniel Halperin mentions the incident reported by Leacock and Leacock (1972: 215) in which "a young woman, whose possession by a spirit named José Tupinambá was questioned (another medium was already possessed by the spirit), called loudly for glowing coals to prove the possession" (1995:

5). As rituals of revelation and unmasking of the public secret of spirit possession, they have a similar effect and are integral to spirit possession rituals, very much like the magician asking a member of the audience to check whether the black top hat is indeed empty before pulling a rabbit out of it is an integral part of the magician's act.[16] For example, mediums are expected to show visible signs of entering a state of semiconsciousness before the spirit enters their bodies and, after the possession, to appear disoriented as if awakening from a deep sleep, showing signs of having suffered momentary amnesia. Retroactively these overt gestures, which become "performances of proof," may take various forms, but the underlying explanation is common to all: mediums who do not remember what transpired during spirit possession prove that their possession was indeed truthful, that the spirit took hold of their body completely. Of the reactions of Vodou practitioners after possession, Alfred Métraux writes, "The possessed *pretends* to remember absolutely nothing of what he may have said or done. Although some pretense is clearly apparent, his denials in this respect are categorical. *One is not supposed to know* that he has been the receptacle of a spirit until others inform him. Many affect disbelief concerning their actions. A woman whose dress was torn during possession came to ask me about the cause of the damage; her pained surprise *appeared* genuine" (1955: 21; emphasis mine).[17] Métraux is not only implicitly conveying his skepticism about the sudden "amnesia" of the possessed but also expressing his reservations about the need to prove this amnesia, especially since everyone knows that one is not supposed to remember. The words "pretends" and "appear" disclose the theatricality of what I call here "proving performances," of their proving nothing beyond their signaling that no deception had taken place, that the mystery of spirit possession is sustained by moves targeted at dispelling disbelief.

Although the effectiveness and power of spirit possession (like those of divination and healing rituals) depend on performative dramas that defy the existence of any discourse regulating the spontaneity and indeterminacy of possession, overt somatic (prereflective) and hidden discursive (reflective) modes of awareness and unmasking coexist in subtle ways (cf. Csordas 1990, 1993). Via ritual speech, music, and manipulation of objects, these dramas produce apparently unscripted, multilevel sensorial experiences of what I have termed elsewhere "spiritual time" (Romberg 2009).[18] That spirit possession is a mimetic corporeal manifestation driven by the spirits—not the mediums—is reasserted again and again in each and every proof- and test-seeking performance, also conjuring the elusive and insubstantial reality of spirit presence by relentless discursive means.

In a brilliant historical analysis Michel de Certeau ([1970] 1990) explores the joint production of discourses of possession by individuals and institutions in seventeenth-century Loudun, France. He unravels how the particular forms these discourses took, the places in which they occurred, and the agents that produced them shaped not just collective perceptions about spirit possession and the modes for its recognition and interpretation but also individual experiences of it, in particular the apparent ease or difficulty, if not impossibility, for some to become possessed. Following this lead, the ubiquitous if suppressed role of individually produced and collectively circulating commentaries by participants about spirit possession in creating the unique reality of possession becomes apparent. Like the expected testing and proving performances of the possessed during spirit possession, they provide opportunities for openly recognizing that deception always lurks behind the potentially truthful and risky manifestation of the spirits among the living.

Mimetic Corporeality and the Risks of Spirit Possession

Spirit possession has been aptly and succinctly characterized by Marc Augé (1999: 27–43) as a mysterious and risky "double movement" of exit and return.[19] This mysterious movement has been poetically characterized by Temiar mediums in Marina Roseman's ethnography of Malay healing as "remembering to forget" (1991: 152–53). Among Temiars, "everyday knowledge and experience is forgotten, displaced by the remembering of the dream-time and connection with the spirit guide" (152). In this ethnography and many others that have dealt with healing and spirit possession, there is a remarkable similarity in the range of bodily signs that publicly mark the double movement of separation and unification or exit and return of the soul from and to the body of the medium. I am tempted to suggest that a universal concern with this inexplicable mystically inspired corporeal manifestation elicits all sorts of bodily reactions that seem to follow an equally universal bodily grammar.

The exit of the soul of the "horse," for instance, has been described as marked by sudden trembling and jerking movements of the limbs, torso, and head; convulsions; sudden outbursts; heavy breathing and perspiration; distraught, anguished, or drowsy facial expressions; and an overall appearance of drowsiness. After the vital parts of the personality of those possessed exit their bodies, if only for a moment, in order to let the spirits inhabit them, they enter an uncanny, risky state of being: of being alive but not quite living. A sudden, eerie mode of awakening from this torpor, accompanied by convulsive agitation, follows as a preamble to the expected change of personality and gestures that indicate that the possessing spirit is now directing the body of the medium. When the possessed finally recover their own vital force as if from a state of quasi death, the return of the medium's soul is dramatically enacted by sensual markers of confusion and disorientation, such as coughing and the inability to speak or remember, usually accompanied by signs of awakening from a deep sleep (Rouch [1967] 1971, 1978; Stoller 1989). Even though, quite interestingly, the bodily signs of experienced mediums might become fewer and shorter, the dramatic exit and return of the medium's vital force are essential to creating the right atmosphere for the uncanny shift of personality, of remembering to forget, that participants expect to see happening during spirit possession rituals. What is noteworthy is that a similar if inverse drama of arrival and departure of spirits to and from the body of the "horse" is not as elaborately marked as the exit and return of the medium's soul. Or perhaps the medium's changes of body movements and gestures are the indicators of both the exit and return of the soul and the imminent arrival and departure of the spirits. Like the rising and falling of curtains in a play, they frame the beginning and end of spirit possession. The surrender of mediums to the whims of spirits—often after a visible but subtle quivering of the medium about to submit to the will of the spirit—attests to the ultimate sacrifice that mediums make on behalf of their communities of worship; further, it proves that what transpires during spirit possession is the result of the spirit's plan, not that of its human horses. This is how the presence of the spirits and the reality of spirit possession are manifested and its ritual efficacy is publicly assured.

Since the risks of spirit possession for the possessed are high, usually attending assistants encircle mediums to prevent the mediums' body from getting hurt during possession and to ensure that their soul can safely return at the end of possession. I often heard Puerto Rican *brujos* (witch healers) and *santeros* (Santería healers) complain about the weariness of their *materia* (body), following the perils of spirit possession. When I met Tonio, a famous elderly brujo, he said that spirit possession had become too strenuous for his frail body; even his *protecciones* (guardian spirits), which had helped him "overpower any brujo in the past," could not shield him in his condition now.[20] In addition to Spiritist entities, sometimes experienced brujos also "catch" (*cogen*) evil spirits pestering their clients in order to exorcise them from the bodies of their victims. Usually, as such evil spirits possess a brujo, another assisting brujo conducts a proxy exorcism performed with the aim of subduing them. Through a series of questions (startlingly similar to those reported by de Certeau in seventeenth-century exorcisms at Loudon), assistants endeavor to identify the evil spirit pestering the victim and then to induce them, through a series of intimations and commands, to leave their victim's body forever and depart to the celestial mansions. Contributing to the technologies of spirit presence, assistants also have the role of translating the messages of the spirits to participants of spirit possession rituals. In Afro-Latin spiritual gatherings these messages are given in *bozal* (broken Spanish of unbaptized slaves)—a familiar language to habitués but always in need of ritual translation. Adding to the reality of the soul's exit during spirit possession, assistants also report to mediums what transpired while they were possessed as they recover from possession in a state of disorientation and confusion, not knowing what had happened. Indeed one of the important purposes of the various corporeal, nondiscursive markers of the soul's exit performed at the beginning of possession is to publicly indicate that the spirits have taken over the consciousness of the possessed and that they—not the medium—are responsible for whatever transpires during spirit possession. This shift of authorship confers a timeless and spaceless veracity to the words spoken by the spirits (through the body of the horse), who reveal what is otherwise concealed from humans (see Crapanzano 1980; Bauman and Sherzer 1974; Du Bois 1993; Romberg 2009). The resulting dramatic and poetic exchanges between the visiting spirit and the community of practitioners establish a unique reality predicated upon prereflective practical beliefs: spirit possession is neither learned nor intentional, it occurs spontaneously among some and might be impossible for others, and the particular script of spirit possession rituals is essentially indeterminate.

Far from being unproblematic, however, the ability of some and inability of others to become possessed raise intriguing questions about the idea of possession and its mysterious workings. In one of the chapters of Umberto Eco's *Foucault's Pendulum* (1989), two fictional characters illustrate some of the tensions between the spontaneity expected of spirit possession and any attempts to induce it intentionally. At an Umbanda *gira* (spiritual gathering) in Rio de Janeiro, mediums become effortlessly possessed by different *orixás* (deities) and *egúns* (spirits of the dead) to the increasingly fast and loud beat of drums. A blond German psychologist—a habitué of these gatherings—stands out in the group, having failed to become possessed despite her exceedingly energetic attempts, moving with her eyes closed to the changing beats of the ritual drums (211–12).[21] In contrast, Amparo—a Marxist student of political science who is of mixed indigenous, African, and European ancestry—becomes possessed against her will by the very spirits she refuses to believe in "for being another opium of the plebeians" (214–15). Her refusal to become possessed could be seen as inversely analogical to the German woman's desire to be possessed. As two sides of the same coin, they reassert the simultaneous visceral yet uncontrollable reality of spirit possession as well as their possible enslaving or liberating effects in either Marxist or psychological terms.[22]

The visceral theatricality of spirit possession and its potentially enslaving and liberating powers particularly in the colonial context have been noted and documented by several ethnographers and artists since the 1930s (Leiris 1958, [1939] 1988, 1996; Métraux 1955; Rouch 1955; Stoller 1995; Taussig 1993).[23] Marked by domination and exploitation, colonial encounters provided the stage and the characters that were enacted in tragicomic mimetic theaters of spirit possession (Stoller 1995). As forms of counterhegemonic embodied memories of the colonial past, these mimetic dramas point to both the enslaving and liberating aspects of spirit possession, offering a glance into an otherwise silenced history from below.[24]

The theatricality of spirit possession fascinated ethnographers, especially those influenced by surrealism, for other, more existential reasons as well. A case in point is the confession French ethnographer and writer Michel Leiris makes about his desire to be possessed in his diary/ethnography, *L'Afrique fantôme* (1934), about the Zar, a popular spirit possession cult in Ethiopia (mentioned in Albers 2008). Refusing to adopt the "cold-blooded" distance of the observer suggested to him by his mentor, the French anthropologist Marcel Griaule, Leiris ended up participating in the Zar cult with the hope of overcoming the inherent split of the observer from the observed for the purpose of achieving a very much desired personal unity with the authentic primitive (Albers 2008: 277–78).[25] Yet his fear of being duped by the practitioners of Zar manifests, according to Albers, "an anxiety that is nothing but the inverse of the desire for an absolutely authentic primitive" (287). Indeed, "Leiris consistently believes that he is experiencing something fundamentally inaccessible to him, something that exactly corresponds to his phantasm of a state of '*hors de soi*'" (277). During the spirit possession ritual performed for him, he is assigned a protective male Zar spirit: Leiris "drinks the animal's blood, eats the chicken sacrificed for him and has its entrails strewn upon his head." In spite of almost transcending the borders of spirit possession, Leiris still cannot free himself from the impression of having participated "in a theatrical play staged foremost for him" (quoted in Albers 2008: 278).[26] The mimetic corporeality of that spirit possession ritual evidently was not as convincing as Leiris had expected it to be, and thus that experience was not enough to dispel his skepticism about that spirit presence, or perhaps even the possibility of spirit manifestations altogether. Troubled by the disappointing realization that he may have been duped, Leiris reinterpreted his experiences with the Zar twenty-four years later in *La possession et ses aspects théâtraux chez les Ethiopiens de Gondar* (1958) by drawing an analogy between the performative ambivalence of spirit possession and his assumptions about the authenticity of autobiographic representation. He notes, on the one hand, that "the supposed authenticity of the autobiographical representation is the result of a play, a permanent assimilation of one's behavior with scripted roles" and, on the other, that "there is no 'authenticity' beyond the play" (quoted in Albers 2008: 284). Disenchanted, he reveals his doubts about the authenticity of the performances of the Zar cult, since—like autobiographical writing—they are guided by scripted roles. What previously could be read as suspicions about his being deceived or as the result of his anxiety about not being able to sense the presence of spirits is now reframed within a discussion about the carnivalesque artistry of the cult, which entails creating alternative realities to the everyday through props, dramaturgy, and ecstatic dance. The "theatre" of the possessed, he concludes, "is not a conscious assumption of roles, but an event in which the theatrical character remains hidden from the participants themselves" (quoted in Albers 2008: 286). Coining the term "*théâtre vécu*," or "lived theatre," which he opposes to the European "*théâtre joué*," or "acted theatre," he suggests that in the former "the distinction between theatre and reality collapses." Spirit possession, as a form of lived theater, thereby constitutes a specifically ambivalent space, a "*monde intermédiaire*," in which the distinction between simulated and authentic spirit possession ceases to be relevant.[27]

Even if this proposition seems viable, it still fails to encompass cases in which the reality of the "lived theatre" falls short of congealing or the habitual oscillations between faith and skepticism recorded among participants. Regardless of whether these comments are expressed publicly or not, they do not seem to threaten—as Leiris's suspicions threatened his own experience of spirit possession—the reality of possession. Rather, the expressed evaluations of the possessed by participants pose intriguing questions about the role of skepticism in sustaining the "fiction" of "unconscious" possession in spirit possession rituals (Leacock and Leacock 1972: 208; quoted in Halperin 1995: 13).[28] As shown in figure 9.2, the possessed medium "becomes" the spirit (in this case, Elegua, the child), adopting the character, behavioral gestures, and taste of the possessing spirit. How is the apparent duality of sensuous mimetic corporeality and intrinsic discursive skepticism together with the embodied skepticism (of testing and proving

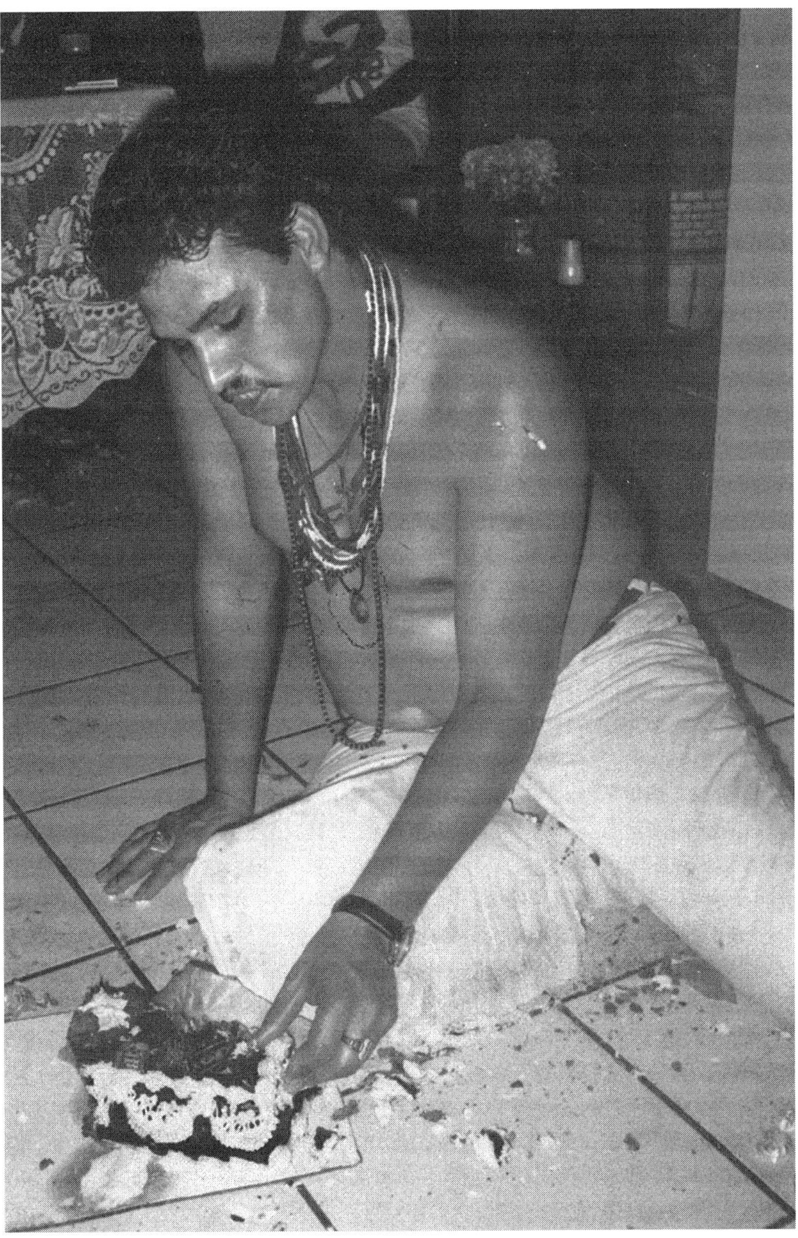

Figure 9.2. "Unconscious" incorporation of Elegua. Photograph by R. Romberg.

performances) resolved in spirit possession rituals? Moving beyond the historically situated relation between the possessed and the pantheon of spirits possessing them, my exploration of the reality of spirit possession here focuses on the interplay between the possessed, the presence of spirits, and the other participants. This approach is inspired by leading works in folklore and anthropology about performance and social life (Abrahams 1968, 1977, 1981; Bauman and Briggs 1990; Bell 1998; Hymes 1975; Tambiah 1985) and about the performance of healing (Laderman and Roseman 1996; Stoller 1995). From an encompassing performative approach to spirit possession rituals, I argue, doubts and any critique about the excellence, veracity, and effectiveness of the possessed as well as all sorts of testing and proving performances of the spirits' presence become intrinsic to the emergent, indeterminate reality of spirit possession. As forms of "skilled revelation of skilled concealment" (Taussig 1998: 222), discursive and embodied expressions of doubt and testing could be seen as complementary manifestations of the mimetic corporeality of the "lived theatre" of spirit possession, which provide indispensable momentary deferrals of both faith and skepticism during spirit possession rituals.

Folk Discourses of Spirit Possession

Cross-cultural evidence shows that historically and geographically specific discourses of spirit possession provide criteria for its control not less than for its evaluation among participants.[29] Whereas folk theories predicate the legitimacy and authenticity of possession on the spontaneity and uncontrollability of the world of spirits, several ethnographic cases attest to the contrary when mediums are coached to learn the proper demeanor of possession, or when conflict arises about which spirit can or should possess a medium. Such instances illustrate the existence of folk discourses and techniques that paradoxically aim at regulating and directing that assumed spontaneity and indeterminacy. In effect, one of the assumptions among the brujos whom I worked with is that not only can one not learn to be a healer—either one is given that god-given gift or not—but also only the spirits can choose whom to possess, even though on certain occasions such as *veladas* (communal nightly séances) brujos "coach" individuals who have shown themselves to be endowed with spiritual gifts and have manifested the early signs of becoming possessed "to let their bodies receive the spirit, to leave their fears and relinquish the control over their bodies."[30]

One of the purposes of specialized classes at Scientific Spiritism cen-

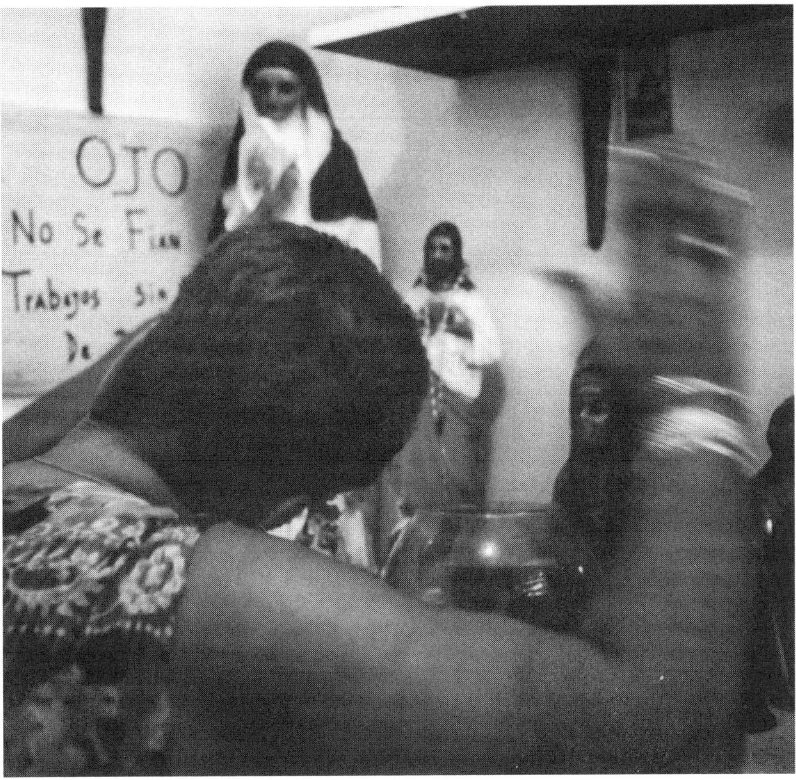

Figure 9.3. "Conscious" incorporation of La Caridad by Haydée (the child) by Armando. Photograph by R. Romberg.

ters and at private *metafísica* workshops in Puerto Rico is to help novice mediums develop their mediumship.[31] In this case, which Halperin characterized as "conscious" possession, mediums do not undergo a total change of personality and behavior as in "unconscious" possession. Instead, they are expected to keep their bodies as composed as possible and just let the spirits speak and deliver messages through them (see figure 9.3). A middle-aged man I met at a *botánica* (a store that sell religious paraphernalia) in Puerto Rico told me he had stopped going to Scientific Spiritism centers because he had been deeply hurt by the remarks of the director of one center, who once arrogantly scolded him for letting "primitive" spirits possess him. He explained, "Apparently my body contorted in overly expressive ways while I was in trance and thus [at the end of trance] the director instructed me to 'educate these wild spirits.' " To me he clarified that "these were my African spirits," and with a tone meant to convey his sarcasm, he concluded, "In no way do they need educating, ha, ha, ha." The proper ways mediums of Scientific Spiritism "channel" spirits are very different from the ways Santería devotees embody their *orishas*.[32] In present-day Puerto Rico (and most surely other places in the Caribbean), where practitioners of related Afro-Latin spirit-possession traditions join in celebrations, the question is how do participants assess "authentic" possession: what for one group might seem appropriate may seem exaggerated for another.

One crucial difference is that Spiritists are expected to learn to "control" the spirits and to deliver their messages in "clear" ways (Halperin's "conscious" possession). During one of the metafísica classes I attended during my fieldwork, I saw an elderly woman get seriously hurt, physically and emotionally, when the instructor-medium—very much like the aforementioned director—instructed the rest of the participants to leave her alone upon her showing the initial signs of fluttering, indicating that trance was about to occur. The point of the instructor's admonition was to demonstrate to the participants how to "educate" a spirit when it "violently descends on" or "takes possession" of their bodies. For this purpose, the instructor had the woman's husband conduct her carefully from her seat in the back of the room to the front. She then began instructing the woman (who had her eyes closed and was trembling) to "control the spirit" while the rest of the class was instructed to pray in litany Hail Marys and Our Fathers. Not being able to control her own body's movements—and as no one was allowed to assist her physically—the woman suddenly fell down; the back of her head hitting the tiled floor with a chillingly troublesome thud. The alarmed participants (myself included) were struck dumb. The instructor's request had clearly contradicted the practices I had observed among brujos, *espiritistas*, and santeros of placing hands a few inches away from the back of the possessed person for the purpose of protecting the "*materia*" from getting hurt. Sensing the tension caused by the unfortunate accident, the instructor explained in quite apologetic terms to the appalled class—while the dazed, crestfallen woman returned to her seat—that "spiritual energies are like children, you have to educate them. You should know when they're about to arrive, and you have to stand up, control them, receive their energy, process it, and then deliver the message."[33] In this context and following the exegetes of Scientific Spiritism (e.g., Amorim and Escudero), the subtext of "to educate" is to avoid letting the spirits dominate the body movements of mediums in a way reminiscent of Afro-Latin forms of spirit possession. According to this perception, spirits need to be taught to communicate only via those encoded forms accepted and institutionalized by Scientific Spiritism (e.g., automatic writing, telekinesis, telepathy, clairvoyance, psychometry, and so forth).

A particular way of speaking during spirit possession that is "direct" and occasionally could become rude and obscene is considered a sign that the spirits, not mediums, are the ones speaking. The very unique ways in which spirits are expected to speak could be one of the many modes of identifying local discourses of spirit possession and make judgments about "authentic" spirit possession. The expectation that spirits mimetically embody the proper ways of speaking of spirits raises essential questions as to who is expected to perform appropriately the speech of spirits—the spirit riding the horse or the horse? Failure to embody these signs might just prove that the medium is not yet ready or mature enough to allow his or her body to articulate publicly and "clearly" the voices of the spirits without any censorship or limits (see Romberg 2009: 157–59). This is what happened to Chini, a Korean shaman novice, whose case—as recounted by Laurel Kendall (1996)—suggests that in addition to having the inspiration of the spirits and receiving their messages, mediums need to be able to appropriately "perform" their voices in public in order to be considered true shamans. "It was the ability to perform that Chini lacked. She failed, the initiating shamans acknowledged, because she was too self-conscious and inhibited. By their logic, she was unable to perform because she could not give herself over to the flow of inspiration conjured by drums beats, dancing, costumes, and by their own suggestive comments—'The spirits are coming!'" (Kendall 1996: 50). In other words, even though mediums are not the ones who speak, they need to let their will over their bodies and voice exit completely and allow the spirits to move their bodies and articulate their messages directly—without any internal censorship. In fact, as I have seen on several occasions among brujos and espiritistas, this is the very goal of mediumship coaching by other more experienced mediums, who constantly cajole novices upon their showing signs of entering trance during such initiatory rituals: "Speak clearly—the santos speak clear!"[34] When the spirits are the ones speaking through the medium's vocal cords, there are usually dramatic shifts of interpretive and emotional frames that call attention to the implied authority, intentionality, and consequence of the spirits' messages; such messages are governed by a unique regime of value and interpretive framing recognized by shamans and healers as well as participants (and perhaps also by spirits). Apart from coaching novices to let their bodies and minds open to the spirits, I have seen and heard brujos also cajole (and coach) the spirits to come through and possess their horses. During veladas and occasionally private consultations, when a person shows signs of becoming possessed, experienced brujos cajole the spirits—speaking directly to them—to come forth, to mount the horse, and to speak clearly through it.

During my fieldwork, Armando, an espiritista-santero from New York, began collaborating with Haydée, the bruja I was working with for more than a year. When Changó's day approached (December 4, also the saint day of Santa Bárbara), Armando decided to throw a lavish party (coronation) in her honor in recognition of her lifesaving intervention. At various points during the coronation festivity for Changó, some of the guests who were also healers expressed to me their doubts about Armando's possession.[35] One healer said that when one is possessed, one does not react so directly to the questions posed by the audience or the behaviors of others as Changó's horse (Armando) did. These comments suggest that folk discourses of spirit possession constitute not only collective perceptions about its authenticity or fakery but also individual judgments of its appropriateness and reality. Days and weeks after a spirit possession ritual, participants might keep commenting (gossiping) about the quality of a past spirit possession ritual and on the messages conveyed by the spirits to the community of practitioners, suggesting that the reality and power of spirit possession depend on and emanate from such discursive reflections no less than its mimetic performative excellence.[36] In this vein, Susan Rasmussen (1993) shows, for example, that the Tuareg people, in effect, re-create spirit possession in their commentaries about its music, singing, and dancing in terms of aesthetic competence as well as curing efficacy.

By the same token, suspicions about "fake" possession, as expressed by participants of spirit possession rituals (and ethnographers), have been widely documented and interpreted in several ethnographies. However, with the exception of Taussig (1998) and Halperin (1995, 1996a), as far as I know, few have placed "fake" spirit possession at the very center of their inquiry unless they were inspired by performance approaches that explored group-specific spirit possession codes and the instances in which they were shaken or broken. It is as if the ethnographic engagement with the visible, empirical, and undeniable "reality" of spirit possession somehow promotes the bracketing of discursive judgments by ethnographers. Perhaps, in keeping with the quest for trust and respect that inform ethnographic encounters, inquiries about the veracity of spirit possession among participants have been mostly self-censored. In quite an exceptional way, Halperin reveals, "Often I observed mediums who seemed to be in the throes of a deeply altered state of consciousness. At other times, I felt less certain about a dancer's 'trance' state and on a few occasions was left with the intuitive impression that a medium was deliberately acting possessed" (1995: 5). Accepting the emic reality of spirit possession would suggest, according to Halperin, accepting also the emic doubts, suspicions, and accusations of practitioners of "faked possession." Rather than eschewing them, he argues that the often ambiguous and fluid ways in which the realities of spirit possession are negotiated—not only among participants but also outsiders—call for the practice of a "delicate science of anthropological exploration." When ethnographers downplay their doubts and those of participants about the authenticity of spirit possession and highlight its mimetic corporeal theatricality—as I sometimes did—they tacitly and unwillingly reproduce the "public secret" (Taussig 1998, 1999) about possession: keeping the secret that I know that you know that I know that you know—that the reality of spirit possession could fail. Yet taking emic doubts seriously might open up a series of discussions about the connection between practical belief and skepticism as well as the ethnographic enterprise in general (Halperin 1996a).

Indeed, occasionally participants of spirit possession rituals openly address the issue of fake possession to ethnographers. For example, Jim Wafer (1991: 34) notes that "false trance" (*equé*) is a familiar phenomenon in Candomblé; his informant, Taís, defined it as a "form of theater." The existence of equé, Wafer explains, does not mean that there is no such thing as genuine trance but "that people have considerable room for maneuver" (34). Wafer therefore avoided considering the "lapses in the performances of Taís's *exuas* [female spirits or *exus*] as evidence of *equé*—although it might have been," because he took it for granted that, "since the three of them [the three *exuas*] used the same body, they would find it hard not to get in each other's way" (34). Here, "fake" does not seem to suggest that it is the result of the horse's intentional deceit but rather the effect of the confusion created by the various spirits entering and exiting the horse's body.

In addition, group-specific idioms (sets of rules) of spirit possession also determine the exact protocol that guides the order and mode in which the appropriate spirit can possess a medium; these protocols in turn reflect on the social structure and dynamics of the group in which spirit possession occurs. For example, Victor Turner (1985), writing about an Umbanda center in Rio de Janeiro, and Michael Lambek (1988b), writing about cases of Mayotte spirit "succession," show that conflict among mediums during spirit possession—whatever the reasons might be—reflect on discourses of spirit possession. In "Conflict in Social Anthropological and Psychoanalytical Theory: Umbanda in Rio de Janeiro" (posthumously published by Edith Turner), Victor Turner draws on Yvonne Velho's *War of Orixá: A Study of*

Ritual and Conflict (1975) to examine the modes in which devastating conflicts among mediums in an Umbanda cult center (*terreiro*) in Brazil were played out through "wars" of spirits during possession.[37] In three months, this center was founded, experienced a crisis, and came to an end. Velho's ethnography shows that although the struggle occurred between two mediums competing for power at the center, the war was launched between the spirits that habitually "ride" these mediums. Such supernatural conflicts provided the idiom through which actual conflicts for important roles and offices in the cult were conducted (V. Turner 1985: 119–20). In Velho's ethnography, the idiom of conflict (*demanda*) or "war between deities" refers to cases in which a medium who has a dispute with another medium mobilizes his or her orixá by means of rituals so that they can harm his or her rival. The target medium then counters the moves of the challenger by mobilizing his or her own orixá and so on. Here, personal competition among mediums within the same center is conducted through the world of spirits, which they manipulate in establishing who the head of the center should be in the future.

Other cases of scripted conflict arising during spirit possession rituals unravel folk theories of possession, which prescribe who can "host" a particular spirit and when. In his study of Mayotte, Lambek refers to the scripted ways in which trance behavior is mediated by a cultural code as "the possession code" (1988b: 712). Such possession codes also define in other spirit possession cults the proper mode and order in which spirits should be summoned in order to possess their horses—by means of specific drumming rhythms, dancing steps, manipulation of ritual objects, or drawing of sacred symbols (*veves*, in Vodou), for example. These techniques (or tricks, if one prefers) may be employed to entice a spirit to descend into the medium's head, giving the mediums (and participants) a measure of control over the world of spirits and the possibility to invite or bargain with a particular spirit to possess a medium or to prevent spirit possession altogether.

There are also rules about the appropriate ways to embody the spirits, which are assumed to be achieved through training, however loosely defined as it might be. Although the process of learning to embody the spirits is not always called initiation, as in the case of *brujería* (witch healing) and Umbanda, mediums are expected to learn to control possession and receive appropriately each type of spirit. Dispelling commonly held stereotypes about the wild nature of ecstatic states, for example, Turner notes the proper etiquette and decorum of trance within Umbanda. When "working the saints," mediums should be able to control the modes in which they are manifested. Similarly to the director of the Spiritist center in Puerto Rico mentioned earlier who had offended my interviewee, Turner (1985: 130) notes that "there is nothing wild about Umbanda trance, except perhaps its first moments when the entranced one jerks and jackknifes galvanically, though never actually falling on the ground"—unlike the poor woman at the metafísica class I mentioned above. Usually, those who do fall on the ground are those who could be candidates for mediumship or are already novices. The process of becoming a medium involves the initiatory ritual known as *fazer cabeça*, literally "to make (or inspire) head." Against the expectations that Leiris had of Zar spirit possession, Brazilian (and Puerto Rican) "mediums are admired for the degree to which they control their trances" (V. Turner 1985: 130).

While working with Puerto Rican brujos—most of whom are espiritistas influenced by Kardec's Spiritism, similar to Brazilian Umbanda practitioners—I was gradually able to distinguish the nuances and modes of spirit possession, their intensity, and their duration. Sometimes these breaks of the quotidian forms of speaking and acting during consultations are so short and enmeshed in divination and healing processes that rather than full-blown spirit possession, they may be better characterized as rapidly shifting trance-induced alternative states of consciousness. Only during formal veladas would spirit/entity possession appear as completely marked and identifiable. During consultations, for instance, one could hear, "It's not me, it's the spirits telling me to tell you," or one could hear intermittently and with few external markers (most commonly after the ringing of bells) the direct voices of the spirits uttered (quoted directly) but not authored by the healer intercepting the words authored by the healer. Often the identity of the entity or entities—composing the *cuadro espiritual* (literally, spiritual frame or spiritual assemblage) of the healer—is not even mentioned or acknowledged. Only the messages of the spirits and their interpretation by the healer to the case in front of them are crucial. In cases when evil spirits are caught by the brujo (an expertise called "*coger muertos*") in order to exorcise them from the bodies of their victims, the evil nature of the spirit is immediately revealed, and the disclosure of its exact name, by means of questions and answers, is the goal of the exorcism ritual (proceeding similarly to the Catholic script). The aim is "to send light" to a low-level spirit and compel it to leave the world of the living (see figure 9.4).

But often trance or spirit possession among brujos is not so dramatic. It occurs without much preamble and ends without much commotion. Some of the major concerns of clients who consult with brujos are not knowing

Figure 9.4. Reina catching an evil spirit, which had been pestering one of the participants, in order to exorcise it. Photograph by R. Romberg.

for certain what the form and sequence of divination and healing rituals will be not knowing whether they will be able to conceal some shameful sides of their lives, and not knowing whether they will learn about some painful truths they would rather keep concealed. From the perspective of brujos, because the dynamics of consultations and rituals actually depend on their ability to summon and manifest the spirits, letting their bodies convey in clear, unambiguous ways the spirits' coded, obscure messages, consultations are ultimately experienced by clients as indeterminate situations, charged with expectations and fears of surprising revelations. After manifesting past, present, and future causes of misfortune, the solutions and advice are also dictated by the spirits through words (uttered by brujos) and via somatic clues (felt in the body of healers) such as sudden aches in specific parts of the body or partial or full-blown trance. These bodily clues are usually interpreted as a manifestation of the *carga negativa* (negative charge) of a client or of the warnings made by the protective spirits of brujos not to continue working for that day if their health could be endangered. These manifestations could be seen as private forms of embodied communication between spirits and healers. Other times, experienced brujos might break into trance without any lengthy preparation or warning, banging suddenly on the table or ringing a bell, in order to sensorially frame what follows as sacred. The unpredictability of such outbursts of spirit presence introduces eerie forms of communication and action in the consultation that transcend everyday speech and behavior. Because of the lack of proper framing and separation, perhaps, these outbursts of spirit presence during consultations may have just as overpowering an effect on skeptics as on believers when the adroitness of what transpires is such that it connects, through invisible chains of resemblance and artifice, the unexpected with causality, the here and now with unseen social and spiritual imaginaries. On those rare occasions when artifice is such that insiders are made to forget impersonation (and cognition), the sensorial excesses of ritual drama and its poetics may transform mere mimetic corporeal manifestations into spiritual realities, aesthetics into emotion, as Thomas Csordas (1990, 1993), Robert Desjarlais (1992, 1996), and Stoller (1989, 1995) would put it.

Drawing on the general poetics of communication sketched by Roman Jakobson (1960) and others of the Prague school, I suggest that such sensorial excesses are orchestrated in mimetically corporeal lived theaters during possession that concurrently address possible doubts about their veracity. Adding the disclaimer "It's not me who is telling you this" and the array of proof and testing performances during spirit possession rituals transform the mere chains of embodied resemblances, correspondences, and parallelisms in discourse, body movement, and manipulation of objects into dramatic rituals of revelation and concealment, increasing our awareness of intangibles and their affectivity, and maybe also mobilizing some into pursuing some form of action. This became evident during my participation in divination, healing, and exorcism rituals when I saw the emotional impact on clients of spirit presence (in whichever form and shape it took) and the unrehearsed spiritual intersubjective reality that it was able to create by means of the puzzling shifting of voices and registers and the overall switching of codes between human and spirit forms of communication.

If within *brujería* multisensorial healing dramas are engineered by the capricious appearance of spirits, in Mayotte and other spirit possession cults, the "possession code" may require a stricter etiquette for distinguishing between the identity of the host and that of the spirit. If they must be recognized as separate, any indication that they have merged might be a sign that possession is fake (Lambek 1988b: 712–13). In particular cases, however, it "might not be clear whether an individual is in trace, speaking as herself or as her spirit; whether she is fully in trance; or whether she is merely confused, lying, imitating possession, or deranged. In theory, and usually in practice, however, host and spirit are clearly distinguished" (ibid.). Although it might not be clear to others (or even the possessed) who the spirit is, it should be clear to all that "it is a member of a specific class of spirits, holding a personal name and identity and a particular status" (713). An individual may be possessed sequentially by more than one spirit, but the spirit can be in only one place at a time (713, 714). Thus, in cases in which two hosts seem to be possessed by the same spirit, the identity of the spirit needs to be negotiated and publicly established. In most cases it entails a process of "succession," which begins before a senior medium dies and relinquishes her own spirit possession activities. It "requires tacit, possibly unconscious agreement by the two hosts and says something about their relationship to each other" (714).

Could spirit possession be also a personal experience, a subjective bodily reaction to some force that is as uncontrollable as blushing, or rather (contra its own discourse) a group-defined and learned aptitude that is amenable to criticism and evaluation? If it is a learned aptitude, one might then ask whether it is our cognition or the body or flesh—as suggested by Eco's Brazilian mediums—that remembers to forget. Even when acquired, "motor habits" might flow seamlessly and effortlessly so that no learning is even suspected and therefore they might need to be forgotten in order to be experienced as "second nature." Like hexis (body memory), the performative memory of spirit possession might be as ingrained as the athlete's "muscle memory" and "feel for the game," concealing its having ever been acquired in the first place. Perhaps mediums need to forget that their bodies remember. Indeed, following Mauss ([1950] 1979) and Bourdieu ([1980] 1990), I submit that, through a form of practical mimesis that involves a kind of amnesia, the body learns from other bodies, moving from practice to practice without passing through discourse and consciousness. The various historical and cross-cultural cases that document the testing and proof-seeking performance aimed at verifying and proving the veracity of spirit possession (Clark 2007; Masquelier 1999: 40, 48) call for a renewed appraisal of the corporeality of possession.

Historical studies of spirit possession in early Catholicism show that testing and searching for proofs of authentic possession were constant preoccupations, yielding numerous theological debates about the evidence required and the modes of testing (de Certeau [1970] 1990; Ferber 2004; Gruzinski 1990; Le Goff 1985; Sluhovsky 2007; Schmitt 1994). The "dramas of discernment" early modern Catholic theologians engaged in attest to the requirement of unequivocally asserting beyond any doubt that corporeal signs were not deceiving. The constant gaze, assessment, and comparison of symptoms of spirit possession show that authentic possession could not be inferred from symptoms alone; they needed testing. Church officials needed to settle and specify which visionaries were genuine and which were fake and whether the supernatural entities possessing them were good or evil (Sluhovsky 2007). One of the pervasive beliefs was that weak individuals, mostly women, would be more likely to be deceived by someone (a person or a spirit granting them otherworldly messages) than adult men and would be more inclined to show the symptoms of "fake" visionary or spirit possession experiences, which officials feared would then lead to "fake" exorcisms. Methodically stipulating what were the signs of genuine or fake possession was therefore crucial. Some concluded that genuine possession was signaled by the sudden knowledge of a foreign language or claims by the spirit to be the soul of a dead person.[38] In contrast, being too talkative and expressive after having a mystical experience raised questions about its veracity among some, because it was assumed that such an experience would result in a postpossession meditative, not vociferous, mood (Sluhovsky 2007: 178).

Interestingly, some of these signs coincide with the proofs of spirit possession sought in Afro-Latin and other cross-cultural cases of possession rituals today.[39] One of the participants in Devī worship and spirit possession rituals in India remembered how her father used to probe real possession of young girls during pilgrimages by placing incense under their nose and seeing whether they flinched or not (Hawley and Wulff 1996: 182). A more extreme form of testing was reported by an elder participant in orisha possession rituals in Trinidad (Lum 2000). He reported that in the past all sorts of tests were used to determine the veracity of a manifestation: swords would be placed in ways that the "horse" of Ogún would not get hurt if he or she touched it only if truly possessed. But nowadays, he added, these sorts of tests are no longer done.

Resonating with these proof-testing narratives, one of the topics of conversation between devotees of Santería I often heard during my fieldwork was about the physical feats performed under possession by some "horses." For example, stories circulated about a heavy old woman who climbed a tree in a flash, a man who inserted his hands in boiling oil without getting scorched, and a man who ran wildly into the street, displaying such superhuman strengths that a group of strong men could not stop him. In his ethnography of spirit possession in Brazilian Candomblé, Wafer (1991: 77) mentions the "*samba de teste*" or "test samba," which is performed to prove that a trance is authentic. When *caboclo* (Amerindian) spirits are in question, it may involve burning gunpowder on the palms of hands or dancing on live coals in order to prove that possession is not false. Métraux observed similar testing performances in Vodou ceremonies. Reflecting on their veracity and effects, he wrote: "In the ceremonies I have attended, the possessed ones did brandish red hot iron rods, but they arranged to take them by the cool end. The *hounsi* who danced in the fire prudently jumped about on logs which the flames had spared. But I have no reason to doubt the testimony of those who have seen the possessed grasp incandescent bars with both hands. . . . As for the Haitian possessed who grind up glass in their mouths, their performance is on the same level as that of our carnival artists" (1955: 31). The question I am tempted to ask is why these testing performances are needed. Who or what is being tested? The medium? The spirit? The information conveyed during spirit possession?

Apparently performances for proving and testing the authenticity of spirit possession, of its uncontrollable nature, are always necessary: they are often enacted, not just commented on, in a sort of unmasking performance that assures that no tricks or deception are involved (cf. Taussig 1998).

One of the ways to prove authenticity is to assert that no learning is at all possible, that it is a gift. Among brujos, for instance—unlike Eco's fictional characters—the reality of their own possession is neither questioned nor viewed as dependent on their belief in spirits. Certainly, it is not viewed as the result of the acquisition of any kind of theological knowledge. Training their bodies to surrender to the will of the spirits is the only type of learning brujos would ever acknowledge. And yet, to assure the effectiveness of their rituals, they do expect their clients to (cognitively) believe. They achieve this via performative means—not unlike the theatricality of spirit possession analyzed by de Certeau—that often conceal this very purpose. One day in the middle of a consultation Haydée suddenly stormed away from the altar (leaving behind the client she was consulting) into the waiting room and harshly asked one of the women waiting, "You! Why are you here? You don't believe! What are you searching for? Are you just being nosy?" Everybody was astonished by these words, for they proved that brujos can "sense" everything (including one's skepticism). Reassuring those women silently and perhaps skeptically waiting to be consulted of the power of brujos to "sense" or "see" beyond (thanks to their spirit protections), the tension between skepticism and belief was dramatically resolved, at least for that time. In repeated acts of revelation during divination consultations, I heard brujos often state, "It's not me; the spirits tell me to tell you." These unmasking rituals resemble those "studied exercises in unmasking" and "skilled revelation of skilled concealment" of shamans who open their mouth or spread their hands for inspection in order to show that they don't conceal anything, that they are not going to cheat (Taussig 1998: 246). These rituals of skepticism and belief, Taussig brilliantly suggests (1998: 235), are required "so as to test and thereby brace the mix by serving not as raw material of doubt positioned so as to terminate as believers, not yet as skeptical manipulators, but as exposers—vehicles for confession for the next revelation of the secret contained in the trick that is both art and technique and thereby real and really made up."

In effect, the boundaries between spirit possession rituals and performances of spirit possession are often blurred (Hagedorn 2001: 116–17). Katherine Hagedorn asks, is it possible that the enactment of the various entities of the Santería pantheon (the orishas) on the stage during a folkloric performance elicit their spiritual presence and sacred corporeal memory? If so, is it with the essence of these traditional characters, not with their mere representation on stage, that local audiences engage during the performance? Are actors actually *possessed* by these characters or are they simply bringing them to life, impersonating them, at each performance? Indeed, performers cannot control the effects of their divinely inspired utterances on the audience, often evoking spirit possession among the faithful who attend folkloric performances, even when the context and the intent of the performance are apparently secular. How could these boundaries ever be fixated?

Illustrating the unexpected yet real and often manifested breaking of boundaries between practical affairs and the games of the gods, Wafer (1991: 189) reported playing snooker with the spirit Corquisa at a local bar in Bahia, Brazil. Perhaps by breaking boundaries that humans create, spirits assert the spontaneous, unique ways in which they choose to manifest themselves. Humans certainly cannot control their ways, which is itself a sign of the authenticity of spirit presence (or possession). Indeed, according to the various cross-cultural discourses of spirit possession, what happens during possession is not the horses' but the spirits' responsibility. The mediums deliver the message, but they are not its authors. Herein lies the ambiguity of possession and its power.

Similar blurring of boundaries between the agency of mediums and that of spirits raises key questions about the theatricality of possession and its assumed agents. In his discussion of the "negotiated reality" of possession in the Tambor de Mina cult, Halperin (1996a: 33) notes that one medium refused to wear the white embroidered apron that acknowledges that the spirit is "taking over" its "horse." But who is making this decision, the medium or the spirit?[40] The leading medium explained to Halperin that "while the spirits themselves are by nature 'pure, authentic beings,' when possessing their imperfect human matter, or 'sinner,' they often manifest in a less than fully genuine or appropriate manner" (34). Addressing this discrepancy and the unresolved ambiguity of the agency of possession, Halperin suggests the analogy "of a great orchestral score played by highly trained artists capable of rendering the spirit of the music, in contrast to mediocre performers who invariably botch the composer's original inspiration." In a similar vein, Métraux (1955: 31) compares the difference between those who show signs of distraction or other lapses during possession and those whose possession is so impressive that it evokes "respect" to the difference between the "rank amateur" and the "great artist." These comparisons resonate with Taussig's discussion, mentioned above, of the spectacular excellence of experienced shamans who manage to turn mere technique into magic trick or art.

What, then, could emic depictions of false, fake, exaggerated possession possibly mean? In some cases, as communicated to me by Paul Stoller, accusations of "fake" possession could be highly problematic in Songhay. In other cases, such as in Santería, doubts are expressed in less harsh terms. The santeros interviewed by Lydia Cabrera (1975) in the 1930s referred, for example, to "exaggerated" possession as "*santicos*" (literally, tiny saints). I often overheard mediums being judged (and slightly dismissed) based upon the degree of "appropriateness" (not truthfulness) of their particular mode of spirit possession, a recurring topic of conversation and gossip among practitioners, as mentioned above. Yet no resolution or final verdict ever seems to be expected. Instead, the indulgence in such speech among practitioners seems to be aimed just at reflecting and maintaining an apparently generalized wariness about the boundary between belief and skepticism in general and between truthful/appropriate and fake/exaggerated possession in particular (reflected also in Eco's depiction of Amparo's and the German woman's possession during the Umbanda ceremony).

Halperin (1995) shows that for participants in Tambor de Mina dance and spirit possession rituals in northern Brazil, the boundaries between "unconscious," "fake," and "conscious" possession are not fixed. Most dancers claim that "unconscious" mediums remember essentially nothing of their trance experiences and speak of "faked" trance as an incomplete form of spirit possession. However, some experienced mediums and religious leaders confidentially acknowledge that "conscious" possession is a more—not less—advanced form of mediumship, suggesting that control over the possessing spirits indicates a higher level of mediumship expertise. As mentioned earlier, among Puerto Rican brujos and espiritistas (Romberg 2003b), elevated forms of mediumship also require mediums to control ("educate") the ways in which spirits manifest their presence and deliver their prophetic messages to humans.

Art, Artifice, and Possession

Such is the power of theatricality and impersonation—devalued, as the senses were by Platonic philosophies, for being deceptive, for diverting us from the apprehension of ultimate realities through our cognition. But sometimes the lived theater of spirit possession is so dramatic and the performances of testing and proving so convincing that participants may forget, if only for a flash, that it is people and not spirits who are moving in front of them and talking to them: mimetic corporeal manifestations are experienced as spiritual presence, and skepticism is momentarily withheld. Indeed, the efficacy of ritual can be paralleled to that of rhetoric (Tambiah 1990: 81–83) in that they depend on artifice and roundabout appeals for inducing desired actions and emotions among both visible and invisible audiences. As Kenneth Burke observes of the "tricks" of the rhetorician, the tricks of spirit possession "are not mere 'bad science'; they are an 'art'" ([1950] 1969: 42). The art of making invisible forces convincingly real is what seems to be at stake here. The following anecdote, mentioned by Alfred Métraux (1955: 36) illustrates this vividly: "A young Zuni Indian, having seen *Katchina* (personages disguised as spirits) without their masks, returned home to announce that he had seen Katchinas wearing the masks of men."

Perhaps what outsiders may call "fake" and insiders "false" or "exaggerated" possession is nothing other than an unsuccessful performance that fails to create the reality of possession by means of skillfully revealing what is skillfully concealed (cf. Taussig 1998: 240). In this sense, the critical comments of participants about the authenticity of the possessed would not be indicative of doubts about the possibility of spirits to manifest themselves among the living. Judgments made about spirit possession from within should thereby be assessed very differently from such judgments made from without. The former may signal that the mimetic theatricality of spirit possession or its density and fluidity were not powerful enough at the corporeal level to "dispel the craving for certainty that secrecy inspires" (250). If mimetic resemblance—between the spirit and its embodiment, or spirit manifestation, among the living—is at stake here, the recognition of authentic spirit presence would be seriously restricted among rapidly-changing heterogeneous communities of practitioners. If "true" mimetic corporeality of spirit possession is constantly measured against an original, originating experience of spirit possession—stemming from a previous manifestation of the spirit, itself measured against a previous manifestation of the spirit—common experiences of this originating experience cannot be assumed among most participants in possession rituals in today's transnational urban centers.

This apparent paradox in judgments of authentic spirit possession brings to the fore the vulnerable, indeterminate nature of vernacular religions: they exist because they are able to change according to the changing needs of their practitioners, but they may cease to exist for the same reason.[41] I suggest here the idea of "mystical indeterminacy" and argue that the very indeterminacy of spirit possession may be a productive, affective force in explaining, promoting, and testifying to spirit presence; it could thus be instrumental in the spiritual transformative processes expected at spirit possession rituals. When brujos reveal that it is not they who speak when they deliver the messages of the spirits, or when they unexpectedly unmask unsuspecting clients waiting to be consulted for being skeptical about the efficacy of magic, they are skillfully performing the theatricality of magic, dispelling the craving for certainty that the secrecy of magic elicits. It is a matter of fact that clients from various backgrounds do feel skeptical at times, fearing deception during spirit possession rituals, often questioning the authenticity of possession when the manifestation of the spirits seems premeditated, movements are too studied—unlike what they had expected from "true" possession.

Even though the reality of spirit possession is predicated on the practical belief that neither learning nor intentional acts other than those of the spirits are involved, the power and drama of possession seem to hinge on its discourse of mimetic resemblance and testing no less than its corporeality, opening up new sets of questions about the limits of innovation, of the spiritual corporeality and mimetic drama and poetics of spirit possession and its lived theatricality.

Mimetic Uncertainty

In sum, when words, gestures, sounds, and things enter an experiential world in which spirits as well as humans mimetically interject each other in unprecedented sensuous interlocutionary dramas and poetics, the truth and reality of ritual indeterminacy might be in itself a transcendent spiritual experience. After all, who can determine the proper ways of the spirits? It is the slight doubt before making a leap of faith that makes the leap all the more dramatic and meaningful. Skepticism lives with practical faith. If mimetic corporeality is assumed as the proof of spirit presence, what are its modes, forms, and limits? Who can really be sure? Indeterminacy and doubt can never disappear. That being the case, the unpredictable manifestation of the spirits—like human creativity—should convince us that in spite of all the testing and proving performances, uncertainty can never be made to disappear;, the most it can do is make us forget to remember.

TEN

Afterword: Recognizing and Misrecognizing Spirit Possession

MICHAEL LAMBEK

This volume provides a series of consistently interesting and innovative essays concerning spirit possession. Not only do they add to our understanding of spirit possession in and of itself, but they make a case, as Paul Johnson states, for bringing spirit possession out of the esoteric ethnographic margins and into the heart of theory, giving it a central place in the genealogy of modernity. I share the sense that spirit possession speaks to fundamental questions of philosophy, such as the nature of selfhood, agency and patiency, action, intentionality, and irony.[1] But Johnson is original in privileging a genealogical and historical approach to the relationship between the central concepts of European philosophy and the nature of spirit possession as encountered, imagined, and shaped by Europeans in their exploitation of the rest of the world. That argument is exciting, but not without its risks, and is one on which I will focus my attention before turning to a number of other themes found in the volume.

In his invigorating (spirited?) and elegant (self-possessed?) introduction and chapter, Johnson interrogates both the "spirit" and the "possession" in spirit possession, thereby partly reviving what has become a more or less dead metaphor. The question of "spirit" challenges Enlightenment, rationalist, and objectivist epistemology, as if it were obvious to separate spirit from matter and to find only the latter reliable. Thus, whereas a decade ago scholars interrogated the mind/body opposition, especially of Descartes (Lock and Scheper-Hughes 1987; Lambek 1998a), now scholars are addressing that of spirit and matter, especially in light of Christianity and its intellectual heritage. Here Johnson's approach is the complement to semiotic materialists like Keane (2007) and also links up to renewed thinking about the concept of animism (Descola 2005) or "material religion" (Houtman and Meyer 2012). A general paradox is that spirit is defined in opposition to matter but can only be manifest in and through matter. Thus spirit and matter are at once opposed in the realm of thought and brought together in the realm of practice. In her chapter in this volume Kristina Wirtz addresses this through her discussion of Pierce's concept of Firstness.[2]

The second big question concerns "possession." Johnson asks why 'possession' emerged as the generic translation of a wide range of diverse acts and what consequences followed from that translation. This is actually at least three questions. Why were a wide range of acts placed under the same generic term? Why was that term "possession"? And what were the consequences? The answer to the last question is still being played out and is evident in some of the chapters in this book; as an ethnographer of something I too have called "spirit possession," I am too much of a native to be able to answer it with any objectivity. The answer to the first question has both a philosophical and a historical dimension. Generic terms seem philosophically preferable to extreme nominalism, and we wouldn't be conversing in the same volume together if we were pure nominalists. Historically, I would say that anthropology works by rendering singular ethnographic phenomena into provisional specific and generic terms for purposes of comparison (Strathern and Lambek 1998; cf. Chakrabarty 2000). Johnson offers us insights into how this started, but to take anthropology seriously, it must also be seen as an ongoing process, subject to various kinds of correction, verification, challenges, and deconstructions, including the discussion in which we are now engaged. Thus it is certainly an interesting idea to link possession to broader discussions of animism but probably wise to continue some forms of differentiation.

Most promising is Johnson's middle question, regarding the term "possession" itself. Johnson links the concept to the possession of property and especially to slaves as property. In early liberal theory, those who were possessed—slaves—could not possess property of their own. Johnson makes the compelling argument that possession by spirits—as Europeans found and imagined it—helped set off by contrast the emergent arguments for the self-possessed modern European individual and indeed for the whole doctrine that C. B. Macpherson so memorably called "possessive individualism." Humanity is divided in effect between the self-possessed possessors of others and those vulnerable to being possessed—by spirits or by other men. If the metaphor of "possession" by spirits was drawn from ideas of property and proprietorship developed by Hobbes and Locke, their ideas of self-possession and autonomy of one's own person were set off in turn against the phenomenon of possession by spirits and served as the foundation for ownership of property. Thus spirit possession was predicated on the idea of persons as a kind of property; the person who is or can be possessed by others (spirits or slaveholders) is contrasted to the autonomous property-owning individual, the modern citizen and liberal subject.

If the encounter with spirit possession shaped European discursive practices and self-conceptions, the same could be said of the encounter with Europeans on the part of the practitioners of spirit possession. In the New World many of the contemporary adepts of spirit possession are descendants of slaves. This raises a number of questions, including whether and to what degree the historical memory of slavery is embedded in New World spirit possession. To what degree is spirit possession shaped by the experience of slavery or conceived on the analogy to slavery? But here one could ask: is it slavery that "possesses" spirit possession or spirit possession that "possesses" slavery? In other words, to what degree does the legacy of slavery determine (or "overdetermine") current practices of spirit possession, or conversely, to what degree is spirit possession an informed response to and an assertion of mastery over this legacy, perhaps an actual transcendence of it? More broadly, to what degree should spirit possession be understood as determined by political and economic forces rather than being understood as a relatively autonomous cultural institution or set of discursive practices of knowledge and power in its own right? Exactly the same question could be asked of possessive individualism (though of course the answer might be different in the two cases).

The major risk of Johnson's argument concerns the original misrecognition of "spirit possession" (by whatever name) on the part of Europeans. What was the actual nature of the phenomenon, and in what respects or to what degree has that original nature escaped or been irreversibly transformed by the act of misrecognition? Insofar as this misrecognition stands in for the whole history of slavery and colonialism, what means or avenues of escape do the misrecognized hold? And how do we ensure that we do not continue to misrecognize practices of "spirit possession" (by whatever name), once again in light of "our" (Euro-American) concerns with our own self-conceptions, self-conceptions now inevitably historically and genealogically informed? Thus, to take literally the statement of an Umbanda priestess that she is a slave (Hayes 2011: 12) could be to exoticize her in exactly the manner of earlier observers. Maybe she is being ironic or means something subtle that we cannot catch. Or perhaps she is deliberately drawing on the discourse to legitimate remarks or actions that would otherwise be suspect.

I am tempted to say, against the spirit of this volume, let's not read too much into the word "possession." I'm not certain that calling something "possession" has radically distorted the way ethnographers of East and West Africa, the Afro-Atlantic, or South and Southeast Asia have conceived or understood their object of study. It's interesting that the term is not used with respect to indigenous Americans or northern and eastern Asia, or at least not as frequently, but I would say it has been no more problematic than the complementary words "shaman" and "shamanism."

Part of me wants to say, let's just look at the philosophies embedded in systems of spirit possession and forget the rhetoric of European philosophy or anthropology. But aside from the intrinsic interest of the latter, Johnson claims that is a false move because spirit possession and European intellectual traditions are not independent phenomena. If philosophy has been influenced by its encounter with and use of the image of possession, he argues even more strongly that possession has been shaped by those uses in Western philosophy.

Spirit possession is for Johnson always already a hybrid form, produced in the encounter with Europe. This is certainly true of the type—"spirit possession"—and of several of the tokens described in this volume—Candomblé, Umbanda, Spiritism, even Pentecostalism. But not all tokens are hybrid products, or at least not hybrid products of the same encounter or the same moment of encounter. Spirit possession in multiple forms surely existed before the arrival of Europeans on the shores of West Africa (or in Europe before the spread of Christianity),[3] even if these forms were not yet under such a generic description and hence different from what is found even in West Africa today. Moreover, misrecognition remains an ongoing problem, and today, as the chapters by McAlister and Selka demonstrate, the primary axis of encounter is not with slavery or colonialism but with aggressive forms of Christianity. The encounter is shaped by powerful streams of contemporary European thought, both the ever more extreme forms of ("neo")-liberalism and the politics of humanitarianism (Fassin 2012). However, if we are not to repeat the mistakes of the past and let our own theories become the strongest vehicles of expropriation or dispossession of all, we need some balance.[4] That is, we need to see what spirit possession itself brings to the encounter. Here is where the power of ethnography becomes significant. The chapters in this book illuminate various sites of encounter and offer the means to explore what spirit possession brings in more depth. I will briefly review some of their contributions, drawing on the concepts of metaphor and mimesis.

Metaphor

Insofar as philosophy is not purified of poetry, as Plato imagined it might be, so we can compare philosophy and spirit possession along a more level epistemological playing field. What are the rhetorical dimensions of Marx, Locke, and Kant? Is Marx's fetish a metaphor? Is Locke's property? Is spirit possession also a metaphor, or the same metaphor as that of commodity fetishism? Whose metaphor is it? These are some of the exciting questions invited by this volume.

The first question raised for me is whether metaphor is not an intrinsic effect of translation. In my ethnographic work I use words like "spirit," "possession," "host," and "medium." None of these have direct counterparts in Kibushy (Malagasy); indeed, Kibushy speakers in Mayotte have no specific word that I know for the person who receives or is possessed by a spirit (though in the Sakalava dialect in neighboring northwest Madagascar there is such a word). Standing outside the "language game" of which practices of possession are a part, I cannot imagine what a literal translation or transliteration of such words or concepts could be. Hence, rather than trying to purify anthropological language of metaphor, we simply need to be more conscious of how we rely on it. The question is not to choose between literal and metaphorical language but to choose the best metaphor and to be self-conscious about it.

When does a metaphor become the thing of which it speaks? Nietzsche described religion as the worship of dead metaphor, metaphor that has come to be taken literally. Insofar as theory (say, liberal theory or anthropological theory) fools itself into thinking it has expunged metaphor, is that not akin to the shouldering, if not the worshipping, of dead metaphor? But what about when the metaphors are alive and used to think or act with rather than to worship or succumb to? What do we want to call the relationship to live metaphor? Is it theory or poetry? Must we choose between these stark Platonic alternatives? Could practices such as Vodou and Candomblé serve as examples of living with and through metaphor?

Even if spirit possession is a dead metaphor when it comes to anthropological theory, it can be a live metaphor in practice. This is especially so because of a double ambiguity. The first has to do with whether it refers to the long-term relationship that a spirit is understood to have with a given host or to the moments of "active possession" (periods of "trance" or "dissociation") when the host or medium is displaced by the spirit who speaks and acts in the host's stead.[5] The second ambiguity concerns who possesses whom. In the usages described by Johnson it is evidently the spirit who possesses—takes possession of—the host. But equally it could be said of a given host that he or she "possesses" one or more spirits who rise when requested and who can serve the host, her family, and her clients.

I do vaguely remember wondering when I began to describe what I called "spirit possession" in Mayotte (in the western Indian Ocean) about its seeming arbitrariness. But I couldn't think of a better term. In fact, I found it more useful than "trance" or, subsequently, "dissociation" insofar as it emphasized the cultural over the natural dimension. In particular, I liked the term for its ambiguity insofar as it does not specify who possesses whom, an ambiguity that I found congruent with the way Kibushy speakers talked and thought about the phenomenon. This ambiguity was deliberate in the title of my first book, *Human Spirits* (1981), and it evokes a tension that lies at the heart of any system of spirit possession and that several of the contributors to this volume note. I consider this a relationship of action and passion (or agency and patiency). I like to compare the medium to the actress who has a repertoire of roles or characters to which she gives life but which equally enliven her. Something similar could be said about the artist or scholar who creates works and is created or enlivened by them. In fact, I think that in its explicit dialectic of action and passion, spirit possession highlights something that is common to all human being in society, akin to what Durkheim referred to as self-transcendence through the social. This may help account for its fascination.

Spirits don't "possess" their hosts in any literal sense, or at least not in the sense of legal ownership, whether by purchase or contract.[6] The dominant idiom is a political rather than an economic one, in the sense of taking something over, as captured in the West African idiom of spirit possession as a horse and rider. (When I say "captured" there is no allusion to slavery or conquest in my dead metaphor.) A rider does not possess a horse in the same sense that she possesses riding boots. To "possess" can also mean simply to "have" rather than to "own."[7] Thus I can say that a host or medium possesses spirits in more or less the way I possess two eyes or two children, an unruly temper, or knowledge of anthropology, without implying they are commodities or that I have specific legal rights over them. However, to say that a spirit possesses its host or medium is not quite the same as to say the spirit or the medium has two eyes. It means some kind of social relationship and generally an encroachment or taking over; my mentor Boura Mwaha represented the period of active possession to me as a coup d'état (Lambek 1993). Possession in this sense is more akin to possessing a political subject, a client, or a colony than possessing a slave or a commodity.

Johnson, in the spirit of Latour, emphasizes the connection to things, whereas the spirits I am familiar with are understood and constituted as persons who engage in social relations with the persons of their hosts, the members of their hosts' families, and the clients of their hosts qua healers or diviners. They may also engage in social relations with other spirits, possessing the same or other hosts. They live in worlds in which one can still speak of a wealth in persons (Barber 1981; Guyer 1993) as well as things. These are worlds in which commodity fetishism or slavery may or may not be present or dominant. Hence I am not sure that I "buy," so to speak, "the observation that notions of property preceded and guided notions of spirits' capacity to 'sit" in flesh' (Johnson, chapter 1 of this volume). That does seem like part of a story Westerners now want to tell themselves; it certainly is provocative and interesting, and it may speak closely to Afro-American experiences of enslavement, but it leaves most Africans themselves strangely silent.

The spirits that I know from the western Indian Ocean have relationships with their hosts and their hosts' families, and they periodically displace the former, using their bodies as vehicles. The relationship is one not of ownership but of initial aggression or love transformed into something more equitable or else one of political subjection. However, if possession subjects the host, it simultaneously empowers her; in fact, the more powerful the spirit, the more celebrated its medium, but equally the more painful or constraining the subjection. Mediums are more tired when they emerge from active possession by a more powerful spirit than a lesser one, and in their daily lives they are subject to more constraints (taboos). Additionally, in Mayotte the power of the spirit is mediated by explicit efforts to render the intrinsically amoral spirits moral and caring, to bind them in social commitments to their hosts. All these relationships are characterized by much more than the episodes of trance, and they have an impact on many more people than the mediums themselves, points that are beautifully brought out in Karen Richman's chapter on analogous features of Vodou.

The power goes both ways. In subjecting herself to the spirit's power, the medium becomes powerful. There is no need—and in fact no possibility—to render this in a simple language of binary distinctions between master and slave, defeat, conquest, or resistance; possession can actually produce all of these conditions or subject positions and perform all of these relations, and many others, in complex polyphony and chronotopic conjuncture (Lambek 2002).

This is ultimately because, intrinsically, possession enables orchestration of voice such that more than one thing may be said or meant at a time. Moreover, there are elaborate and playful twists: as persons, spirits may be no less rational than their hosts and indeed they are sometimes capable of greater objectivity, able to speak about their hosts in the third person with evenhanded appraisal of their strengths and flaws (as well as in anger or love).

In sum, if spirits are conceived as "nonhuman agents," in many instances they are conceived on the image of human persons and are "all too human." There need be no "fetish objects" on which they are based, conceived as somehow ontologically prior to their persons. Thus the issue of property is obviated or offset by the presence of personal voice.

We are back to the question of how metaphorical this animation or personhood is and whether the word "fetishism," now on the analogy of commodity fetishism rather than in any original sense, is called for. One could talk about the mystification of the agency of the host, but it may be better to see spirit possession as a transcending of the host's agency. There is also the constitution of the apparent autonomy of the spirit by means of mystification of the performative acts that produce its identity and distinguish it from that of the host. This in turn gives rise to questions of sincerity, truth, etc., to which I now turn.

Mimesis and Truth

Mimesis has been described in derogatory terms. Johnson discusses the falsity imputed to the fetish and the emptiness of the mimic. The word of the parrot is void, like fool's gold or the word of the man who has no right or means to offer a contract. Yet mimesis is also described as the art of representation, central to literary and art theory. The major questions here are what can be meant by "truth" in the sphere of human creativity (poiesis). What are the criteria by which we establish the difference between different forms of voice or speaking and the criteria relevant to each? Without entering an elaborate discussion of the matter, I will only note that John Austin (1965) forms a useful philosophical starting point for addressing these questions; his *How to Do Things with Words* is famous for showing the limits of a distinction between representational truth and falsity, replacing "truth" in certain contexts with what he terms "felicity." Unlike the absoluteness of truth, the criteria for felicity differ according to the kind of speech act being considered.[8]

Several contributors to the volume address the questions of truth and skepticism in spirit possession. Both Wirtz and Romberg address issues of what actually happens in possession and how this gets talked about and confirmed. Especially critical here is the distinction between *being* possessed and performing *as though* one were possessed: that is, the question of whether possession as a form of mimesis can be recontextualized by considering the mimesis of possession, an issue that practitioners of spirit possession regularly encounter. Where do we, or they, draw the line? Thus Wirtz points to the permeability between "religiously verifiable possession trances" and theatrical enactments and acknowledges the possibility of a slippage between frames. She describes a folklore performance for tourists in which a "real" spirit arrives and refuses to play by the new rules. Here actual possession recontextualizes the events and suggests that it is the folklore performance that is to be judged false. This nicely inverts the mimesis of possession; the actions of the possessed man provide an exemplary critique of the way spirit possession gets trivialized in folklore. Implicit here is the "agency" to be found in the ostensibly unconscious activities of the possessed performer.

Brian Brazeal describes a similar scenario in Brazil where there is a performance of spirit possession for stage and camera. This "folklore" can be recognized by practitioners as a kind of fakery—even when it is performed by the "real" adepts.

Patrick Polk's chapter most explicitly addresses the fascinating qualities of mimesis. In the nineteenth-century United States, minstrels imitate black people on stage; psychic mediums channel them. But the refractions of mimesis are endless. Mediums also channel deceased minstrels imitating black people, and the minstrels then perform imitations of spiritualist séances. Minstrels become spirit mediums, and spirit mediums take on the features of burlesque performers. On a different kind of stage, in the United Kingdom, a medical doctor's Charcot-like display of his patients provokes the appearance of the same personages and their music. Most fascinating of all is the comparison with literature. How did Harriet Beecher Stowe come to write in the voices of black people? How did she think she did? How do we describe the process of mimesis in "high brow" literature no less than in "low" burlesque? How do we distinguish high from low here (Stallybrass and White 1986)? Mindful of the racism and appropriation, Polk is skeptical of the whole business. But what of possession in Brazil or

West Africa, where the spirits can be white colonials or indigenous Native Americans? Would we take the same tone? In fact, Polk's chapter illustrates the limited choices that nineteenth-century Americans had with respect to psychic performances—to take them literally or dismiss them as frauds. It is an ambition of anthropological and historical scholarship to transcend this dichotomy and find a third way.

While we could examine the stereotypes as particular to American racism of the period, I think it would be fair to add that spirit possession frequently entails mimesis of the cultural "Other" and that such mimesis generally entails features of stereotype and caricature. From Africa one can turn to Fritz Kramer's *The Red Fez* (1993) or Janice Boddy's *Wombs and Alien Spirits* (1989) for numerous examples (cf. Taussig 1993). Then there is Jean Rouch's film *Les maîtres fous*, which could be said to mimetically stereotype the Hauka's mimetic caricature. Whether mimesis is racist or not depends on the context, the local hierarchies, etc., not the practice per se.

So spirits imitating minstrel acts is quite wonderful but, from a comparative perspective, not wholly surprising. Also extremely interesting is the use of the mimesis of the photograph to reinforce the mimesis of the spirit—in the case of Spiritualism a visual appendage to what, as Stephan Palmié notes, is primarily an auditory mode. And it's particularly clever that the images are only partially developed, much like the ghostly presence of the voices.

One question to ask is whether in all this impersonation and caricature there was also some room for a voice of protest or a critique of race. If burlesque reinforced "the prevailing logics of corporeality and race," did spiritualism simply do the same, or did it also offer the means to pry apart and rethink prevailing dichotomies? Did the mediums sometimes channel southern white slave owners and the like or give voice to diverse opinions about race and slavery? It would be good to know more about black spiritualists and whether they sometimes voiced white folk and how these practices shifted over time. For example, how did all this change during and after the Civil War?

Mimesis can be extolled and valued or despised and feared. I have several e-mail messages purporting to be from my bank, the daughter of Gadhafi looking for a place to secure her money, and an American soldier in Iraq with the same problem. Depending on my mood I am irritated or I admire the ingenuity of the mimesis. However, both irritation and admiration are possible only insofar as the mask slips and the audience is given a glimpse of the actor, writer, or producer. Much literature plays with this idea explicitly, and possession in the areas I have observed it sometimes highlights rather than attempts to dispel the irony intrinsic to it. Spam filters attempt to detect it.

Brian Brazeal takes up the question of fraud head on, making a nice analogy with the trading of gemstones. He shows that in Brazil, as in most places where possession is found, the central issue is not the existence of spirits or the possibility of possession in general but the plausibility of any given practitioner and performance in the face of many unknowns.[9] He makes the important point that "the existence of deceivers . . . reinforces the value of the putatively genuine article," thereby illustrating that there is a whole economy of truth at work here. Sellers of emeralds and of healing work to deceive and convince, and there is a lively language of deception or what would count for Austin as kinds of infelicity. Moreover, both the mining and marketing of gemstones and the activities of spirit possession are marked by a play of concealment and revelation. Here, as for Heidegger, truth is best exemplified as unconcealment.[10]

Brazeal argues that what possession services and gemstones have in common is that their value is difficult to assign or perceive. It is only when the mica is cut away and the emerald revealed that we can discern its value. Maybe we can then discern its market price, but not why emeralds are valuable in the first place. And what of the genuine price or value of spirits and their mediums? The Brazilians are concerned with deeper questions of value, ultimately not measured in money but grounded in human life. In this respect, gemstones and spirits are perhaps not simply analogies of one another or simply the product of market relations but part of a unified circuit of life force. In other words, if market relations help describe the practice of spirit possession, perhaps possession in turn recontextualizes the market.

In sum, there is a whole hermeneutics and politics of mimesis that attempts to distinguish the true from the false performance. Of local concern to market traders or healers and their clients, this also speaks to much larger issues of creativity and social theory. An issue central to any form of mimesis is the relation or balance of agency to patiency, or action to passion—and our ideas about that. Is the better poet the one who works at her craft, endlessly revising, or the one who writes almost effortlessly, "as if possessed," but then only when the mood takes her? Is the better actor the one who is self-conscious or the one who loses himself in the role? Is one of these modes understood as truer, more authentic, difficult, or dangerous?

These various themes are woven together in original ways in Raquel Romberg's chapter. She asks what depictions of false possession could mean and addresses the question implied in Polk's chapter, namely, What is the difference between who copies whom? In her answers Romberg speaks fascinatingly of "ritual piracy" and of Leiris's distinction between lived and acted theater. But most important, she takes us to the perceptions and commentary of the mediums themselves.

We should not be surprised by the skepticism among practitioners. As scholars we engage in a profession in which we evaluate each other all the time. I comment on these chapters and consider the strength and comprehensiveness of the arguments. You evaluate the quality of my remarks. Do I know what I am talking about, have I understood the papers, am I convincing, fair, professional? Am I merely playing the game, more or less successfully reproducing what a good anthropologist looks like, rather than actually being one? How bad an anthropologist do I have to be before I become reclassified as a *false* one?

In fact, these questions seem to be more salient for spirit mediums than they are for anthropologists; their performance is always subject to criticism, and the distinctions between the "lived" and the "acted" are drawn more sharply. They distinguish in their own ways between competence and performance and appraise the felicity conditions for effective performativity. How ungrammatical or infelicitous does a performance have to be before it is discarded as a failure? Does a failed performance necessarily indicate falsehood? Do local appraisals draw from primarily aesthetic or ethical criteria or from ones we could call scientific, or critical in the Marxist sense, with respect to mystification and false consciousness? Romberg concludes that possession is not bad science but an art, a point with which I largely concur. But of course there is plenty of bad art around. When do we say that a bad singer or actor isn't merely bad, but faking it?[11] To recognize that some learning is more embodied than memorized obviously does not release it from criteria of evaluation or distinguish a good dancer from a brilliant one, a painter of tourist art from a master.

A locally relevant question might be, Who is accountable for a given poor performance? Does the fault lie with the spirit or with the medium, or is it attributable to some other factor, perhaps sorcery conducted by a third party to undermine the event? A different local question would be why some people become possessed rather than others; is this attributable to the whims of the spirits or the qualities or capacities of the mediums? And how is any given active appearance of a spirit attributed to the agency or intentionality of the spirit or the medium or both?

A theoretically relevant question might be, When does artifice become art, virtuality become reality, mimesis its object? How does one successfully perform unintentionality? How do mediums overcome their own uncertainty or skepticism and realize the truth of their performances?[12] Conversely, when is art reduced to artifice, reality to its copy? When and how does the tension sustained in performance or irony break down?

Romberg makes the point that along with the implicit grammar of possession as a cultural phenomenon come certain explicit conventions for interpreting and criteria for evaluating specific performances. Such criteria are shaped by multiple sources, including traditional modes of understanding and *techniques du corps* as well as current forms of objectification and rationalization. Like most human practices, possession is constituted by means of both implicit, or nondiscursive, and explicit, or discursive, conventions and criteria. We might broaden this dichotomy to speak about the subdiscursive and metadiscursive, as well as the extradiscursive, paradiscursive, or simply nondiscursive.

Somatic and discursive modes of attention need not be understood as contradictory or mutually exclusive. In my experience, the ostensible spontaneity of possession is often regulated or performed; the questions of evaluation raised above are all relevant to spontaneous no less than planned events or instances of possession. Indeed, it's not immediately evident what "spontaneity" means, either in any given context or theoretically. Romberg is right to speak of the "risky 'double movement' of exit and return," which is certainly central to the experience of both mediums and onlookers.

I once wrote a paper called "Graceful Exits," which described a medium whose exiting from trance was all wrong (Lambek 1988a). The spirit stayed around for too long and was too drunk. Contrary to convention, the medium herself retained the signs of alcohol after the spirit left. I suggested we might evaluate the performance of spirit mediums at three levels: as the more or less compelling personification of a particular character from the spirit repertoire in a given performance; as a medium who integrates the moves in and out of possession and handles relations with audience and clients, etc., more or less gracefully; and as a person who integrates possession in her life more or less well. The criteria of evaluation differ at each level.

Romberg points out that possession is often exhausting, painful, and risky for the medium. Perhaps this is the hidden exploitation of labor. But doubtless there are also hidden benefits.

Spiritual Warfare

The stakes of evaluation are often not only aesthetic or ethical but highly political, especially in contexts of religious pluralism and conflict. As such they take us from the analysis of mimetic performance to questions of broader social forces. Cubans, Brazilians, and Puerto Ricans have long been afforded the juxtaposition or competition between traditions or disciplines of possession that are more continuously African and those that are more of a European hybrid ("Spiritism"). Recently a much greater challenge to spirit possession has come from the rise of evangelical Pentecostal Christianity, as vividly illustrated in the chapters by Stephen Selka and Elizabeth McAlister. As they point out, one of the interesting features of this challenge is that it comes not from rationalism but from a strong spiritual orientation. Thus it is a matter of what in some contexts is explicitly referred to as "spiritual warfare." Pentecostalism may be less different from the practices it attacks than it cares to think, illustrating once again the principle that proximity produces conflict (the narcissism of microdifferences). In other words, both Spiritism and Pentecostalism offer spirit-based critiques of spirit possession, arguing not that the latter is false or inauthentic but that it makes use of the wrong spirits, bad ones. As both Selka and McAlister describe it, spirit possession can be vulnerable to the onslaught of Pentecostalism, albeit in this respect it is not alone; Roman Catholicism too has suffered large losses in Latin America and elsewhere, as have other "mainstream" Protestant churches. Moreover, it is interesting—or from my perspective, equally disquieting—that in parts of Africa spirit possession suffers similarly from the onslaught of newly popular movements of "reformist" Islam (Masquelier 2001; Janice Boddy, personal communication).

Returning to some of the opening themes of the volume, Selka points out that the relationship of spirituality to materiality is central to Pentecostalism. Pentecostalism is also a radical means to divest of certain spiritual and social relations and to become the self-possessed individual of capitalist modernity overnight. But this appears to be accompanied by a strong dependence on the church or the charisma of certain preachers, and it occurs in a context in which concerns with fakery and theft ought to be even more striking than in the context described by Brazeal. Certainly, the church at hand has become very wealthy. What Selka does not tell us, though, is how the practitioners who remain within Candomblé view the Pentecostalists. The question is whether Candomblé's spirit possession is simply more inclusive and open-minded than that of the evangelical Christians or whether Candomblé too attempts to discredit its rival. Is Pentecostalism ever put on the defensive?

McAlister picks up the theme of Selka's chapter as played out in Haiti and shows explicitly the kind of transnational spiritual warfare taking place "in the name of Jesus" against ancestral spirits. Like Selka she also insightfully notes the similarities between these forms of religious practice, and here again I would question whether there is not also the difference that where one is inclusive the other is exclusive, one pluralist and the other colonizing, one relatively modest and the other insatiable. McAlister ups the ante: "possession" here is now about possessing the entire earth in the name of Jesus. In her astonishing piece, we see the strength of evangelism in its ability to offer services and hope in the camps set up in the wake of the earthquake. More disquietingly, evangelism appears to take advantage of the event to blame Vodou for Haiti's misery. As she says, "These Haitian believers fought the most profound and abject dispossession with the most direct form of possession, by the Holy Spirit itself." Of course, "these Haitians" are equally possessed by the determination and money of American missionaries.

Presence and Perspicience

Stephan Palmié and Kristina Wirtz complement or challenge both the metaphor and the mimesis models by focusing more closely on the embodied and materially effective qualities of possession. Wirtz nicely coins the term "perspicience" to describe a kind of bodily knowledge, like the pricking of my thumb. Wirtz rightly points out that active possession is not the only means through which spirits are present and shows the ways in which mediums can feel or indicate their presence. Thus the "ceding of control at the heart of spirit possession serves as a model for the susceptibility of the entire physical and human world to the influence of spirits." She points too to the way the spirits in Cuba get invested in material "power objects," such as statues on altars. However, whereas European-influenced Spiritism emphasizes the ethereal through materials like water, perfume, flowers, and candles, the more directly African practices engage with the "messy materiality" of blood and meat. Here we can see how a European bias might affect the discernment of what is considered properly "religious."

Stephan Palmié has an ear for technology, comparing spirit possession and technological instruments as forms of mediation, but he is also interested in how they draw upon each other. Unlike so many studies of modern media that concern questions of reproduction, Palmié claims that Cuban *abakuá*—like the Catholic Mass—is each time an original "instantiation of presence beyond time." This is mediation "that results in 'pure presence' or immediacy" rather than the copy. Thus for Palmié what is at issue is precisely not mimesis, in the sense of reproduction. To put this another way, Palmié is concerned less with what is said in ritual than in what is done, and what is done, in the first instance, is bringing the numinous (here the spirits) into presence. For Palmié, it is important to understand the "ritual work necessary to effect the vanishing of mediators and media into the message."

Palmié attends in his chapter primarily to the aural. This is a departure not only from the usual emphasis on the visual but, with respect to spirit possession, a departure from a focus on the oral dimension of voice, that is, on what can be spoken, or given voice, for the aural, or what can be heard or received as voice. Palmié claims that in both the Cuban practices and the modern West there has been a process of what he calls "ensoniment." In homage but contrast to Weber, he argues that there has been a "Weberian enchantment of the very technological means of rational sound propagation and reproduction," and in an argument reminiscent of Polk's chapter, he links the rise of North American Spiritism directly to the production of first the telegraph and then the phonograph. Indeed, he joins a number of other historians in arguing that the first scientists often considered their discoveries or inventions in continuity with older ideas about spirits rather than as a moment or index of their defeat. Interestingly, he proposes that phonograph records were originally more shocking than photographs to North Americans in their ostensible ability to enable an audition of the voices of the dead and ultimately "to relativize mortality itself." Spiritualism then drew on the same idea, becoming another "enchanted technology in the service of rationalizing the numinous."

The Sociality of Spirit Possession

Several of the chapters supplement Johnson's central argument by pointing out that there have actually been at least two prominent European responses to spirit possession, namely, the rationalist and the romantic. Both are inadequate for understanding the practices at issue, although they do serve as useful concepts with respect to European ideas of selfhood. In particular, Karen Richman lucidly argues that Haitian spirit possession has not only been used to set off the individual modern self, as described by Johnson, but has also been imagined as the source of the "authentic" self that individual Westerners can go to Haiti to find. As she puts it, "The assumption of the spirits' universality is the corollary of the modern notion of the abstract, equivalent individual. . . . (Protestantism takes the homogenizing process a democratic step further by installing a direct line of communication from any person to the deity). The application of the concept of the individual to experiencing Vodou is that, since all persons are free and equivalent, any person (and ultimately the researcher her- or himself) can have access to any spirit; there are no ontological barriers preventing communication. This communication is then focused inwardly on self-knowledge rather than communal interaction." She then proceeds to show how radically different this idea is from the actual practice of Haitian subjects. In an argument that is in a sense the next step of Johnson's, Richman also points out that "the focus on auto communication [by other writers] was reinforced by the rhetorical burden of the term 'possession' itself, meaning private ownership and unilateral control."

Hence the arguments in other chapters concerning skepticism and authenticity take on a new valence in this one. We see the very real historical effects of a specific kind of interpretation of possession by outsiders, producing a whole tradition of scholarship, and possibly practice, that itself could, from a certain perspective, be understood as inauthentic.[13] But rather than dwell on past misreadings, Richman uses her ethnographic skills to show in detail why possession is a rich social practice in its own right and one that we should be able to understand reasonably well without appropriating it. This chapter is thus doubly valuable, first, in offering a much-needed critique of the semipopular literature on Vodou, some of which has actually entered the anthropological canon, and, second, in returning Vodou to its primary practitioners or at least to its rural practitioners in one part of Haiti.

As is evident from her citations, Richman's analysis of possession among "real" Haitians—here not excluding transnational migrants—resonates with my ethnography of Mayotte, on the far side of the globe from Haiti. In particular, Richman shows the way possession in Haiti articulates the reproduction of the descent group. However, it is significant that she does not make the argument about an unbroken tradition from Africa but rather locates an original formation in the aftermath of the Haitian revolution and the emergence of landowning groups. Here then is another way in which spirit possession articulates with our ordinary understanding of property. We may say that ancestors, land, and spirits are all part of the family estate.

Richman makes a very important point, one largely missing in the other chapters, about viewing possession as intersubjective exchange, and she illustrates this through case material concerning the ritual performed for a migrant living in Miami. It is striking that an individual *lwa* possesses only one person at a time, for that person's lifetime, but has a relationship with—and confers protection over—a larger group. These are practices that need to be understood as being as fully ethical as they are artistic. Working out the ethnographic details still holds as much fascination as the postcolonial and genealogical deconstructions of the European high traditions. And it is work that needs to be done before we can make confident assertions about fetishism, historical trauma, and the like. Viewed from the position of Haitian peasants, these abstractions are no doubt *our* fetishes.

This volume is especially welcome for making questions of spirit possession central to modernity and to anthropology, specifically to the genealogy of the modern individual, as agent and subject, as well as continuing the argument, made by a number of postcolonial scholars, that the development of European thought can only be understood in relation to colonial activity. Johnson moves back from colonialism per se to the mercantile period and especially the transatlantic traffic in human beings that is evidently one of the major events of the last half millennium and one whose repercussions are still with us. If some kinds of people could be possessed by spirits, why could they not also be possessed by other human beings, the kind who were themselves ostensibly invulnerable to spirits? In taking this view it seems it was the Europeans who took possession literally. But those who had been possessed as slaves continued and renewed their practice of being possessed by—or possessing—spirits. And curiously, the descendants of slave owners themselves took on a new form of Christianity, itself influenced by slave religion, that emphasized possession by the single Holy Spirit, and they then took this new religion as the medium through which to possess the descendants of the slaves a second time.

Spirit possession is not simply a creation of European thought, and to suggest so would be the ultimate act of expropriation, more extreme in its erasure than the attempts by evangelical Christians to exorcize the spirits. Hence, although this book starts off with a genealogical approach, by the end it has provided sufficient ethnographic portraits to show the historical reality of something that, whatever one's misgivings about its classification or label, has substance and energy.

The philosopher Alasdair MacIntyre (1990) once discerned three forms of moral inquiry, which he named the encyclopedic, the genealogical, and the traditional. Whereas MacIntyre depicted these as "rival versions," hence implicitly as mutually exclusive, I take anthropological analysis to be constituted through the sustained interplay of all three (Lambek 2011). That is to say, anthropological depiction and analysis must shift among these three perspectives—viewing phenomena as objective entities or activities, available for comparison and classification; examining these classifications skeptically as the products of specific genealogies of knowledge and power; and trying to understand the phenomena (ideas and practices) "from the natives' point of view" while at the same time translating them into language that makes sense "from the readers' point of view." The exceptionally interesting chapters that make up this volume elegantly manage this complex task of juxtaposition. The authors ask powerful questions in new ways and make extremely valuable, original, and provocative transections across the theoretical landscape. Paul Johnson's contribution in particular is original, adding a genealogical analysis of spirit possession that has been absent from the literature, which has hitherto relied entirely on encyclopedist and interpretive perspectives.

One of the claims sometimes made by genealogists (though not by Johnson) or by critics of a genealogical approach is that it undermines both the specific categories by which the discipline has operated ("totemism," "taboo," "belief," not to mention "culture") and, possibly, the very project of objective comparison itself. But the actual effect of the genealogical approach is to change one object of inquiry into another: as the previously imputed signified dissolves, the once transparent signifier becomes held up for inspection and turned into a signified object in its own right. However, doing this alongside the other approaches means that the genealogical examination of the signifier can be pursued without completely dissolving the signified. Instead, it gets put under a new description. Hence we end up with multiple objects, both "spirit possession" and spirit possession (or its replacement in a new language), and in fact these play off each other, neither being fully stable or static but seen as part of a mutual history. Thus one of the central strengths of this volume is to reprise the conversation or interaction between Europe and its former colonies and to show that cultural practices and ideas on each side, even the seemingly most formative and continuous ones, have been disturbed by or formulated in relation, reaction, or response, to the other. This operates at the most abstract level of the philosophy of liberalism and at the most embodied and visceral level of the incarnation of spirits, as well as at the abstract level of spiritual ontologies and the embodied practices of liberal subjects. Across this continuum we can observe the mimetic faculty at work as well as its limitations as a satisfactory mode of analysis for, and transcendence by, practitioners themselves.

It is fascinating to follow Johnson and consider how the modern bounded individual may have been forged in relation to or against a conceptualization of spirit possession. In Kant's project of distinguishing, and perhaps purifying, human reason from sensory impression, possession exemplifies the remainder that is passion. In Locke and Hobbes the project is presumably also about distinguishing the (possessive) individual from various forms of dividualism. One thing these chapters illustrate is that these debates are not simply a matter of the past; they remain contemporary issues of the highest salience—in debates over the relationship between science and religion, in the progress of neoliberal agendas to disparage and undermine forms of sociality, and, to deliberately invoke questionable words, in attempts by some proponents of the monotheistic religions to quash forms of polytheism or animism.

NOTES

INTRODUCTION

Epigraph: Machado's full sentence reads, "Assim é que um espírito, desde que tenha sido reencarnado na tartaruga, logo que se desencarne, pode voltar novamente encarnado no *bond* elétrico." September 23, 1894, *Gazeta de Notícias*, Rio de Janeiro. Machado was writing satirically in this passage, yet the satire indicates how common and publically known spirit possession phenomena were in 1890s Brazil, as well as the convergence of possession religions with new technological affordances.

1. As Talal Asad (2006: 523) wrote, "The liberal idea is that it is only when this individual sovereignty is invaded by something other than the representative democratic state, which represents his individual will collectively, and by something other than the market, which is the state's dominant civil partner (as well as its indispensable electoral technique), that free choice gives way to coerced behavior."
2. This idea is different from and potentially much more destabilizing than the currently fashionable modernity-sorcery nexus. A retuned genealogy of "possession," as a metaphor of property applied to bodies and ritual practices, offers a point of access for thinking about how early modern philosophies of property exchange (of lands and minerals, but also of persons, in the Atlantic slave trade) and "modern" notions of rational autonomy were forged in relation to the dangers of "possession," located above all in African and Afro-American religions. By juxtaposing spirit possession and materiality, we also revisit Herskovits's (1956) characterization and critique of a theoretical-geographical split in which Afro-American studies favored the study of religion to a fault, and African studies favored the study of economic production and social structure, neglecting religion to a fault. Herskovits argued that both needed to become more "rounded" in their approach. This book "rounds" by a different method, namely, by locating "religion" and material production as inseparable rather than discrete domains, whether in Africa or the African Americas.
3. Writes LaCapra (2001: 90): "In memory, one is both back there and here at the same time, and one is able to distinguish between (not dichotomize) the two. In other words, one remembers—perhaps to some extent still compulsively reliving or being possessed by—what happened then without losing a sense of existing and acting now."

   Henry Miller was, in turn, possessed by those who occupied the home before him: "Là, habitaient Dali, Antonin Artaud et Foujita. Derain venait juste de déménager. Je passai la nuit chez ce gentil *fol* qui ne pensait qu'à la mort. Quelqu'un pour me plaire! C'était ma première entrevue avec la Villa Seurat et comme vous savez, j'ai repris plus tard l'appartement qu'Artaud venait de quitter et j'y ai vécu jusqu'à aujourd'hui" (Dali, Antonin Artaud, and Foujita lived there. Derain had just moved in. I passed the night with that wonderful madman who thought of nothing but death. And liked him! It was my first encounter with the Villa Seurat. As you know, later I took the apartment that Artaud had just left, and I've lived there until today). Letter to Joseph Delteil, April 1939, http://faustroll.net/soutine/page08.htm#sdendnote6sym, consulted on April 4, 2011.

4. As a matter of the ethnography of ritual practices, we regard the state of "being possessed" as part of a continuum of self-consciousness, a subjectively and collectively determined status rather than as a definitive state. Though forensic judgments are often levied as to the "authentic" presence of a god or spirit, or lack thereof, such commentaries are themselves a key part of ritual practice. The study of "actual" consciousness, whatever that might mean, is beyond the pale of cultural anthropology and religious studies and is not of interest here.
5. Though Bastide in certain respects imposed categories drawn from his early investigations of Christian mysticism, he was alert to the subtleties of the emic glossary for spirit possession. In Brazil, he noted, for example, that the possessions caused by a spirit of the dead, during, say, an *axexe*, or funerary rite, are not to be understood as "mystical trance" in the same way as the ritual appearance of a deity (*orixá*) but rather via other terms like "obsession," or "encostar" (to lean against) or "rodear" (circle around) (1953: 46).
6. The full text of article XXVIII reads: "We declare slaves to be incapable of possession any thing except to the use of their master; and whatever they may acquire, either by their own industry, or the liberality of others, or by any other means, or under whatsoever title, shall be and accrue to their respective master in full property, in bar of all claim to the same by the children, parents, or relations, of such slaves, or any other persons, free or slaves, by any deed of gift or grant, or by inheritance or succession, or last will and testament: we declare all such dispositions null and void; as well as all promises, engagements, and obligations, made or entered into by such slaves; the same being deemed to have been made, entered into, and given, by persons incapable of contracting and disposing in their own name."
7. As Arjun Appadurai (1996: 189) notes, "The nation-state relies for its legitimacy on the intensity of its meaningful presence in a continuous body of bounded territory. It works by policing its borders, producing its people . . . , constructing its citizens, defining its capitals, monuments, cities, waters, and soils, and by constructing its locales of memory and commemoration, such as graveyards and cenotaphs, mausoleums and museums." Crucial to the production of nation-state presence is the carefully crafted treatment of the dead and their memory or, if one likes, "spirits."
8. The semantic chain of *slave:body:possessed* replicated in a new form the early sociophysiological map of Aristotle's *mind:master :: body:slave* in his prescriptive writing on the polis: "For that which can foresee by the exercise of mind is by nature intended to be lord and master, and that which can *with its body* give effect to such foresight is a subject, and by nature a slave" (*Politics*, book I, pt. II). At times African intellectuals have themselves embraced and celebrated the opposition of European rationality versus African emotion and naturalness: Consider Léopold Senghor's famous declaration, inspired by the writing of the German ethnologist Leo Frobenius: "L'émotion est nègre comme la raison est hellène" (1939: 295). For Senghor,

at least, this was an attempt to counter the "rationality" of European colonization and militarization.

9. The risk of such a claim is that it is, strictly speaking, at once too general, in consideration of the history of primitivist stereotypes of Africa as "a place possessed," and too specific, since many societies not of African descent act in relation to spirits. One could argue plausibly that the interanimation of enslavement—the body possessed—and spirit possession is particular to the histories of those societies descended from the context of plantation slavery in the New World, though Suzanne Preston Blier (1996), to take just one example, has demonstrated the centrality of ideas and arts of binding in religious practice in West Africa itself.
10. "Comparable," we might say, in at least the following three senses: that they (1) derive from a relatively delimited geographic range of societies of African origin, from which slaves were taken, especially from the West African ports in the Bight of Benin to the Bight of Biafra and from the Central African ports surrounding Luanda; (2) have shared socioeconomic beginnings in plantation systems with roughly equivalent climates and plant resources; and (3) increasingly share self-identification with "African diaspora" traditions, where their formal and aesthetic similarities are reinforced. The chapters in this volume are primarily concerned with the second and third of these issues of comparability, though the horizon of relatively shared African "origins" remains in play implicitly, not least in the selection of chapters to include in the book.
11. For De Certeau (1975), it is the absolute alterity of the dead, their final and absolute silence (which can be nevertheless be given voice) that constitutes history as a specific discipline in the West. In this sense history is analogous to forensics, the search to discern meaning in a corpse. If anthropology's constituting Other was "the primitive," for the discipline of history it was "the dead." The continuing life and speech of spirits from the past, who are not really past at all, present not only epistemological but also disciplinary conundrums for historians, especially those, noted Chakrabarty, whose aim is to let the subaltern speak.
12. "Spirits of history" is another strange, and strangely commonplace, phrase we can define only in relation. Spirits of history are those memories of the "modern" dead (or the moderns' dead), considered to have done things in their lives that continue to exert force in the present. They are unlike ancestors who are fully incorporated by the living in "possession," on one hand, and the simply unremembered, on the other. They are actively present but indirectly or prosthetically so, acting through the things they left behind.
13. The male-gendered term for human beings in general is used deliberately in this case, because the character of the rational, accountable, contract-worthy, and possessing man in political philosophy from Hobbes and Locke through the mid-twentieth century was male. Children and women, like savages, were to be possessed.
14. On this score, Price (2007: 294–97) has analyzed how divination (including that of spirit possession) in the hands of a specialist like Tooy efficiently focuses and sometimes shifts historical horizons for the Saramaka.
15. Fifth rule of "Greater Discernment of Spirits": "We ought to note well the course of the thoughts, and if the beginning, middle and end is all good, inclined to all good, it is a sign of the good Angel; but if in the course of the thoughts which he brings it ends in something bad, of a distracting tendency, or less good than what the soul had previously proposed to do, or if it weakens it or disquiets or disturbs the soul, taking away its peace, tranquility and quiet, which it had before, it is a clear sign that

it proceeds from the evil spirit, enemy of our profit and eternal salvation" (http://www.ccel.org/ccel/ignatius/exercises.xix.ii.html).

16. As Stefania Capone reports, "Since his death in 1996, Verger's spirit has become an Egungun, a worshiped ancestor, though not exactly a 'possessing' spirit. Egunguns manifest themselves without taking possession of initiates. Verger's Egungun is called Baba Efunladê and an annual festival is dedicated to him in the Ilê Axé Opô Aganju of Lauro de Freitas (Salvador de Bahia, Brazil)" (personal communication, e-mail of July 26, 2012).

17. Lambek notes in his study of Sakalava possession in Madagascar, that the key part of the notion of spirit possession as theater is not so much performance as irony, the fact of multiple voicings that together refute a singular idea of truth as self-evident (2002: 266).

18. What is key is that this is not just the summoning of the past for purposes in the present, to take the familiar refrain, because it is also a summoning of the present into the past, a ritually produced retreat from demands for individually accountable causation. This is no mean feat, requiring techniques of estrangement like speaking with a different voice—amplified or with antiquated terms, or absent—donning ancestral garb, or showing knowledge of events unknown to the living. When the present is thrown "back," into the domain of ancestors' recognizable acts, it is alienated from individual authorship. Multiple voices can now intervene; causation is blurred by generations of potential agents and crisscrossing lines of accountability.

19. Brazeal's chapter, like Elizabeth McAlister's chapter on "spiritual mapping" in Haiti, illustrates the persistence in the contemporary moment of specific imbrications of spirits and things that first emerged under the slave trade and the plantation economy. The problem of reading the interiors of precious metals (a question of things) and of reading the interior persons of their traders (a question of spirits) were tightly interwoven on Africa's West Coast throughout the seventeenth and eighteenth centuries. Gold contracts required the determination of at least partly shared valuations of metal and of personal trust over time, and the "problem" of spirits and spirit possessions both helped to construct and radically threatened the ability to posit and affix cross-cultural values both monetary and moral.

20. Alfred Russel Wallace prefaces the third edition (1896) of *Perspectives in Psychical Research* with the ironclad evidence that "what are termed spirit-photographs . . . have now been known for more than twenty years. Many competent observers have tried experiments successfully" (xiv). On the spirit powers of photographs, see Meyer (2010) and P. Johnson (forthcoming).

    Similarly, the notion of "the social" and "the individual" were thoroughly permeated by and hybridized with the electrical imagination in the decades of the formation of sociology. Here is Emile Durkheim describing the notion of self-consciousness (1908: 275): "L'excitation extérieure, au lieu de se décharger immédiatement en mouvements, est arrêtée au passage, soumise à une élaboration *sui generis*, et un temps plus ou moins long s'écoule avant que la réaction motrice apparaisse. Cette indétermination relative n'existe pas là où il n'existe pas de conscience, et elle croît avec la conscience" (External excitation is stopped, instead of being immediately discharged in movements, and submitted to a sui generis elaboration. It takes time for the motor reaction to appear. This indetermination does not exist where there is no consciousness; it grows with consciousness).

21. The phrase is from Tzvetan Todorov, "La tyrannie de l'individu," *Le Monde*, March 27, 2011, 18.

22. The scholarship on Candomblé has long cast Candomblé de Caboclo as inventive and personalized in relation to spirit possession and its cast of characters compared to "traditional" (i.e., *nagô*) Candomblé, which is taken to be conservative, even monotonous (e.g., Carneiro 1961).
23. Sansone's work has been attentive to zones of selective "Africanness" in Brazil and to the desirability of engaging selective Africanness in varying contexts. Not surprisingly, the Candomblé temple (terreiro) is the domain where Africanness is most valued, emphasized, and embraced even by those who reject that framing of identity in other contexts. Aisha Khan's work (2004) also helpfully opens up the consideration of zones and degrees of blackness in the Caribbean and its uneven relation to ethnic identifications.
24. For example, as we learned during the last presidential campaign, Governor Sarah Palin enlisted the help of Kenyan pastor Thomas Muthee during his 2005 visit to Alaska to cast out the spirits that hindered her career. The *New York Times* elaborated, "Ms. Palin has long associations with religious leaders who practice a . . . brand of Pentecostalism known as 'spiritual warfare.' Its adherents believe that demonic forces can colonize specific geographic areas and individuals. . . . Critics say the goal of the spiritual warfare movement is to create a *theocracy*" (Goodstein 2008, my emphasis). Of interest here is the way in which this particular story on Palin's trafficking with spirits was presented as bizarrely anachronistic and both a civil risk and political liability.
25. The global surge of spirit-based Christianities and, as a corollary revival, the burgeoning literature on the anthropology of Christianity and on the "sorceries" of modernity have to some degree altered the perspective of spirit possession as an anachronism. Yet one might argue that the anthropology of Christianity only gained traction through the study of Pentecostalism, which, with its ritual events devoted to (Holy) spirit possession, appeared sufficiently "primitive" to warrant anthropological scrutiny. In that sense at least, the recent anthropological study of Christianities serves as much to fortify the view of spirit possession as anachronistic as much as to subvert it.

CHAPTER ONE

A different, shorter version of this essay appeared in *Comparative Studies in Society and History* (P. Johnson 2011). Parts of it are reprinted here with the permission of Cambridge University Press.

1. "But what do I see apart from hats and coats, under which it may be the case that there are automata hidden?" (Descartes 2003: 29). The metaphor of the automaton, a person "resembling machines, automatic," first appears around the same period, in 1607 (*Online Etymological Dictionary*, consulted March 19, 2009); the OED locates the earliest citation in 1625.
2. Jack Goody has documented that the terms of "property" were applied to slaves before they were applied to land in human history (in Palmié 1996).
3. *Religion*, Jonathan Smith argued, was a process of domestication, transforming pathos to ethos in the domain of civil discourse and commerce (1982: 104). Webb Keane (2007: 73–76) called attention to the performative discourses of the free, sincere individual and the ways in which discursive practices of freely embraced beliefs themselves work as a powerfully constraining habitus and political regime.
4. "Chronotope" is Bakhtin's (1981: 84) term that "expresses the inseparability of space and time." Note that while spirit possession has often worked as a chrono-

tope of Africa, and rational personhood was equally chronotopic of Europe, Locke alleged the latter to be precisely utopic, or antichronotopic. Rational personhood, he wrote, consists of "a thinking intelligent being, that has reason and reflection, and consider itself as itself, the same thinking thing, *in different times and places*" ([1689] 1975, book II, ch. XXVII, part 9; my emphasis). The appearance of rational personhood as universal, despite its radical specificity to a certain time-place, is what has made it especially pernicious.

5. Hobbes had a stake in the Virginia Company from 1622 until 1624, when it became a royal colony of James I, and attended thirty-seven meetings of its governing body. He also had investments in the Somers Islands Company, which organized the settlement of the Bermudas. Both were acquired through his employer William Cavendish, the Earl of Devonshire (Malcolm 1996: 20). Locke's work for his patron Lord Ashley (who became the Earl of Shaftesbury) entailed being secretary to the Lords Proprietors of the Carolinas from 1668 to 1671, during which time he wrote a constitution giving owners absolute powers over their slaves. He also owned shares in the Royal Africa Company and the Bahamas Adventurers, two slave-trading companies (Uzgalis 2002: 82). Kant wrote many passages framed in terms of racial hierarchy, among them this passage from *Physical Geography* (1804): "Humanity is at its greatest in the race of the whites. The yellow Indians do have a meager talent. The Negroes are far below them and at the lowest point are a part of the American peoples" (in Bernasconi 2002: 147). He was silent about slavery other than to note that "Negroes" are only apt for "slave culture."
6. Judaism's tradition is itself rich and varied, providing the vocabulary of *ru'ah*, wind, and a standard word for spirits; *maggid*, "a heavenly mentor granted to great kabbalists"; the *ibbur*, "a usually undetected additional righteous soul that came to help rectify one's sins"; *gilgul*, a soul that moves from dead to live bodies; and more recently, *dybbuk*, a "malevolent spirit, generally that of a dead person, that adheres to and controls and unwilling subject" (Goldish 2003: 12–13). The proliferation of terms of possession in Judaism roughly paralleled the possession idiom in Christianity—or preceded it, as Hobbes had it. In the Greek version of Hebrew scriptures, the Septuagint, *ru'ah* is rendered as *pneuma* and distinguished from *daimon*, an early distinction of the good breath of God (in-spiration) linked to wisdom, *sophia*, versus the pernicious, often violent enthusiasms of the devil, daimon (Heron 1983: 33–35). Islam, of course, has its own lineage. Here I'm trying to think through the doxic rules of the West, which then informed translations of diverse ritual events into the problem of spirit possession.
7. Concomitantly, as Marion Gibson (1999) has argued, the English genre of the "witchcraft pamphlet," which flourished from 1597 to 1602, began to be purged of the issue of possession after 1612. Witchcraft pamphlets thereafter speak little of possession, as though possession had delegitimized the genre (perhaps by emphasizing the victimhood of the "perpetrator").
8. Note the accusation of fraud in his formulation. He proceeds to write that some men, "faining themselves to be possessed with a devil, will deceive the said witches, as their wives have been deceived by them."
9. Consider the play of "possession" in modern novelistic applications to sexual congress as a salve to alienation, the best example of which appears in a text like Alberto Moravia's 1961 *La Noia* (Boredom, or the Empty Canvas), where the painter-protagonist sexually penetrates his accomplice over and over again ad nauseam in a desperate attempt to possess "her." His staring blank canvas is the crush-

ing reminder of his failure, as well as of the elusiveness of just where "she" resides. Or Rousseau in his *Confessions*: "When I possessed her I felt she still was not mine; and the single idea that I was not everything to her caused her to be almost nothing to me" ([1781] 1953: 395).

10. From Montaigne's interviews with three Tupi circa 1560, on the basis of which he composes one of his most famous essays, "De Caniballes" (1580). Just a few decades later, Shakespeare used the text in Gonzalo's descriptions of the ideal commonwealth, in *The Tempest* (act 2, scene 1). In the following century, Rousseau depended heavily on it, ending the *Discourse on the Origins of Inequality* with the words of Montaigne's Tupi, by then so famous as to require no citation whatsoever.
11. By the late eighteenth century, possession phenomena began to appear more frequently as a constitutive component of orientalist writing about South Asia (Hugh Urban, oral communication, April 16, 2009). In chronological terms, writing on spirit possession always indexed colonial lands possessed. Frederick M. Smith (2006) argues that in India, spirit possession has always been marginalized by purifying efforts by Brahmins to generate values of control, self-awareness, and a discrete self (4–8, 12). But "spirit possession" as such was rarely addressed in a frontal attack, even by British colonial authorities (23).
12. Pieter de Marees described the *fetisso* in his *Description and Historical Account of the Gold Kingdom of Guinea* ([1602] 1987). The German surgeon Andreas Joshua Ulsheimer noted the use of the word *futisse* on the Cape Coast of Africa, on his voyage of 1603–4 (in Chireau 2003: 40). Peter Logan (2009: 18) notes early versions in multiple European languages: Old French *faitis*, "well made"; Middle English *fetis*, used for example in Chaucer to describe beautiful people and their actions; *fetisly*, or "ful fetys damyseles two"; and the Anglo-Norman *fetiz*. This set of terms bridged the issues of the qualities of persons or objects and the effects those persons or objects produce in us. See also Roger Sansi's excellent essay "Sorcery and Fetishism in the Modern Atlantic" (2011).
13. The entry for "fétiche" was written by M. l'Abbé (Edme François) Mallet, who died in 1755—at least if the *Encyclopédie*'s attributions can be trusted, which seems at times unclear after the revocation of the royal license in 1759. His source for the entry was Dapper's 1686 travelogue (Sansi 2011). Diderot confirmed de Brosses's "discovery" in a 1757 letter: "Vous avez raison, le fétichisme a certainement été la religion première, générale et universelle. Les faits doivent nécessairement être d'accord avec la philosophie. . . . Vous avez complété la démonstration de l'Histoire naturelle de la religion de David Hume. Connaissez-vous ce morceau? Il est tout à fait dans vos principes" (You are correct, fetishism was certainly the first general and universal religion. Facts by necessity agree with philosophy. You have completed the demonstration of David Hume's *Natural History of Religion*. Do you know that piece? It is very consistent with your principles) (David 1981: 131).
14. The first place de Brosses invoked *fétiche* and *fétichisme* was in his 1756 *Histoire des navigations aux terres australes* (2:377), in relation to the practices of "ce people nègres des Philippines," who are in every way (climate, hair, lips, color, fetishism ("Ils adorent des pierres rondes, des troncs d'arbres & diverse autres espèces de *fétiches*") just like "les nègres Africaines." But the terms weren't developed until *Du culte de dieux fétiches*. De Brosses mentions his sources for Africa in that work as being Bosman, Atkins, and Des-Marchais, but Bosman is earlier and more substantial than Atkins, and Des-Marchais seems largely derivative. Atkins (1735: 116, 123) cites Bosman, also noting the use of the fetish in business affairs, but refines Bos-

man too: the fetish is the thing contractors first see after determining upon an affair, or sometimes as *that which determines them to conduct that affair* (119). Atkins also equates "Fetish" with "Deity," recounts stories about fetish worship and human sacrifice (about which he is doubtful), and wonders whether snake worship might endanger "our factories" (118). He also softens fetishism as "reverence improved for creatures" (117) and discusses how "Fetish-women" use "fits and distortions" in a kind of fakery.

15. Engels's introduction to *The Origin of the Family*, which he composed largely from Marx's notes, reports his and Marx's wide reading of nineteenth-century anthropological literature—especially Lewis Henry Morgan, but also Bachhofen, Tylor, Lubbock, and others. Morgan's *Ancient Society*, the key text that Engels engaged, described African society as "in an ethnical chaos of savagery and barbarism" and said nothing else.

16. T. K. Oesterreich's *Possession: Demoniacal and Other* is exemplary: "I shall begin with primitive civilization, as regards which the data concerning spontaneous possession are still exceedingly scanty. The majority of the relevant documents which I can produce relate to Africa, where happily the main regions furnish their contribution so well that we may consider possession as a frequent phenomenon widely disseminated throughout this giant continent" ([1921] 2003: 132).

    Latour (1993) and Keane (2007) demonstrate how purification efforts inevitably yield new hybrids. "Purification" already appears as a term applied in relation to possession phenomena in Kant's early work on Swedenborg, *Dreams of a Spirit Seer*.

17. David Hume made a similar move in linking superstition and enthusiasm as the two corruptions of "true religion," in his essay of 1741: "That the corruption of the best things produces the worst, is grown into a maxim, and is commonly proved, among other instances, by the pernicious effects of superstition and enthusiasm, the corruptions of true religion." Ultimately, though, he placed superstition and enthusiasm as opposed forces, with the only the former leading to political tyranny: "My third observation on this head is, that superstition is an enemy to civil liberty, and enthusiasm a friend to it" ("Of Superstition and Enthusiasm," http://infomotions.com/etexts/philosophy/1700–1799/hume-of-738.htm, accessed May 7, 2009). The association of Africa with a lack of developed personhood was occasionally inverted, as in Swedenborg's 1758 *Treatise Concerning the Last Judgement, and the Destruction of Babylon*, where he identifies Africa's interior lands with persons of the greatest interiority, precisely because they receive spiritual communications in unmediated form, unlike "Mahometans and Papists" (64): "The Africans are a more interior people than the rest" (64). Noteworthy is how geography and anthropology are understood to mirror and replicate each other. See Rotberg (2005).

    Keane (2007) has best articulated the relationship between ideas and practices related to the status of "things" and notions of personhood.

18. For example: "And for that part of Religion, which consisteth in opinions concerning the nature of Powers Invisible, there is almost nothing that has a name, that has not been esteemed amongst the Gentiles, in one place or another, a God, or Divell; or by their Poets feigned to be inanimated, inhabited, or possessed by some Spirit or other" ([1651] 1985: 173).

19. The idea of the self as a possession to be gained is reprised, albeit in a different sense, by Sartre's version of existentialism, among others: "Mais si vraiment l'existence précède l'essence, l'homme est responsable de ce qu'il est. Ainsi, le première dé-

marche de l'existentialisme est de mettre tout homme en possession de ce qu'il est et de faire repose sur lui la responsabilité totale de son existence" (If existence truly precedes essence, man is responsible for what he is. The first step of existentialism is to give every man possession of what he is, and to place the responsibility of his existence completely on him) (1996: 31).

20. During the same period, Christian salvation was translated into the terms of property: Richard Vickers, the Quaker, wrote a tract in 1697 about how to acquire and keep the "Heavenly Possession," for example.
21. Raymond Williams traces the emerging ideas about the idea of "the individual" and what is "private," in the sense of exclusive and with limited access, in the sixteenth and seventeenth centuries at the intersection of economic, social, and religious ideas about the self and society (1985: 161–65; 242–43).
22. Hobbes asserts that the two things assuring contracts are (1) the fear of "Invisible Spirits" and (2) pride ([1651] 1985: 194–200).
23. In de Léry's account, "being tormented by evil spirits" is described with the term "passions." Thanks to Michael Lambek for directing my attention to the close proximity between passions and possessions in various philosophical texts.
24. The "propensity to truck, barter and exchange one thing for another" was likewise for Adam Smith the central distinction of the human from the animal: "Nobody ever saw a dog make a fair and deliberate exchange of one bone for another with another dog" ([1776] 1976: 1:ii).
25. If an object is not anyone's property, that object is "annihilated" in a practical respect; it becomes nothing. Kant goes on to discuss property of three types (6:247–48, 260): First is the right to a thing, to corporeal objects in space, or land. The second is the right against a person, the right to coerce that person to perform an action, or *contract right*. The third is the "right to a person akin to a right to a thing," including spouses, children, and servants (cf. Hobbes [1651] 1985: 253). Here we see how legal and civil ideas about possession entail also a social theory of relation.
26. Noted Braudel, inter alia: "Countries producing gold and silver were almost always primitive, even savage places" (1992: 197).
27. Leibniz's *New Essays* (1704) refuted Locke's thought experiment of the prince and the cobbler with his own experiment in metempsychosis: Say you become the king of China, in the process losing all your present memories. Would you as a person continue to exist? Against Locke, Leibniz's answer was no; personhood is inseparable from the perceiving body. Future rewards and punishments could not have meaning or any systematic character without the preservation of memory and personal identity; thus any idea of justice depends on the firm union of consciousness and body (in Perkins 2007: 145).
28. "It came in my head to ask him an idle question, because I thought it not very likely for me to see him again, and I had a mind to know from his own mouth, the account of a common, but much credited Story, that I had heard so often from many others, of an old Parrot he had in *Brasil*, during his Government there, that spoke, and ask'd, and answer'd common questions like a reasonable creature; so that those of his Train there, generally concluded it to be Witchery or Possession; and one of his Chaplains, who liv'd long afterwards in *Holland*, would never from that time endure a Parrot, but said, They all had a Devil in them" (Temple 1692: 76–77). Locke quotes the story at length from William Temple's *Memoirs of what past in Christendum*.

29. The sovereign, argued Hobbes, may be installed by either institution (consensual establishment of the so-called Rules of Propriety) or acquisition ([1651] 1985: 234, 228, 251ff). On the question of the proper disciplining of spirits, an exemplary text is Locke's *Some Thoughts Concerning Education,* far and away the most important English pedagogical treatise of its time and for the century that followed: "Having by gentle degrees, as you find him capable of it, settled such an idea of God in his mind, and taught him to pray to Him, and praise Him as the Author of his being, and of all the good he does or can enjoy; *forbear any discourse of other spirits.*" ([1692] 1996: 103, part 9, sec. 137; my emphasis).
30. Le Bon's use of "la foule" seems inspired by Tocqueville's. For example, "The more equal conditions become, the less strong men are individually, the more they allow themselves to go along with the crowd, and the harder they find it to adhere by themselves to an opinion the crowd has abandoned" (Tocqueville 2004: 603).
31. "La renaissance de la magie," *Revue Scientifique,* March 26, April 2, 1910; "Le spiritisme et la science," *La Nature,* no. 1962, December 31, 1910.
32. Cuba underwent very similar processes, aggravated by repeated witch hunts against Afro-Cuban religions, whose practitioners were accused of cannibalizing white children. As the Havana newspaper *El Día* reported in 1918: "Until after the triumph of the revolution blacks raised white children without eating or abusing them. The war has ended . . . Cuba has been liberated from Spanish tutelage, legal equality and rights of all citizens have been recognized and those people have begun to drink the blood of white girls, and even to martyrize their own daughters, under the impression that they are the tainted members of the family. Where is progress, then, where is civilization?" (in Bronfman 2004: 39). "Proxemics" is Edward Hall's term ([1966] 1990).
33. Nina Rodrigues says that this is "unfortunately" said by others but nevertheless lamentably true.
34. The specter of possession was not only useful to philosophers thinking about personhood, rationality and the like. It was also associated with spectacular popular displays of science, above all through the trajectory from demons to ventriloquist stage shows. As Leigh Schmidt's article "From Demon Possession to Magic Show" documents, the key moment in this shift came with the publication of Joannes Baptista de La Chapelle's 1772 *Le Ventriloque, ou engastrimythe,* a text that systematically set out to debunk the history of spirits speaking through persons. It became the anchor of entries in encyclopedias such as the *Britannica* (1797) and was hastily translated into multiple languages. Supernatural voices speaking from the belly (the *ventre*) were now a natural phenomena explained by the generation of aural illusion by the throat and tongue. If the wave of debunking spectacles that followed in nineteenth-century Europe and the United States were first and foremost a showcase of gender relations, with scientific men exposing deceitful women, Schmidt shows how the new theater of evidence also quickly interpolated savage religions—taking forms ranging from Eskimo shamans to disrupted black revival meetings. Just as Kant had invested substantial time and money in his investigations of Swedenborg from 1763 to 1766, later scholars of religion from Tylor to William James were frequently in the audience of Spiritualist séances. As in the earlier example of Locke's thought-experiment that split the identities of "man," "soul," and "person," at once defining the rational person and deeply problematizing it by showing its gaps, mimicry, and fabrications, the unending modern freak show of possession hinted that the real and the perceived are not easily discerned and may not be separable

whatsoever. James' "pragmatic" approach to religious experience may be read in a sense as a response to this conundrum.

35. Andrew Willford (2006: 91) argues something similar: "In Freud, it is not simply that narcissistic and animistic residues are uncanny in their inevitable returns—that is, the surmounted pasts in the service of the ego-ideal. Rather, it is the frightening 'automaton' of socially conditioned reason that is the uncanny alien 'double' within, with its contingent morality overwhelming and enveloping the subject through its impossible demand for obedience."

36. Here is Freud on the uncanny:

> It is true that the writer creates a kind of uncertainty in us in the beginning by not letting us know, no doubt purposely, whether he is taking us into the real world or into a purely fantastic one of his own creation. He has, of course, a right to do either; and if he chooses to stage his action in a world peopled with spirits, demons and ghosts, as Shakespeare does in *Hamlet*, in *Macbeth* and, in a different sense, in *The Tempest* and *A Midsummer Night's Dream*, we must bow to his decision and treat his setting as though it were real for as long as we put ourselves into this hands. But this uncertainty disappears in the course of Hoffmann's story, and we perceive that he intends to make us, too, look through the demon optician's spectacles or spy-glass—perhaps, indeed, that the author in his very own person once peered through such an instrument. (Freud [1919] 1955: 230)

Or consider this passage from Morgan's *Ancient Society* (1907: 6), where property is described as a germ that takes possession of the brain: "The idea of property was slowly formed in the human mind, remaining nascent and feeble through immense periods of time. Springing into life in savagery, it required all the experience of this period and of the subsequent period of barbarism to develop the germ, and to prepare the human brain for the acceptance of its controlling influence. It not only led mankind to overcome the obstacles which delayed civilization, but to establish political society."

37. As Geertz put it, "The ability of anthropologists to get us to take what they say seriously has less to do with either a factual look or an air of conceptual elegance than it has with their capacity to convince us that what they say is a result of having penetrated (or, if you prefer, been penetrated by) another form of life." (1988: 4). West (2008: 109) notes that "[Janice] Boddy has similarly compared ethnographic fieldwork and writing to spirit possession, telling us that both are 'rooted in the conviction that knowledge is achieved through transcendence of the self in the other.' "

38. To take just one of many examples, consider Judy Rosenthal's recent writing on the Ewe of West Africa: "My own writerly presence here is obviously not mine in the property sense, and it is not present in any metaphysical way. Like Ewe and Gorovodu being, it is a nexus of 'Others,' crisscrossing personhoods, stories, political events, cultural transformations, bodies and spirits both dead and alive, and so many other texts" (1998: 3); thus, "this is a text issued from the vodus" (7). "I was seduced by all I saw and heard and I wanted very much to merge into the trance state with the spirit hosts" (7). Spirit possession is a set of techniques for "becoming Foreign Others" (30); thus, "Vodu identity is peculiarly and radically modern (or post-modern)" (31); "My longing is for the gorovodus to remain positioned to seize or possess theory"(32).

39. In Candomblé, initiated spirit holders are also understood, in some sense, to possess the tutelary deities seated in their head, as in "Tom's Xangô," expressing the

particularity and interdependency of every human-divine relationship (e.g., Capone 2010: 20). This complexity does not invalidate the basic semantic links between possession and servitude, though it makes them more ambiguous.

40. Slavery appears elsewhere in Hayes's description as well: the exús are "slaves" of the orixás, for example (2011: 253; Capone 2010: 44–45). Analogously, Rosalind Shaw's (2002) work has shown how contemporary notions of sorcery, as the "consumption" of people, is a direct legacy of the slave trade.
41. Reis (2011) documents a legal case arising in nineteenth-century Bahia of an African-born priest of Candomblé named Candeal who allegedly tried to sell someone else's slave who was now under his *ritual* authority. Here, the slave-master relationship was contested but not by any simple acquisition of free will or liberty of movement.

CHAPTER TWO

1. A note on spelling: rather than standardizing the orthography of abakuá terminology, I have chosen to retain the (inconsistently) hispanicized spelling found in abakuá "libretas" (notebooks) and utilized by my interlocutors in Regla (e.g., "abakuá" instead of "abacuá" and "Sikan" instead of "Sican" but "enquico" instead of "enkiko" or "Nasacó" instead of "Nasakó").
2. This is a once common heteronym for abakuá, nowadays uniformly rejected by its members.
3. The four *obones* (highest titles) are *Illamba, Mocongo, Isué,* and *Insunecue*; the *indiobones* (next high-ranking titles) are *Empegó, Ecueñón,* and *Enkrícamo.*
4. Obviously, interpreting a North American newspaper account from the turn of the twentieth century in light of Cuban ethnographic evidence from the turn of the twenty-first century comes dangerously close to the kind of ahistorical exercises deriving "African" origins from comparisons of New World data with decontextualized Africanist ethnography that I myself have repeatedly criticized.
5. In the former case, my own fieldwork in Havana's "municipio" of Regla since 1996 will serve as the major source of data; in the latter case, I will rely on an eclectic sample of publications that issued forth from the social networks surrounding Bell's Volta laboratory and Thomas Edison's Menlo Park as well as a copious secondary literature.
6. This, of course, makes perfect sense to anyone familiar with the ethnographic literature on Nigeria's Cross River region and its secret societies, which have been consistently (if somewhat problematically—see Palmié 2008) been pinpointed as abakuá's African "antecedents." The number of such cognoscenti nowadays includes members of abakuá who have read, for example, Fernando Ortiz's or Lydia Cabrera's writings on these matters, though they would never have heard a leopard's voice outside Havana's Jardín Zoológico. Note also that in both contemporary mythical accounts and visual representations, *llebengó,* the tiger, has become Ecueñón's primordial beast of prey.
7. "To attain their supernatural condition," writes Fernando Ortiz (1952–55: 4: 42), all ritual objects "first have to pass through a rite of reanimation. To effect this, at the beginning of a plante, the ritual specialist marks the floor with a magical chalk sign that reaches from the seclusion of *écue* to the temple's door, and he puts the four principal drums on the part of the hieroglyph designating [the position of] *écue.* He places the *empegó* [drum] on top of *écue,* above it the *ekueñón* [drum], then

the *eribó* [a silent drum], and on top of them all the *enkríkamo*." The *itones* (staffs of office) are likewise activated through sacred writing; even the *afoíreme* (body masks) have to be ritually attended to in order to enable their wearers not to enact the liturgical functions of íremes but to embody them.

8. "Oye la campana pero no sabe donde sueña" (he hears the church bells, but doesn't know where they are ringing) an abakuá proverb has it. Although it aims to make a distinction between common obonécues and "plazas" (the first do not get to visually apprehend Écue, the latter do), it neatly circumscribes abakuá's phonic esotericism: women, foreign anthropologists, bystanders, or even the police will hear Écue's voice. But how could they possibly grasp the portent of its utterances?

9. Here significant ritual differences exist between the *ramas* (branches) of efó and efí (given that the mystery was originally discovered in the territory of efó and only incompletely transmitted to the efí), abakuá potencias pertaining to the rama efó do not need to go out and search for the voice, which "lives" in a *tinaja* (water-filled jar) on the potencia's altar. In the efó version of the baroco, the voice begins to sound as soon as Ecueñón begins to chant.

10. Which, most of my informants agree, they carried in or on their bodies (e.g., in the form of bracelets that were not taken from them upon enslavement).

11. Details omitted to respect the esoteric nature of the process.

12. To be sure, contemporary Cuban obonécues strenuously deny the possibility that Écue's voice could have been transmitted across Atlantic waters after its initial arrival at the dockside of Itía Ororó Cande, where African slaves belonging to the "cabildo de los bricamó ápapa efí" first managed to transmit Écue's voice to New World sonic space. Yet the questions this may raise are neither particularly interesting for my argument (I have no intention to prove or disprove whether the Leal's Temple of the Ancient Grace was *really* an abakuá potencia), nor are they, in fact, accessible to historical verification. Besides, contemporary Cuban obonécues themselves ultimately resort to secondary rationalizations in trying to argue that even photographic evidence (such as, for example, in the Spanish criminologist Rafael Salillas's images taken at the turn of the twentieth century in the Spanish presidio of Ceuta; see Palmié 2008) could not prove the presence of a functioning "potencia" outside of Cuba. Who would have authorized its birth? they will ask. How could the transmission of the voice have been achieved? But, of course, since Écue itself did come to Cuba, the matter nowadays seems to be conditioned by a fear of unauthorized reproduction—including not only a break in the chain of "transmisiones" but the possibility that a "copy" might take the place of the "original." Perhaps the paradox at the heart of this matter is best expressed in the *negue* (ritual question) "If Nasacó swore in the first thirteen obones in Usagaré, who then swore in Nasacó?" to which the answer must be given "The men he swore in."

13. But see Corbett (1994), Chude-Sokei (1997), or Eshun (1998) for suggestive analytical leads in such directions. Most intriguingly, Henriques, too, speaks of the sonic dominance characterizing sound-system situations as effecting multiple "transductions" (e.g., from electromagnetic frequencies into sonic and ultimately kinetic and affective modalities).

14. In Webb Keane's (2003, 2008) sense of a metapragmatics regimenting socially routinized practices of attaching relatively specific sign values to the materiality of semiotic forms, in this case sonic vibrations registered as auditory apperceptions.

15. See Schmidt's (2000: 19–31) astute but generous critique of the Pauline theology of

the word underlying Ong's lament for the desacralization of audition in the course of the rise of secular visualism and Sterne (2003: 16–19) on its relation to Derrida's critique of a metaphysics of presence.

16. Such as an auditory surveillance system aptly designated as a panacousticon by Zielinski (2006: 129).
17. See, for example, Scharlau (1969) and Ullmann (2002) for systematic expositions of Kircher's acoustic and musicological theories. An illustration of this technology from Kircher's *Phonurgia nova* (1673) is available at http://diglib.hab.de/drucke/xb-4827/start.htm?image=00163.
18. Francis Bacon reported on the "ear trumpet" or "otoacousticon" as early as 1629, and Robert Hooke introduced its principle to the Royal Society in 1688 on the analogy of the microscope as a technology to extend sensory reach (Gouk 1982). According to the OED, it was in 1684 that the word "microphone" first appeared in print in English. Closely intertwined though they historically are, I am concerned with megaphony rather than microphony here.
19. These included (among quite a few others) Charles Wheatstone's speaking machine, which is said to have inspired the young Bell; Joseph Faber's "Euphonia"; and, as the endpoint of this series of "dead technologies," George René Joseph Marie Marage's artificial larynx siren with buccal resonators in 1911 (Hankins and Silverman 1995).
20. *Fernschreiben*, as it still is called in the indicative German gloss. *Fernsprechen* (telephony) and *Fernsehen* (television) were, and are, an entirely different matter. Aschoff (1987) provides a lucid history of telegraphy before Morse.
21. Himself a deeply pious man, "convinced that he was a divinely chosen instrument for the furtherance of communication," Morse had arguably laid the groundwork for the enchantment of telegraphy by selecting a biblical verse ("What hath God wrought," Numbers 23:23) for the first message transmitted from the US capitol building to Baltimore's Mount Clare railway station (Harlow 1936: 99). Indeed, within less than ten years, on January 6, 1851, Andrew Jackson Davis, "the Poughkeepsie Seer," received a lengthy message from the spirit of Benjamin Franklin claiming that it was Franklin who, over the course of the good half century since his body had died, had invented the celestial telegraph (Sollors 1983: 988–89) and had merely, as the medium and spiritualist historian Emma Hardinge later put it, taken time in finding an earthy location "charged with the aura requisite to make it a battery for the working of the telegraph" between the hereafter and the world of the mortals (Sconce 2000: 36). Compare the inaugural moments of the telephone and phonograph: Bell shouting, "Watson, come here! I want you"; Edison reciting, "Mary had a little lamb." Of course, it didn't matter much. Their inventions became "haunted" within no time.
22. A project he had inherited from his father Alexander Maxwell Bell who had designed one of the more important early phonetic scripts—"visible speech"—for the same purposes.
23. Or, according to his own, rather more colorful version (Edison 1948: 44) a boyhood encounter with an aggressive train conductor.
24. Frow (1982: 21) features a photograph of Edison's personal disc phonograph with highly visible bite marks. Commenting on the above passage, Peters (2004) notes, "There is a perverse logic in Edison's chomping on the machine, because the phonograph (as opposed to the gramophone, which is ROM or read-only) also achieved the reversibility of mouth and ear, of recording and playback."

25. See the examples given in Read and Welch (1959: 18–24).
26. Characterizing the auditory ideology that guided initial receptions of phonography, Brady (1999: 46–47) writes:

    > In European and American cultures, hearing has been poetically and philosophically understood as the most ephemeral and evocative of sensory impressions, retrievable only through the mutable workings of memory. Western writers and thinkers in an unbroken line extending to St. Augustine back through Aristotle portray memory as a voiced entity. Marcel Proust writes figuratively of voices trapped in an inanimate object, lost to us unless we unwork the magic. 'Then they start and tremble, they call us by their name, and as soon as we have recognized their voice, the spell is broken.' The poignancy of this image lies in Proust's suggestion that this moment is a fairy-tale instant that for most of us never arrives. . . . But the wax cylinder, crude as it was, challenged the finality of this image, offering just such a spell to release the lost voices. An inanimate object, the cylinder bore the traces of past events in its very grooves and was capable of reanimating the event's lost voices and wrenching time out of the linear conformation of the Western mind, projecting past into present.

    This may well have been so, but surely only among those whose prior representational economies and auditory ideologies predisposed them toward enchanting the relation between audible sonic copies and their absent "originals."
27. By the 1920s, the Panamanian Cuna (who never seem to have been much taken aback by sound recording) were positively resisting the "civilizing" impact foisted upon them by the canal authority, which forced their women to attend dances with canal workers—to the tunes of American phonograph records (Taussig 1993: 196). And even though the phonograph does seem to have played some role in the emergence of the northern Rhodesian Lozi kingdom under British rule (Strickrodt 2007) by relaying the voice of a suitably collaborative chief to his future subjects, this episode, too, betrays rapid understanding and routinization of the technology's capacity to transcend time and space in the absence of any sustained supernatural interpretations.
28. Speaking about the prolific metaphors of male birth and mechanic infancy that permeate both Bell's and Edison's early popular (and even private) writings, Sterne (2003: 181) puts his finger on a "child is father to the man" moment when he notes that once "machines come into the world through singular moments of birth, they can have 'impacts.' They take on a little bit of humanity by becoming autonomous agents coming from outside the world of human activity to affect it, even as the birth metaphor deprives them of their greater humanity as products of human endeavor."
29. Though Edison soon abandoned his theory of "etheric force," he continued dabbling in electrical medicine, inventing, among other things, a medicinal electrifier ("Edison Therapeutic Sinusoidal Machine") and a patent medicine ("Edison's Polyform") designed to alleviate neuralgia by restoring electrical balance to facial nerves. As Nye (1983: 142) tells us, the "Edison formula contained one dram of peppermint oil mixed with small quantities of chloroform, morphine, alcohol, and other substances. Applied externally to the face, it worked on the theory that mucous membranes excrete an alkaline fluid, and serous membranes produce an acid, thus together producing electricity as a kind of battery. Polyform restored normal electrical exchange."
30. Of course Edison would not be the first materialist to change his mind in the afterlife. In 1924, Michael Faraday, perhaps one of the fiercest opponents of Victorian

Spiritualism, posthumously dictated an entire book titled *The Evolution of the Universe*.

31. See Porter (2005) and Vasconcelos (2008) for particularly lucid expositions of the relationship between Spiritualism and positivism.
32. One thinks of the likes of the eminent chemists Sir William Crooke and Robert Hare, the Nobel Prize–winning physiologist Charles Richet, Darwin's competitor in the development of the theory of evolution Alfred Russell Wallace, the physicist Oliver Lodge, the pioneer of transatlantic telegraphy Cromwell Fleetwood Varley, the Italian founder of "positive" criminology Césare Lombroso, psychologist and philosopher William James, folklorist Andrew Lang, or Comte's translator and social critic Harriet Martineau but also such distinguished figures as US Supreme Court Justice John C. Edmunds, industrialist and social reformer Robert Owen, the *New York Tribune* editor Horace Greeley, writers as famous as Harriet Beecher Stowe, Sir Arthur Conan Doyle, or Mark Twain, the composer Richard Wagner, and Mary Todd Lincoln, the wife of the slain US president.
33. And notionally sometimes even before then: after all, Ben Franklin had been laboring mightily in the afterlife before he managed to find the right conditions for the passing the telegraph from the afterlife to the sublunar world in Rochester, New York!
34. It took a full twenty-two years between the invention of daguerreotypy and William H. Mummler's 1861 announcement that he had successfully photographed a spirit.
35. Compare the reproduction of Bell's 1876 sketches of the first liquid-based telephone in Bruce (1973: 179, 180, 183).
36. This, of course, is exactly what differentiated both the emergent secularist consumers of phonographic entertainment and Spiritualist users of electroacoustic technology from psychotics who just as eagerly began to harness telephony and (to a perhaps lesser extent) phonography to the expression and elaboration of their personal delusions. See Gitelman (1999: 62–96) for examples drawn from the correspondence received by Edison's lab.
37. As the *New York Times* (March 16, 1860) article described it, the "instrument was nothing less than a great reservoir for the collection of sound, connected with a series of distributing pipes for conveying to many different ears at once. . . . The funnel-shaped vessel is placed before the pulpit, and catches the words as fast as they drop from the speaker's lips. From the bottom of the funnel, pipes are laid beneath the floor, to the various parts of the house occupied by those whose hearing is defective, and these terminate in ear-pieces attached to the side of the pew."
38. Were the "spools" gaily floating in the water induction coils? Was the "pagoda" a device to capture and funnel sound? Might the mouthpiece into which Leal is seen speaking in the photograph in the *North American* have been furnished with a microphonic diaphragm? Was the water acidulated? Would the wemba or mocuba used in contemporary abakuá work as an electrolyte or medium to vary impedance? While the answer to the last question is an unequivocal yes, the others are historical imponderables.
39. Walter Benjamin (1969: 217–51) of course famously caught on to this cultural moment: Is not the very notion of "auratic loss" an artifact of an ideology of mediation that simply could not have been developed in the absence of technical reproducibility? As he puts it (ibid.: 243n2), "To be sure, at the time of its origin, a medieval picture of the Madonna could not have been said to be 'authentic.' It became 'au-

thentic' only during the succeeding centuries and perhaps most strikingly so during the last one."

40. On this issue see Thompson's (1995) analysis of phonographic advertisement copy and her account of how Edison's "Tone Test Campaign" (concert performances in which audiences were exposed to both "live" singers—the term "live music" originated in these contexts—and phonographic recordings of their voices) between 1915 and 1922 systematically cultivated a new culture of (technologically enhanced) auditory "realism" among the American public. Though much less dramatically so than in the case of photographic "realism" (see Mnookin 1998), the awareness of staged or otherwise manipulated "copies" without originals was part and parcel of that moment right from the start (Feaster 2001): as early as 1878, Edison himself produced the equivalent of spirit photographs by recording several times over the same strip of tinfoil, and while the phonograph did see battle in Cuba during the Spanish-American War, the Victor record "The Battle of Santiago" made extensive use of sound effects. As Feaster (ibid.: 86) well puts it, the "kettle drums in 'The Battle of Santiago' do not sound much like the naval cannons used during the Spanish American War, but when prefaced by the command, 'Fire the starboard thirteen-inch gun at the enemy's flagship!,' the striking of a drum can readily be interpreted as the firing of a cannon." Readily, perhaps, but *only* once one has been inculcated into the auditory semiotic ideology that was dawning at the time.
41. In Heidegger's (1977) sense of technology as both "techne" and "poiesis."

CHAPTER THREE

1. For more about the remarkable career of Frances Conant, see Putnam (1872) and Day (1873).
2. The advertising broadside in question belongs to the Harvard Theatre Collection, Houghton Library. An image of the work can be viewed on the Uncle Tom's Cabin & American Culture website sponsored by Stephen Railton and the University of Virginia, http://utc.iath.virginia.edu/onstage/bills/tsbills15f.html.
3. Much has been written on the history and practice of Anglo-American minstrelsy. For background information presented here, I rely on standard works such as Rice (1911), Toll (1974), Boskin (1986), Lott (1993), Cockrell (1997), Mahar (1999), Lhamon (1998), Tosches (2001), Pickering (2008), and S. Johnson (2012).
4. See R. Laurence Moore (1977), Oppenheim (1985), Barrow (1986), Carroll (1997), Winter (1998), Cox (2003), Kucich (2004), and Bennett (2007). The anonymous author's juxtaposition of "spirit knocking" with "women's rights" seemingly foreshadows much recent work on the intersections of Spiritualism, gender, and power. See, for example, Braude (2001), Owen ([1989] 2004), McGarry (2008), and Tromp (2006).
5. The best discussion of this fascinating history is found in Winter (1998).
6. For example, the British journal the *Medium and Daybreak* records "negro entertainments" or performances "in character" associated with spiritualist activities: vol. 16, no. 815 (November 13, 1885): 733 and vol. 16, no. 777 (January 9, 1885): 28.

CHAPTER FOUR

My first debt of gratitude is to the Cuban folk practitioners, scholars, and skeptics alike who have generously facilitated my long-term ethnographic engagement in the city of Santiago de Cuba, becoming cherished friends in the process. Although I go against her wishes in refusing to reveal her identity for reasons that I have not yet successfully translated, Josefina's loving insistence that I learn from her made this essay possible: Madrina, te felicito y te agradezco con todo mi corazón. I also thank her cabildo and all of its spiritual commissions for permitting me to create these material traces. On the no less important mundane plane, I thank the researchers of the Casa de Caribe as well as Sarah Hill, Diana Espirito Santo, Jalane Schmidt, Stephan Palmié, two anonymous reviewers, and especially Paul Christopher Johnson for their insights and intellectual support. My 2006–11 fieldwork was supported by generous internal grants from Western Michigan University.

1. Original in Spanish; translation is mine, although the film also has English subtitles.

CHAPTER FIVE

1. Saltpeter (potassium nitrate) is a main ingredient in black gunpowder.
2. I use *santo* as a general term for all the spirits and deities of Afro-Brazilian religion and Brazilian popular Catholicism in accordance with local usage in the sertão.
3. One hundred reais were worth about fifty-five dollars that day.
4. One US dollar bought 1.82 Brazilian reais on August 6, 2009. Therefore R$850 = USD 467.03; R$28,000 would be USD15,385. A carat is equal to 0.2 grams.
5. G and VS1 are measurements of the color and clarity of diamonds.
6. Nicolau's story was told to me by one of his backland disciples. Whether or not it is true, it functions as a potent morality tale.
7. This information is available from the Instituto Brasileiro Geográfica e Estadística at http://www.ibge.gov.br/cidadesat/.
8. This research has been sponsored by a Fulbright-Hays fellowship and the California State University, Chico, Office of Research and Sponsored Programs.

CHAPTER SIX

1. Among neo-Pentecostals in general, the emphasis on exorcism or "deliverance" does not always go hand in hand with an emphasis on property; some neo-Pentecostals disdain the prosperity teachings (see for example Annacondia 2008; Bottari 2000; D. Prince 1998).
2. In contrast to Brazil and Africa, there is little emphasis on deliverance from demons among North American prosperity preachers. In addition, some who stress the material dimension of salvation do so from a leftist perspective (e.g., Volf 2011; Boff 1978) that is opposed both to consumerism and the idea that demons are the primary cause of society's ills.
3. Oro (2006) refers to the IURD as "neopentecostalismo macumbeiro" and calls its tendency to absorb other religions "religiofagia."
4. An older Pentecostal denomination that was founded in the United States and reached Brazil via missionaries in the early twentieth century.
5. Various versions of this testimony are available on the Internet as well. For example, see http://www.youtube.com/watch?v=GpSS1jNFgEU.
6. Interestingly, luxury vehicles also figure prominently in the Comaroffs' discussion of the IURD in South Africa. They mention advertisements for BMWs adorning the altar of an IURD church, for instance, and they cite an informant who claims that Satanists love to speed around in fast cars (Comaroff and Comaroff 2000).

CHAPTER SEVEN

The names of small organizations and people have been changed to protect their privacy and security. I am grateful to Pastor Yvette and her congregation for welcoming me into their space, to Pastor John for bringing me there, and to Jim and Faith

Chosa, Pastor Joel Jeune, Pastor Maurice, Peter Wagner, and Rev. J. L. Williams for interviews. I am grateful to Paul C. Johnson and the members of the Atlantic Studies Initiative at the University of Michigan for their comments, and I also thank Attiya Ahmad, Maxwell E. Bevilacqua, Ron Cameron, Annalise Glauz-Todrank, Henry Goldschmidt, Peter Gottschalk, Laura Harrington, Jason Craige Harris, Jeffrey Kahn, Justine Quijada, and Mary-Jane Rubenstein.

1. Romans 8.
2. The term "evangelicalism" can describe many broad branches of Christianity and has recently come to include leftist ideologies as well as the more commonly known politically conservative ones. In general, evangelicalism of all stripes is characterized by four features: (1) biblicalism, or the ultimate authority of the Bible; (2) the born-again experience, or the sense of having been reborn through a direct experience of the presence of Jesus Christ; (3) activism, or the duty to witness and spread the gospel; and (4) crucicentrism, or the focus on Christ's crucifixion as the sole path to salvation. This definition is drawn from D. W. Bebbington, *Evangelicalism in Modern Britain: A History from the 1730s to the 1980s* (London: Unwin Hyman, 1989), 2–17, and endorsed by Mark A. Noll, *America's God: From Jonathan Edwards to Abraham Lincoln* (New York: Oxford University Press, 2002), 5. While there is great debate about terms and definitions, I use the term "renewalism" to refer to a broad category containing branches of evangelicals, fundamentalists, Pentecostals, and charismatics that are expanding rapidly on a global scale. (Pew Forum on Religion & Public Life, "Spirit and Power: A 10-Country Survey of Pentecostals" [Washington: Pew Forum on Religion and Public Life, 2006]).
3. This popular train of thought emerges from evangelical seminaries such as the Fuller Theological Seminary, the Dallas Theological Seminary, Trinity Evangelical Divinity School, and the Wagner Leadership Institute, and its rhetorical style focusing on transformation and restoration has been taken up by a wide range of groups and public speakers, including, in the United States, Rick Warren of Saddleback Church and Glen Beck on Fox News. Journalists have written about the movement since discovering Sarah Palin's involvement, yet social scientists have not yet researched its thought and lived dimensions to the extent that it merits. Other prominent Americans affiliated with the movement include Ted Haggerty, former head of the National Association of Evangelicals; Mike Bickle's International House of Prayer; Rick Joyner; and the loose network calling themselves Joel's Army.
4. Many quotations here are from Jim Chosa's work because I attended a spiritual warfare training seminar with him at the Wagner Leadership Institute in Colorado Springs. However, he shares this theology with other major thinkers whose writings are variations on a common theme. For focused attention on legalism, see Larson (1999).
5. Following Charles Taylor's notion of the "social imaginary," I am interested in analyzing the way "ordinary people 'imagine' their social surroundings," often in ways that are not theorized but rather conveyed in images and through storytelling and the like. When shared widely, a social imaginary can form the basis of practices and identities and give rise to new social forms (Taylor 2002: 106).
6. It is undeniably true that third-wave evangelicals seek to eradicate Afro-Creole traditional religion, which they see as anti-Christian, demonic, and responsible in large measure for Haiti's problems. As a researcher with multiple investments in Vodou, I forcefully reject this position and its project, even as I respect and admire the evangelicals I have met. Their anti-Vodou stance is all the more reason to work to under-

stand their structures of thought, for they seem to be gaining converts among the Haitian majority and middle classes at a rapid rate and to be influencing renewalist thought worldwide.

7. I have heard a difference of opinion on Satan's legal standing in the Christian era. Some maintain his activity on earth is illegal, while others insist that as long as humans continue to commit sin, Satan derives legal rights on earth as a result.
8. The quotation is from a woman in the US Virgin Islands rather than Haiti, but it is such a fine and wonderfully illustrative example of the rhetorical flair and certainty of members of renewalist movements that I cite it here.
9. Wagner (1992: 143) also points out that this area is the center of other "demonic religions" such as Buddhism, Confucianism, Hinduism, Shintoism, and Taoism.
10. "For so hath the Lord has commanded us, saying, I have set thee to be a light of the Gentiles, that thou shouldest be for salvation unto the ends of the earth." (Acts 13:47).
11. It is worth noting that demon possession and exorcism is a central Christian theme and has come in and out of practice in various forms of Christianity in different periods.
12. The ad probably addresses domestic Bahamian anxieties about Haitian migrants, known as "the Haitian problem" in the local media, as much as it does support for spiritual warfare in Haiti itself. I am grateful to the anonymous reviewer for the University of Chicago Press who pointed this out.
13. Comments from Bishop Joel Jeune, whom I interviewed in 2001 and 2010.

CHAPTER EIGHT

1. An earlier version of this chapter was presented at the panel "The Work of Possession" at the Moments of Crisis: Decision, Transformation, Catharsis, Critique conference of the Society for the Anthropology of Religion and the Society for Psychological Anthropology, Pacific Grove, California. I wish to express my gratitude to panel organizer Paul Johnson and discussant Michael Lambek for their comments.
2. In addition to Mauss's concept of "the gift," Marx's idea of "appropriation" is another well-know example of this approach. See also Carrier (1999); Taussig (1993); and Wernick (1991).
3. Unlike Mama Lola and others in the Haitian immigrant community in Brooklyn described by Karen McCarthy Brown (1991), many in South Florida have not endeavored to serve or feed their spirits in the host society. Rather, those in Palm Beach County practice long-distance worship, anchored in the sacred landscape of the family land back home. The earlier movement to New York involved many migrants from the city of Port-au-Prince who were already a generation (or more) removed from their "inheritance" and may have already been affiliated with urban temple congregations based on voluntary association rather than descent. Yet as Brown (1991) explains, people who serve their spirits in New York are nonetheless occasionally enjoined through spiritual affliction to return home to worship.
4. Migration of a spirit's "chosen" similarly prevents the spirit from appearing in his or her "person" until that person returns. Nor can the lwa claim another member as long as the migrant is alive. See Richman and Rey (2009) for a discussion of this issue.

CHAPTER NINE

1. Following the agonistic notion of play and opposition developed by Richard Burton (1997), I am thinking about the mimetic dances that slaves used to perform in

yards, mimicking the steps of dancing parties they saw being performed in salons of white planters, which later developed into the dancing styles of postemancipation black countercultures.

2. See also Jean Rouch's *Les maîtres fous* (1955).
3. For the Anglo-American case of "playing Indian," see Abrahams (1995).
4. Homi Bhabha and other postcolonial writers stress the inherent existential (structural) tragedy of imperfect copies for colonial subjects who, to paraphrase Bhabha, have been required to be like white but could never be quite white. Following Bhabha (1994) I suggest elsewhere (Romberg 2005, 2011) that the violence that every act of irreverent impersonation had generated for hegemonic institutions in colonial times stemmed in part from their dependence on keeping social and moral categories separate and clear—not tarnished by illegitimate imitation and the dangers of "passing" (pretense).
5. The European witch craze offers another context for examining the fascination and fear of the assumed magic of polluting others—in this case of marginal groups within their own societies. See Larner (1984), Macfarlane (1970), Middelfort (1972), Monter (1976, 1983), and K. Thomas (1971). Following these lines of inquiry, recent scholarship on early modern witch hunts points to alleged witches (often but not only older women) as scapegoats for the ills of society at a time of rapid and fundamental changes, whether demographic, economic, political, or religious (Ankarloo, Clark, and Monter 2002; Roper 2004).
6. Similarly, the feared Haitian "zombie" and the West Indian Obeah man in the Caribbean owe their frightening deadly power to the nightmares of slavery (see Dayan 1995; Fernández Olmos and Paravisini-Gebert 1997).
7. Translation from Spanish is mine.
8. I'm referring to modernist artistic movements such as afrocubanismo—Ortiz's ethno-musicological work of the 1940s is a case in point (see, for example, Robin Moore 1997, 1994).
9. For example, dancers and artists such as Maya Deren ([1953] 1983) and Katherine Dunham (1969) focused on the African-based dances and movements of creole possession and initiation rituals, bracketing any information about the social conditions in which participants lived at the time of their observations and participation.
10. These kinds of explanations suggest that some practitioners simulate possession for sheer material interests, which in turn reflects on the widely held romantic assumption that when money (as commodity) is involved, religious inauthenticity is the outcome.
11. Often, incorporated mediums perform all sorts of potentially harmful feats and voice all sorts topics that are usually taboo or unspeakable. I am aware that what I interpret here as proof and testing performances, psychological approaches to spirit possession might interpret as reflecting some repressed aspects of the possessed or specific socially taboo behaviors (see Albers 2008: 284). Métraux goes as far as characterizing the impunity with which the possessed in Haiti can get away with "shocking indiscretions" as analogous to that resulting from the effects of alcohol or drug "intoxication in America" (1955: 28).
12. Indeed, Halperin notes (1995: 5), "Directly charging another medium with false possession is no minor matter, and I did not observe at first-hand any such incidents. Mina dancers occasionally gossip, however, that other mediums 'aren't with anything at all' when, for example, some members of the more traditional, and typically more subdued, centers critique the newer terreiros where, they claim, 'ev-

erybody jumps and rolls around and yelps . . . but they don't really "have anything [receive spirits]."' "

13. Métraux notes that some are better than others at representing (or, should I say, becoming) a *loa*. About a woman who was known in Vodou circles to embody Erzulie in an exceptional way, Métraux reports, people made comments such as: "You should see her as Erzulie" (1955: 25).
14. I use "discourse" here to mean local rules governing the speech about possession and "embodied discourses" to talk about the embodied, nondiscursive dispositions and conventions governing possession.
15. Here I am inspired by the work of Boddy (1994), Desjarlais (1992, 1996), Halperin (1996a, 1996b), Lambek (1988b, 2000), and especially Taussig (1998, 1999). Kristina Wirtz's "representational economy of spirit presence" in Afro-Cuban religions (this volume) is relevant here, especially in relation to the specific semiotics that helps constitute the reality of possession.
16. These performances are very different from the "proofs" (*comprobaciones* or *confirmaciones*) brujos claim after something that they divined actually happens. These are meant to be *manifestaciones* (manifestations) of their spiritual powers (see Romberg 2009).
17. Notably, this "amnesia" or "reticence," Métraux adds (1955: 21), is not extended to the preliminaries of possession; many describe how they felt just before possession. But apparently this kind of revelation does not become central to the technologies of presence in possession rituals.
18. I discuss the idea of "spiritual time" and the multilevel sensuous drama and poetics of possession, divination, and healing rituals extensively in Romberg (2009).
19. For a recent discussion of the "displacement" and "fusion" models of possession, see Cohen and Barrett (2008).
20. Tonio thus referred me to Haydée, "a very positive medium and powerful *espiritista bruja*" and one of his spiritual godchildren, with whom I would go on to work intensely as an apprentice.
21. The difficulty of falling into trance is widely reported. See Rouch ([1967] 1971) and Stoller (1989).
22. A different view, which I find highly problematic, argues that there is a physiological explanation. According to the ritual healing theory endorsed by McClenon and Nooney, "those more suggestible were healed more often by shamanic rituals; as a result, they passed on their genes to future generations more frequently than those not benefiting from healing rituals. The evolutionary processes selecting for these genotypes shaped the physiological basis for religiosity" (2002: 47). Eco's Amparo would have been very disturbed by this theory, but the German woman would have found solace in knowing that it was not just her fault.
23. Albers (2008) notes the influence of Julius E. Lips's ideas—introduced as early as 1937 in his *The Savage Hits Back; or, The White Man through Native Eyes*—about the mockery of Europeans in African art as an ironic mirror of colonialism on works that have stressed the theatricality of possession since.
24. In a recent critique of the counterhegemonic interpretation of Hauka possession in Rouch's film *Les maîtres fous*, Paul Henley (2006) revisits the film by comparing it to Rouch's own book about Hauka possession.
25. Rouch's trancelike experiences as camera operator in the series of Sigui films, most notably in *Tourou et Bitti* (1971, filmed in 1967), inspired in him a feeling of pro-

found communion similar to that of possession with the people in and around the camera's eye that he called "cine-trance."

26. Indeed, during the last weeks of his stay in Gondar, his suspicions were confirmed. Someone told him that "the women presumably did not show him the true cult but only a reduced version, that they fooled him and that their trances were faked in exchange for the promise of money and presents" (Albers 2008: 280–81).
27. The influence of Métraux's work (1955) on Leiris (1958) is well documented but is most evident in this idea of the "lived theatre." Indeed, revolutionizing how possession rituals would be interpreted in the years to come, Métraux argued some three years before Leiris that the "similarities between possession and theater must not make us forget that in the eyes of the public no possessed person is truly an actor. He does not *play* a person, he *is* that personage through the trance" (1955: 25).
28. Daniel Halperin (1995) analyzes the discourses of unconscious versus conscious possession among participants of Tambor de Mina, Brazil, explaining the influence of Kardecism on their notion of conscious possession as more elevated than the unconscious form (similarly to my discussion here of mediumship development in Scientific Spiritism centers inspired by Kardec).
29. See, for example, Wirtz's semiotics of spirit presence in Afro-Cuban religions in this volume.
30. I have recorded several such instances during my fieldwork in Puerto Rico (see Romberg 2003b, 2009).
31. In Puerto Rico today, when people say they go to metafísica workshops, they refer to classes in mediumship, some of which combine in various ways the teachings of Kardec and his contemporary exegetes as well as those of paranormal and New Age esoteric schools.
32. See note 28.
33. The stress here is on verbalization, which could include other forms of coded communication such as the scribbling of *claves* (automatic writings) on a piece of paper; Spiritist mediums might also deliver the messages of the spirits through body movements, but these are considered by some, like this instructor, to be just the signs of undeveloped forms of mediumship characteristic of novices. The racist and evolutionist connotations of these assumptions are developed elsewhere (Romberg 1998, 2003a).
34. See also Wirtz, this volume.
35. Changó, the orisha owner of lightning and drumming, is associated with Santa Bárbara in Puerto Rican *brujería*.
36. See Wirtz (2007) for the constitutive nature of discursive evaluations of possession in Santería.
37. Spirits also battle among themselves in order to own the head of their horses. In the case recounted by Wafer (1991: 32), two female spirits—Corquisa and Sete Saias—competed over the head of Taís.
38. One of the friends who shared with Palmié his doubts about the man possessed by Yemayá claimed that had this man been really possessed, he should have recognized him as a santero and greeted him ritually as is customary.
39. How past discourses on possession enter into the performative experience of ritual in the here and now is an intriguing question, albeit outside the scope of this essay; it adds to other questions that have been addressed by scholars of possession such as how events in the past enter into the present (Stoller 1995) and how current

socioeconomic contexts reshape possession rituals (Romberg 2003b) and modes of transmission and succession (Lambek 2000).

40. Likewise, who was refusing Palmié's pesos? Was it Yemayá or an impostor spirit?
41. The doubts raised by a group of Malaysian traditional healers about the innovations of Cik Su, an urban healer, and the charges they made about her inauthenticity seem to have crept also into the mind of the anthropologist Carol Laderman, working with both types of healers (1997). The "traditional" shamans told her that Cik Su was "clever" but not to be "trusted" and, criticizing her ways of healing, advised Laderman to throw the tapes of Cik Su away as worthless for not being representative of "traditional" Malaysian shamanism. Unlike traditional female shamans, Cik Su had adopted the ceremonial dress of men when conducting healing performances: "Her spirit guide was masculine," and her "expressions of fury when under his influence were far from normal" (1997: 336) for a female healer. If the spirit she embodied was masculine, the charges made against the medium were certainly unfounded in terms of the reality of spirit presence but, culturally speaking, understandable from the perspective of the politics of healing practices. A very different position about spirit reality and the role of the anthropologist is offered by Edith Turner (E. Turner et al. 1992; E. Turner 1993).

CHAPTER TEN

1. There has been a gradual shift in my own work from drawing on Western concepts to illuminate spirit possession to drawing on spirit possession to illuminate and develop Western concepts.
2. My own view is that we need distinct starting points from both spirit and matter. Their relationship can never be fully resolved insofar as it represents a fundamental incommensurability in the human condition. To reprise (but invert) the argument I made about mind and body (Lambek 1998a), if you start from matter, spirit and matter have to be rigorously distinguished; however, if you start from spirit, they are inextricable. Hence, it is a matter of either/or and of both/and—a paradox. One might in this respect compare science to religion (or parascience) or chemistry to alchemy.
3. The history of spirits in Christian Europe is another, related story.
4. Of our theoretical options, isn't genealogy the strongest form of disappearance (expropriation)?
5. Any evaluation or explanation of possession, whether by local people or by theorists, ought minimally to distinguish between which of these phenomena it is referring to. But frequently there is a failure to do so.
6. Of course, something along the same lines can be said of slavery; persons are a false commodity in Polanyi's sense. Such contracts would be open to the same questions of falsehood as possession has been subject to—and with more justification.
7. I hope capitalism has not yet extended so far that we can no longer imagine a form of having that is not commoditized.
8. For further discussion in philosophy, see Cavell ([1969] 1976) and in anthropology Tambiah (1985), Rappaport (1999), and Lambek (2010).
9. Compare Walsh (2004) on uncertainty in the sapphire trade in Madagascar.
10. Strictly speaking, the relationship between what is seen and unseen, or concealed and unconcealed, is not the same in various kinds of practices. In the case of the emerald, the surrounding mica must be chipped away, whereas in the case of possession, the spirit is manifest in the body of the host as the body of the host is mani-

fest in the presence, and as the vehicle, of the spirit. Possession is characterized as much by irony as by mystification.

11. Sometimes the "fakes" can appear better than the "real thing"; witness the reception of the works of Castaneda.
12. If, as Romberg reports, Puerto Ricans say you cannot learn deliberately to be possessed, people can acquire the confidence to know they *are* possessed (Lambek 2007).
13. The outsiders whom Richman discusses, notably Maya Deren and Katherine Dunham, were dancers. It would be equally interesting to see Richman's take on the more recent appropriations of Haitian knowledge by the ethno-botanists, who also write in a popular and heroic mode.

BIBLIOGRAPHY

Abrahams, Roger D. 1968. "Introductory Remarks to a Rhetorical Theory of Folklore." *Journal of American Folklore* 81 (319): 143–58.

———. 1977. "Toward an Enactment-Centered Theory of Folklore." In *Frontiers of Folklore*, edited by William R. Bascom, 79–120. Boulder, CO: published by Westview Press for the American Association for the Advancement of Science.

———. 1981. "Ordinary and Extraordinary Experience." In *The Anthropology of Experience*, edited by Victor W. Turner and Edward M. Bruner, 45–72. Urbana: University of Illinois Press.

———. 1995. "Making Faces at the Mirror: Playing Indian in Early America." *Southern Folklore* 52 (2): 121–35.

Adorno, Rolena. 2008. *The Polemics of Possession in Spanish American Narrative*. New Haven, CT: Yale University Press.

Albers, Irene. 2008. "Mimesis and Alterity: Michel Leiris's Ethnography and Poetics of Spirit Possession." *French Studies: A Quarterly Review* 62 (3): 271–89.

Ankarloo, Bengt, Stuart Clark, and William Monter. 2002. *The Period of the Witch Trials* Witchcraft and Magic in Europe 4. Philadelphia: University of Pennsylvania Press.

Annacondia, Carlos. 2008. *Listen to Me, Satan!* Lake Mary, FL: Charisma House.

Anonymous. 1838. "University College Hospital: Animal Magnetism." *Lancet* 26 (May): 282–88.

Anonymous. 1850. "Bad Spirits on the Tap." *Literary World* 163 (March 16): 276.

Anonymous. (1854) 1858. "Obituary, Not Eulogistic: Negro Minstrelsy Is Dead." *Journal of Music* 13 (18):118.

Anonymous. 1856. "A Talk about Popular Songs." *Putnam's Monthly* 7 (40): 401–15.

Anonymous. 1876. *Various Revelations with an Account of the Garden of Eden*. Boston: n.p.

Anonymous. 1877. "Uncle Tom's Cabin: Its Early Days, and the People Who Played in It." Amusement Annals, Clipper series, no. 4. *Clipper* (February 10).

Anonymous. 1878. "A Spiritualistic Séance in the Trongate, Glasgow." *Medium and Daybreak* 9 (438) (August 23): 533–34.

Anonymous. 1882. *Confessions of a Medium*. New York: E. P. Dutton.

Anonymous. 1882. "A Singular Superstition." *Gleason's Monthly Magazine* 6 (9): 400.

Anonymous. 1885. "Prof. Kershaw's Mesmeric Experiences." *Medium and Daybreak* 16 (780) (March 13):163–64.

Anonymous. 1898. "The Stage." *Munsey's Magazine* 19 (4): 617–26.

Apgaua, Renata. 1999. "A Dadiva Universal—Reflexões em um Debate Ficcional." Master's thesis, Universidade Federal de Minas Gerais.

Appadurai, Arjun. 1986. "Introduction: Commodities and the Politics of Value." In *The Social Life of Things: Commodities in Cultural Perspective*, edited by Arjun Appadurai, 3–63. Cambridge: Cambridge University Press.

———. 1996. *Modernity at Large: Cultural Dimensions of Globalization*. Minneapolis: University of Minnesota Press.

Argüelles Mederos, Anibal, and Ileana Hodge Limonta. 1991. *Los llamados cultos sincreticos y el espiritismo*. Havana: Editorial Academia.

Asad, Talal. 2006. "Trying to Understand French Secularism." In *Political Theologies: Public Religions in a Post-Secular World*, edited by Hent de Vries and Lawrence E. Sullivan, 494–523. New York: Fordham University Press.

Aschenbrenner, Joyce. 2002. *Katherine Dunham: Dancing a Life*. Urbana: University of Illinois Press.

Aschoff, Volker. 1987. *Geschichte der Nachrichtentechnik*. Berlin: Springer.

Ashforth, Adam. 2005. *Witchcraft, Violence, and Democracy in South Africa*. Chicago: University of Chicago Press.

Atkins, John. 1735. *A voyage to Guinea, Brasil, and the West-Indies; in His Majesty's Ships, the Swallow and Weymouth*. London.

Aubrée, Marion, and François Laplantine. 1990. *La table, le livre et les esprits: Naissance, évolution et actualité du mouvement social spirite entre France et Brésil*. Paris: J. C. Lattès.

Augé, Marc. 1999. *The War of Dreams: Studies in Ethno Fiction*. London: Pluto.

Austen, A. W. (1932) 2006. "Woman Who Was a Medium for Fifty-Two Years." *Psypioneer* 2 (6) (June): 127–30. Originally published in *Psychic News*.

Austin, J. L. 1965. *How to Do Things with Words*. New York: Oxford University Press.

Babbitt, Edwin Dwight. 1881. *Religion as Revealed by the Material and Spiritual Universe*. New York: Babbitt.

Bakhtin, M. M. 1981. *The Dialogic Imagination: Four Essays*. Translated by Caryl Emerson and Michael Holquist. Austin: University of Texas Press.

Baptista, José Renato de Carvalho. 2007. "Os Deuses Vendem Quando Dão: Os Sentidos do Dinheiro nas Relações de Troca no Candomblé." *Mana* 13 (1): 7–40.

Barber, Karin. 1981. "How Man Makes God in West Africa: Yoruba Attitudes towards the Orisa." *Africa* 51 (3): 724–45.

Barbot, Jean. 1732. *A Description of the Coasts of North and South Guinea*. London: A. and J. Churchill.

Barnett, Steve, and Martin Silverman. 1979. *Ideology and Everyday Life: Anthropology, Neomarxist Thought, and the Problem of Ideology and the Social Whole*. Ann Arbor: University of Michigan Press.

Barrow, Logie. 1986. *Independent Spirits: Spiritualism and English Plebeians, 1850–1910*. London: Routledge and Keegan Paul.

Bartlett, George C. 1891. *The Salem Seer: Reminiscences of Charles H. Foster*. New York: United States Book.

Bastide, Roger. 1953. "Cavalos dos Santos: Esboço de uma Sociologia do Transe." In *Estudos Afro-Brasileiros*, 3:29–60. São Paulo: Universidade de São Paulo.

Bates, Emily Catherine. 1887. *A Year in the Great Republic*. Vol. 1. London: Ward and Downey.

Bayle, Pierre. 1704. *Réponse aux questions d'un provincial*. Rotterdam: Reinier Leers.

Bauman, Richard, and Charles L. Briggs. 1990. "Poetics and Performance as Critical Perspectives on Language and Social Life." *Annual Review of Anthropology* 19:59–88.

Bauman, Richard, and Joel Sherzer, eds. 1974. *Explorations in the Ethnography of Speaking*. Cambridge: Cambridge University Press.

Beard, George M. 1881. *American Nervousness: Its Causes and Consequences*. New York: G. P. Putnam's Sons.

Beighle, Nellie. 1903. *Book of Knowledge: Psychic Facts*. New York: Alliance.

Bell, Catherine. 1998. "Performance." In *Critical Terms for Religious Studies*, edited by Mark C. Taylor, 205–24. Chicago: University of Chicago Press.

Bell Telephone Company. 1908. *The Deposition of Alexander Graham Bell in the Suit Brought by the United States to Annul the Bell Patents*. Boston: American Bell.

Bellah, Robert, Richard Madsen, William Sullivan, Ann Swidler, and Steven Tipton. 1985. *Habits of the Heart: Individualism and Commitment in American Life*. New York: Harper and Row.

Benjamin, Walter. 1969. *Illuminations*. New York: Schocken.

Bennett, Bridget. 2007. *Transatlantic Spiritualism and Nineteenth-Century American Literature*. New York: Palgrave Macmillan.

Benz, Ernst. 1972. "Ergriffenheit und Besessenheit als Grundformen religiöser Erfahrung." In *Ergriffenheit und Besessenheit*, edited by Jürg Zutt. Berne and Munich: Francke.

Bernasconi, Robert. 2002. "Kant as an Unfamiliar Source of Racism." In *Philosophers on Race: Critical Essays*, edited by Julie K. Ward and Tommy L. Lott, 145–66. Oxford: Blackwell.

Berry, Catherine. 1876. *Experiences in Spiritualism: A Record of Extraordinary Phenomena, Witnessed through the Most Powerful Mediums, with Some Historical Fragments Relating to Semiramide, Given by the Spirit of an Egyptian Who Lived Contemporary with Her*. London: James Burns, Spiritual Institution.

Berti, Daniela, and Gilles Tarabout. 2010. "Possession." In *Dictionnaire des faits religieux*, edited by Régine Azria and Danièle Hervieu-Leger, 941–47. Paris: Presses Universitaires de France.

Besson, Jean. 1984. "Family Land and Caribbean Society: Toward an Ethnography of Afro-Caribbean Peasantries." In *Perspectives on Caribbean Regional Identity*, edited by Elizabeth M. Thomas-Hope, Monograph Series no. 11, 57–83. Liverpool: Centre for Latin American Studies, University of Liverpool.

———. 2002. *Martha Brae's Two Histories: European Expansion and Caribbean Culture Building in Jamaica*. Chapel Hill: University of North Carolina Press.

Bhabha, Homi K. 1994. "Of Mimicry and Man: The Ambivalence of Colonial Discourse." In *The Location of Culture*, edited by Homi Bhabha, 85–92. London: Routledge.

Blake, Clarence J. 1878. "The Use of the Membrana Tympani as a Phonautograph and Logograph." *Annals of Ophthalmology and Otology* 5:108–13.

Blier, Suzanne Preston. 1996. *African Vodun: Art, Psychology, and Power*. Chicago: University of Chicago Press.

Boddy, Janice. 1989. *Wombs and Alien Spirits: Women, Men, and the Zar Cult in Northern Sudan*. Madison: University of Wisconsin Press.

———. 1994. "Spirit Possession Revisited: Beyond Instrumentality." *Annual Review of Anthropology* 23:407–34.

Boff, Leonardo. 1978. *Jesus Christ Liberator: A Critical Christology for Our Time*. Maryknoll, NY: Orbis Books.

Bornstein, Erica. 2003. *The Spirit of Development: Protestant NGOs, Morality, and Economics in Zimbabwe*. New York: Routledge.

Boskin, Joseph. 1986. *Sambo: The Rise & Demise of an American Jester*. New York: Oxford University Press.

Bosman, Willem. 1705. *A New and Accurate Description of the Coast of Guinea*. London: J. Knapton.

Bottari, Pablo. 2000. *Free in Christ: Your Complete Handbook on the Ministry of Deliverance*. Lake Mary, FL: Charisma House.

Bourdieu, Pierre. (1980) 1990. *The Logic of Practice*. Translated by Richard Nice. Stanford, CA: Stanford University Press.

Bourguignon, Erika. 1970. "Review of *Island Possessed* by Katherine Dunham." *American Anthropologist* 72:1132–33.

———. 1973. *Religion, Altered States of Consciousness, and Social Change*. Columbus: Ohio State University Press.

———. 1976. *Possession*. Novato, CA: Chandler and Sharp.

Boyer, Veronique. 1999. "O pajé e o caboclo: De homem a entidade." *Mana* 5 (1): 29–56.

Boyle, Robert. 1979. *Selected Philosophical Papers of Robert Boyle*. Edited by M. A. Stewart. New York: Manchester University Press.

Brady, Erika. 1999. *A Spiral Way: How the Phonograph Changed Ethnography*. Jackson: University Press of Mississippi.

Braude, Anne. 2001. *Radical Spirits: Spiritualism and Women's Rights in Nineteenth-Century America*. 2nd ed. Bloomington: Indiana University Press.

Braudel, Fernand. 1992. *The Wheels of Commerce*. Vol. 2 of *Civilization and Capitalism, 15th–18th Century*. Berkeley: University of California Press.

Broad, Charles Dunbar. 1962. *Lectures on Psychical Research*. London: Routledge and Keegan Paul.

Bronfman, Alejandra. 2004. *Measures of Equality: Social Science, Citizenship, and Race in Cuba, 1902–1940*. Chapel Hill: University of North Carolina Press.

Brosses, Charles de. (1760) 1970. *Du culte des dieux fétiches; ou, Parallèle de l'ancienne religion de l'Egypte avec la religion actuelle de Nigritie*. England: Westmead, Farnborough, Hants.

———. 1756. *Histoire des navigations aux Terres Australes*. Paris: Durand.

Brown, David H. 2003. *The Light Inside: Abakuá Society Arts and Cuban Cultural History*. Washington, DC: Smithsonian Institution Press.

Brown, Karen McCarthy. 1991. *Mama Lola: A Vodou Priestess in New York*. Berkeley: University of California Press.

Bruce, Robert V. 1973. *Bell: Alexander Graham Bell and the Conquest of Solitude*. Boston: Little, Brown.

Buarque de Holanda, Sérgio. 1968. *História Geral da Civilização Brasileira*. Vol. 1, *A Época Colonial*. São Paulo: Difusão Européia do Livro.

Burke, Kenneth. (1950) 1969. *A Rhetoric of Motives*. Berkeley: University of California Press.

Burton, Richard D. E. 1997. *Afro-Creole: Power, Opposition, and Play in the Caribbean*. Ithaca, NY: Cornell University Press.

Bush, Luis. n.d. "The 10/40 Window: Getting to the Core of the Core." AD2000 and Beyond Movement. http://www.ad2000.org/1040broc.htm.

Cabrera, Lydia. (1954) 1975. *El Monte: igbo, finda, ewe orisha, vititi nfinda; notas sobre las religiones, la magia, las supersticiones y el folklore de los negros criollos y el pueblo de Cuba*. Miami: Ediciones Universal.

———. 1969. *La sociedad secreta abakuá: narrada por viejos adeptos*. Miami: Ediciones C and R.

Caciola, Nancy. 2003. *Discerning Spirits: Divine and Demonic Possession in the Middle Ages.* Ithaca, NY: Cornell University Press.

Campos, L. S. 1997. *Teatro, Templo e Mercado: Organizaçao e Marketing de um Empreendimento Neo-Pentecostal.* Petrópolis: Vozes.

Capone, Stefania. 2010. *Searching for Africa in Brazil: Power and Tradition in Candomblé.* Durham, NC: Duke University Press.

Carneiro, Edison. 1961. *Candomblés da Bahia.* Rio de Janeiro: Conquista.

Carrier, James. 1995. *Gifts and Commodities: Exchange and Western Capitalism since 1700.* New York: Routledge.

Carroll, Bret. E. 1997. *Spiritualism in Antebellum America.* Bloomington: Indiana University Press.

Cavell, Stanley. (1969) 1976. *Must We Mean What We Say? A Book of Essays.* Cambridge: Cambridge University Press.

Chakrabarty, Dipesh. 2000. *Provincializing Europe: Postcolonial Thought and Historical Difference.* Princeton, NJ: Princeton University Press.

Chesnut, Andrew. 1997. *Born Again in Brazil: The Pentecostal Boom and the Pathogens of Poverty.* New Brunswick, NJ: Rutgers University Press.

———. 2007. *Competitive Spirits: Latin America's New Religious Economy.* Oxford: Oxford University Press.

Chireau, Yvonne. 2003. *Black Magic: Religion and the African American Conjuring Tradition.* Berkeley: University of California Press.

Chosa, Jim, and Faith Chosa. 2004. *Thy Kingdom Come Thy Will Be Done in Earth: A First Nation Perspective on Strategic Keys for Territorial Deliverance and Transformation.* Privately printed.

Christensen, C. P. 1915. "Hypnotism and Its Use." *Spiritualist* 1 (4): 11–22.

Christy, Edwin Pearce. 1851. *Christy's Plantation Melodies.* Philadelphia: Fisher and Brother.

Chude-Sokei, Louis. 1997. "The Sound of Culture: Dread Discourse and Jamaican Sound Systems." In *Language, Rhythm, and Sound: Black Popular Cultures into the Twenty-First Century,* edited by Joseph K. Adjaye and Adrianne R. Andrews, 185–202. Pittsburgh: University of Pittsburgh Press.

Clark, Mary Ann. 2007. *Santería: Correcting the Myths and Uncovering the Realities of a Growing Religion.* Westport CT: Praeger.

Coates, James. 1897. *How to Mesmerize.* Chicago: National Institute of Science

Cockrell, Dale. 1997. *Demons of Disorder: Early Blackface Minstrels and Their World.* Cambridge: Cambridge University Press.

Cohen, Emma, and Justin L. Barrett. 2008. "Conceptualizing Spirit Possession: Ethnographic and Experimental Evidence." *Ethos* 36 (2): 246–67.

Cole, Jennifer. 2001. *Forget Colonialism? Sacrifice and the Art of Memory in Madagascar.* Berkeley: University of California Press.

Coleman, Simon. 2010. "An Anthropological Apologetics." *South Atlantic Quarterly* 109:791–810.

Comaroff, Jean. 1985. *Body of Power, Spirit of Resistance: The Culture and History of a South African People.* Chicago: University of Chicago Press.

Comaroff, Jean, and John L. Comaroff. 1993. *Modernity and Its Malcontents: Ritual and Power in Postcolonial Africa.* Chicago: University of Chicago Press.

———. 1999. "Occult Economies and the Violence of Abstraction: Notes from the South African Postcolony." *American Ethnologist* 26 (2): 279–303.

———. 2000. "Millennial Capitalism: First Thoughts on a Second Coming." *Public Culture* 12 (2): 291–343.

———. 2002. "Alien-Nation: Zombies, Immigrants, and Millennial Capitalism." *South Atlantic Quarterly* 101 (4): 779–805.

———. 2006. "Law and Disorder in the Postcolony: An Introduction." In *Law and Disorder in the Postcolony*, edited by Jean Comaroff and John L. Comaroff, 1–56. Chicago: University of Chicago Press.

Comte, Auguste. 1891. *The Catechism of Positive Religion*. Translated by Richard Congreve. London: K. Paul, Trench, Trübner.

Conant, Frances M. 1857–70. *The Banner of Light*. Boston: Banner of Light Publications.

Connelly, James. H. 1891. "Calling Araminta Back." *The Path* 6 (5): 102–9, 143–49.

Connolly, William. 2005. "The Evangelical-Capitalist Resonance Machine." *Political Theory* 33 (6): 869–86.

Connor, Steven. 1999. "The Machine in the Ghost: Spiritualism, Technology, and the 'Direct Voice.'" In *Ghosts: Deconstruction, Psychoanalysis, History*, edited by Peter Buse and Andrew Stott, 203–25. New York: Macmillan.

Conot, Robert. 1979. *A Streak of Luck*. New York: Seaview Books.

Corbett, John. 1994. *Extended Play: Sounding Off from John Cage to Dr. Funkenstein*. Durham, NC: Duke University Press.

Corin, Ellen. 1998. "Refiguring the Person: the Dynamics of Affects and Symbols in an African Spirit Possession Cult." In *Bodies and Persons: Comparative Perspectives from Africa and Melanesia*, edited by Michael Lambek and Andrew Strathern, 80–102. Cambridge: Cambridge University Press.

Cossard-Binon, Giselle. 1970. "Contribution à l'étude des Candomblés au Brésil: Le Candomblé Angola." PhD diss., University of Paris.

Costa, Esdras Borges. 1979. "Protestantism, Modernization and Cultural Change in Brazil." PhD diss., University of California, Berkeley.

Cox, Robert S. 2003. *Body and Soul: A Sympathetic History of American Spiritualism*. Charlottesville: University of Virginia Press.

Crapanzano, Vincent. 1980. *Tuhami: Portrait of a Moroccan*. Chicago: University of Chicago Press.

Crapanzano, Vincent, and Vivian Garrison, eds. 1977. *Case Studies in Spirit Possession*. New York: Wiley.

Crary, James W. 1989. *Communication as Culture: Essays on Media and Society*. Boston: Unwin Hyman.

Csordas, Thomas J. 1990. "Embodiment as a Paradigm for Anthropology." *Ethos* 18 (1): 5–47.

———. 1993. "Somatic Modes of Attention." *Cultural Anthropology* 8 (2): 135–56.

Daaku, Kwame Yebua. 1970. *Trade and Politics on the Gold Coast, 1600–1720*. London: Oxford University Press.

Daniel, Yvonne. 2005. *Dancing Wisdom: Embodied Knowledge in Haitian Vodou, Cuban Yoruba, and Brazilian Candomblé*. Urbana: University of Illinois Press.

Daniels, J. W. 1856. *Spiritualism versus Christianity; or, Spiritualism Thoroughly Exposed*. New York: Miller, Orton and Mulligan.

Dapper, Olfert. 1670. *Africa: Being an Accurate Description. . . .* London: Johnson.

David, M. V. 1981. "Le president de Brosses historien des religions et philosophe." In *Charles de Brosses, 1777–1977*, edited by Jean-Claude Garreta, 123–40. Geneva: Slatkine.

Day, John W. 1873. *Biography of Mrs. J. H. Conant, the World's Medium of the Nineteenth Century*. Boston: William White.

Dayan, Joan. 1992. "Dessalines, Dessalines Démembré: Hero, Detritus, and God." Conference of the University of Virginia, April 8.

———. 1995. *Haiti, History, and the Gods*. Berkeley: University of California Press.

Deans, Joseph. 1883. "Spiritism." *Morning Light*, 6 (290) (July 21): 281–82.

De Certeau, Michel. (1970) 1990. *The Possession at Loudun*. Translated by Michael B. Smith. Chicago: University of Chicago Press.

———. 1975. *L'Écriture de l'histoire*. Paris: Gallimard.

Deflem, Mathieu. 2003. "The Sociology of the Sociology of Money: Simmel and the Contemporary Battle of the Classics." *Journal of Classical Sociology* 3 (1): 67–96.

De Heusch, Luc. 2006.*La Transe*. Brussels: Éditions Complexe.

De Marees, Pieter. (1602) 1987. *Description and Historical Account of the Gold Kingdom of Guinea*. Translated by Albert van Dantzig and Adam Jones. Oxford: Oxford University Press.

Deren, Maya. (1953) 1983. *Divine Horsemen: The Living Gods of Haiti*. London: McPherson.

Derrida, Jacques. 1989. *Of Spirit: Heidegger and the Question*. Translated by Geoffrey Bennington and Rachel Bowlby. Chicago: University of Chicago Press.

Descartes, René. 2003. *Meditations and Other Metaphysical Writings*. London: Penguin.

Descola, Philippe. 2005. *Par-delà nature et culture*. Paris: Gallimard.

Desjarlais, Robert R. 1992. *Body and Emotion: The Aesthetics of Illness and Healing in the Nepal Himalayas*. Philadelphia: University of Pennsylvania Press.

———. 1996. "Presence." In *The Performance of Healing*, edited by Carol Laderman and Marina Roseman, 143–64. New York: Routledge.

Dewey, John. 1885. "The Revival of the Soul." *The University* 219 (December 5): 6–7.

Dianteill, Erwan. 2008. "Le caboclo surmoderne: Globalisation, possession et théâtre dans un temple d'umbanda à Fortaleza (Brésil)." *Gradhiva* 7:24–37.

Dickson, George. 1885. "Dudley Colliery." *Medium and Daybreak* 16 (817) (November 27): 762–63.

Dijk, Rijk van. 1998. "Pentecostalism, Cultural Memory and the State: Contested Representations of Time in Postcolonial Malawi." In *Memory and the Postcolony: African Anthropology and the Critique of Power*, edited by Richard Werbner, 155–81. London: Zed Books.

Dodson, Jualynne E. 2008. *Sacred Spaces and Religious Traditions in Oriente Cuba*. Albuquerque: University of New Mexico Press.

Drewal, Margaret Thompson. 1992. *Yoruba Ritual: Performers, Play, Agency*. Bloomington: Indiana University Press.

Du Bois, John W. 1993. "Meaning without Intention: Lessons from Divination." In *Responsibility and Evidence in Oral Discourse*, edited by Jane H. Hill and Judith T. Irvine, 48–71. Cambridge: Cambridge University Press.

Dunham, Katharine. 1969. *Island Possessed*. Chicago: University of Chicago Press.

Dupuy, Alex. 1997. *Haiti in the New World Order: The Limits of the Democratic Revolution*. Boulder, CO: Westview.

———. 2010. "Disaster Capitalism to the Rescue: The International Community and Haiti after the Earthquake." *NACLA Report on the Americas* (July–August): 14–19.

Duranti, Alessandro. 2009. "The Relevance of Husserl's Theory to Language Socialization." *Journal of Linguistic Anthropology* 19 (2): 205–26.

Durkheim, Emile. 1908. "Representations individuelles et representations collectives." *Revue de métaphysique et de morale* 6:273–302.
Eco, Umberto. 1989. *Foucault's Pendulum*. Translated by William Weaver. San Diego: Harcourt Brace Jovanovich.
Edison, Thomas A. 1878. "The Phonograph and Its Future." *North American Review* 126 (262) (May–June): 527–36.
———. 1888. "The Perfected Phonograph." *North American Review* 146 (379) (June): 641–50.
———. 1910. "'No Immortality of the Soul' Says Thomas A. Edison." Interview by Edward Marshall. *New York Times*, October 2, 1, 15.
———. 1911. "Thomas A. Edison on Immortality: The Great Inventor Declares Immortality of the Soul Improbable." Interview by Edward Marshall. *Columbian Magazine* 3 (4).
———. 1920. "Edison Working on How to Communicate with the Next World." Interview by Bertie C. Forbes. *American Magazine* 90:10–11, 85.
———. 1948. *The Diary and Sundry Observations of Thomas Alva Edison*. Edited by Dagobert D. Runes. New York: Philosophical Library.
Eisenlohr, Patrick. 2009. "Technologies of the Spirit: Devotional Islam, Sound Reproduction and the Dialectics of Mediation and Immediacy in Mauritius." *Anthropological Theory* 9:273–96.
Eliade, Mircea. 1964. *Shamanism: Archaic Techniques of Ecstasy*. London: Routledge and Kegan Paul.
Elliotson, John. 1846. "Mesmerism Not to Be Trifled With." *Zoist* 15 (October): 388–405.
Ellis, Alfred Burdon. (1883) 1970. *The Land of Fetish*. Westport, CT: Negro Universities Press.
Emerson, Harry. 1946. *Listen, My Son: An Epistle to My Soldier Son, Bearing an Account of the Mediumship of Hunter Selkirk*. London: Psychic.
Engelke, Matthew. 2007. *The Problem of Presence: Beyond Scripture in an African Church*. Berkeley: University of California Press.
Enns, Anthony. 2005. "Voices of the Dead: Transmission/Translation/Transgression." *Culture, Theory, and Critique* 46:11–27.
Eshun, Kodwo. 1998. *More Brilliant Than the Sun: Adventures in Sonic Fiction*. London: Quartet Books.
Espirito Santo, Diana. 2010. "Spiritist Boundary-Work and the Morality of Materiality in Afro-Cuban Religion." *Journal of Material Culture* 15 (1): 64–82.
Evans, Wainwright. 1963. "Scientists Research Machine to Contact the Dead." *Fate* 16 (4): 38–43.
Evans-Pritchard, Edward E. 1937. *Witchcraft, Oracles, and Magic among the Azande*. Oxford: Clarendon.
Fanon, Frantz. 1967. *Black Skin, White Masks*. New York: Grove.
Fassin, Didier. 2012. *Humanitarian Reason: A Moral History of the Present Times*. Berkeley: University of California Press.
Feaster, Patrick. 2001. "Framing the Mechanical Voice: Generic Conventions of Early Phonograph Recording." *Folklore Forum* 32:57–102.
Ferber, Sarah. 2004. *Demonic Possession and Exorcism in Early Modern France*. New York: Routledge.
Fernández Olmos, Margarite, and Lizabeth Paravisini-Gebert. 1997. *Sacred Possessions:*

Vodou, Santería, Obeah, and the Caribbean. New Brunswick, NJ: Rutgers University Press.

Fields, Annie. 1898. *Life and Letters of Harriet Beecher Stowe*. Boston and New York: Houghton, Mifflin.

Foster, George M. 1987. *Tzintzutzan: Mexican Peasants in a Changing World*. Long Grove, IL: Waveland.

Foucault, Michel. (1962) 1999. "Religious Deviations and Medical Knowledge." In *Religion and Culture*, edited by Jeremy R. Carrette, 50–57. New York: Routledge.

Freitas, Edith Alves. 2004. *História da Freguesia Velha de Santo Antônio Campo Formoso*. Salvador: Secretaria de Cultura e Turismo.

Freston, Paul. 1994. *Evangélicos Na Política Brasileira: História Ambígua e Desafio Ético*. Curitiba: Encontrão Editora.

Freud, Sigmund. [1919] 1955. "The Uncanny." In *The Standard Edition of the Complete Psychological Works of Sigmund Freud*, vol. 17, translated and edited by J. Strachey. London: Hogarth.

Frobenius, Leo. 1909. *The Childhood of Man: A Popular Account of the Lives, Customs and Thoughts of the Primitive Races*. Translated by A. H. Keane. London: Seeley.

Frow, George L. 1982. *The Edison Phonographs and Diamond Disks: A History with Illustrations*. Sevenoaks, Kent, UK: G. L. Frow.

Fuentes Guerra, Jesús, and Grisel Gómez Gómez. 1994. *Cultos Afrocubanos: Un estudio etnolingüístico*. N.p.: Editorial Ciencias Sociales.

Garoutte, Claire, and Anneke Wambaugh. 2007. *Crossing the Water: A Photographic Path to the Afro-Cuban Spirit World*. Durham, NC: Duke University Press.

Geertz, Clifford. 1988. *Works and Lives: The Anthropologist as Author*. Stanford, CA: Stanford University Press.

Gell, Alfred. 1998. *Art and Agency: An Anthropological Theory*. Oxford: Clarendon.

Geschiere, Peter. 1997. *The Modernity of Witchcraft: Politics and the Occult in Postcolonial Africa*. Charlottesville: University Press of Virginia.

Ghachem, Malick. 2003. "The Slave's Two Bodies: The Life of An American Legal Fiction." *William and Mary Quarterly*, 3rd ser., 60 (4): 809–42.

Gibson, Marion. 1999. *Reading Witchcraft: Stories of Early English Witches*. New York: Routledge.

Gitelman, Lisa. 1999. *Scripts, Grooves, and Writing Machines: Representing Technology in the Edison Era*. Stanford, CA: Stanford University Press.

Giumbelli, Emerson. 2007. "Um Projecto de Cristianismo Hegemônico." In *Intolerancia Religosa: Impactos do Neopentecostalismo no Campo Religioso Afro-brasileiro*, edited by Vagner Gonçalves da Silva, 149–69. São Paulo: ESUSP.

Goffman, Erving. 1976. "Replies and Responses." *Language in Society* 5:257–313.

Gold, Herbert. 1991. *Best Nightmare on Earth: A Life in Haiti*. New York: Touchstone.

Goldberg, Alan Bruce. 1981. "Commercial Folklore and Voodoo in Haiti: International Tourism and the Sale of Culture." PhD diss., Indiana University.

Goldish, Matt. 2003. *Spirit Possession in Judaism: Cases and Contexts from the Middle Ages to the Present*. Detroit: Wayne State University Press.

Goodman, Amy. 2010. "Thousands of Haitians Face Forcible Evictions from Temporary Camps." *Democracy Now*, August 17. http://www.democracynow.org/2010/8/17/thousands_of_haitians_face_risk_of.

Goodstein, Laurie. 2008. "YouTube Videos Draw Attention to Palin's Faith." *New York Times*, November 25, A-13.

Gouk, Penelope. 1982. "Acoustics in the Early Royal Society 1660–1680." *Notes and Records of the Royal Society of London* 36:155–75.

———. 1999. *Music, Science, and Natural Magic in Seventeenth-Century England*. New Haven, CT: Yale University Press.

Graeber, David. 2005. "Fetishism as Social Creativity; or, Fetishes Are Gods in the Process of Construction." *Anthropological Theory* 5 (4): 407–38.

Gruzinski, Serge. 1990. *La Guerre Des Images*. Paris: Fayard.

Guareschi, P. A. 1995. "Sem Dinehiro Não Ha Salvação: Ancorando o Bem e o Mal Entre os Neopentecostais." In *Textos em Representações Sociais*, edited by Pedrinho Guareschi and Sandra Jovchelovitch, 191–223. Petrópolis: Vozes.

Gunewardena, Nandini. 2008. "Human Security versus Neoliberal Approaches to Disaster Recovery." In *Capitalizing on Catastrophe: Neoliberal Strategies in Disaster Reconstruction*, edited by Nandini Gunewardena and Mark Schuller, 3–16. Lanham, MD: Altamira.

Guyer, Jane. 1993. "Wealth in People and Self-Realization in Equatorial Africa." *Man* 28: 243–65.

Hagedorn, Katherine J. 2001. *Divine Utterances: The Performance of Afro-Cuban Santería*. Washington, DC: Smithsonian Institution Press.

Haldeman-Julius, Emanuel. 1948. "Name Your Poison." Glenn Carrington Collection, Schomburg Center for Research in African American Culture, New York.

Hall, Edward T. (1966) 1990. *The Hidden Dimension*. New York: Anchor Books.

Halperin, Daniel. 1995. "Memory and Consciousness in an Evolving Brazilian Possession Religion." *Anthropology of Consciousness* 6 (4): 1–17.

———. 1996a. "A Delicate Science: A Critique of an Exclusively Emic Anthropology." *Anthropology and Humanism* 21 (1): 31–40.

———. 1996b. "Trance and Possession: Are They the Same?" *Transcultural Psychiatry* 33 (1): 33–41.

Hankins, Thomas L., and Robert J. Silverman. 1995. *Instruments and the Imagination*. Princeton, NJ: Princeton University Press.

Harding, Rachel. 2000. *A Refuge in Thunder: Candomblé and Alternative Spaces of Blackness*. Bloomington: Indiana University Press.

Harkins-Pierre, Patricia. 2005. "Religion Bridge: Translating Secular into Sacred Music; A Study of World Christianity Focusing on the U.S. Virgin Islands." In *The Changing Face of Christianity: Africa, the West, and the World*, edited by Lamin Sanneh and Joel A. Carpenter, 21–44. New York: Oxford University Press.

Harlow, Alvin F. 1936. *Old Wires and New Waves: The History of the Telegraph, Telephone, and Wireless*. New York: D. Appleton–Century.

Hastings, Horace Lorenzo. 1890. *Ancient Heathenism and Modern Spiritualism*. Boston: Scriptural Tract Repository.

Hastings, Wells Southworth, and Brian Hooker. 1911.*The Professor's Mystery*. Toronto: McLeod and Allen.

Hawley, John S., and Donna M. Wulff, eds. 1996. *Devī: Goddesses of India*. Berkeley: University of California Press.

Hayes, Kelly E. 2011. *Holy Harlots: Femininity, Sexuality, and Black Magic in Brazil*. Berkeley: University of California Press.

Hegel, G. W. F. 1956. *Philosophy of History*. Mineola, NY: Dover.

Heidegger, Martin. 1962. *Being in Time*. New York: Harper and Row.

———. 1977. *The Question Concerning Technology and Other Essays*. New York: Garland.

Henley, Paul. 2006. "Spirit Possession, Power, and the Absent Presence of Islam: Reviewing 'Les maîtres fous.'" *Journal of the Royal Anthropological Institute* 12 (4): 731–61.

Henriques, Julian. 2003. "Sonic Dominance and the Reggae Sound System Session." In *The Auditory Culture Reader*, edited by Michael Bull and Les Back, 451–80. Oxford: Berg.

Heron, Alasdair I. C. 1983. *The Holy Spirit*. Philadelphia: Westminster.

Herskovits, Melville. 1956. "The Social Organization of the Afrobrazilian Candomblé." *Phylon* 17:147–66.

Hess, David J. 1991. *Spirits and Scientists: Ideology, Spiritism, and Brazilian Culture*. University Park: Pennsylvania State University Press.

Hirschkind, Charles. 2006. *The Ethical Soundscape: Cassette Sermons and Islamic Counterpublics*. New York: Columbia University Press.

Hobbes, Thomas. (1651) 1985. *Leviathan*. London: Penguin.

Holbraad, Martin. 2005. "Expending Multiplicity: Money in Cuban Ifa Cults." *Journal of the Royal Anthropological Institute* 11 (2): 231–54.

———. 2008. "Definitive Evidence, from Cuban Gods." *Journal of the Royal Anthropological Institute* 14, supplement: S93–S109.

———. 2012. *Truth in Motion: The Recursive Anthropology of Cuban Divination*. Chicago: University of Chicago Press.

Hollywood, Amy. 2011. "Enthusiasm." *Freq.uenci.es, a collaborative genealogy of spirituality*, September 1. http://freq.uenci.es/2011/09/01/enthusiasm/.

Houtman, Dick, and Birgit Meyer, eds. 2012. *Things: Religion and the Question of Materiality*. New York: Fordham University Press.

Hughbanks, Leroy. 1945. *Talking Wax; or, The Story of the Phonograph, Simply Told for General Readers*. New York: Hobson Book Press.

Hulme, Peter. 1986. *Colonial Encounters: Europe and the Native Caribbean, 1492–1797*. London: Methuen.

Hume, David. (1739) 2006a. *A Treatise of Human Nature*. eBooks@Adelaide. http://ebooks.adelaide.edu.au/h/hume/david/h92t/index.html. Accessed May 21, 2009. Adelaide: University of Adelaide Library.

———. 2006b. *Essays Moral, Political, and Literary*. New York: Cosimo.

Hunt, C. J., Mrs. 1875. "Mrs. Stewart, Out of the Mouths of Many Witnesses the Truth Is Established." *Spiritual Magazine* 1 (9) (September): 399–400.

Hurston, Zora Neale. (1935) 1968. *Mules and Men*. Bloomington: Indiana University Press. Reprint, New York: Harper Perennial, 1990.

———. (1937) 2006. *Their Eyes Were Watching God*. New York: Harper.

———. (1938) 1990. *Tell My Horse: Voodoo and Life in Haiti and Jamaica*. New York: Harper.

Hymes, Dell. 1975. "Breakthrough into Performance." In *Folklore: Performance and Communication*, edited by Dan Ben Amos and Kenneth Goldstein, 11–74. The Hague: Mouton.

IBGE (Instituto Brasileiro de Geographia e Estatística). 2005. http://www.ibge.gov.br.

Irvine, Judith. 1996. "Shadow Conversations: The Indeterminacy of Participant Roles." In *Natural Histories of Discourse*, ed. Michael Silverstein and Greg Urban, 131–59. Chicago: University of Chicago Press.

Ivy, Marilyn. 1995. *Discourses of the Vanishing: Modernity, Phantasm, Japan*. Chicago: University of Chicago Press.

Jackson, Michael. 2012. *Lifeworlds: Essays in Existential Anthropology*. Chicago: University of Chicago Press.

Jakobson, Roman. 1960. "Closing Statement: Linguistics and Poetics." In *Style in Language*, edited by Thomas A. Sebeok, 350–77. Cambridge, MA: MIT Press.

James, William. (1901) 1961. *The Varieties of Religious Experience*. New York: Macmillan.

James Figarola, Joel. 1999. *Los Sistemas Mágico-Religiosos Cubanos: Principios Rectores*. Caracas: UNESCO.

Jameson, Frederic. 1981. *The Political Unconscious: Narrative as a Socially Symbolic Act*. Ithaca, NY: Cornell University Press.

Jardilino, P. 1994. "Neo-Pentecostalismo: Religiao na Fronteira da Modernidade." *Reves do Avesso* (Nov.–Dec.): 42–50.

Johnson, Paul Christopher. 2002. *Secrets, Gossip, and Gods: The Transformation of Brazilian Candomblé*. New York: Oxford University Press.

———. 2006. "Secretism and the Apotheosis of Duvalier." *Journal of the American Academy of Religion* 74 (2): 420–45.

———. 2007. *Diaspora Conversions: Black Carib Religion and the Recovery of Africa*. Berkeley: University of California Press.

———. 2011. "An Atlantic Genealogy of 'Spirit Possession.'" *Comparative Studies in Society and History* 53 (2): 393–425.

———. Forthcoming. "'The Dead Don't Come Back like the Migrant Comes Back': Many Returns in the Garifuna Dügü." In *Passages and Afterworlds: Anthropological Perspectives on Death and Mortuary Rituals in the Caribbean*, edited by Maarit Forde and Yanique Hume. Durham, NC: Duke University Press.

Johnson, Stephen, ed. 2012. *Burnt Cork: Traditions and Legacies of Blackface Minstrelsy*. Amherst: University of Massachusetts Press.

Kant, Immanuel. (1766) 2002. *Dreams of a Spirit Seer*. West Chester, PA: Swedenborg Foundation.

———. (1791) 1960a. *Religion Within the Limits of Reason Alone*. New York: Harper and Row.

———. (1797) 1996. *The Metaphysics of Morals*. Translated and edited by Mary Gregor. Cambridge: Cambridge University Press.

———. 1960b. *Observations on the Beautiful and the Sublime*. Translated by John T. Goldthwait. Berkeley: University of California Press.

Keane, Webb. 1997. *Signs of Recognition: Powers and Hazards of Representation in an Indonesian Society*. Brekeley: University of California Press.

———. 2003. "Semiotics and the Social Analysis of Material Things." *Language and Communication* 23:409–25.

———. 2007. *Christian Moderns: Freedom and Fetish in the Mission Encounter*. Berkeley: University of California Press.

———. 2008. "The Evidence of the Senses and the Materiality of Religion." *Journal of the Royal Anthropological Institute* 14, supplement: S110–S127.

———. 2012. "On Spirit Writing: Materialities of Language and the Religious Work of Transduction." *Journal of the Royal Anthropological Institute* 19 (1): 1–17.

Keller, Mary. 2002. *The Hammer and the Flute: Women, Power, and Spirit Possession*. Baltimore: Johns Hopkins University Press.

Kendall, Laurel. 1996. "Initiating Performance: The Story of Chini, a Korean Shaman." In *The Performance of Healing*, edited by Carol Laderman and Marina Roseman, 17–58. New York: Routledge.

Khan, Aisha. 2004. *Callaloo Nation: Metaphors of Race and Religious Identity among South Asians in Trinidad*. Durham, NC: Duke University Press.

Kirsch, Thomas G. 2008. *Spirits and Letters: Reading, Writing and Charisma in African Christianity*. New York: Berghahn Books.

Kittler, Friedrich. 1999. *Gramophone, Film, Typewriter*. Translated by Geoffrey Winthrop-Young and Michael Wutz. Stanford, CA: Stanford University Press.

Kramer, Eric. 1999. "Possessing Faith: Commodification, Religious Subjectivity, and Community in a Brazilian Neo-Pentecostal Church." PhD diss., University of Chicago.

Kramer, Fritz. 1993. *The Red Fez: Art and Spirit Possession in Africa*. London: Verso.

Kraft, C. H. 1994. *Behind Enemy Lines: An Advanced Guide to Spiritual Warfare*. Ann Arbor, MI: Serant.

Kraut, Anthea. 2008. *Choreographing the Folk: The Dance Stagings of Zora Neale Hurston*. Minneapolis: University of Minnesota Press.

Kucich, John. 2004. *Ghostly Communion: Cross-Cultural Spiritualism in Nineteenth-Century American Literature*. Hanover, NH: Dartmouth College Press.

LaCapra, Dominick. 2001. *Writing History, Writing Trauma*. Baltimore: Johns Hopkins University Press.

Laderman, Carol. 1997. "The Limits of Magic." *American Anthropologist* 99 (2): 333–41.

Laderman, Carol, and Marina Roseman, eds. 1996. *The Performance of Healing*. New York: Routledge.

Lambek, Michael. 1981. *Human Spirits: A Cultural Account of Trance in Mayotte*. Cambridge: Cambridge University Press.

———. 1988a. "Graceful Exits: Spirit Possession as Personal Performance in Mayotte." *Culture* 8 (1): 59–69.

———. 1988b. "Spirit Possession/Spirit Succession: Aspects of Social Continuity among Malagasy Speakers in Mayotte." *American Ethnologist* 15 (4): 710–31.

———1993. *Knowledge and Practice in Mayotte: Local Discourses of Islam, Sorcery and Spirit Possession*. Toronto: University of Toronto Press.

———. 1996. "The Past Imperfect: Remembering as Moral Practice." In *Tense Past: Cultural Essays in Trauma and Memory*, edited by Paul Antze and Michael Lambek, 235–54. New York: Routledge.

———. 1998a. "Body and Mind in Mind, Body and Mind in Body: Some Anthropological Interventions in a Long Conversation." In *Bodies and Persons: Comparative Perspectives from Africa and Melanesia*, edited by Michael Lambek and Andrew Strathern, 103–23. Cambridge: Cambridge University Press.

———. 1998b. "The Sakalava Poiesis of History: Realizing the Past through Spirit Possession in Madagascar." *American Ethnologist* 25 (2): 106–27.

———. 2000. "Nuriaty, the Saint and the Sultan: Virtuous Subject and Subjective Virtuoso of the Post-Modern Colony." *Anthropology Today* 16 (2): 7–12.

———. 2002. *The Weight of the Past: Living with History in Mahajanga, Madagascar*. New York: Palgrave Macmillan.

———. 2003. "From Rheumatic Irony: Questions of Agency and Self-Deception as Refracted through the Art of Living with Spirits." *Social Analysis* 47 (2): 40–61.

———. 2007. "On Catching Up with Oneself: Learning to Know That One Means What One Does." In *Learning Religion*, edited by David Berliner and Ramon Sarró, 65–81. Oxford: Berghahn.

———. 2009. "Traveling Spirits: Unconcealment and Undisplacement." In *Traveling Spirits: Migrants, Markets and Mobilities*, edited by Gertrud Hüwelmeier and Kristine Krause, 17–35. London: Routledge.

———. 2010. "Towards an Ethics of the Act." In *Ordinary Ethics: Anthropology, Language, and Action*, edited by Michael Lambek, 39–63. New York: Fordham University Press.

———. 2011. "Anthropology's Ontological Anxiety and the Concept of Tradition." *Anthropologica* 53 (2): 317–22.

Larner, Christina. 1984. *Witchcraft and Religion: The Politics of Popular Belief*. Oxford: Basil Blackwell.

Larson, Bob. 1999. *Larson's Book of Spiritual Warfare*. Nashville: Thomas Nelson.

Latour, Bruno. 1993. *We Have Never Been Modern*. Translated by Catherine Porter. Cambridge, MA: Harvard University Press.

Leacock, Seth, and Ruth Leacock. 1972. *Spirits of the Deep: A Study of an Afro-Brazilian Cult*. American Museum of Natural History. Garden City, NY: Doubleday Natural History.

Le Bon, Gustave. 1894. *Les lois psychologique de l'évolution des peuples*. Paris: Félix Alcan.

———. 1895. *Psychologie des foules*. Paris: Félix Alcan.

———. 1898. *The Psychology of Peoples*. New York: Macmillan.

Lee, Benjamin. 1997. *Talking Heads: Language, Metalanguage, and the Semiotics of Subjectivity*. Durham, NC: Duke University Press.

Le Goff, Jacques. 1985. *L'Imaginaire médiéval*. Paris: Gallimard.

Lehman, Amy. 2009. *Victorian Women and the Theatre of Trance*. Jefferson, NC: McFarland.

Leiris, Michel. 1934. *L'Afrique fantôme*. Paris: Gallimard.

———. (1939) 1988. *L'Âge d'homme*. Paris: Gallimard.

———. 1958. *La possession et ses aspects théâtraux chez les Éthiopiens de Gondar*. Paris: Librairie Plon.

———. 1996. *Miroir de l'Afrique*. Edited by Jean Jamin. Paris: Gallimard.

Leo Africanus, Joannes. 1600. *A Geographical Historie of Africa*. Collected and translated by John Pory. London: G. Bishop.

Léry, Jean de. (1578) 1990. *History of a Voyage to the Land of Brazil*. Translated by Janet Whatley. Berkeley: University of California Press.

Lévi-Strauss, Claude. 1966. *The Savage Mind*. Chicago: University of Chicago Press.

Lewis, I. M. 1971. *Ecstatic Religion: An Anthropological Study of Spirit Possession and Shamanism*. London: Penguin.

Lhamon, W. T. 1998. *Raising Cain: Blackface Performance from Jim Crow to Hip Hop*. Cambridge, MA: Harvard University Press.

Lifschitz, Edward. 1988. "Hearing Is Believing: Acoustic Aspects of Masking in Africa." In *West African Masks and Cultural Systems*, edited by Sidney L. Kasfir, 221–29. Tervueren: Koninklijke Museum voor Midden-Afrika.

Linton, Charles. 1855. *The Healing of the Nations*. New York: Society for the Diffusion of Spiritual Knowledge.

Lippitt, Francis James. 1888. *Physical Proofs of Another Life: Given in Letters to the Seybert Commission*. Washington DC: A. S. Witherbee.

Lips, Julius E. 1937. *The Savage Hits Back; or The White Man through Native Eyes*. New Haven, CT: Yale University Press.

Lobb, John. 1907. *Talks with the Dead: Luminous Rays from the Unseen World*. London: John Lobb.

Lock, Margaret, and Nancy Scheper-Hughes. 1987. "The Mindful Body: A Prolegomenon to Future Work in Medical Anthropology." *Medical Anthropology Quarterly* 1:6–41.

Locke, John. (1680) 2003. *Two Treatises of Government and a Letter Concerning Toleration*. Edited by Ian Shapiro. New Haven, CT: Yale University Press.

———. (1689) 1975. *An Essay Concerning Human Understanding*. 4th ed. New York: Dover.

———. (1692) 1996. *Some Thoughts Concerning Education and Of the Conduct of the Understanding*. Edited by Ruth Grant and Nathan Tarcov. Indianapolis: Hackett.

Logan, Peter Melville. 2009. *Victorian Fetishism: Intellectuals and Primitives*. Albany: State University of New York Press.

Lott, Eric. 1993. *Love and Theft: Blackface Minstrelsy and the American Working Class*. New York: Oxford University Press.

Lowenthal, Ira. 1987. "'Marriage Is 20, Children Are 21': The Cultural Construction of Conjugality and the Family in Rural Haiti." PhD diss., Johns Hopkins University.

Lukes, Steven. 1985. "Conclusion." In *The Category of the Person: Anthropology, Philosophy, History*, edited by Michael Carrithers, Steven Collins, and Steven Lukes, 282–301. Cambridge: Cambridge University Press.

Lum, Kenneth Anthony. 2000. *Praising His Name in the Dance: Spirit Possession in the Spiritual Baptist Faith and Orisha Work in Trinidad, West Indies*. New York: Routledge.

MacCormack, Sabine. 1993. "Demons, Imagination, and the Incas." In *New World Encounters*, edited by Stephen Greenblatt, 101–26. Berkeley: University of California Press.

Macfarlane, Alan. 1970. *Witchcraft in Tudor and Stuart England*. London: Routledge and Kegan Paul.

Macintyre, Alasdair. 1990. *Three Rival Versions of Moral Enquiry*. London: Duckworth.

Maggie, Yvonne. 1992. *Medo do feitiço: relações entre magia e poder no Brasil*. Rio de Janeiro: Arquivo Nacional.

Mahar, William J. 1999. *Behind the Burnt Cork Mask: Early Blackface Minstrelsy and Antebellum American Popular Culture*. Urbana: University of Illinois Press.

Malcolm, Noel. 1996. "A Summary Biography of Hobbes." In *The Cambridge Companion to Hobbes*, edited by Tom Sorrell, 13–44. Cambridge: Cambridge University Press.

Malinowski, Bronislaw. 1948. *Magic, Science and Religion, and Other Essays*. New York: The Free Press.

Mariano, Ricardo. 1996. "Os Neopentecostais e a Teologia da Prosperidade." *Novos Estudos* 44 (March): 24–44.

———. 1999. *Neopentecostais: Sociologia do Novo Pentecostalismo no Brasil*. São Paulo: Edições Loyola.

———. 2004. "Expansão Pentecostal no Brasil: o Caso da Igreja Universal." *Estudos Avançados* 18 (52): 121–38.

Mariz, Cecília. 1994. "Libertação e Ética: Uma Análise do Discurso de Pentecostais que se Recuperaram do Alcoolismo." In *Nem Anjos Nem Demônios: Interpretações sociológicas do Pentecostalismo*, edited by Alberto Antoniazzi, 204–24. Petrópolis: Vozes.

———. 1997. "Reflexões Sobre a Reação Afro-Brasileira á Guerra Santa." *Debates do Núcleo de Estudos da Religião* 1 (1): 96–103.

Marryat, Florence. 1891. *There Is No Death*. New York: Lovell, Coryell.

Marshall, Paule. 1983. *Praisesong for the Widow*. New York: Penguin.

Martins dos Santos, Osmar. 2009. "Os Bens Minerais Região de Campo Formoso Estado da Bahia: Destaque Para Esmeralda Potencial de Produção e Transformação. Locais Avaliados Carnaiba—Municipio de Pindobaçu, Socotó—Municipio de Campo Formoso, Estado da Bahia." Unpublished manuscript prepared for the Cooperativa Mineral da Bahia.

Masquelier, Adeline. 1999. "The Invention of Anti-Tradition: Dodo Spirits in Southern Niger." In *Spirit Possession, Modernity and Power in Africa*, edited by Heike Behrend and Ute Luig, 34–50. Madison: University of Wisconsin Press.

———. 2001. *Prayer Has Spoiled Everything: Possession, Power, and Identity in an Islamic Town of Niger*. Durham, NC: Duke University Press.

———. 2002. "Road Mythographies: Space, Mobility, and the Historical Imagination in Postcolonial Niger." *American Ethnologist* 29 (4): 829–56.

Marx, Karl. 1977. *Capital*. Vol. 1. Translated by B. Fowkes. New York: Vintage.

Masuzawa, Tomoko. 2000. "Troubles with Materiality: The Ghost of Fetishism in the Nineteenth Century." *Comparative Studies in Society and History* 42 (2): 242–67.

Mather, Cotton. 1697. *Memorable providences, relating to witchcrafts and possessions a faithful account of many wonderful and surprising things, that have befallen several bewitched and possessed persons in New-England. . . .* Boston: n.p.

Mattoso, Katia M. de Queirós. 1986. *To Be a Slave in Brazil, 1550–1888*. Translated by Arthur Goldhammer. New Brunswick, NJ: Rutgers University Press.

Maurer, Bill. 2000. *Recharting the Caribbean: Land, Law, and Citizenship in the British Virgin Islands*. Ann Arbor: University of Michigan Press.

Mauss, Marcel. (1924) 2000. *The Gift: The Form and Reason for Exchange in Archaic Societies*. New York: Norton.

———. (1950) 1979. "Body Techniques." In *Sociology and Psychology: Essays*, edited by Marcel Mauss, 95–123. London: Kegan Paul.

Mayes, Elizabeth. 1995. "Spirit Possession in the Age of Materialism." PhD diss., New York University.

Mazzarella, William. 2004. "Culture, Globalization, Mediation." *Annual Review of Anthropology* 33:345–67.

McAlister, Elizabeth A. 1995. "A Sorcerer's Bottle: The Art of Magic in Haiti." In *Sacred Arts of Haitian Vodou*, edited by Donald J. Cosentino. Los Angeles: UCLA Fowler Museum of Cultural History.

———. 2002. *Rara! Vodou, Power, and Performance in Haiti and Its Diaspora*. Berkeley: University of California Press.

———. 2005. "Globalization and the Religious Production of Space." *Journal for the Scientific Study of Religion* 44 (3): 249–55.

———. 2012. "From Slave Revolt to a Blood Pact with Satan: The Evangelical Rewriting of Haitian History." *Studies in Religion/Sciences Religieuses* 41 (2): 187–215.

———. 2013. "Humanitarian Adhocracy, Transnational New Apostolic Missions, and Evangelical Anti-Dependency in a Haitian Refugee Camp." *Nova Religio: The Journal of Alternative and Emergent Religions* 16 (4) (May): 11–34.

McClenon, James, and Jennifer Nooney. 2002. "Anomalous Experiences Reported by Field Anthropologists: Evaluating Theories Regarding Religion." *Anthropology of Consciousness* 13:46–60.

McGarry, Molly. 2008. *Ghosts of Futures Past: Spiritualism and the Cultural Politics of Nineteenth-Century America*. Berkeley: University of California Press.

McKittrick, Katherine, and Clyde Woods. 2007. "No One Knows the Mysteries at the Bottom of the Ocean." In *Black Geographies and the Politics of Place*, edited by Katherine McKittrick and Clyde Woods, 1–13. Cambridge, MA: South End.

McNeal, Keith E. 2011. *Trance and Modernity in the Southern Caribbean: African and Hindu Popular Religion in Trinidad and Tobago*. Gainesville: University Press of Florida.

Métraux, Alfred. 1955. "Dramatic Elements in Ritual Possession." Translated by James H. Labadie. *Diogenes* 3:18–36.

———. 1958. *Voodoo in Haiti*. Translated by Hugo Carteris. New York: Oxford University Press, 1959.

Meyer, Birgit. 2010. "'There Is a Spirit in That Image': Mass-Produced Jesus Pictures and

Protestant-Pentecostal Animation in Ghana." *Comparative Studies in Society and History* 52 (1): 100–130.

Middelfort, H. C. Erik. 1972. *Witch Hunting in Southwestern Germany, 1562–1684*. Stanford, CA: Stanford University Press.

Miller, Daniel. 2001. "Possessions." In *Home Possessions: Material Culture behind Closed Doors*, edited by Daniel Miller, 107–22. Oxford: Berg.

Mills, Mara. 2009. "When Mobile Communication Technologies Were New." *Endeavor* 33:140–46.

Mintz, Sidney. 1961. "Pratik: Haitian Personal Economic Relationships." In *Proceedings of the 1960 Annual Spring Meeting of the American Ethnological Society*, edited by V. Garfield, 54–63. Seattle: American Ethnological Society.

———. 1973. "A Note on the Definition of Peasantries." *Journal of Peasant Studies* 1 (1): 91–106.

———. 1974a. *Caribbean Transformations*. Chicago: Aldine.

———. 1974b. "The Rural Proletariat and the Problem of Rural Proletarian Consciousness." *Journal of Peasant Studies* 1 (3): 291–325.

Mintz, Sidney W., and Michel-Rolph Trouillot. 1995. "The Social History of Haitian Vodou." In *Sacred Arts of Haitian Vodou*, edited by Donald J. Consentino, 123–47. Los Angeles: UCLA Fowler Museum of Cultural History.

Mnookin, Jennifer L. 1998. "The Image of Truth: Photographic Evidence and the Power of Analogy." *Yale Journal of Law and the Humanities* 10:1–74.

Modern, John Llardas. 2011. *Secularism in Antebellum America*. Chicago: University of Chicago Press.

Monceil, Theodore, Count de. 1879. *The Telephone, the Microphone, and the Phonograph*. New York: Harper and Brothers.

Monter, E. William. 1976. *Witchcraft in France and Switzerland: The Borderlands during the Reformation*. Ithaca, NY: Cornell University Press.

———. 1983. *Ritual, Myth and Magic in Early Modern Europe*. Brighton, Sussex: Harverster.

Montero, Paula. 2006. "Religião, Pluralismo e Esfera Pública no Brasil." *Novos Estudos* 74:47–65.

Moore, Henrietta L., and Todd Sanders. 2001. *Magical Interpretations, Material Realities: Modernity, Witchcraft and the Occult in Postcolonial Africa*. New York: Routledge.

Moore, R. Laurence. 1977. *In Search of White Crows: Spiritualism, Parapsychology, and American Culture*. New York: Oxford University Press.

Moore, Robin. 1997. *Nationalizing Blackness: Afrocubanismo and Artistic Revolution in Havana, 1920–1940*. Pittsburgh: University of Pittsburgh Press.

———. 1994. "Representations of Afrocuban Expressive Culture in the Writings of Fernando Ortiz." *Latin American Music Review/Revista de Música Latinoamericana* 15 (1): 32–54.

Moravia, Alberto. 1961. *L'ennui*. Translated by Claude Poncet. Paris: Flammarion.

Moreland, Samuel. 1671. *Tuba Stentoro-Phonica: An Instrument of Excellent Use as well at Sea as at Land*. London: W. Godbit.

Morgan, Lewis H. 1907. *Ancient Society*. New York: Henry Holt.

Moseley, Sidney A. 1919. *An Amazing Séance and an Exposure*. London: Sampson Low.

Mosse, David. 2006. "Possession and Confession: Affliction and Sacred Power in Colonial and Contemporary South India." In *The Anthropology of Christianity*, edited by Fenella Cannell, 99–133. Durham, NC: Duke University Press.

Murray, Gerald. 1977. "The Evolution of Haitian Peasant Land Tenure." PhD diss., Columbia University.

———. 1980. "Population Pressure, Land Tenure and Voodoo: The Economics of Haitian Peasant Ritual." In *Beyond the Myths of Culture: Essays in Cultural Materialism*, edited by Eric Ross, 295–321. New York: Academic.

Murray, James. 1884. "Hetton-Le-Hole." *Medium and Daybreak* 15 (734) (April 25): 270.

Napier, A. David. 1986. "Masks and Metaphysics: An Empirical Dilemma." In *West African Masks and Cultural Systems*, edited by Sidney L. Kasfir, 231–40. Tervueren: Koninklijke Museum voor Midden-Afrika.

Nassau, Robert Hamill. 1904. *Fetichism in West Africa: Forty Years' Observation of Native Customs and Superstitions*. New York: Negro Universities Press.

Nina Rodrigues, Raymundo. (1896) 1935. *A animismo fetichista dos negros bahianos*. Rio de Janiero: Civilização Brasileira.

———. (1932) 2008. *Os africanos no Brasil*. São Paulo: Editora Madras.

Novaes, Regina, and Maria da Graca Floriano. 1985. *O Negro Evangélico*. Rio de Janeiro: Instituto de Estudos de Religião.

Nye, David E. 1983. *The Invented Self: An Anti-Biography, from Documents of Thomas A. Edison*. Odense: Odense University Press.

Ochoa, Todd Ramón. 2007. "Versions of the Dead: Kalunga, Cuban-Kong Materiality, and Ethnography." *Cultural Anthropology* 22 (4): 473–500.

Oesterreich, T. K. [1921] 2003. *Possession: Demoniacal and Other*. Translated by D. Ibberson. Whitefish, MT: Kessinger Reprints.

Ollman, Bertell. 1971. *Alienation: Marx's Conception of Man in Capitalist Society*. Cambridge: Cambridge University Press.

Ong, Aihwa. 1987. *Spirits of Resistance and Capitalist Discipline: Factory Women in Malaysia*. Albany: State University of New York Press.

Ong, Walter J. 1982. *Orality and Literacy: The Technologizing of the Word*. London: Methuen.

Oppenheim, Janet. 1985. *The Other World: Spiritualism and Psychical Research in England, 1850–1914*. Cambridge: Cambridge University Press.

Oro, Ari Pedro. 1996. *Avanço Neo-Pentecostal e Reação Catolica*. Petrópolis: Vozes.

———. 1997. "Neopentecostais e Afro-brasileiros: Quem Vencerá esta Guerra?" *Debates do Núcleo de Estudos da Religião* 1 (1): 10–36.

———. 2001. "Neopentecosalismo: Dinheiro e Magia." *Revista da Antropologia* 3 (1): 71–85.

———. 2004. "A Presença Religiosa Brasileira no Exterior: O Caso da Igreja Universal do Reino de Deus." *Estudos Avançados* 18 (52): 139–55.

———. 2006. "O 'Neopentecostalismo Macumbeiro.'" *Revista USP* 68:319–22.

Ortiz, Fernando. (1906) 1916. *Hampa afro-cubana: Los negros esclavos*. Havana: Revista Bimestre Cubana.

———Ortiz, Fernando. 1906. *La hampa Afrocubana: Los negros brujos*. Madrid: Librería de Fernando Fe.

———. (1906) 1973. *Los negros brujos*. Miami: Ediciones Universal.

———. 1952–55. *Los instrumentos de la música afrocubana*. Havana: Cárdenas y Cía.

Otis, George, Jr. 1993. "An Overview of Spiritual Mapping." In *Breaking Strongholds in Your City*, edited by C. Peter Wagner, 29–48. Ventura, CA: Regal Books.

Owen, Alex. (1989) 2004. *The Darkened Room: Women, Power, and Spiritualism in Late Victorian England*. Chicago: University of Chicago Press.

Palmié, Stephan, ed. 1996. *Slave Cultures and the Cultures of Slavery*. Knoxville: University of Tennessee Press.

———. 2002. *Wizards and Scientists: Explorations in Afro-Cuban Modernity and Tradition*. Durham, NC: Duke University Press.

———. 2004. "'Fascinans' or 'Tremendum'? Permutations of the State, the Body, and the Divine in Late-Twentieth-Century Havana." *New West Indian Guide* 78 (3–4): 229–68.

———. 2006. "A View from Itía Ororó Kande." *Social Anthropology* 14:99–118.

———. 2008. "*Ecué*'s Atlantic: An Essay in Methodology." In *Africas of the Americas: Beyond the Search for Origins in the Study of Afro-Atlantic Religions*, edited by Stephan Palmié, 179–222. Leiden: Brill.

———. 2010. "Now You See It, Now You Don't: Santería, Anthropology, and the Semiotics of 'Belief' in Santiago de Cuba." *New West Indian Guide* 84 (1–2): 87–96.

———. Forthcoming. "Historicist Knowledge and Its Conditions of Impossibility." In *The Social Life of Spirits*, edited by Ruy Llera Blanes and Diana do Espirito Santo. Chicago: University of Chicago Press.

Patterson, Thomas C. 2009. *Karl Marx, Anthropologist*. Oxford: Berg.

Peel, John David Yeadon. 1994. "Historicity and Pluralism in some Recent Studies of Yoruba Religion." *Africa* 64 (1): 150–66.

Peirce, Charles Sanders. 1940. *The Philosophy of Peirce: Selected Writings*. Edited by Justus Buchler. London: Routledge and Kegan Paul.

———. 1997. *Pragmatism as a Principle and Method of Right Thinking: The 1903 Harvard Lectures on Pragmatism*. Albany: State University of New York Press.

Perkins, Franklin. 2007. *Leibniz: A Guide for the Perplexed*. London: Continuum.

Pernet, Henry. 1992. *Ritual Masks: Deceptions and Revelations*. Columbia: University of South Carolina Press.

Perrone-Moisés, Beatriz. 2008. "L'alliance normando-tupi au xvie siècle: La célébration de Rouen." *Journal de la Société des Américanistes* 94 (1): 45–64.

Peters, John Durham. 1999. *Speaking into the Air: A History of the Idea of Communication*. Chicago: University of Chicago Press.

———. 2004. "Helmholtz, Edison, and Sound History." In *Memory Bytes: History, Technology, and Digital Culture*, edited by Lauren Rabinovitz and Abraham Geil, 177–98. Durham, NC: Duke University Press.

Pickering, Michael. 2008. *Blackface Minstrelsy in Britain*. Aldershot: Ashgate.

Pierruci, Antônio Flávio, and Reginaldo Prandi. 2000. "Religious Diversity in Brazil: Numbers and Perspectives in a Sociological Evaluation." *International Journal of Sociology* 15 (4): 629–40.

Pierson, Charles O. 1895. "A Series of Séances at Washington." *Borderland* 2 (10) (October): 349–53.

Pietz, William. 1985. "The Problem of the Fetish, I." *Res* 9:5–17.

———. 1987a. "The Phonograph in Africa: International Phonocentrism from Stanley to Sarnoff." In *Post-structuralism and the Question of History*, edited by Derek Attridge, Geoff Bennington, and Robert Young, 263–85. Cambridge: Cambridge University Press.

———. 1987b. "The Problem of the Fetish, II." *Res* 13:23–45.

———. 1988. "The Problem of the Fetish, IIIa." *Res* 16:105–23.

———. 1994. "The Spirit of Civilization: Blood Sacrifice and Monetary Debt." *Res* 28:23–38.

Plummer, Brenda. 1990. "The Golden Age of Tourism: U.S. Influence in Haitian Cultural and Economic Affairs, 1934–1971." *Cimarrón* 2 (3): 49–63.

———. 1992. *Haiti and the United States: The Psychological Moment*. Athens: University of Georgia Press.

Polk, Patrick A. 2010. "Black Folks at Home in the Spirit World." In *Activating the Past: History and Memory in the Black Atlantic World*, edited by Andrew Apter and Robin Derby, 371–414. Newcastle: Cambridge Scholars.

Porter, Jennifer E. 2005. "The Spirit(s) of Science: Paradoxical Positivism as Religious Discourse among Spiritualists." *Science as Culture* 14:1–21.

Prandi, Reginaldo. 1995. "Raça e Religião." *Novo Estudos* 42:113–29.

Premawardhana, Devaka. 2012. "Transformational Tithing: Sacrifice and Reciprocity in a Neo-Pentecostal Church." *Nova Religio: The Journal of Alternative and Emergent Religions* 15 (4): 85–109.

Price, Richard. 1998. *The Convict and the Colonel: A Story of Colonialism and Resistance in the Caribbean*. Boston: Beacon.

———. 2007. *Travels with Tooy: History, Memory, and the African American Imagination*. Chicago: University of Chicago Press.

Prince, Derek. 1998. *They Shall Expel Demons: What You Need to Know about Demons—Your Invisible Enemies*. Ada, MI: Chosen Books.

Prince, Walter Franklin. 1921. "A Survey of American Slate-Writing Mediumship." *Proceedings of the American Society for Psychical Research* 9:315–592.

Promey, Sally M., ed. 2014. *Sensational Religion: Sensory Cultures in Material Practice*. New Haven, CT: Yale University Press.

Putnam, Allen. 1872. *Flashes of Light from the Spirit-Land, through the Mediumship of Mrs. J. H. Conant*. Boston: W. White.

Ramos, Artur. (1934) 1988. *O Negro Brasileiro*. Vol. 1, *Etnografia Religiosa*. São Paulo: Compania Editora Nacional.

Ramsey, Kate. 2000. "Melville Herskovits, Katherine Dunham, and the Politics of African Diasporic Dance Anthropology." In *Dancing Bodies, Living Histories: New Writings about Dance and Culture*, edited by Lisa Doolittle and Anne Flynn, 196–216. Banff, AB: Banff Centre.

———. 2002. "Without One Ritual Note: Folklore Performance and the Haitian State, 1935–1946." *Radical History Review* 84:7–42.

———. 2011. *The Spirits and the Law: Vodou and Power in Haiti*. Chicago: University of Chicago Press.

Rappaport, Roy. 1999. *Ritual and Religion in the Making of Humanity*. Cambridge: Cambridge University Press.

Rasmussen, Susan J. 1993. "Creativity, Conflict, and Power in Tuareg Spirit Possession." *Anthropology and Humanism* 18 (1): 21–30.

Read, Oliver, and Walter L. Welch. 1959. *From Tin Foil to Stereo: Evolution of the Phonograph*. Indianapolis: H. W. Sams.

Reis, João José. 2011. "Candomblé and Slave Resistance in Nineteenth-Century Bahia." In *Sorcery in the Black Atlantic*, edited by Roger Sansi and Luis Nicolau Parés, 55–74. Chicago: University of Chicago Press.

Rey, Terry, and Karen E. Richman. 2010. "The Somatics of Syncretism: Tying Body and Soul in Haitian Religion." *Studies in Religion/Sciences Religieuses* 39 (3): 379–403.

Rice, Edward Le Roy. 1911. *Monarchs of Minstrelsy, from "Daddy" Rice to Date*. New York: Kenny.

Richman, Karen E. 2005. *Migration and Vodou*. Gainesville: University Press of Florida.

———. 2007. "Peasants, Migrants and the Discovery of the Authentic Africa." *Journal of Religion in Africa* 37 (3): 1–27.

———. 2008. "Innocent Imitations? Mimesis and Alterity in Haitian Vodou Art." *Ethnohistory* 55 (2): 203–28.

———. 2010. "Religion at the Epicenter: Religious Agency and Affiliation in Léogane after the Earthquake." Paper presented at the annual meeting of the Haitian Studies Association, Brown University, Providence, RI, November 11–13.

Richman, Karen E., and Terry Rey. 2009. "Congregating by Cassette." *International Journal of Cultural Studies* 12 (1): 53–70.

Robbins, Joel. 2003. "On the Paradoxes of Global Pentecostalism and the Perils of Continuity Thinking." *Religion* 33:221–31.

———. 2004. "The Globalization of Pentecostal and Charismatic Christianity." *Annual Review of Anthropology* 33:117–43.

Romberg, Raquel. 1998. "Whose Spirits Are They? The Political Economy of Syncretism and Authenticity." *Journal of Folklore Research* 35 (1): 69–82.

———. 2003a. "From Charlatans to Saviors: Espiritistas, Curanderos, and Brujos Inscribed in Discourses of Progress and Heritage." *Centro Journal* 15 (2) (Fall): 146–73.

———. 2003b. *Witchcraft and Welfare: Spiritual Capital and the Business of Magic in Modern Puerto Rico*. Austin: University of Texas Press.

———. 2005. "Symbolic Piracy: Creolization with an Attitude?" *New West Indian Guide* 79 (3–4): 175–218.

———. 2007. "Today, Changó Is Changó; or, How Africanness Becomes a Ritual Commodity in Puerto Rico." In "Afro-Caribbean Religions, Culture, and Folklore," special issue, *Western Folklore* 66 (1–2) (Winter–Spring): 75–106.

———. 2009. *Healing Dramas: Divination and Magic in Modern Puerto Rico*. Austin: University of Texas Press.

———. 2011. "Creolization or Ritual Piracy?" In *Creolization: Cultural Creativity in Process*, edited by Ana Cara and Robert Baron, 109–36. Jackson: University Press of Mississippi.

———. 2012a. "Sensing the Spirits: The Healing Dramas and Poetics of Brujería Rituals." *Anthropologica* 54 (2): 211–25.

———. 2012b. "Uncertainty and the Performance of Unmasking and Revelation: Spiritual Power and Healing Dramas in Puerto Rican Brujería." Paper presented at the annual of the European Association of Social Anthropology, Nanterre University, France, July 7–13.

Roorbach, Orville A. 1875. *Minstrel Gags and End-Men's Hand-Book*. New York: Fitzgerald.

Roper, Lyndal. 2004. *Witch Craze: Terror and Fantasy in Baroque Germany*. New Haven, CT: Yale University Press.

Rose, Thomas. 1829. "The Slave Ship." *Imperial Magazine* (June): 537–41.

Roseman, Marina.1991. *Healing Sounds from the Malaysian Rainforest: Temiar Music and Medicine*. Berkeley: University of California Press.

Rosenthal, Judy. 1998. *Possession, Ecstasy, and Law in Ewe Voodoo*. Charlottesville: University Press of Virginia.

Rotberg, Robert I. 2005. "The Swedenborgian Search for African Purity." *Journal of Interdisciplinary History* 36 (2): 233–40.

Rothenbuhler, Eric W., and John Durham Peters. 1997. "Defining Phonography: An Experiment in Theory." *Musical Quarterly* 81:242–62.

Rothman, A. D. 1921. "Mr. Edison's 'Life Units': Hundred Trillion in Human Body May Scatter after Death—Machine to Register Them." *New York Times*, January 23, 1, 6.

Rouch, Jean. 1955. *Les maîtres fous*. Documentary film. Icarus Films.

———. 1960. *La religion et la magie Songhay*. Paris: Presses Universitaires de France.

———. (1967) 1971. *Tourou et Bitti, les tambours d'Avant*. Documentary film. Centre National de la Recherche Scientifique.

———. 1978. "On the Vicissitudes of the Self: The Possessed Dancer, the Magician, the Sorcerer, the Filmmaker, and the Ethnographer." *Studies in the Anthropology of Visual Communication* 5 (1): 2–8.

Rouget, Gilbert. 1985. *Music and Trance: A Theory of the Relations between Music and Possession*. Chicago: University of Chicago Press.

Rousseau, Jean Jacques. (1781) 1953. *The Confessions*. Translated by J. M. Cohen. London: Penguin Books.

Routon, Kenneth. 2008. "Conjuring the Past: Slavery and the Historical Imagination in Cuba." *American Ethnologist* 35 (4): 632–49.

Sahlins, Marshall. 1981. *Historical Metaphors and Mythical Realities: Structure in the Early History of the Sandwich Islands Kingdom*. Ann Arbor: University of Michigan Press.

Sanchez, Rafael. 2008. "Seized by the Spirit: The Mystical Foundation of Squatting among Pentecostals in Caracas (Venezuela) Today." *Public Culture* 20 (2): 267–305.

Sansi, Roger. 2007. "'Dinheiro Vivo': Money and Religion in Brazil." *Critique of Anthropology* 27 (3): 319–39.

———. 2011. "Sorcery and Fetishism in the Modern Atlantic." In *Sorcery in the Black Atlantic*, edited by Luis Nicolau Parés and Roger Sansi, 19–40. Chicago: University of Chicago Press.

Sansone, Livio. 2003. *Blackness without Ethnicity: Constructing Race in Brazil*. New York: Palgrave.

Saraiva, Clara. 2010. "Afro-Brazilian Religions in Portugal: Bruxos, Priests and Pais de Santo." *Etnográfica* 14 (2): 265–88.

Sartre, Jean-Paul. 1965. Preface to *The Wretched of the Earth*, by Frantz Fanon, xlii–lxii. New York: Grove.

———. 1996. *L'existentialisme est un humanisme*. Paris: Gallimard.

Scharf, John Thomas, and Thompson Westcott. 1884. *History of Philadelphia, 1609–1884*. Vol. 2. Philadelphia: L. H. Everts.

Scharlau, Ulf. 1969. *Athanasius Kircher als Musikschriftsteller: Ein Beitrag zur Musikanschauung des Barock*. Marburg: Görich und Weiershäuser.

Schieffelin, Edward. 1996. "On Failure and Performance: Throwing the Medium Out of the Séance." In *The Performance of Healing*, edited by Carol Laderman and Marina Roseman, 59–89. New York: Routledge.

Schmidt, Leigh Eric. 1998. "From Demon Possession to Magic Show: Ventriloquism, Religion, and the Enlightenment." *Church History* 67 (2): 274–304.

———. 2000. *Hearing Things: Religion, Illusion, and the American Enlightenment*. Cambridge, MA: Harvard University Press.

Schmitt, Jean-Claude. 1994. *Les revenants*. Paris: Gallimard.

Schuller, Mark. 2007. "Deconstructing the Disaster after the Disaster." In *Capitalizing on Catastrophe: Neoliberal Strategies in Disaster Reconstruction*, edited by Nandini Gunewardena and Mark Schuller, 17–27. Lanham, MD: Altamira.

———. 2010. "Falling through the Cracks, or Unstable Foundations?" *Huffington Post*, August 8. Accessed August 10, 2010. http://www.huffingtonpost.com/mark-schuller/falling-through-the-crack_b_675004.html.

Schwartz, Regina M. 1997. *The Curse of Cain: The Violent Legacy of Monotheism*. Chicago: University of Chicago Press.

Sconce, Jeffrey. 2000. *Haunted Media: Electronic Presence from Telegraphy to Television*. Durham, NC: Duke University Press.

Selka, Stephen. 2008. "The Sisterhood of Boa Morte in Brazil: Harmonious Mixture, Black Resistance and the Politics of Religious Practice." *Journal of Latin American and Caribbean Anthropology* 13 (1): 79–114.

———. 2010. "Morality in the Religious Marketplace: Evangelical Christianity, Candomblé and the Struggle for Moral Distinction in Brazil." *American Ethnologist* 37 (2): 291–307.

Semán, Pablo. 2001. "A Igreja Universal do Reino de Deus: Um Ator e as Suas Costuras da Sociedade Brasileira Contemporânea." *Debates do Núcleo de Estudos da Religião* 2 (3): 87–97.

Senghor, Léopold. 1939. "Ce que l'homme noir apporte." In *L'homme de couleur*, edited by Jean Verdier, 291–313. Paris: Librairie Plon.

Sered, Susan. 1994. *Priestess, Mother, Sacred Sister: Religions Dominated by Women*. New York: Oxford University Press.

Seybert, Henry. 1920. *Preliminary Report of the Commission Appointed by the University of Pennsylvania to Investigate Modern Spiritualism*. Philadelphia: J. B. Lippincott.

Shapiro, Michael J. 1994. "Moral Geographies and the Ethics of Post-Sovereignty." *Public Culture* 6:479–502.

Sharp, Lesley A. 1993. *The Possessed and the Dispossessed: Spirits, Identity, and Power in a Madagascar Migrant Town*. Berkeley: University of California Press.

Shaw, Rosalind. 2002. *Memories of the Slave Trade: Ritual and the Historical Imagination in Sierra Leone*. Chicago: University of Chicago Press.

Sherman, Loren Albert. 1895. *The Science of the Soul*. Port Huron, MI: Sherman.

Silva, Vagner Gonçalves da. 1995. *Orixás da Metrópole*. Petrópolis: Vozes.

———. 2007. "Entre a Gira da Fé e Jesus de Nazare: Relações Sócio-estruturais entre neo-Pentecostalismo e Religiões Afro-brasileiras." In *Intolerancia Religosa: Impactos do Neo-pentecostalismo no Campo Religioso Afro-brasileiro*, edited by Vagner Gonçalves da Silva, 191–260. São Paulo: ESUSP.

Simmel, Georg. 1990. *The Philosophy of Money*. 2nd ed. Edited by David Frisby. Translated by Tom Bottomore and David Frisby. New York: Routledge.

Sjöberg, Kjell. 1993. "Spiritual Mapping for Prophetic Prayer Actions." In *Breaking Strongholds in Your City: How to Use Spiritual Mapping to Make Your Prayers More Strategic, Effective, and Targeted*, edited by C. Peter Wagner, 108–9. Ventura, CA: Regal Books.

Sluhovsky, Moshe. 2007. *Believe Not Every Spirit: Possession, Mysticism, and Discernment in Early Modern Catholicism*. Chicago: University of Chicago Press.

Smith, Adam. (1776) 1976. *An Inquiry into the Nature and Causes of the Wealth of Nations*. Edited by R. H. Campbell and A. S. Skinner. Oxford: Clarendon Press.

Smith, Frederick M. 2006. *The Self Possessed: Deity and Spirit Possession in South Asian Literature and Civilization*. New York: Columbia University Press.

Smith, Jonathan Z. 1982. *Imagining Religion: From Babylon to Jonestown*. Chicago: University of Chicago Press.

Snyder, Charles. 1974. "Clarence John Blake and Alexander Graham Bell: Otology and the Telephone." *Annals of Otology, Rhinology and Laryngology* 83, supplement 13:3–31.

Sodré, Muniz. 1988. *O terreiro e a cidade: A forma social negro-brasileiro*. Petrópolis: Vozes.

Sollors, Werner. 1983. "Dr. Benjamin Franklin's Celestial Telegraph, or Indian Blessings to Gas-Lit American Drawing Rooms." *Social Science Information* 22:983–1004.

Spinoza, Benedict de. 1996. *Ethics*. Translated by Edwin Curley. New York: Penguin Classics.

Stallybrass, Peter, and Allon White. 1986. *The Politics and Poetics of Transgression*. Ithaca, NY: Cornell University Press.

Sterne, Jonathan. 2003. *The Audible Past: Cultural Origins of Sound Reproduction*. Durham, NC: Duke University Press.

Stoler, Ann Laura. 2008. *Along the Archival Grain: Epistemic Anxieties and Colonial Common Sense*. Princeton, NJ: Princeton University Press.

Stoller, Paul. 1985. "A Performative Approach to Ritual." In *Culture, Thought, and Social Action: An Anthropological Perspective*, edited by Paul Stoller, 123–66. Cambridge, MA: Harvard University Press.

———. 1989. *Fusion of the Worlds: An Ethnography of Possession among the Songhay of Niger*. Chicago: University of Chicago Press.

———. 1995. *Embodying Colonial Memories: Spirit Possession, Power, and the Hauka in West Africa*. New York: Routledge.

Stolow, Jeremy. 2009. "Wired Religion: Spiritualism and Telegraphic Globalization in the Nineteenth Century." In *Empires and Autonomy: Moments in the History of Globalization*, edited by Stephen M. Streeter, John C. Weaver, and William D. Coleman, 79–92. Vancouver: University of British Columbia Press.

———. 2013. *Deus in Machina: Religion, Technology, and the Things in Between*. New York: Fordham University Press.

Stowe, Harriet Beecher. 1852. *Uncle Tom's Cabin: A Tale of Life among the Lowly*. London: George Routledge.

Strathern, Andrew, and Michael Lambek. 1998. Introduction to *Bodies and Persons: Comparative Perspectives from Africa and Melanesia*, edited by Michael Lambek and Andrew Strathern, 1–25. Cambridge: Cambridge University Press.

Streiff, John. 2009. "Edison, Psycho-Phone and ITC Technology." Accessed November 29, 2010. http://www.sdparanormal.com/f/Edison_Psychophone_and_ITC_Technology.pdf.

Strickrodt, Silke. 2007. "The Phonograph in the Jungle: Magic and Modernity in the African Encounter with the Talking Machines." In *Magical Objects: Things and Beyond*, edited by Elmar Schenkel and Stefan Welz, 109–26. Leipzig: Galda and Wilch.

Swedenborg, Emanuel. (1758) 1788. *A Treatise Concerning the Last Judgement*. . . . London: R. Hindmarsh.

"The Talking Phonograph." 1877. *Scientific American* 37 (25) (December 22): 384–85.

Tambiah, Stanley J. 1970. *Buddhism and the Spirit Cults in North-east Thailand*. Cambridge: Cambridge University Press.

———. 1985. *Culture, Thought, and Social Action: An Anthropological Perspective*. Cambridge, MA: Harvard University Press.

———. 1990. *Magic, Science, Religion, and the Scope of Rationality*. Lewis Henry Morgan Lectures 1981. Cambridge: Cambridge University Press.

Taussig, Michael. (1980) 1983. *The Devil and Commodity Fetishism in South America*. Chapel Hill: University of North Carolina Press.

———. 1987. *Shamanism and Colonialism and the Wild Man: A Study of Terror and Healing*. Chicago: University of Chicago Press.

———. 1992. *The Nervous System*. New York: Routledge.

———. 1993. *Mimesis and Alterity: A Particular History of the Senses*. New York: Routledge.

———. 1997. *Magic of the State*. New York: Routledge.

———. 1998. "Viscerality, Faith, and Skepticism: Another Theory of Magic." In *In Near Ruins: Cultural Theory at the End of the Century*, edited by B. Nicholas Dirks, 221–56. Minneapolis: University of Minnesota Press.

———. 1999. *Defacement: Public Secrecy and the Labor of the Negative*. Stanford, CA: Stanford University Press.

Taylor, Charles. 1989. *Sources of Identity: The Making of the Modern Self*. Cambridge: Cambridge University Press.

———. 2002. "Modern Social Imaginaries." *Public Culture* 14 (1): 91–124.

———. 2007. *A Secular Age*. Cambridge, MA: Belknap.

Temple, William. 1692. *Memoirs of what past in Christendom, from the war begun 1672 to the peace concluded 1679*. London: Printed by R. R. for Ric. Chiswell.

Terry, Walter. (1956) 1971. *The Dance in America*. New York: Harper and Row.

Thevet, André. (1575) 1986. *André Thevet's North America: A Sixteenth-Century View*. Edited and translated by Roger Schlesinger and Arthur Phillips Stabler. Kingston, ON: McGill-Queen's University Press.

Thomas, John F. 1929. *Case Studies Bearing upon Survival*. Boston: Boston Society for Psychic Research.

Thomas, Keith. 1971. *Religion and the Decline of Magic*. New York: Oxford University Press.

Thompson, Emily. 1995. "Machines, Music, and the Quest for Fidelity: Marketing the Edison Phonograph in America, 1878–1925." *Musical Quarterly* 79:131–71.

Tocqueville, Alexis de. [1835–40] 2004. *Democracy in America*. New York: Library of America.

Toll, Robert C. 1974. *Blacking Up: The Minstrel Show in Nineteenth Century America*. London: Oxford University Press.

Tosches, Nick. 2001. *Where Dead Voices Gather*. Boston: Little, Brown.

Toussaint, Gregory. 2009. *Jezebel Unveiled*. Miami: High Way.

Tromp, Marlene. 2006. *Altered States: Sex, Nation, Drugs, and Self-Transformation in Victorian Spiritualism*. Albany: State University of New York Press.

Turner, Edith B. 1993. "The Reality of Spirits: A Tabooed or Permitted Field of Study?" *Anthropology of Consciousness* 4:9–12.

Turner, Edith B., with William Blodgett, Singleton Kahona, and Fideli Benwa. 1992. *Experiencing Ritual: A New Interpretation of African Healing*. Philadelphia: University of Pennsylvania Press.

Turner, Victor W. 1985. "Conflict in Social Anthropological and Psychoanalytical Theory: Umbanda in Rio de Janeiro." In *On the End of the Bush: Anthropology as Experience*, edited by Edith Turner, 119–50. Tucson: University of Arizona Press.

Tylor, Edward Burnett. (1871) 1958. *Primitive Culture*. 2 vols. New York: Harper.

Ullmann, Dieter. 2002. "Athanasius Kircher und die Akustik der Zeit um 1650." *NTM Zeitschrift für Geschichte der Wissenschaften, Technik und Medizin* 10:55–67.

Uzgalis, William. 2002. "'An Inconsistency Not to Be Excused': On Locke and Racism." In *Philosophers on Race: Critical Essays*, edited by Julie K. Ward and Tommy L. Lott, 81–100. Oxford: Blackwell.

Vasconcelos, João. 2008." Homeless Spirits: Modern Spiritualism, Psychical Research, and the Anthropology of Religion in the Late Nineteenth and Early Twentieth Centuries." In *On the Margins of Religion*, edited by Frances Pine and João de Pina Cabral, 13–37. Oxford: Berghahn.

Velho, Y. M. 1975 *Guerra de Orixa: Um Estudo de Ritual e Conflito*. Rio de Janeiro: Zahar Editores.

Volf, Miroslav. 2011. *Public Faith: How Followers of Christ Should Serve the Public Good*. Ada, MI: Brazos.

Wafer, James. 1991. *The Taste of Blood: Spirit Possession in Brazilian Candomblé*. Philadelphia: University of Pennsylvania Press.

Wagner, C. Peter. 1991. *Engaging the Enemy: How to Fight and Defeat Territorial Spirits*. Ventura, CA: Regal Books.

———. 1992. *Warfare Prayer: What the Bible Says about Spiritual Warfare*. Ventura, CA: Regal Books.

Wall, Cheryl. 1989. "Mules and Men and Women: Zora Neale Hurston's Strategies of Narration and Visions of Female Empowerment." *Black American Literature Forum* 23 (4): 661–80.

Wallace, Alfred Russel. (1896) 1975. *Perspectives in Psychical Research*. 3rd ed. New York: Arno.

Walmsley, Peter. 1995. "Prince Maurice's Rational Parrot: Civil Discourse in Locke's Essay." *Eighteenth-Century Studies* 28 (4): 413–425.

Walsh, Andrew. 2004. "In the Wake of Things: Speculating in and about Sapphires in Northern Madagascar." *American Anthropologist* 106 (2): 225–37.

Ward, Martha C. 2003. *A World Full of Women*. 3rd ed. Boston: Allyn and Bacon.

Warrick, F. W. 1939. *Experiments in Psychics: Practical Studies in Direct Writing, Supernormal Photography and Other Phenomena, Mainly with Mrs. Ada Emma Deane*. London: Rider.

Watson, Thomas A. 1926. *Exploring Life: An Autobiography*. New York: D. Appleton.

Weber, Max. (1904) 2003. *The Protestant Ethic and the Spirit of Capitalism*. Translated by Talcott Parsons. New York: Dover.

Wernick, Andrew. 1991. *Promotional Culture: Advertising, Ideology, and Symbolic Expression*. London: Sage.

West, Harry G. 2007. *Ethnographic Sorcery*. Chicago: University of Chicago Press.

Wheeler, H. H. 1902. *Up-to-Date Minstrel Jokes*. Boston: Up-To-Date Publishing.

Willford, Andrew C. 2006. *Cage of Freedom: Tamil Identity and the Ethnic Fetish in Malaysia*. Ann Arbor: University of Michigan Press.

Williams, Raymond. 1985. *Keywords: A Vocabulary of Culture and Society*. Rev. ed. New York: Oxford University Press.

Williamson, Judith. 1978. *Decoding Advertisements: Ideology and Meaning in Advertising*. London: Marion Boyars.

Wills, Ian. 2009. "Edison and Science: A Curious Result." *Studies in the History and Philosophy of Science* 40:157–66.

Winter, Alison. 1998. *Mesmerized: Powers of Mind in Victorian Britain*. Chicago: University of Chicago Press.

Wirtz, Kristina. 2005. "'Where Obscurity Is a Virtue': The Mystique of Unintelligibility in Santería Ritual." *Language and Communication* 25 (4): 351–75.

———. 2007. *Ritual, Discourse, and Community in Cuban Santería: Speaking a Sacred World*. Gainesville: University Press of Florida.

———. 2011. "Cuban Performances of Blackness as the Timeless Past Still among Us." *Journal of Linguistic Anthropology* 21 (1S): E11–E34.

———. Forthcoming. "Spirit Materialities in Cuban Folk Religion: Realms of Imaginative Possibility." In *The Social Life of Spirits*, edited by Diana Espirito Santo and Ruy Llera Blanes. Chicago: University of Chicago Press.

Wyndham, Horace. 1937. *Mr. Sludge, the Medium: Being the Life and Adventures of Daniel Dunglas Home*. London: G. Bles.

Zammito, John H. 2002. *Kant, Herder, and the Birth of Anthropology*. Chicago: University of Chicago Press.

Zielinski, Siegfried. 2006. *Deep Time of the Media: Toward and Archaeology of Hearing and Seeing by Technical Means*. Cambridge, MA: MIT Press.

Zorzo, Francisco Antonio. 2001. *Ferrovia e Rede Urbana na Bahia: Doze Cidades Conectadas pela Ferovia no Sul do Recôncavo Baiano (1870–1930)*. Feira de Santana: Universidade Estadual de Feira de Santana.

CONTRIBUTORS

BRIAN BRAZEAL is a professor of anthropology at California State University, Chico. His research specialties include Afro-Brazilian religions, the international trade in emeralds, and anthropological digital cinema production. He founded and directs the Advanced Laboratory for Visual Anthropology at CSU, Chico.

PAUL CHRISTOPHER JOHNSON is professor of history and Afroamerican and African studies and director of the Doctoral Program in Anthropology and History at the University of Michigan, Ann Arbor. He is author of *Secrets, Gossip, and Gods: The Transformation of Brazilian Candomblé* (2002) and *Diaspora Conversions: Black Carib Religion and the Recovery of Africa* (2007).

MICHAEL LAMBEK holds a Canada Research Chair in Anthropology at the University of Toronto. He has been following spirit possession ethnographically in the Western Indian Ocean (Mayotte and northwest Madagascar) and thinking about and with it for over thirty years, recently as a lens to appreciate the ethical dimension of human sociality.

ELIZABETH MCALISTER is professor of religion at Wesleyan University in Middletown, Connecticut. She is author of *Rara! Vodou, Power, and Performance in Haiti and Its Diaspora*, a book and CD (2002). She is also coeditor of *Race, Nation, and Religion in the Americas* (2004) with Henry Goldschmidt. McAlister has produced the Afro-Haitian religious music albums *Rhythms of Rapture* (Smithsonian Folkways) and *Angels in the Mirror* (Ellipsis Arts).

STEPHAN PALMIÉ is professor of anthropology at the University of Chicago. He is author of *Das Exil der Goetter: Geschichte und Vorstellungswelt einer afrokubanischen Religion* (1991), *Wizards and Scientists: Explorations in Afro-Cuban Modernity and Tradition* (2002), and *The Cooking of History: How Not to Study Afro-Cuban Religion* (2013) and editor of several volumes.

PATRICK A. POLK received his PhD in folklore and mythology from the University of California, Los Angeles. He is curator of Latin American and Caribbean Popular Arts at the Fowler Museum at UCLA and also serves as a lecturer for the UCLA Department of

World Arts and Cultures. His primary research interests are folk religion, material behavior, popular culture, and urban visual traditions. His publications include *Haitian Vodou Flags* (1997), *Botánica Los Angeles: Latino Popular Religious Art in the City of Angels* (2004), and *The Beautiful Walls: Photographic Elevations of Street Art in Los Angeles, Berlin, and Paris* (2010).

KAREN RICHMAN is a cultural anthropologist. She is author of *Migration and Vodou* (2005) and numerous articles and book chapters on Haitian and Mexican migration, religion, labor and expressive culture. Richman won the 2009 Heizer Award for ethnohistory for "Innocent Imitations? Mimesis and Alterity in Haitian Vodou Art." In 2012, she coedited a special volume on Haitian Religion for *Studies in Religion*. She is the academic director of the Institute for Latino studies, a member of the anthropology and Romance languages departments and a fellow of the Kellogg and Eck Institutes at the University of Notre Dame.

RAQUEL ROMBERG is a cultural anthropologist and author of *Witchcraft and Welfare: Spiritual Capital and the Business of Magic in Modern Puerto Rico* (2003) and *Healing Dramas: Divination and Magic in Puerto Rico* (2009). Her work on the modernity of brujería, the moral economy of consumerism and heritage, spiritual capital, the poetics of ritual, embodiment, ritual indeterminacy, and creolization has appeared in various journals and edited volumes. She currently teaches anthropology at Tel Aviv University.

STEPHEN SELKA is a cultural anthropologist who received his PhD from the State University of New York at Albany in 2003. His first book, *Religion and the Politics of Ethnic Identity in Bahia, Brazil* (2007), explores the various ways that Afro-Brazilians in both Christian and Candomblé communities construct their ethnic identities and engage with Brazil's *movimento negro*. His current research explores how Afro-Brazilian religion has been framed as cultural heritage and what this means for local practice. Selka is currently an associate professor of religious studies and American studies at Indiana University.

KRISTINA WIRTZ, a linguistic and cultural anthropologist, is associate professor of anthropology at Western Michigan University. Her ethnographic research on folk religion, ritual and folklore performance, racialization, and the meaning of "Blackness" in Cuba has been published in journals such as *American Ethnologist, Journal of the Royal Anthropological Institute, Journal of Linguistic Anthropology, Text and Talk,* and *Religion in Africa* and in the monograph *Ritual, Discourse, and Community in Cuban Santería* (2007).

INDEX

Page numbers followed by the letter *f* refer to figures.

abakuá, 49–50, 58, 73–78, 271; phonation and audition in contemporary, 51–58
accumulation, 135, 153, 157, 159, 167, 171–75
ackamarackus, 136
acoustic mask, 50, 56, 76–78. *See also* masks
action, 257, 262, 267. *See also* possessed action
aestheticism. *See* estheticism and spirit possession
affliction, 155, 157, 159, 165, 174, 215–19; ancestors, spirits, and mediation of transnational, 219–22
agency: patiency and, 257, 262, 267; of spirits, 100, 107, 109, 112–19, 124, 127–29
alienation, 208, 216
altars, Cuban folk religion and, 104, 105f, 106f, 107, 110, 118, 122
ancestors, 11, 190, 216, 217; caused to appear in various performative modes, 10; as lived history, 20; as potential spirits, 11; role of, 215, 217, 222; worshipping, 215. *See also* ancestral spirit(s)
ancestral chronotope, mediated belonging characteristic of the, 16
ancestral sin, 188, 189
ancestral spirit(s), 11, 15, 53, 190, 192, 207, 216–17, 222, 223; demonic, 181, 187, 190, 192, 200; and mediation of transnational affliction, 219–22; New Apostolic movement and, 181, 187–92, 196; process of becoming an, 14; spiritual warfare against, 270. *See also* ancestors
animal sacrifice. *See* sacrifice
animism, 26, 40
anthropologists and spirit possession, 229, 232, 237
Aristotle, 10–11
art, artifice, and possession, 254–56, 268–69
Assembleia de Deus (Assembly of God), 161
"atavistic," as descriptor for possession, 21
Atkins, John, 30
aural, the, 272
authenticity of autobiographical representation, 238
authenticity of spirit possession, 143, 154, 232, 238; assessing, 11, 229, 231, 240, 242–45, 253, 255–56; downplaying doubts about, 245; proof of, 123, 124, 128, 136, 232, 233, 251, 252
authentic primitive, 237
authentic vs. false trances in Candomblé, 245, 251
authentic vs. fraudulent practitioners/charlatans, 131, 132, 136, 142, 145, 231–32. *See also* charlatans
autonomy, 6; possession and, 1, 6–7, 17, 24, 32, 44, 159, 173, 174, 258–59, 264

Babbitt, Edwin Dwight, 93
backlands, 131, 133, 135, 136, 142, 150, 154
bad faith, 131, 142
Bahian Recôncavo, 159–60
baroco, 49, 51–54, 77
baroco llansao, 55, 57
baroco ninllao, 56, 57, 78
Bartlett, George C., 96–97
Batista Betel (Bethel Baptist), 161
Bayle, Pierre, 29
Beard, George M., 79
Bell, Alexander Graham, 61–63, 72
Bible, 179, 190, 195, 198; land and the, 178, 184, 185, 195, 197, 203–4; "possession" in, 195
biblical law, 184–88, 194
biblical promises of prosperity, 157, 158, 173–75
blacks, possession and, 82–91. *See also* minstrel shows; *Uncle Tom's Cabin* (Stowe)
blood, sacrificial, 63, 150, 188, 192, 237
blood covenant, 188
blood pact, 192. *See also* Bois Caïman ceremony
bodily sensation, 110, 116, 117, 124, 125, 128
body movements and gestures of the possessed, 232–36, 238, 242, 243, 249, 256. *See also* embodiment
Bois Caïman ceremony, 188, 192
Bosman, Willem, 30, 38
Boston, strange relations in, 79–83
Bourguignon, Erika, 3, 209, 211
Brasil Para Cristo (Brazil for Christ), 162
Brown, David H., 53, 77
Brown, Karen McCarthy, 14, 209, 296n3
búzio, jogos de, 145

caboclo, 142–45, 149, 150, 251
cachaça, 133, 144
Cachoeira, 136, 142–43, 145, 160, 161; caboclos and, 142; Campo Formoso and, 134, 135; children in, 143; churches and religious denominations in, 155, 161; economics, 134–36, 146; evangelical churches in, 155, 161; IURD and, 155, 156, 162–64; media in, 135, 156; overview, 133–34, 160; research in, 155, 164, 165. *See also* Candomblé
Cachoeirans, 162, 166–67
Campo Formoso: Afro-Brazilian religions in, 135; Cachoeira and, 134, 135; economics, 134, 136, 139, 146–47, 152, 153; emerald trade in, 134, 137, 139, 153; gemstones in, 132, 134, 138–39; overview, 133–34; Protestant churches in, 152
Candomblé, 14, 20, 44, 135, 143–45, 155, 159, 160, 168–70; civil risks related to, 41; evangelical Christianity and, 252, 257, 259, 261; evangelicals' views of, 162, 165–68; false vs. authentic trances in, 245, 251; gods of, 150–51; historical and cultural context, 153; IURD and, 158–59, 162, 164, 165, 174, 175; leaving, 167–68; magic in, 148; money, economics, prosperity, and, 131, 134, 135, 144, 145, 150–51, 158–60, 164, 169, 174, 175; Pentecostalism, neo-Pentecostalism, and, 20, 159, 162, 165, 174, 270; possession and, 41, 156, 157, 163, 164, 167, 168, 175, 251, 260, 270, 281n22, 287n39; slavery and, 44, 149, 151, 153
Capone, Stefania, 19, 280n16
Carnaiba, 134, 137–39, 147, 152, 153
charlatans, 131–33, 136, 142–44, 154, 156, 227. *See also* authentic vs. fraudulent practitioners/charlatans
Christensen, C. P., 90
Christian demonology. *See under* demonology
Christianity, conversion to, 167, 168, 173, 190, 191, 227. *See also specific topics*
Christian renewalism. *See* renewalism
Christy, George N. (George Harrington), 81, 83, 84, 86–89, 92, 94–97
Christy and Wood's Minstrels, 83, 84, 86, 88, 92. *See also* Christy's Minstrels
Christy's Minstrels, 80, 82, 83, 90, 92. *See also* Christy and Wood's Minstrels
Cidade da Macumba, 133, 135. *See also* Cachoeira
Cimarrón, 113, 114
clairvoyance, 124–25
Coates, James, 88
colonial representations of spirit possession, 225–28, 237

commodities, 133, 136, 137, 146, 154; conversion into spiritual gifts, 229; mineral, 133, 134, 140, 154; money and, 133, 136, 154, 229, 297n10; possession and, 208, 262–63
commodity fetishism, 75, 214, 263, 264
communication: moral, 222; ritual, 208, 215, 218, 222; spirits and, 118, 128, 207–9, 214, 217, 219, 221–23 (*see also specific topics*); terminology, 208
Comte, Auguste, 29
Conant, Frances "Fanny," 81, 84
concealment and unconcealment, 267, 300n10
conocimiento, 124, 125
contact and spirit possession, 225, 226
contagion, 41. *See also* society: and the specter of the horde
contracts, possession in relation to, 33–35. *See also* pacts/covenants
conversion to Christianity, 167, 168, 173, 190, 191, 227
correctors (corretores), 138, 140
covenants. *See* pacts/covenants
cowry, 112, 118, 135, 145, 149
creativity, 264, 267
cross-cultural instances of spirit possession, 228–31, 240, 250, 251, 253
Cuba: Santiago de Cuba, 99–100, 113–15, 118; a sensorium of Cuban spirits, 103–8
Cuban folk religion: altars and, 104, 105f, 106f, 107, 110, 118, 122; practitioners, 102–4, 107, 113, 114, 116–18, 121–22, 124, 125, 127, 128. *See also* Cuban Spiritism; Reglas de Palo; representational economies of spirit presence; Santería; Spiritism
Cuban Revolution, 102
Cuban Spiritism, 99, 103, 104, 105f, 106f, 113, 115, 121–26

dances: "fetish," 30; mimetic, 296n1
dancing, 10, 47, 84, 297n9; Cachoeira and, 142–43; ethnography and, 210–11; spirit possession and, 14, 25–26, 190, 208–11, 213–14, 217–18, 220, 222–23, 228, 231, 238, 243–46, 251, 254; Vodou and, 213
Dancing Wisdom (Daniel), 211
Daniel, Yvonne, 211
de Brosses, Charles, 29–31
deception, 12, 131, 133, 136, 140–42, 146, 154, 267. *See also* charlatans
deliverance, 178; from demons, 157–59, 164, 175, 294n2; IURD and, 157–59, 174, 175; prayer and, 198; religious emphasis on, 159, 294nn1–2. *See also* exorcism; liberation
demonic afflictions: IURD's promise of relief from, 155, 157, 159, 162, 175. *See also* affliction; exorcism
demonic entrenchment, 187, 189, 191
demonic infestation, slavery and, 191–92
demonic nations, 202
demonic pacts, 166, 183, 187, 192. *See also* devil: pacts with
demonic possession, evangelical legal mythography of, 192. *See also* possession; spirit possession
demonic script, Christian, 12, 26
demonic territory, 185, 187, 188
demonology: Christian, 16, 25 (*see also under* demons); medicalization of, 12, 28; New Apostolic theology and, 188, 191–92, 195, 200, 201
demons, 148, 149, 181, 194; Boa Morte and, 166; evangelicalism and, 166, 188, 189, 191–93; God and, 173, 184; Haiti and, 188, 189, 191–93, 198; Haitian Vodou and, 189, 190, 194–95, 198, 199; Jesus Christ and, 187–89, 199; money and, 157, 159, 162, 163, 166, 173; Pentecostalism, neo-Pentecostalism, and, 157, 173, 174; racism and, 191–92, 194; relationships with, 172, 187, 188; Satan and, 184–85, 187, 191, 192, 197–98, 200. *See also* exús; *and specific topics*
Deren, Maya, 9, 43, 118, 210–11, 297n6
Derrida, Jacques, 26, 65
Descartes, René, 12, 23, 36
descent groups, 209, 215–20, 222–23
Deus é Amor (God is Love), 162
devil, 162, 169–72, 188, 189, 191; pacts with, 171–72, 193 (*see also* Satan: pacts/covenants with)
devils, 25, 153

Dewey, John, 94
direct voice manifestations, 271–73
discursive and somatic modes of attention, 232, 233
disease. *See* illness
disembodiment, 50, 61, 67, 71, 86
dissociation, 5
divination, 125, 247–49, 252, 279n14; cowry-shell, 135, 149
divination ceremonies (*jogos de búzio*), 145
Divine Horsemen (Deren), 9, 43, 210–11, 214
dizimo (tithe), 158, 172
doubts about spirit presence, 230, 238, 240, 244, 245, 249, 254–56. *See also* skepticism
drama of spirit possession, 230, 231, 233, 235–38, 249, 256. *See also* "lived theatre"; theater: possession and
"dramas of discernment," 250
drumming, 48, 49; Écue and, 51–58, 73, 74; spirit possession and, 26, 51, 115, 128, 142, 228, 231, 236, 243, 246
drumskins, 52–55, 77
dualism, 5, 108
Dunham, Katherine, 211, 212, 297n6

ear-phonautograph, 61–62
echo, 47–48, 51, 57, 58, 74, 77. *See also* Écue
economic policies, neoliberal, 180–84
economics: of Cachoeira, 134–36, 146; of Campo Formoso, 134, 136, 139, 146–47, 152, 153; of Candomblé, 131, 134, 135, 144, 145, 150–51, 158–60, 164, 169, 174, 175. *See also* money; prosperity
economic value, 35, 44, 45, 132, 133, 153, 182
ecoria ñene abakuá, 52, 55, 56, 77
écue, 288n7
Écue, 52, 54–57; as biotechnology, 52, 53, 75, 77, 78 (*see also* Leal brothers: Écue and); drumming and, 51–58, 73, 74; voice of, 51, 53–57, 73, 75, 77, 78, 289n12
Ecueñón, 49, 51–53
Edison, Thomas Alva, 63–65, 71, 290n24, 291nn28–29; attempts to record and preserve messages from the dead, 64–65; communications in afterlife, 70, 291n30; on etheric force, 68, 291n29; phonograph, 63–66, 75, 290n24; Spiritualism and, 72; Tone Test Campaign, 293n40; transductive cosmology, 65–71
Edisonian technology, 76–77. *See also* Edison, Thomas Alva
efficacy, 133, 136, 145; ritual, 133, 135–37, 144, 145, 199, 235, 255
Egunguns, 14, 280n16
egúns, 148, 149, 151, 236
Einstellung (orientation), 111, 117, 124, 128
Ejamba, 47–49, 73, 76. *See also* Illamba
electroacoustic technology, 50, 58, 60, 66, 73, 74, 77, 78. *See also* Edison, Thomas Alva; phonograph
Eleggua, 99–100, 125, 126
Elliotson, John, 89–90
embodiment, 104, 109, 117, 118; bodily sensation, 110, 116, 117, 124, 125, 128. *See also* perspicience
embori, 52, 55, 56
"enchantment" by evil spirits, 12
energy and spirits, 102–4, 107, 118–21, 125
Enllenisón, 50, 51, 56, 57, 77
Enquico (rooster), 49, 51
ensoniment, 58, 272; dialectic of, 59, 70, 75
Eribangandó, 52, 54
eritaj (heritage), 190, 222; interdependence, possession, and, 215–19
Espirito Santo, 120–21
estheticism and spirit possession, 228, 244, 249
ethnicity and spirit possession, 228. *See also* cross-cultural instances of spirit possession; *and specific topics*
ethnography, 44–45, 210–13, 237–38
Eucharist, 51, 57, 64
evangelical Christianity, 161; Candomblé and, 252, 257, 259, 261. *See also* Pentecostalism
evangelical churches in Cachoeira, 155, 161
evangelical discourses about prosperity, 169–72
evangelicalism: demons and, 166, 188, 189, 191–93; expansion, 178–80, 202;

features, 295n2; Haiti earthquake and, 177–78, 193, 271; spirit possession and, 191, 192, 270. *See also* Pentecostalism; renewalism; Universal Church of the Kingdom of God
evangelical possession of land, 195, 197, 199
evangelicals, 180, 183–84, 188, 191; and Afro-Creole traditional religion, 295n6; in Brazil, 153, 156, 159, 161, 162, 164, 165; exorcism and, 164, 274; in Haiti, 188, 189, 191–95, 197, 199, 202, 295n6; Haitian Vodou and, 188, 190–93, 198, 204, 295n6; slavery and, 191–92; spiritual mapping and its cosmology, 184–89; spiritual warfare, 178, 184, 192; third-wave, 157, 162, 179, 181, 185–87, 190, 191, 193–97, 202–4, 295n6; views of Candomblé, 162, 165–68. *See also* New Apostolic movement; renewalism
evangelical seminaries, 295n3
evil, profit and the problem of, 146–50
exit and return, 234, 235, 269
exorcism, 162–65, 188, 274. *See also* deliverance; liberation
exoticism, 211, 213, 225, 226; spirit possession and, 225, 226
exús, 134, 148, 149, 151, 154, 164, 245

"faked" trance, 254
fake possession, 10–13, 41; nature of, 229, 245, 254, 255; signs of, 249–51; suspicions of, 11, 229–32, 244, 245, 250, 254
Feast of the Assumption, 165
feeding spirits, 118, 121–22, 150, 192, 217, 219, 220. *See also* offerings: of food; sacrifice
feitiço, 26, 148, 164
fetiches, 29, 30
fetishism, 29–30, 41; commodity, 75, 214, 263, 264
fetishist possession, 30
fidelity, 71–78
Fields, Annie, 91
Firstness (metaphysical state), 102, 110–12, 128–29
Flannery, Matthew (Matt Peel), 81
folk discourses of spirit possession, 240–54. *See also* Cuban folk religion
Foster, Stephen C., 86
Foucault, Michel, 12
Freemasonry, spirit of, 181, 194
Freemasons, 166
free will, as a possession state, 42–43
Frobenius, Leo, 8–9
fundamentos, 165

garimpeiros, 133, 141, 153
gems, 132, 137–40, 142, 145
gemstones, 16–17, 82, 133, 145, 152, 267. *See also under* Campo Formoso
gestures of the possessed, 232, 233, 235, 238, 256
"gifts of the Holy Spirit," 161
"gifts of the spirit," 202
God: demons and, 173, 184; Haiti earthquake as judgment/punishment from, 184, 193, 201, 202, 204; Kant on, 34, 39; offerings to, 172, 173; vs. Satan, 184, 186, 187, 200
gods: of Candomblé, 150–51; caused to appear in various performative modes, 10
Goffman, Erving, 113, 118
"Graceful Exits" (Lambek), 269
guides, spirits as, 1, 95, 97, 100, 117, 128, 234, 300n41
Gypsy spirits, 100, 101f, 103, 104

Haiti: demons and, 188, 189, 191–93, 198; dispossession in, 181–84; eritaj, 190, 215–19, 222; evangelicals in, 188, 189, 191–95, 197, 199, 202, 295n6; missions to, 183–84, 196–97; Protestantism in, 177–79, 214, 272; renewalism in, 186, 189, 199, 296n6; Satan and, 188, 189, 191–93; slavery in, 191–92, 198, 208–9, 215; spiritual geography, 189–94; spiritual warfare and, 178–80, 184, 191, 193, 198, 296n12
Haitian carnival, 177, 178
Haitian descent groups, 209, 215–20, 222–23
Haitian Vodou, 44, 190, 198–99, 272–73; ceremonies, 251; demons and, 189, 190, 194–95, 198, 199; devil and, 191; evangelicals and, 188, 190–93, 198,

Haitian Vodou (*continued*)
204, 295n6; Haiti earthquake and, 177, 193, 271; historical perspective on, 189–90, 210, 211, 213–14, 227; legislation regarding, 192–93; literature on, 210, 211; lwa and, 214 (*see also* lwa); Maya Deren and, 9, 118; overview, 187–89; priests and priestesses, 192–93; scheme of ritual reciprocity and, 199; spirit possession and, 14, 44, 194–95, 198, 207, 222, 233; spiritual warfare and, 198
Haiti earthquake of 2010, 177–78, 180, 209; aftermath, 177–78, 180–84, 189, 194, 199, 203; destruction caused by, 177, 181–82; evangelicalism and, 177–78, 193, 271; as God's judgment/punishment, 184, 193, 201, 202, 204; spiritual warfare and, 178–80, 184; Vodou and, 177, 193, 271
Haiti tent encampments, 181–84, 194, 195; dispossession and possession in a refugee camp, 199–205
Haldeman-Julius, E., 91
Harrington, George (George N. Christy), 81, 83, 84, 86–89, 92, 94–97
Havana, 49, 77, 78
healing, 161, 162
"health and wealth" gospel, 157. *See also* prosperity: theology of
Hegel, Georg Wilhelm Friedrich, 29–30
Hirschkind, Charles, 58, 59
historicity, spirits and, 104, 107–9, 117
Hobbes, Thomas, 24, 32, 33, 38
Holbraad, Martin, 99, 108
Hooker, Isabella Beecher, 87
horse and rider metaphor of spirit possession, 115–16, 208, 229, 231, 243–46, 251, 253, 262; arrival and departure of spirits to and from body of "horse," 234; lwa and, 221
Horsemen (Deren). See *Divine Horsemen* (Deren)
Hume, David, 29, 36, 39
Hurston, Zora Neale, 43, 212–13
Husserl, Edmund, 111, 117, 124

identity, 34–37; the problem of, 11. *See also* self
idolatry, 29, 41
idol possession, 30
Ignatius Loyola, 12
Igreja Universal do Reino de Deus (IURD). *See* Universal Church of the Kingdom of God
Illamba, 49, 52, 54, 55, 73. *See also* Ejamba
Illamba (abakuá title), 49, 288n1
illness, 157, 188–89, 216–17
immediation, 64, 77
indeterminacy, 12, 229–31, 233, 236, 248; emergence and, 231, 240; "mystical," 255–56; ritual, 256. *See also* mimetic uncertainty
indexicality, 50, 57, 73–74, 110–12
Indians, 138–39, 142, 146
Indio, spirit manifestation of the, 232f
individualism, 212, 214, 273–76; possessive, 43, 259
infinition, 99, 128
initiation, 55, 135, 144, 155, 160, 170, 190, 212, 243, 246
íreme, 49, 52, 54, 55
irony, 14, 257, 267
Islam, 270
IURD (Igreja Universal do Reino de Deus). *See* Universal Church of the Kingdom of God

Jesus Christ: demons and, 187–89, 199; spiritual warfare and, 188–89, 193, 198
John, Gospel of, 28, 44

Kant, Immanuel, 285n25; autonomy and, 44; on fetishism, 29, 38, 39; on God, 34, 39; illuminism and, 34, 39; possession and, 24, 33–34, 39, 45, 275–76; on racial hierarchy, 25, 282n5; on reason, 275; Swedenborg and, 33, 39
Keane, Webb, 102, 108–9, 281n3, 284nn16–17, 289n14
Keeler, Pierre Louie Ormand Augustus, 95, 96, 96f, 97
Kibushy (Malagasy) speakers, 218, 261
Kircher, Athanasius, 59

Lambek, Michael, 16, 209, 218, 245, 246, 280n17, 300n2

land: and the Bible, 178, 184, 185, 195, 197, 203–4; evangelical possession of, 195, 197, 199; Pentecostalism and, 184, 294n1. *See also* "possessing the land"; property
lapidaries, 133, 138, 140
law, 34, 37; biblical, 184–88, 194; legislation regarding Vodou, 192–93
laying on of hands, 161, 163
Leal brothers, 48–51, 57–58; Écue and, 57–58, 73–75, 77, 78; technoreligious experiments, 72–78; Temple of the Ancient Grace, 49, 58, 61, 78, 289n12
Leay brothers. *See* Leal brothers
Le Bon, Gustave, 39, 40
legal imaginary, 179–80, 202–3
legitimacy of practitioners, 136, 145. *See also* authentic vs. fraudulent practitioners/charlatans; charlatans
Leibniz, Gottfried Wilhelm, 34
Lenin, Vladimir Ilyich, 2, 7
liberation, 155, 157, 167, 173, 212, 237. *See also* deliverance; exorcism
"lived theatre" (*théâtre vécu*), 238, 240, 249, 254, 256
Locke, John, 32, 36–38, 42, 45
Lucumí, 118, 120, 123
lwa (deities/archetypal spirits), 190, 208, 209, 217–21; access to, 207; ancestors and, 216–18, 222; feeding of the, 217; illness caused by, 216–17; as nature spirits, 9, 215, 222; personalities, 217; and possession, 273; powers, 215; as protagonists of a cult of affliction and healing, 217; as universal, 207, 214, 215, 222

Macedo, Edir, 156
macumba, 131, 135, 155, 166
magic, 148–49, 227, 254, 256; as antimodern, 227–28; colonial persecution of, 227; features of African, 29–30
Magno de Miranda, Carlos, 156
Malagasy (Kibushy) speakers, 218, 261
Malinowski, Bronislaw, 14, 15
marmotagem, 145
masks, 47–49, 55, 56, 76, 79, 266; acoustic, 50, 56, 76–78; and unmasking, 233, 252, 255, 256
materiality, 2, 35, 117–24
materialization and spirits, 99, 100, 102, 107–10, 129. *See also* materiality
Mather, Cotton, 12
Mayotte, 245, 246, 249, 261–63, 273
mediation, 52–54, 56–58, 73–74, 77, 78, 271–72
medium(s): becoming a, 247; controlling possession, 246–47; "Graceful Exits," 269; minstrels and, 265; psychological screening and licensing of, 42; Spiritist, 299n33; trumpet, 72; vital force, 235. *See also* possessed, the; *and specific topics*
megaphony, 48, 58, 59, 69–70, 72, 74
metaphor, 261–64
Miller, Henry, 2, 3
mimesis, 10–13; magic and, 227; power and, 225–28, 231–33, 244, 255, 256; transgression and, 225, 227; truth and, 264–69
mimetic corporeality: dangers of, 234–40; politics of alterity and, 225–28; vs. spirit possession discourse, 231–34
mimetic faculty: emotions and, 225, 226, 232, 249, 255; persecution and, 226–28
mimetic fascination, 225–27, 237
mimetic performances, 225, 244. *See also* folk discourses of spirit possession; mimetic corporeality; spirit presence: reality of
mimetic resemblance, 229–30, 248, 249, 252, 255, 256
mimetic uncertainty, 256
mind/body opposition, 257
miners, 132, 133, 137, 140, 147–53
minstrel acts, spirits imitating, 266
minstrels as spirit mediums, 265
minstrel shows, 87–91, 94–97; back in blackface, 83–87; spirits in Uncle Tom's cabinet, 91–94; strange relations in Boston, 79–83
Mintz, Sidney, 214–15, 227
misreading, 273
missions (to Haiti), 183–84, 196–97
mob psychology. *See* society: and the specter of the horde
modernity, 227–28; the individual, nature, and possession in, 213–15; sorcery and, 277n2, 281n25

money, 132, 133, 135–37, 145–49; commodities and, 133, 136, 154, 229, 297n10; demons and, 157, 159, 162, 163, 166, 173; laying up treasures in heaven, 150–53; profit and the problem of evil, 146–50; sacrifice of, 158, 172. *See also* Candomblé; economics; prosperity
moral accountability, 19–20
moral community, 203, 222
moral economy, 133, 146, 215. *See also* profit: and the problem of evil
moral geographies, 193–94, 203
moral inquiry, forms of, 274–75
morality, 150–54, 159, 172, 174–75, 209
Morse, Samuel, 61
Morse code, 63, 71
Moseley, Sydney A., 92
muertos, 103, 113–17, 122–24, 127, 128. *See also* spirits
Murray, Gerald, 215
mystification, 264

Nasacó, 52–54, 62
neoliberal agendas, 276
neoliberal capitalism, 157–58, 188
neoliberal economic policies, 180–84
neoliberal globalization, 174
neoliberalism, 202, 281–82
neo-Pentecostalism, 157, 159, 162, 164, 165, 172–74. *See also* Universal Church of the Kingdom of God
neo-Pentecostals, 162, 174, 178, 180, 294n1 (chap. 6)
New Apostolic movement, 181, 183; ancestral spirits and, 181, 187–92, 196
New Apostolic Reformation, 179, 181, 194, 196, 200
New Apostolic theology, 188, 200, 203
New Apostolic thought, 184, 191–92, 195, 197, 203
Nina Rodrigues, Raymundo, 4, 27, 30, 40–42

obonécues, 52, 54–58, 78, 289n12
obones, 52–53, 78, 289n12
obrigações, 160, 163. *See also* sacrifice
obsession vs. possession, 12
occult economies, 158
offerings, 110, 118–20, 148, 217, 220–21; in Candomblé, 160; of food, 118, 119f, 120f, 122, 160, 217; functions and goals of, 110, 120; to God, 172, 173; monetary, 173; of sound and music, 110, 119, 120; transubstantiation into spiritual energy, 121
Old Testament. *See* Bible
orichas, 99–100, 103, 104, 107, 114, 115, 117–22
orishas and the possessed, 253
orixás, 149–51, 160, 166, 236, 245–46. *See also* santos (saints)
Ortiz, Fernando, 21, 27, 40, 48–49, 54, 55, 228; on Cuba's "mala vida," 41; possession and, 21, 30, 41, 49, 54; on ritual objects, 288n7
Ouidah, cult of, 31

pacts/covenants: blood, 192 (*see also* Bois Caïman ceremony); demonic, 166, 183, 186, 192; with devil, 171–72, 193; with Satan, 183, 187. *See also* contracts
Palmié, Stephan, 104, 127, 229, 266, 271–72
Palo. *See* Reglas de Palo
participant footing, 113
participation roles in spirit possession, 113
Partridge, Charles, 86
patiency and agency, 257, 262, 267
Peel, Matt (Matthew Flannery), 81
Peirce, Charles Sanders, 75, 76, 102, 110–12, 128
Pentecostalism, 59, 152, 157–59, 161, 162; in Cachoeira, 155; Candomblé and, 20, 159, 162, 165, 174, 270; demons and, 157, 173, 174; First and Second Waves, 162; land and, 184, 294n1; materiality, spirituality, and, 108, 270; spirit possession and, 157, 260, 270. *See also* evangelical Christianity; neo-Pentecostalism
performance, felicitous, 264, 265, 267, 268. *See also* possession performances
performances of proof. *See* proof and testing performances
personae, 19
personhood, 35–38
persons, things, and person-things, 5–9. *See also* property: persons as

perspicience: and conocimiento, 124, 125; and spirit presence, 124–27, 271–72
Peters, John Durham, 63, 64, 290n24
Philadelphia, 47, 48, 50, 78
Philadelphia North American, 47, 51, 58, 74
phonautograph, 61–62
phonograph, unmasked, 71–78
polyphony, 264
possessed, the: from the Indian to the African, 28–32; topography of, 28–32. *See also specific topics*
possessed action: vs. individual action, 1; meanings and connotations, 1–3
"possessing the land," 177, 178, 181, 184, 195, 196. *See also* Haiti tent encampments
possession, 45; frenzy of (*see* society: and the specter of the horde); origin of the term, 23; parameters of, 1–3; in relation to property, person, and society, 32–40; terminology, 3–5, 42, 208–10, 262; who possesses who, 261–62. *See also* spirit possession; *and specific topics*
possession discourse. *See* spirit possession discourse
possession performances, 14–16, 19, 21, 142, 207, 209, 222
potencia(s), 50, 53, 55–57, 78
power, 263–64; mimesis and, 225–28, 231–33, 244, 255, 256; of spirit possession, 231–34, 244, 253, 256
prayer warrior movement. *See* spiritual mapping; spiritual warfare
presence, 51, 73, 271–72; ancestral, 51–53; beyond time, 54; biotechnology and, 77; illusion of real, 64; the problem of, 67; pure, 57, 77. *See also* representational economies of spirit presence
presences, masks and, 49, 76. *See also* Écue
primitive cultures, 39
profit, and the problem of evil, 146–50. *See also* economics; money
proof, of authenticity, 123, 124, 128, 136, 232, 233, 251, 252. *See also* mimetic uncertainty
proof and testing performances, 233, 249–52, 254–56, 297n11
proof-seeking performance, 250
property: persons as, 45, 258–59, 263, 264 (*see also* slavery); possession in relation to, 32–33, 35. *See also* land; "possessing the land"
property ownership and slaves, 5–6, 32, 258, 259, 278n6, 281n2
prosperity: biblical promises of, 157, 158, 173–75; evangelical discourses about, 169–72; IURD and, 157–59, 162, 164, 165, 173–75; paths to, 159, 166, 173, 174; spirits and, 165; theology of, 157, 158. *See also* Candomblé; economics; money
protectors, spirits as, 103
Protestant churches, 133, 150, 152. *See also specific denominations*
Protestant ethic, 152, 153
Protestantism, 39, 154, 158, 161; in Haiti, 177–79, 214, 272. *See also specific denominations*
Puerto Rican brujos and espiritistas, 235, 247, 254
Puerto Rico, 241–42, 299nn30–31

quijilas, 138

railroads, 134
reciprocal shock, 10
Regla, 56, 288n5
Reglas de Palo, 103, 117
religion, 23–24, 30, 43; traditional, 39–40
renewalism, 179, 180, 182; defined, 295n2; expansion, 178–79; in Haiti, 186, 189, 199, 296n6. *See also* Pentecostalism
renewalist movement, charismatic, 182
renewalists: ritual practices, 203; spiritual warfare, 184
renewalist vision of the global order, 187
representational economies of spirit presence, 108–12; agency, 113–17; materiality, 117–24; perspicience, 124–27
ritual efficacy, 133, 135–37, 144, 145, 199, 235, 255
ritual families, 132, 135, 143, 150, 151
ritual offerings. *See* offerings
"ritual piracy," 227
Roorbach, Orville A., 87–88
Root, George Frederick, 86–87
Royal Road (Brazil), 134

sacrifice: animal, 48, 49, 52, 55, 119f, 120f, 121, 150, 160, 192, 210, 217, 220, 221, 237; human, 63, 211; as leading to remuneration, 159; of money, 158, 172. *See also* obrigações
sacrificial blood, 63, 150, 188, 192, 237
sacrificing embori, 52, 55
Santería, 100, 103, 115, 118, 119, 121, 251, 254. *See also* orichas; orishas and the possessed; santeros
santeros (Santería healers), 114, 118–20, 122–23, 242, 244, 254; channeling spirits, 102–3; and the relationship between people and spirits, 107, 109–10; Scientific Spiritists contrasted with, 121; spirit possession and, 109–10, 115–17, 235; testing and proving spirit presence, 109, 115
Santiago de Cuba, 99–100, 113–15, 118
santo bruto, 19
santo jinetero, 229
santos (saints), 103, 104, 120–22, 137, 165, 168; defined, 294n2 (chap. 5). *See also* orixás
santos de cachaça (saints of liquor), 144
santos de mentira (saints of lies), 143
Sartre, Jean-Paul, 27
Satan: demons and, 184–85, 187, 191, 192, 197–98, 200; and the Fall of Man, 185; vs. God, 184, 186, 187, 200; Haiti and, 188, 189, 191–93; IURD and, 157–59; legal standing in Christian era, 185, 189, 296n7; pacts/covenants with, 183, 187; sin and, 185, 188; slavery and, 192, 197–98; spiritual warfare and, 184–88, 191, 195; Vodou and, 195. *See also* demons
science, 137–40
Scientific Spiritism, 121, 122, 240–43
séances, 87–88; "cabinet"/"curtain," 86, 95–97; Kaluli spirit, 231; race and, 81–83, 265; sound and music in, 81, 83, 86, 95–97; Spiritualist, 81, 93, 95, 265, 286n34; *Uncle Tom's Cabin* and, 92, 93
Secondness (metaphysical state), 102, 110–12, 128–29
self, 36–37; lack of properly bounded, 40; loss of, 19. *See also* identity
semiotic ideologies, 17, 58, 67, 73, 75
semiotics: mediation, 102, 108–12, 117–18, 121, 122, 124, 126–29; metaphysical degrees of reality, 102, 110–12, 128. *See also* Peirce, Charles Sanders
senses. *See* embodiment
sensual markers of spirit possession, 235
sertão, 134–36, 153
shamanism, 4–5
Sikan, 50–52, 56, 57
sin: ancestral, 188, 189; Satan and, 185, 188; slavery and, 191–92
Sisterhood of Our Lady of Good Death, 165, 168
skepticism, 237–40, 248, 252, 254, 256, 265; brujos and, 252, 256; emic doubts and, 245; of Alfred Métraux, 233; among practitioners, 265, 268; santeros and, 115; as the sole intrinsic feature of spirit possession rituals, 230. *See also* doubts about spirit presence
slave-master relations, 44, 122, 278n8, 282n5, 288n41. *See also* slaves: regarded as things
slave owners, Christian descendants of, 274
slave revolts and revolutions, 86, 192, 216
slavery, 88, 227, 263, 278n8, 282n5, 288n40; Candomblé and, 44, 149, 151, 153; and demonic infestation, 191–92; evangelicals and, 191–92; in Haiti, 191–92, 198, 208–9, 215; history, 6–7, 44–45; legacy of, 259; New Apostolic thought and, 191–92; Satan and, 192, 197–98; sin and, 191–92; slave trade, 5, 6, 20, 38, 44, 85–86, 280n19, 282n5, 288nn40–41; Spiritism and, 104; spirit possession and, 4–5, 20, 27, 44, 45, 117, 259, 278n8, 279n9; Vodou and, 44
slaves, 56; as possessed, 5–6, 274; property ownership and, 5–6, 32, 258, 259, 278n6, 281n2; regarded as things, 5–6, 19, 20, 23, 258, 278n6, 300n6; religious practices, 40, 42, 117, 190, 208–9; spirits of, 113; in *Uncle Tom's Cabin*, 93
Smith, Adam, 34–35
sociality of spirit possession, 272–74
society: possession in relation to property, person, and, 32–40; and the specter of the horde, 38–41

somatic and discursive modes of attention, 232, 233
sorcerers, 132, 134; moral economies and, 133, 146
sorcery, 149, 153–54, 170, 227; dangers associated with, 132, 134, 148–49, 227; defined, 148; economics, 132, 133, 146, 148, 149, 154; modernity and, 277n2, 281n25. *See also* witchcraft
sound: origins of, 60, 74; semiotics of, 67. *See also* drumming
sound box, 70
sound system, 58, 74
sound transmission, 50, 52, 59–62; Alexander Bell and, 62–63, 72; Leal brothers and, 48, 74, 75, 77. *See also* Écue; Edison, Thomas Alva; phonograph
speaking trumpets. *See* trumpets: speaking
spectral duplicity, 26
Spinoza, Benedict de, 38
spirit guides, 1, 95, 97, 100, 117, 128, 234, 300n41
Spiritism, 270–72; Cuban, 99, 103, 104, 105f, 106f, 113, 115, 121–26; Kardecist, 174, 247. *See also* Scientific Spiritism; Vieira, Francisco
Spiritist mediums, 299n33
spirit materialization. *See* materialization and spirits
spirit possession, 1, 45; choice and use of the term, 3–5; comparative exploration of, 228, 250, 253–54; constitutive elements of, 230; dialogic representations of, 225; experience of, 230–34, 237–38, 250–51, 255; and the governance of twentieth-century Americas, 40–44; as pathological and criminal, 228; power of, 231–34, 244, 253, 256; public secret of, 230–33, 245; reality of, 228–31, 244, 245, 252, 253, 255, 256 (*see also* mimetic corporeality); sacredness of, 231, 248, 253; visible signs of, 233 (*see also* body movements and gestures of the possessed). *See also* possession; spirit possession rituals; *and specific topics*
spirit possession discourse, 225, 228; mimetic corporeality and, 231–34, 256 (*see also* mimetic corporeality). *See also* folk discourses of spirit possession
spirit possession rituals: attending assistants in, 235; gossip about, 232, 244, 254; paradox about, 232; participants of, 228–32, 234–36, 238, 242–46, 254, 255; practitioners of, 225, 227–29, 254, 255; risks of, 234–40; and risks of failure, 231, 232, 236, 243, 245, 255. *See also specific topics*
spirit presence: authenticity of (*see* authenticity of spirit possession); reality of, 228–31. *See also* technologies of presence
spirits, historical challenge presented by, 8. *See also specific spirits and specific topics*
spirits' words, shifts of authorship of the, 236, 247
spirit trumpets. *See* trumpets: spirit
spiritual energy/energies, 102–4, 107, 118–21, 125
spiritual geography of Haiti, 189–94
Spiritualism, 87, 89, 92, 93, 95; Anglo-American, 82; birth of, 61; and irrationality of the modern crowd, 40; minstrelsy and, 82, 86, 97; photographs and, 266, 272; race, color, and, 17, 84, 90, 97, 266; Harriet Beecher Stowe and, 91–94; technology and, 61, 70–73; in Venezuela, 199
Spiritualist séances, 81, 93, 95, 265, 286n34
spiritual mapping, and its cosmology, 184–89. *See also* spiritual warfare
spiritual warfare, 180, 198–200, 269–71, 281n24, 295n4; evangelicals and, 178, 184, 192; Haiti and, 178–80, 184, 191, 193, 198, 296n12; "Jericho march," 178; Jesus and, 188–89, 193, 198; terminology, 179, 184, 186, 189, 270. *See also* spiritual mapping
spiritual warfare movement, theocracy as goal of, 281n24
Sterne, Jonathan, 58–62, 74, 75, 291n28
Stowe, Harriet Beecher, 91–94
strategic-level spiritual warfare, 179, 186. *See also* spiritual mapping; spiritual warfare
"superstitions": as antimodern, 227–28; colonial persecution of, 227–28
Swedenborg, Emanuel, 33, 39

Taussig, Michael, 226, 230–31, 240, 252
technologies of presence, 232, 236; denial of, 232; and efficacy, 232; recognition of, 232. *See also* spirit presence
telegraphy, 61–63, 71, 272
telephone, 62–64, 73, 75
Temple of the Ancient Grace, 49, 58, 61, 78, 289n12
testing of spirit presence, 228–30, 232–34, 238–40, 249–52, 254–56. *See also* proof and testing performances
theater, 81–82, 92, 113, 115; "lived" vs. "acted," 238 (*see also* "lived theatre"); possession and, 233, 237, 244, 245, 252–56, 280n17, 299n27; spirits in the theater of history, 18–21. *See also* minstrel shows
theaters, haunted, 82
"theatre" of the possessed, 238
theatricality: art, artifice, and possession, 254–56, 269; ethnographers and, 237–38; of "proving performances," 233; spirit possession and, 14, 17, 89–90, 113, 115, 128, 233, 237, 245, 252–56
Thirdness (metaphysical state), 102, 110–12, 128, 129
third-wave evangelicals. *See* evangelicals: third-wave
Tio Chico (Francisco Vieira), testimony of, 168–75
tourism, 127, 143, 165, 166, 168, 169, 210
tradition, 21
trance, 51, 52, 56, 62
trances, 89–90; exiting from, 269; "faked," 254; false vs. authentic, in Candomblé, 245, 251; Maya Deren and, 210–11; mediums and, 254; spirit agency and, 113–15; spirit possession and, 3, 102, 113–16, 241–49, 254, 261–63, 269; terminology, 3, 262. *See also specific topics*
transduction, 8
transductive cosmology of Edison, 65–71
trumpet mediums, 72
trumpets: speaking, 47, 58, 59, 72, 74; spirit, 72, 73
truth, 264–65, 267; mimesis and, 264–69
Tylor, E. B., 26, 29, 42–43

Umbanda, 157, 159, 164, 174, 236, 245–47
Uncle Tom's Cabin (Stowe), 92–94
Universal Church of the Kingdom of God (Igreja Universal do Reino de Deus [IURD]), 155–59; Cachoeira and, 155, 156, 162–64; Candomblé and, 158–59, 162, 164, 165, 174, 175; deliverance and, 157–59, 174, 175; exorcism in, 162–65; promise of relief from demonic afflictions, 155, 157, 159, 162, 175; prosperity and, 157–59, 162, 164, 165, 173–75; Satan and, 157–59; scandals, 156, 172
Usagaré, 51, 52, 57, 77

value, 146, 182, 266–67; of commodities, 136, 154, 267; economic, 35, 44, 45, 132, 133, 153, 182; of a ritual service, 136; social, 109, 111
values, 154, 215; moral, 153–54
vantagem, 133
ventriloquism, 45
Vieira, Francisco (Tio Chico), testimony of, 168–75
vital force: of mediums, 235; of the possessed, 235
Vodou. *See* Haitian Vodou
voice: disembodied, 50, 71, 86; of Écue, 51, 53–57, 73, 75, 77, 78, 289n12; of the mystery, 50, 51; orchestration of, 264

Wagner, C. Peter, 184, 186, 197–98, 296n9
Watson, Thomas A., 68, 71
wealth. *See* money; prosperity
wealth in persons, 263
West, Luke, 79–84
witchcraft, 133, 148–50, 164, 188, 189. *See also* feitiço; sorcery
"witchcraft pamphlets," 282n7

Yemayá, spirit manifestation of, 229